MOZAMBIQUE

BEYOND THE SHADOW

By Ellie Hein

Rodney and Ellie Hein
AFRICA WA YESU
P.O. Box 1510
Mutare,
Zimbabwe, Africa.

MOZAMBIQUE

BEYOND
THE SHADOW

Dedicated to the people of Mozambique
whose footprints of pain have forever
marked the scorched earth of their ravaged nation
while they bravely reached beyond the shadow...
to the light filtering through.

Also to all who helped us shine the
light in the darkness
especially to our children
Tammy, Dustin and Deborah.
We Love You!

– Ellie

ACKNOWLEDGMENTS

This book would not be what it is without the magnificent support and teamwork of our friends at Christ For The Nations. Together they picked up our heartbeat and laid it out on paper. With extreme care they operated on the soul of the book, and without losing a beat, set it to a more systematic pace.

Our special thanks to Mrs. Freda Lindsay for believing in us and determining to see this story put into print. Mrs. Lindsay, we are forever grateful to you for your support and encouragement during the last fifteen years of our ministry. You have made a great difference in our lives.

To Anna Jeanne Price, our sincere thanks and respect for your sensitivity and amazing dedication in giving your best while editing the African-style text. You have allowed us to remain who we are.

Thanks to Sandra Geldenhuys, for your input and encouragement in getting the printing process started, and to Shirley Lindsay for proofreading the text.

Our thanks to Vicky Sanz for an excellent job in typesetting and layout of pages, photos and cover design. We could not have imagined anything better.

Thanks also to all our family and friends who continually urged us to write this follow-up to our first book, "Mozambique, The Cross And The Crown."

To God be the Glory.

Rodney and Ellie Hein

FOREWORD

By:
Professor André Eam Thomashaussen Dr. Jur (Kiel)
Institute of Foreign and Comparative Law
University of South Africa

It would not be an overstatement to say that without Rodney and Ellie Hein, the long and difficult process of negotiations and the conclusion of the General Peace Accord for Mozambique of 4th October, 1992 might not have been possible.

Their mission work in Northern and Central Mozambique, especially in Renamo areas and with the soldiers and leadership of that movement, during the 80s and on to the peace negotiations in 1989, laid the very groundwork for peace to become possible. The Heins have brought the message of Christianity, love and respect for all human life, to thousands who have never heard of Christ. They gave new hope to entire peoples, often preaching to thousands of brutalized and abandoned people at a time. **In particular, their mission achieved the miraculous conversion to the Christian faith of several of the Renamo leadership.** It was due to this achievement that the Renamo leadership agreed in 1989, for the first time after 12 years of a most cruel and devastating civil war, to meet with a delegation of Mozambican leaders to discuss the possibilities of a framework for peace with the government of that country.

When the peace negotiations began in earnest, it was Rodney, with his 35-year-old Piper Aztec, who ensured that the Renamo negotiators could actually depart from their strongholds and hidden camps, and arrive at an international airport, to finally make their way to Rome, Italy, where the negotiations were taking place. More than once, factions of the Mozambican government opposed to peace negotiations bombarded the makeshift airstrips in Sofala and opened fire on Rodney's plane. Many people, myself included, have been strengthened in their faith just by witnessing, again and again, the truly miraculous escapes from injury or death during these flights. Rodney was the only person Renamo leaders trusted to have knowledge of their exact whereabouts and to fly them.

The strain on the Hein family during those years was enormous. The highest representatives of the most powerful nations would relentlessly rely upon them, demanding that with their meagre means and their old airplane, they would ensure transport and communications with an otherwise inaccessible people, without any remuneration.

This might be illustrated by the mere fact that throughout the entire negotiation process, until as late as two months before the signing of the Peace Accord, Renamo had no general accessible means of telecommunications at their disposal. Every document and every proposal for the total of eight lengthy protocols, which make up the Peace Accord, had to be received and conveyed to Renamo by Rodney and Ellie. And even when the Renamo leadership finally received a portable satellite telephone in August 1992, they (and with them the world powers and negotiators of the United Nations), had to rely on Rodney's plane to ensure the supply of petrol for the generator.

Rodney and Ellie neither sought credit nor publicity. To the contrary, they have patiently endured accusations and defamation, harassment and threats, and the hate of those who envied them for the confidence which they had built up in Mozambique simply by continuing to set examples of love and faith.

Following the conclusion of the Peace Accord in October 1992, Mozambique and most neighboring countries suffered the worst drought ever recorded. Millions were at risk of dying from lack of water and food. Rodney and Ellie spent every moment and resource possible to try and alert the world, to fight for relief aid, and when it was not forthcoming, to themselves take food and medicines to the dying populations. In a most cruel and merciless war of hunger, where the government was deliberately preventing relief supplies from reaching the interior of the country (where Renamo had ruled), Rodney's plane became the only sign of hope. With its maximum payload of half a ton, the plane would find up to 4,000 people gathering around a landing strip, waiting for help and food. The cruelty of this experience of not being able to do more than making a gesture, day after day, was most painful for him.

The Heins continue to be known in the villages, by the hundreds of pastors whom they have motivated to take up mission work, by the patients they helped and the students of the Bible School they have built up at Inhaminga.

My belief and trust in the Hein family and in their integrity and competence is unconditional.

From **Rev. Wayne Myers**
Missionary to Mexico and to the nations

From time to time we encounter people who make a profound impact on our lives. They challenge, unintentionally, our thinking and our lifestyle. Such are Rod and Ellie Hein. Having been privileged to know hundreds of fine missionaries worldwide in over 50 years of dedication to missions, I feel that on a scale of one to ten they would be at the top. Words are inadequate to fully express my admiration for the daring courage and dedication of this Godly young couple, whose costly sacrifices and sensitivity to the Holy Spirit's guidance have affected an entire nation's history, both politically and spiritually. May this book inspire all of us to re-evaluate our priorities and redirect our efforts to things eternal.

CONTENTS

PART THREE: BEAUTY FOR ASHES

INTRODUCTION

This is a story of ordinary people of no particular qualification or talent, caught up in an extraordinary drama that would affect a nation's history and change the destiny of many souls. It is simply a story of lives surrendered to God, not of any great personal achievement. Controversial and challenging, it is deeply sad in parts and ecstatically joyous in others. Most of all, it's true – every bit of it – and it's current, tracking right over into 2000.

Posted on our wall are the words of a famous 20th-century author:

To Be A Good Writer

First there must be talent... Next there must be discipline.
Then there must be a conception of what it can be,
and an absolute conscience to prevent faking.
The writer must be intelligent.
Time is short; he must survive and get his work done.
I should like to read what such a writer would write.
–Ernest Hemingway

It has helped me to read those lines often, as I have struggled and wished for more intelligence to make a complicated story plain. Because it is true, and not a novel, I couldn't change anything to make it flow or work out better. Fact is fact, and fact can be stranger than fiction.

As for the discipline part, how easily I have been distracted, perhaps due to emotions connected with each chapter's content. Pleasant or painful, they are intense; and *I always needed one more cup of tea!*

Rodney has been a constant encouragement, his patience endless in providing needed help. I do not have a good relationship with the computer and without Rod's help and perseverance I would have given up a hundred times. Together we have laughed and cried as we recalled some of the incidents. We dug out timeworn memos and documents to make sure I recorded it all accurately.

We are thankful to have survived to pour out our hearts on these pages, squeezing out every drop that might touch another heart and make it easier for someone to see clearly the love, power, and greatness of our God.

- Ellie Hein

* *Before reading, please note the definitions furnished on page 445.*

Part One

WHO WILL LOVE
MY CHILDREN?

"I could scarcely breathe.
My heart pounded in my chest
as I felt the AK-47 automatic rifle
pressing into my back
and heard a rough voice say, 'Start Walking!'
Oh God, I don't want to die. Oh God, my children!
Who will love my children?"
-Ellie Hein

I heard the voice of the Lord saying,
"Whom shall I send and who will go for us?"
Then I said , "Here am I! Send me."
Isaiah 6:8

One

A Bullet in a Bag

The brilliant African sun glistened on the blue wings of the Piper Aztec as Rodney levelled the plane across the treetops. Sandbanks shimmered beside the mirror of water as the aircraft dipped even lower for a closer view of the hippos lazing in the Zambezi River. A monstrous crocodile sunning himself on the bank lurched at the rude awakening of the twin-engine roar and slithered into the concealing depths. Twitching their small ears the hippos shifted their great hulks just a little at the giant steel bird with the deafening cry.

Rodney's heart surged with the joy of it all. This was Africa at its best. Unspoiled. One could for a brief moment forget that this was a time of war.

Dark, hidden danger lurked beneath unsuspecting wings. Camouflaged in the grass and scrub of the riverbank a band of soldiers waited, the cold metal of their weapons held in deadly grip. Within seconds, a barrage of deadly venom spewed out at the target. Rodney tensed as the burst of automatic firing erupted above the engine noise. A second succession of shots dealt a dull thud to the fuselage.

Rod quickly scanned the instrument readings to see if any damage to vital parts showed up on the panel. Nothing, yet. Most important, the engines were still running. Leaning over to check first the right wing then the left, he could see no leaking fuel – but would leaking be visible? Detecting no apparent problem, Rodney increased speed to reach the bush strip as quickly as possible. "Thank you, Father God. You have covered me with your feathers and under your wings have I taken refuge."

Twenty minutes later Rodney's trained eye picked out the narrow clearing in the thick of the forest. Friendly soldiers, this time, filtered out of the bush to stand with their weapons ready along the rough runway, on the alert to both welcome and protect. Carrying out the landing checks, Rodney approached the slit in the forest. Would the wheels come out into position? Yes! The green lights flashed as the wheels were released. Thankfully, the undercarriage held firm and remained intact as the wheels hit the dirt and the plane settled in a rush of dust and leaves. Rod breathed thanks, mopping his brow in sweaty relief.

The Renamo soldiers grinned a cheery welcome, gripping the hand of their friend "Joseph", some giving him a hug. Here was a link to the outside world. A world with no war, where people lived without fear of being bombed and attacked. A world where there were shops and things to buy, where peace and sanity were the order of the day. A group of church leaders and Christians also moved forward to greet Pastor Joseffo, (alias Rodney or Joseph). They had walked a long way to be at this place today where they had been told to wait for the gifts that would come in the missionary's plane. They laughed and chattered excitedly; a reunion was extra special when life was fraught with the perils of war.

Out came the boxes of Bibles for the churches that have no copy of the Word of God. Through the door came bolts of cloth, covering for the women and girls whose half-naked bodies were shamefully kept hidden in huts and behind trees as they had no clothes. Finally, the bags of seed, without which there would be no crop for survival this year. What a haul of treasure from the heavens today!

As the last bag was dragged out, a trail of seeds poured through a shredded hole in the sacking. Whoever plants this bag of seed will find a metal object among the seeds. He might not be too surprised, for after all, this is the time of war. Who knows where the next bullet may hit?

With the plane now empty, Rodney checked for evidence of the firing and found a bullet hole in the belly of the plane. Close scanning of the angle of the hole showed its route of passage. The rear elevator control cables had been missed by just half an inch, the bullet lodging in the bottom bag of seeds directly behind the front seat. The plane suffered only one hit out of numerous automatic discharges. Rodney estimated that at least eight weapons were firing. It only takes one bullet, however, to bring a plane down. Once more God had spared Rod's life. *"You shall not be afraid ... of the arrow that flies by day" Psalm 91:5.*

Guerrillas In The Bush

When I was a child in Rhodesia (Zimbabwe) I asked my mother "Will there be a war in my lifetime?" Talk of 'during the war' (reference to World War II) had at times reached my ears, and I was sure I could never be brave enough to endure the terror and hardships of a war. My mother had comfortingly assured me, "I don't think so." How wrong we all were!

My first experience of war-related violence occurred just a few years later when a gasoline bomb was thrown through the window of the junior boys' dormitory at the boarding school I attended in Chipinge. Screams of terror brought us running to the windows to see terrified little boys fleeing across the grass towards our dorm.

That night, each of us seniors had a trembling little girl in our beds with us, their dorm having been cleared out for the boys to sleep in. There was nothing left of the boys' dorm. Only one boy, Johnny, on whose bed the bomb had fallen, was badly burned. My cousin, Francois, suffered minor burns on his hands when he bravely beat out the flames on Johnny.

Our last war incident to date was in 1994.

The Rhodesian bush war raged at various levels of intensity from 1965 - 1980. Rodney and I were married in 1971, just prior to the acceleration of the war to its fiercest heights. The horrors of war fractured the lives of both Black and White communities, shocking the world with its brutal atrocities committed by all sides. Ambushes, land mines, mortar attacks on homes, brutal murders became regular occurrences. Families were torn apart by repeated separations as the men reported for military call-ups. How we hated those separations. Friends and acquaintances were buried monthly, sometimes weekly. High security fencing surrounded our homes, the windows guarded by grenade screens. We drove in a mine-proofed vehicle with bullet-proofed glass.

The turning point in our lives came when my father was caught in an ambush attack. In agony and bleeding profusely from five gunshot wounds, he bravely hung onto life, trying to convince my mother that he was OK. To us, "Pa" was invincible. He shot his first elephant at the age of twelve. He was the toughest of the tough. He couldn't just die like that! But he did.

We were shocked to the core. The funeral was awful; painfully empty, except for grief which was full to overflowing. We were suddenly faced with the fact that we were spiritually ignorant and didn't really know what followed death. We believed in God, but had no personal experience of knowing Him. Rodney pulled a dusty Bible from the shelf and together we tried to find answers. We couldn't. But into the depths of our devastation and hopelessness God dropped the seed of searching, which would within a year grow into a glorious discovery and acceptance of Jesus as our Lord and Saviour... not only for us, but for my mother, my sisters and their families too. Bereft of our beloved earthly father, we learned to lean hard on the Everlasting Arms of a loving, eternal heavenly Father.

In 1980 the Rhodesian war ended with Ian Smith's White government finally being replaced by the Black government of President Robert Mugabe. By this time our loyal allegiance to our homeland had been shifted from an earthly to a heavenly country. We were totally sold out to the cause of Christ. He had become our very reason for being, and we were passionately in love with Him. While thousands of White Rhodesians fled from the prospects of living under a Black government to the borders of a still White South Africa, God clearly showed us to stay. He had a purpose for our lives right where we were.

How great our deliverance, to be free of the bitterness and anger created by years of animosity and fighting. Jesus had washed away our pain and sorrow, and the chains of rancor had fallen away. We had grown up and lived in an atmosphere akin to apartheid, and now we felt the call to take the Gospel to those who had been our enemies. The cessation of the war brought in also a freedom of movement. Where we had previously been restricted from taking the Gospel to the bush areas because the army forbade entrance into these regions, we could now come and go as we liked. We became missionaries to our own country, taking the Gospel to the villages, discovering Black brothers and sisters in Christ who had been set free just like us.

Our season of peace was short-lived. Evenings spent in prayer and intercession birthed a vision and placed an incredible burden upon our hearts. It was for Mozambique that our souls agonized this time. A nation that was suffering beyond imagination, the Marxist government having persecuted and put to death countless Christians. The blood of the martyrs seeped up from the ground, crying out to God. Thousands upon thousands perishing without having heard the Gospel of Jesus Christ. Civil war raged rampant, leaving a path of death and destruction far more devastating than any that had scorched our own soil.

To this we would go, straight into another hostile war zone. Only this time there would be no ambush or mine-proofed vehicle. There would be no grenade screens and pro-tective fences, no help on call. There would be only God, and the sword of the Lord, which is the Word of God. These would prove again and again to be far more powerful than any earth-ly weapons of warfare.❖

"If you live for the next world you get this one in the deal; but if you live only for this world you lose them both"

C.S. Lewis

Two

THE FORGOTTEN PEOPLE

When the Marxist Frelimo government came into power in Mozambique in 1975, the border with Rhodesia was closed. Frelimo wanted no dealings with the "West" as we were then. But when Rhodesia became Zimbabwe, that all changed, President Mugabe being a chief supporter of Marxism and a close friend of the Communist Frelimo government. The border to Mozambique was opened and we were able to cross, but not without some difficulty and restrictions.

In 1982, a token move toward religious freedom was made and the ban on churches was lifted. However, the rigidly Communist government of Mozambique did not welcome missionaries, and though persecution was less severe many were still to die for their faith. We had to enter the country on some pretext **other** than preaching. Initially, if we wanted to take Bibles we had to smuggle them. All forms of Christian literature were classed as "subversive material".

With the help of Jethro, a Zimbabwean friend, we visited several small churches. Always we were deeply moved by their enthusiastic welcome and tears of joy. "We have not received visitors for many years. People are afraid to come here because of the war. We know God loves us, and cares for us, because He sent you to us. We thought we had been forgotten by the world." One old man stood shakily to his feet, leaning on his stick while he spoke in a quivering voice. "Now I am ready to die, for my eyes have seen the salvation of the Lord. God has not forgotten us. Many times I have been close to death, but God has kept me alive to see this day."

It was humbling to see the response to the small gifts we brought. Bibles held tenderly to the breast; soap sniffed and exclaimed over, caressed as if these were bars of gold. Clothes were reverently draped over tattered rags. The Christians hung onto every word we said, so eager for contact with the outside world and hungry to hear the Word of God. It was an enriching experience for us, but we were saddened by the conditions in which they were living. We longed to clothe this naked church with the garments of praise.

The oppressive spirit of Communism cloaked the nation. The few cars one saw on the run-down roads were old and dilapidated. The streets were devoid of real life and activity, the people walking about with eyes averted to the ground, speaking or laughing very little. Most of the shops were closed and the few that were open had little to offer. Rows of empty shelves with a few goods of no real use scattered about depicted the state of the heart and soul of Mozambique under Marxist rule.

We determined to give our best to the people of this nation. Already we had seen the difference that Jesus makes in the lives of those who put their trust in Him. The Christians looked different, were different. Their faces, though they lived in troublesome times, were not darkened with the hopelessness of those around them. We would preach the Gospel, encourage the churches and win souls for Christ, no matter what the cost.

This was easier said than done. The days of a steady income were long gone. Rodney used his many talents to do odd jobs until we had enough money to fill the tank of our old pickup truck as well as some extra cans, as one could seldom buy diesel in Mozambique. We would buy as many Bibles as we could afford, perhaps twenty or so, a box of soap and a few pens and notebooks. Old clothes that we were always collecting were packed in bags, then off we'd go.

Sometimes we felt embarrassed at the meagre supply of goods we were taking to people who had nothing. Our truck was unreliable and not cut out for long rough journeys on deserted roads. The few people whose lives we touched and the little we achieved did not in the natural justify the risk and effort involved in making these journeys. But in spiritual value the risks measured as nothing. Jesus shed His blood for the souls of men. Even just one soul was worth a trip. It was never just one soul though; we were amazed at what God did with the little we had. He spoke to Rodney's heart, "Take what you have and I will multiply it." Little is much when God is in it.

For three years we worked in this manner, visiting as many places as we could. We were constantly frustrated by the limited time the Frelimo government allowed us to stay in the country. Just a few days at a time and then only in certain areas, where our every move was watched by SNASP agents, the Mozambican equivalent of the KGB. We were not permitted to evangelize or do any significant work. We devised a plan that would give us more time and allow us to visit other regions by applying for transit visas en route to Malawi. This allowed us to drive through other regions and as our truck broke down frequently, we always had an excuse for taking extra days on a transit journey. We would stop off along the way, establishing contact with church groups of all denominations and preaching wherever we went. Once we reached Malawi we would cross over for just a few hours and have our passports stamped, to prove we had been there, then start back on our transit journey home.

TRAVEL IN THE WAR ZONE

Traveling through a war-torn country was no joke. The Mozambique Resistance army (Renamo), in their attempt to bring an end to Communist rule, majored in the destabilization and destruction of everything that moved in the name of the Frelimo government. Trains were derailed, deep trenches dug across the roads to stop traffic, vehicles ambushed and land mines planted. As we drove along, avoiding the large potholes and still larger land mine holes, our eyes were peeled for any sign of an unexploded mine. Sometimes we could detect a disturbance of the ground where one had been planted. At intervals, the burnt out shells of vehicles that had been ambushed and set afire littered the sides of the road. Some were quite old, already rusting, but others had obviously been in very recent attacks. We saw few civilian cars but a number of army trucks full of Frelimo soldiers patrolling the roads. There were some isolated checkpoints and we always felt uneasy when the Frelimo soldiers advanced towards us with AK-47 guns in hand, to ask questions. They were suspicious and edgy, checking our documents again and again. We could never be certain they would let us through.

The fighting was escalating and the rebel army gaining more and more territory in Mozambique. So much so, that only the major towns were considered not to be under the control of the rebels. With 85% of the population living in the rural areas, we were not reaching the majority of unreached peoples at all. Something had to be done if we were to see God's promise to us fulfilled in our lives... *"Ask of me, and I will give you the nations for your inheritance, and the uttermost parts of the earth for your possession. Psalm 2:8"* (Amplified)

Our inheritance, the souls of men, women and children, was hidden far away in the bush, in rebel territory. How were we to get to them? It was forbidden by law to enter those regions and it was impossible to claim our inheritance without doing so.

We were consumed with an urgency to preach the Gospel in the regions beyond. The implications were uncertain. Reports of the fierceness of the Renamo rebels had reached our ears. What would they do if they found us in their territory? Perhaps more alarming was the question of what the Frelimo government would do with us if they found we had been in rebel territory. Either way, we were running the gauntlet.

We didn't spend too much time pondering these things; the compelling desire to *"go into all the world"*, to win the lost at any cost had been too strong for too long. I remembered a dream God had given me when we first started our work in Mozambique.

In this dream, I was standing on the banks of a wide river, watching in horror as soldiers fought in the water, which began to turn red with the blood of the wounded and dying. On the other side of the river, a crowd of terrified women and children watched, their pitiful cries and wailing rising above the noise of the fighting. They were painfully thin, dressed in dismal rags; their faces bore the look of abject terror and despair.

My heart ached for them. I knew I had to help, but to reach them I had to pass through that river and the killing soldiers. Haltingly, I stepped into the river, aghast as the water began to stain my clothes a sickening red. I kept my eyes on the faces on the other side, I knew I had to go on. I continued deeper and deeper until I was completely covered by the bloody water. I knew I had to be willing to be submerged into that blood-bath in order to gain entrance into the lives and hearts of those people. I had to identify with them as Christ had identified with people during His ministry on this earth, becoming partakers of their lives and suffering. I had to risk being shot as well as contaminated by the waters. There was no other way.

I passed through the waters, unharmed by the soldiers. I climbed up the bank, weeping, and embraced the women and children, giving what comfort I could.

1985 arrived, and we took a trip that would forever change our lives and ministry. We left our three children, Tammy, Dustin & Deborah in the care of our family in Zimbabwe. It was a difficult goodbye for us, as we did not know how long we would be gone or what lay ahead. For the children it was an adventure; they loved staying at home on the farm and were well loved and cared for. Nobody knew of our plan to enter rebel country; we kept this secret as the crossing would be illegal and we did not want any of our family implicated should we be caught. There was no way we could do this trip through normal channels.

We had opted to cross the border into Mozambique from Malawi. It was too difficult from Zimbabwe, as the borders were patrolled by Zimbabwean soldiers, and to be caught on an illegal crossing would be risky. This meant driving through Mozambique into Malawi in the regular way, then crossing again into Mozambique in a highly irregular way.

The drive through Mozambique was tougher than usual. At the roadblocks the soldiers were exceptionally unfriendly. We also met up with some army trucks full of Zimbabwean soldiers who were now helping the Frelimo government fight the rebels. The Zimbabwe army had started running a convoy system where all vehicles traveled together under military escort for protection. At this time traveling in convoy was optional; later it became compulsory. The Zimbabweans did not like seeing us on the road and the commander leaped out, yelling at us. "What are you doing on this road. Don't you know it is dangerous?" We replied calmly that we were on our way to Malawi. "You should not use this road without army escort. Why are you traveling alone? You must be friends of the bandits!" We weren't. Not yet, anyway, but they weren't convinced and ranted and raved their objections. Eventually they said "Go! Go!"

The truck groaned and complained over the potholes and broke down several times on the lonely road. Rodney with his toolbox worked a series of miracles but at dusk we broke down again, this time in a stretch of road that suffered frequent attacks. It was our policy not to travel at night but each breakdown had cost us precious time; now night was falling and it didn't feel good. Finally, with headlights blazing to all in the bush that there was a lone car on the road, we limped the last thirty kilometres into Tete, where we camped for the night by the Zambezi River. Two days later we reached Nsanje, the southernmost tip of Malawi, where Pastor Chakanza and a group of his church members awaited our arrival.

WAITING

The Shire River forms the border between Malawi and Mozambique for miles. Dugout canoes ferry a few passengers back and forth. Here where the land is so flat, the river flows slowly, forming swamps that harbor hoards of mosquitoes of unbelievable size.

We were glad to have Pastor Chakanza as our guide. He knew these parts and had made several preaching trips into the region where we were headed, by canoe and on foot. He took us to one of his churches at Kalumbi village where we were housed in the mud and thatch church, "Just for one night, then we will make the journey into Mozambique by canoe. I must make arrangements with one of the canoe men to take us across very early in the morning before it is fully light so nobody can see your white skins," he told us. It was not a problem for Mozambicans or Malawians to cross the border in this manner, but why would white people want to go into the wilds? Such a suspicious-looking event would surely be reported to the police and customs officials.

The Shire valley must be one of the hottest places in Africa. The day droned on with the flies sticking as close as the humidity that clung damply to our skins. This was the wet season and rain fell several times a day and at night, adding steam to the closeness of the atmosphere. We were eager for nightfall that would bring a slight drop in temperature, send the flies to bed and usher in the event for which we had driven all this way. All we could think of was Mozambique and how close we were to fulfilling the long-awaited dream of entering the forbidden regions. We pushed aside the feelings of uncertainty and possible trouble. We had not come this far to turn back now.

Nightfall brought small relief from the heat; the very ground breathed out the hot rays absorbed during the day and the flies were replaced by the mosquitoes, which caused far more discomfort. We hardly slept, so anxious were we for the call that would say, "Come now; it is almost morning, we must move." The call never came, and we sat and waited as the flies took over duty from the mosquitoes at morning light.

Finally Pastor Chakanza and his men arrived to tell us that the boatman was away for two days and we would have to wait till his return. "Why can't we find another boatman?" "No, no. This is the one we can trust. He will take us secretly and will tell no one." Who were we to argue? We did not know any- thing, so we submitted and waited for another two days.

The two days turned into a week, the excuses becoming more and more prolific, only we ceased to believe them. This was a typical example of African delaying-tactics. The African is incredibly affable and will do his best not to offend or disap- point. He will avoid telling you straight what he knows you don't want to hear, and will embark on tactics of evasion that border vaguely on the truth while he thinks of a better way to let you in on the picture. He does this for your own good and peace of mind, and if it is a form of lying he does not see it that way. After a few more days of this considerate treatment, we were at our wits' end and tempted to turn back, mission unac- complished. Finally, we realized they were afraid to take us and I even wondered if perhaps God didn't want us to go after all — a sure sign of resolve being whittled away by agitation. We announced that tonight was to be the night. If they did not take us, we would find a canoe and go by ourselves. The widening of their eyes showed us they believed we meant business, and sure enough, just before morning light we heard the voice, "Come, very quietly, it is almost light."

We swished through the long grass to the black mud that framed the water's edge. There we waited for some time with- out even a whisper, slapping softly as possible at the mosqui- toes, which were even more merciless in their swamp home- land. A pink and gold dawn was already lighting up the sky when the gentle splashing of water heralded the arrival of two canoes. First our supplies were loaded on. Back packs with blankets, a few clothes and personal items. Our tea box with cups and plates, tea, coffee, sugar, and some packets of soup.

Next, the valuable cargo of Bibles. We splodged ankle-deep through the black porridge and climbed into our boat. On the bottom was a mat of reeds to sit on. We soon discovered that this mat was wet; there was a pool of water under it as most of these canoes leak. One boatman stood at the helm with a long pole digging into the mud and the other sat at the rear with a single paddle. The first boatman began to pole us on our way while some of our team helped by pushing, knee deep in the muddy water. It was a great sensation when we felt the water lift us off the mud bottom, then we wobbled precariously as the men who had been pushing climbed over the side and sat in single file behind us on the reed mat.

It was a beautiful ride. Our excitement and anticipation were enhanced by the quivering of the canoe as the light currents swirled this way and that against the dugout trunk. Hippos grunted and blew through their nostrils. Lily-trotters danced from one lily pad to another in pursuit of their early morning breakfast. A brilliant blue kingfisher hovered, then darted with a splash into the water, emerging with a silvery prize. Then to our surprise, a tiger fish jumped right into the canoe. Black stripes against a shimmering body thrashed on the reed mat. Delightedly, one of the team seized it. "Ho. The Lord has provided!" It was a good sign of blessing.

The boatmen maneuvered the canoes around the large floating islands inhabited by storks, plovers and a variety of water birds. We marvelled at the way the men knew their way around. To us, the river was a maze of reeds and islands, the narrow channels between floating vegetation adding to our confusion.

We traveled for over an hour, passing a couple of canoes full of Mozambicans on their way to Malawi. They exclaimed in shocked surprise when they saw us but were reassured by Pastor Chakanza's "Don't worry, these are friends, not enemies. They come in the Name of Jesus."

Pastor Chakanza had explained to us that he had sent a

messenger with a note some days ago to the Renamo army base on the Mozambique side. In the letter he had asked permission to bring some foreigners into Renamo territory for the purpose of preaching the Gospel. A message had finally come back saying yes, but that we were to be taken to a certain point on the river bank and remain there until some of the soldiers came in person to talk with us. Presumably, they wanted to check us out before allowing us to roam around at liberty.

"We have arrived," said Pastor Chakanza as we rounded another bend, and the boatmen turned towards the riverbank. Glad to stretch our stiff legs, we stepped out into more mud and slush, this time knee-deep. For a considerable way we slipped and sloshed, fighting to keep our balance. By the time we got to firm ground it was difficult to tell the difference between us and our black fellowmen. Waiting for us were the messengers that had been sent ahead and a couple of churchmen from the area. Seeing the sweat drip from their faces gave us an idea what we must look like too, the broiling sun beating heavily upon our backs. "We must wait here," we were told. There was not a tree in sight, and though the ground was firm it was wet. There was absolutely no place to sit, so we stood and waited, swatting flies, wilting and growing weary on our legs. We wondered how long we would have to wait in this place and position.❖

Three

CAPTURED

We waited and waited. Finally, one of the church members felt sorry for us and said he would take us to his village where we could wait for the soldiers in the shade. We walked for about half an hour to some small huts nestled under the welcoming shade of paw-paw and banana trees. It felt so good to sit on an animal-hide chair in the shade with a mug of cold water to drink. This respite turned out to be a big mistake! We were not following orders as they had been given, and we were yet to learn how crucial it was to follow orders.

Out of nowhere, a bicycle ridden by two armed soldiers came flying around a hut. Sweeping the corner they skidded in the mud and in the attempt to dismount with a flourish, the soldier perched on the back lost his balance, and they both tumbled into the mud right in front of us. It was like a scene out of a movie. We desperately wanted to laugh, but one look at their faces, and we dared not. Ego badly bruised, the soldiers began yelling unintelligibly at us, then pointed to the guide that had received us on the Mozambique side. They bound him hand and foot and knocked him about some, just enough to scare us. They certainly scared me; I was sure this was it, finito! A tirade of thoughts rushed through my head. "We made a mistake in insisting to come across when God was putting obstacles in our way to stop us. It had been such a fight to come all this long way, why didn't we listen? Oh, Lord, I'm sorry!" All the usual negative stuff that follows when things go wrong.

"Who will love my children?" I was in anguish. If we went to prison for years or if we were shot, someone else would have to raise our darling children. Although Rodney and I had discussed all this, knowing it was a real possibility, now facing the actual reality of it turned my blood cold. Our children would be loved and cared for by my family, but nobody could love them like we do.

SPIES!

The two soldiers grabbed our rucksacks and emptied everything out onto the muddy ground, inspecting each item piece by piece. They raised their voices in angry affirmation of our guilt as they pointed at our tea box. They thought we were spies sent by Frelimo and that box would surely prove it.

During the Rhodesian war we had accumulated various army items which Rod had to use on call-ups. Olive green rucksacks, water bottles and best of all, a metal box for our tea things – sturdy, strong and waterproof. We had never foreseen that this very useful box would cause us so much trouble; the problem being that it was an old **ammunition** box. The soldiers leaped upon it in anticipation. Yanking the lid open, their expectant expressions turned to disgust as all they found was our tea supplies. Not to be deterred, they began pointing at the other army articles, exclaiming "Militar, militar!"

We knew we were in trouble. We spoke no Portuguese but we did speak Shona and though this was a Sena-speaking area, we attempted to explain to them our mission. Preaching our hearts out we told them "we had come because God had sent us to tell them of the love of Jesus; this was their day of salvation. We loved Mozambique and the people were in our hearts; that was why we had come at risk; it was to bring them a message of peace and hope in a time of war." We said a whole

lot more, as much and as fast as we could. To our amazement
the Commander replied in Shona. He understood us! We were
later to learn that most of the Renamo soldiers spoke some
Shona. What a break! "You speak Shona? Where are you
from?" He told us that he had worked on a plantation at
Chipinge in Zimbabwe. "That's where we come from. I was
born in Chipinge", I said, putting out my hand to greet him as a
friend. He put out his hand too. Here in the wilds, a long way
from home two groups had met and found they had a common
ground. The atmosphere was defused to some extent. "I am
Commander Chidoko," he said.

They untied the pastor and explained that because we had
not followed their instructions to wait at the river, they thought
we were enemy spies slipping through into their territory. They
helped us repack our bags and said that we were to go with
them. We realized that our problems were by no means over.

For two hours they walked us through the bush, AK-47's
held close to our backs. We still had to prove our innocence.
Speaking to them in Shona had done wonders, but that did not
mean we were absolved of suspicion. Finally we reached the
outskirts of Shire Base, the Renamo regional base camp.

THE COMMANDER RECEIVES CHRIST

Mozambique's colonization by the Portuguese had
brought in a strong Roman Catholic influence. This and ani-
mism were mostly all the people knew about religion. While the
soldiers questioned us in detail concerning what we did, where
and why we did it, we took the opportunity to preach the Word
in our replies. The fact that we white people had left comfort
and a high standard of living in Zimbabwe to come to a place
like Mozambique, this bush region in particular, made some
impact and clearly puzzled them. We challenged the soldiers
concerning their own spiritual condition, and after some dis-
course a wonderful thing happened. Commander Chidoko
said, "Yes, I want God to forgive my sins. I want to receive
Jesus into my life." He put down his gun and removing his cap,

knelt down in the dirt and prayed with us. Here was this proud soldier who had been so angry at the humiliation of falling off his bicycle into the mud, willingly humbling himself before God and the group of people standing by. This acceptance of Christ by the first Renamo soldier we met gave us a real boost. To us it was a sign that God was with us all the way in this venture and that we would see many souls won for His Kingdom.

We were given permission to move on to a village where meetings had been arranged by Pastor Chakanza. It was a great time and people walked miles to come and listen. Some were interested in the message and others were interested in seeing the white strangers who had dared to cross the river. Bush telegraph—word of mouth—is very effective and any unusual news spreads like wildfire.

In Frelimo Communist-controlled areas, villagers were moved away from their homes and placed in communal villages or camps from which they went out daily to labor in the collective fields. The Communist system took most of the crop produced, leaving little for the people. Here the people told us they had been liberated from Communism by Renamo and were free to live in their own villages and keep their own fields as families used to do before the Communist takeover. They brought food for us daily and though the crops were rotting due to excessive rain, they managed to find a few treats for us such as an occasional pineapple or paw-paw. The women took turns bringing clay pitchers of water for our washing. A young girl with a hunchback worked especially hard to minister to us. Her name was Fagi, and she was always the first one to jump up to carry water from the river, search for firewood to cook the food, doing whatever she could for us. The women showed their warm welcome by acts of kindness, taking our coming to their region as a sign of peace and hope for the future. But at all times, two armed soldiers were unobtrusively standing near, watching. We were not fully aware at this time that **we were prisoners**, so discreet was the manner of the soldiers. As far as we were concerned, we were simply waiting for permission from a higher order to proceed further into the heart of Mozambique.

Our meetings were immensely blessed. The hunger for the Word of God was inspiring. "Even if you were free of Communism and oppression, you can never be truly free without Christ. Jesus is the true Liberator, the one that will set you free from the bondage of Satan." Many received Jesus as Saviour and brought their witchcraft fetishes, charms and artifacts to be burned. There is no doctor around except the witch doctor who dispenses powders of dried blood and ground-up bone tied in a little ball of cloth, to hang around the neck on a string. This supposedly brings not only healing, but also wards off evil spirits.

After three days more soldiers arrived. Commander Chidoko's saluting and stamping in their honor clearly showed that these were of higher rank. One soldier was of slight build, with a quiet but calculating manner. He carried a pistol on his hip. We would come to know him as Commander Dique. The other had thick woolly hair twirled into fringes, wild eyes and an untamed look. This was Mario. Carrying a transistor radio in a leopard skin pouch slung over one shoulder, an AK-47 over the other and a chrome plated pistol on his left hip, he cut a classic bandit-figure. We were surprised at the ultra polite greeting as they stretched out their hands to ours and said "Please, you must come with us now." The rain had brought up the level of the rivers and we waded almost waist-deep through what was normally an ankle-deep stream while porters carried our rucksacks and blankets on their heads. It was almost dark when we arrived back at the edge of the Renamo Shire Base. Our stuff was dumped at a hut surrounded by a maize field on one side and tall jungle grass and bush on the other. The heavy clouds threatened another deluge and already a few large drops were falling while thunder rolled ominously. Knowing that most bush huts harbored a variety of creeping creatures we usually chose to sleep outside, but with this storm coming we took cover inside to spend **one of the worst nights of our lives.**

Eleven bodies packed like sardines lay on the mud floor. Several sonatas of snoring competed against each other, intercepted by loud grunts and groans and unintelligible exclamations. This didn't bother any of the other bodies; we were the only ones not accustomed to such midnight entertainment. The heat from the bodies so closely packed together with the heat of the fire built on the floor sent stifling waves over us. Smoky fires help ward off the mosquitoes, but some continued to whine around our ears and nibble consistently at us. Sleep finally came, only to be dispelled by a huge rat that ran over my chest, digging its sharp little claws into my neck.

Was ever a morning so welcome? The rain had temporarily ceased, and at first light we moved outside to stretch our cramped legs and gasp in the fresh air. Bush telegraph had rippled from hut to hut that the missionaries had been moved to another location, and it was not long before both Christians and non-believers began to arrive to see about us. Unbeknown to us they were very worried about us; the big guys from the big base had come and taken us off, and who was to know what would happen to us now? Sounds of voices communicating over a radio floated across a bushy area. We could not hear what was being said but guessed we were the topic of interest as Commander Dique communicated with his home base and with the Gorongosa Headquarters of the Renamo army.

THE NOOSE TIGHTENS

From out of the bush came two wooden chairs and a table. These were placed under the shade of the paw-paw trees as Commander Dique followed and sat on one of the chairs. We were called forward for questioning, but one at a time; we could not go together. We were drilled with many questions. Where we had come from, at what churches had we been preaching in Malawi, had we spent any time in the Frelimo areas, what was our purpose for coming to Renamo, Mozambique? Truthful answers gave opportunity to preach the Gospel all the way. When I was unsure what to say, I simply said, "I don't know; I am only a woman, I do what my husband tells me." This impressed them as it is right in line with African custom for a woman to refer questions to her husband.

After the interrogation we were sure we would go free, but we had a surprise in store. All our possessions except for a change of clothes and toiletries were taken away. We were dismayed at the retention of our passports; a man without a passport is a man without a country. We wouldn't miss our watches much; what is the meaning of time in Africa anyway? We were allowed to keep only our Bibles, which was of greatest importance. To our questions of why our things were being taken away, they simply said we would get everything back once we were released. They had some investigations to do first.

The days passed slowly while the soldiers did indeed investigate. Through the "bush telegraph" transmitted by the local Christians who were still allowed to visit and worship with us, we learned that runners had been deployed to Malawi to check out our story at the places we had visited. We wished we could understand the voices floating from the radio transmitter stationed in the Renamo base camp nearby, but all messages were coded. The unceasing activity of the radio left us in no doubt that we were a hot topic.

WITCH DOCTORS GET INVOLVED

For a prison it was not bad, but the uncertainty together with the humidity, rain, flies and mosquitoes began to rasp on our nerves. Our meals were sparse, a little rice with pumpkin leaves. We used our tea bags again and again, drying them in the sun during the brief intervals that the sun shone. I became very ill with amoebic dysentery, and at one point was sure I was dying. This was a direct attack from the devil and we found out later that a group of witch doctors had converged to come against us in the spirit. They did not like the light that was coming into their dark territory through the Word of God.

Our bathroom was a mealie field (corn field), where we took our showers from a clay jar in the midst of shoulder-high maize while the other kept watch. We were not allowed more than a few meters from our shelter. Armed guards were present day and night. We forgot what it felt like to be dry; the rain dripped through the sparse thatch of our shelter and though we huddled under a piece of plastic, our blankets were damp and smelly. At night we lay dreaming up scrumptious menus with such intensity that we could smell the steak on the grill and fresh bread in the oven.

At times we were too weak and discouraged to pray. We asked God to alert His intercessors. We needed someone to fight for us. The Lord gave us a word that the prayers from the West would draw us out of the East. Other times we were full of hope and courage, convinced that God was working out a marvelous plan for our lives. He was. One by one the soldiers came to ask us about our faith and about the Bible. We enjoyed great Bible studies together and were glad that Pastor Chakanza and the rest of the team had opted to stay with us. They could have left at any time but said, "No, we are together. We cannot leave you here alone. Where you are, that is where we will be also." Some of the local Mozambican villagers also stayed close by to be with us. They fetched firewood and carried water from a stream for us to bathe, cooked our food and served us with great care. Fagi was one of them. We will ever remember her quiet strength and the love of Jesus shining through her.

FREE AND ENDORSED BY THE PRESIDENT

Two weeks after our first contact with the soldiers, the word for our release came. Not only were we free to go, but we were free to go anywhere in Mozambique. A personal message from Afonso Dhlakama, the President of Renamo was relayed to us. "You are welcome in Renamo zones. Please preach the gospel to the people and to my soldiers also; they too need to know about Jesus. Please bring as many Bibles as you can. The Christians need Bibles and my soldiers also."

We were wild with joy! Our belongings were returned with embarrassed smiles and a chicken was cooked with rice and tomatoes for the best celebration meal of our lives. We were assured that we could immediately proceed on our journey inland. But we had one priority in mind – to get back to our children. We promised we would return before long to continue with ministry further inland. It poured rain all the way on our walk back to the river, but we didn't care. Huge banana leaves served as umbrellas and at least kept the water out of our eyes so we could see where we were going.

The Shire River was dark from the reflection of the black thunder clouds and night was not far off, but there was no way we were going to hang around for another night. The wind blew strong, and we prayed the storm would hold off as we climbed into the canoes. It did, and with relief we disembarked safely in Malawi and set off to find our pickup parked under the bushes.

This incident was the launching pad for some of the most exciting, rewarding, fruitful years of our lives. What if we had grown tired of waiting at Kalumbi village? How easy it is to take a wrong turn at a crossroad of life.

It was wonderful to hug Tammy, Dustin and Deborah. They seemed doubly precious now, and we couldn't get enough of them. We told nobody about our experience and smilingly nodded yes when we were asked, "Did you have a good vacation?" We would have to keep our lips tightly sealed if our mission was to be continued successfully.❖

LION TERRITORY

While we rejoiced at all God was doing and the incredible opportunities He was opening for us, we faced some serious problems. Because Zimbabwe had troops fighting for the communist Frelimo army trying to eradicate Renamo, we were in danger. Should our contact with Renamo be discovered, it would be the end for us. Zimbabwe newspapers warned that if any Zimbabwean was found to have links with Renamo, they would be considered traitors and enemies of the state. The death penalty was reserved for traitors. It was better that our friends and family should know nothing lest they become endangered as collaborators.

For almost three years we operated from Zimbabwe through Frelimo Mozambique, into Malawi and over again into Renamo Mozambique. We established a good church network in each region. Amazingly, we were showing the *JESUS* film in the Zimbabwe army camps as well as in the Renamo camps. Rodney had asked one of the Commanders if he would like the film shown to the soldiers. The Commander had been very keen, and we took every opportunity to reach anyone we could, regardless of what side they were on. Frelimo would not allow religion in their camps, declining our offer to show them the film, but we witnessed to them as much as we could when we saw them along the roads. We were playing a cat and mouse game, and sometimes the cat got so close you could smell it. We knew that at any moment the police or army could step in; but the Word of God was reaching places and people where it would not be possible any other way. God gave us peace, and we did not live in fear. Sometimes we made foolish mistakes that could have blown our cover, but the Lord in His faithfulness always undertook. It was our business to do the work, and it was His business to protect us.

The devil took every opportunity to try and scare us off. One day when I was alone at home in Zimbabwe, an army jeep full of Frelimo soldiers roared up to the gate. My first thought was to hide, but instead, with pounding heart, I greeted them at the door trying to look like I had not a worry in the world. I asked if I could help them, and the leader replied that he was in town for a visit and was looking for one of his relatives who was working for us. Sure enough, Chico claimed him as a relative. I was glad I hadn't done something silly like run out the back door. I had experienced God's courage at the sound of the lion's growling. If our love for God is greater than our fear of Satan, he cannot defeat us by his roar.

When we were in the interior of Mozambique with the Renamo soldiers, some of them had asked us to take pictures of them. Most of them had never had a picture of themselves, so this would be a special treat. They posed with their guns, looking as military in their garb of odd bits of uniform mixed with civilian rags would allow. Some posed proudly with their new Bibles. We had the shots developed in another country, as it was not safe to have them exposed in Zimbabwe. The soldiers were easily recognizable as Renamo, and many of the pictures showed us standing with them, as well as preaching and handing out Bibles. We were now in possession of very incriminating material, and we were not happy about carrying it on our journeys with us. However, we could not bring ourselves to disappoint our photographed friends. There was only one thing to do: ask God to help us keep them hidden from the eyes of those who sought to do us harm.

We took them on our next trip and hid them, praying that the customs and guards that carried out routine searches on cars would not find them. We slipped them through the border check OK but after several hours on the road were stopped at a roadblock not far from the town of Tete. This roadblock was manned by Zimbabwean soldiers operating in Mozambique. They were aggressive and shouted at us. "Why do you travel so often on this road? We know you are friends of Renamo! Today we are going to get you. We are going to search this car, even strip the paneling off till we find evidence against you!"

Of course they did not know we had contact with Renamo; it was the father of lies speaking through them to terrify us. It amazes us how often Satan speaks half-truths through people who have no way of knowing anything about our situation.

It isn't easy to look innocent when a stranger's accusation is partly factual. The soldiers ordered us to the army barracks some way off at Tete. One of them jumped into the front of the vehicle with us, holding his gun ready, while we had to travel with an army truck hot on our heels. It was not a good feeling. We tried to be friendly to our escort and asked where he had received his efficient training. He told us he had been trained with many other Frelimo soldiers in Romania, but he was not very conversational. We prayed fervently from the heart. With this guy in front of us we couldn't have even eaten the photographs. They were hidden under my seat and I sat tight.

All too soon we arrived at the army barracks. While several soldiers stood guard at our vehicle, others went inside to register their suspicions about us to officers of higher rank. We were more than a little scared, but God had it all under control. We watched as the Colonel came down the steps. **We knew this man!** The Lord had marvelously worked things out. We had met him on several occasions in a Mozambican Refugee camp in Zimbabwe. He welcomed us warmly with, "Come and have a cup of coffee with me in my office." We accepted with relief as he assured the soldiers that we were his friends and were not to be bothered anymore. How faithful God is to silence the roar of the lion.

SOWING TEARS, REAPING SOULS

"They that sow in tears shall reap in joy.
He that goeth forth and weepeth, bearing precious seed,
shall doubtless come again with rejoicing,
bringing his sheaves with him." Psalm 126:5,6 (KJV)

The canoe crossings became second nature to us and the people welcomed us gladly each time we returned. Boxes of Bibles and bags of clothes were ferried across and carried on heads of couriers further and further inland. We were usually met on the river bank by Mr. 'X', a real character whose wizened features were hidden under an enormous straggly straw hat. He worked with Renamo as a type of spy-come-coordinator. He knew the river like the back of his hand and was an excellent boatman. We never tried to discover his real name though all the locals knew who he was.

We loved the warmth of the African people and enjoyed observing their customs, which are parallel to many biblical customs. They eat together seated on the ground around a common pot, sharing whatever is available. Strangers are well received and automatically are served something to eat. Lengthy salutations with repetitious inquiries concerning the health of the visitor and welfare of family members are considered essential in displaying good manners. One thing the African person has much more of than the wealthy westerner is time; one of the most precious and elusive things in life, the one thing which once lost, can never be recovered. When someone dies, everyone gathers from far and wide to mourn together, sharing each other's pain. If someone is ill, friends and relatives walk for days to come and inquire about his health. They are never in a hurry and carry out their activities in a relaxed manner. All seem to work together, old and young, telling stories and teaching one another. There is never a worry about whether or not a task will get done; it can always wait for tomorrow!

Children are a vital part of family life. The older ones carry the smaller ones on their backs and play together. Since there are no shops and no toys to buy, they make their own entertainment. The boys use bits of bone and stones for cattle and goats; the girls use corncobs for dolls. All have to help with chores from an early age, herding goats, collecting firewood, pounding corn, carrying water in clay jars on their heads for long distances. We are always humbled by a visit in the villages. The people honor us, always giving their best. To see the suffering and hardship they endure with patience is a great lesson to us.

TERROR AND TORMENT

Physical conditions in the bush of Mozambique are almost beyond description. Most of the country is of low altitude, intersected by rivers that dry up during drought, and flood their banks during rainy seasons. The sun is intensely hot, vast swamps and dank forests are infested with malaria-carrying mosquitoes. It seems there is a pest or destructive agent standing ready to demolish anything you have or make. Termites eat the poles or wood of buildings, locusts destroy the crops, ants eat your books and clothing, and inhabit your food. Rats and field mice are prolific and very active at night. Shoes and clothing must be shaken vigorously to dislodge spiders and scorpions before being put on. Crocodiles hide in riverbanks ready to drag an unsuspecting person under the water for a meal. A dark curse prevails, fed by the satanic activities of witchcraft that rules many lives. Surely the light of Christ is all that can dispel this darkness.

Death from natural causes is unknown. The people believe that death, disease, drought, lightning, attack from wild beasts, any type of misfortune is caused solely by magical powers; by curses, witches, or the vengeance of ancestral spirits who have been annoyed. The distressed African knows only one source of help and escape. He seeks out the cleverest witch doctor in whom he places his implicit faith.

The witch doctor rules the village, having greater power

even than the chief, for his power is spiritual. He judges at trials, divining judgment and accusations and solving mysteries while seated on a goat skin. He throws his bones, shells, animal teeth and various other artifacts while he chants his communication with the ancestral spirits. He carefully studies the position of his tools; their related position will tell him what he wants to know.

The circle of faces gathered around him is tense, no one knows who will be found guilty. The incantation goes on, then suddenly he stiffens. Pointing to a man or woman in the crowd he shouts, "There is the one responsible for all this trouble!" The accused person screams and runs madly. He or she may be perfectly innocent, or may indeed be collaborating with the devil. The witch doctor may prescribe the poison test, the belief being that if innocent, the person will survive. Few survive the deadly concoction of the poison cup, innocent or otherwise. Or he may pronounce a curse on them. This is equally deadly but by slower means. The accursed is gripped by a deadly fear and frequently wastes away and dies, though from a physical standpoint there is no cause of death. Often the miserable soul unable to live with his fear, hangs himself – to get it over and done with. Frequently blood sacrifices are called for. A pigeon or chicken, a goat if it's a serious case, and ultimately, though it is seldom spoken of, a **human** sacrifice. Parts of the human body are considered to have great powers. The witch doctor also requires payment. He or she is the most feared and hated person in the village, but considered vitally necessary to the survival and well-being of the tribe.

NO MEDICAL FACILITIES

These remote areas have absolutely no medical facilities. If someone is wounded or ill, they have two choices: go to the witch doctor or believe God for a miracle. There are so few that know the name of Jesus, they turn to the witch doctors, usually with disastrous results. People died almost daily in the villages. It seemed that in every village we entered families were mourning for or burying a loved one.

We learned that the most effective way of giving comfort is simply through identifying with the people in whatever situation they are. Laugh with those who laugh, mourn with those who mourn. We have to become partakers of their sufferings as well as of their joys. When there is no way to help, nothing we can do for the sorrowing, just to love them and weep with them helps to bring healing.

Early in this learning experience while walking to a village for a meeting, we passed a group of people carrying two men on stretchers made out of branches. They were emaciated and barely conscious. Their feet were bound with dirty rags and flies buzzed around them. "What happened to these men?" we asked in dismay. "They were walking to their fields when they stepped on anti-personnel mines that had been planted by the communists. We have been walking with them for three weeks, from near Quelimane. We are trying to get them to a place where they can be treated." It was awful; we had no help to give them but to pray and offer encouraging words. I wept.

Day by day we discovered Jesus in a new way as we found ourselves identifying with events we read about in the Gospels. *"The Son of man has no place to lay His head."* At times we slept along the side of a footpath, no hut, no blanket, no food, no water. *"And Jesus, being moved by compassion, stretched forth His hand and healed them."* It is exciting to see the miraculous hand of God move when people believe Him for healing. Many physical problems are related to the spiritual problems that abound through witchcraft. Sometimes deliverance from demons is all it takes to see a person miraculously healed. How desperate the need for teaching, and how great the tragedy of leaving converts unequipped for their new life in Christ. The seeds of equipping nationals as leaders to teach the people were planted deep into our hearts from the start.

The joy of harvesting a soul is a wondrous experience, but true to the Word, sowing in tears precedes the bringing in of the sheaves. There is a price to pay. A sense of urgency stirred within us, and we were driven by an urge to go further, to visit new villages not yet reached. The pioneering spirit was strong in us and would not be satisfied with staying close to the shores. The words of David Livingstone were never far from our hearts, "I see the smoke of a thousand villages where the Gospel has never been preached."

IN REBEL CAMPS

"I will both lie down in peace and sleep;
For You alone, O Lord, make me dwell in safety." Psalm 4:8

Living among the Renamo soldiers challenged us, soldiers in God's army. Here were men and women enacting a level of discipline, commitment and unity that we as Christians should be proud to emulate. We were amazed at their dedication and willingness to pay the price for freedom in their nation. They displayed a genuine love and commitment to their President, Afonso Dhlakama, speaking highly of him. They were of one accord. The military camp felt strange at first. I would wake up at night and think to myself, "Here I am, the only white woman in a rebel camp." But I never feared the Renamo soldiers – even when Rod was away. They always treated me graciously and with respect. My comfort was in knowing that *"the angel of the Lord encamps all around those that fear Him, and delivers them." Psalm 34:7*

There was always a lot of saluting, stamping of feet and military etiquette. We were given a place at the officers' table at meal times and were served by waiters who first held out a basin of water for us to wash our hands (an African custom). We had the liberty to move around as we pleased, but if they considered it necessary, we were given armed escorts to accompany us as we trailed through the bush from village to village. Sometimes we requested to go without escorts but were told that they were for our protection as had been ordered by President Dhlakama. Fanning out from the camps, we visited the civilian population in their villages. They always welcomed us freely, and it was obvious that the relationship between Renamo and the povo (people) was a good one. Grateful for liberating them from the communist plots imposed by Frelimo, the citizens accepted Renamo as the ruling government of the province.

We ministered to the soldiers on a one-to-one basis as well as in group studies. We held large evangelistic meetings, preaching while they stood at attention after morning parade. We baptized several soldiers in the river; what a privilege to lead these men to Jesus and see them receive the Holy Spirit. They were hungry for life, for hope and peace and received the Word with gladness.

We watched as the men trained for fitness and endurance. They ran up and down the mountain carrying out various maneuvers, often training during the night hours. One morning at about 2:00 am, we woke up to the sound of hundreds of feet pounding the ground as they ran by. The ground literally shook as they shouted and chanted and stamped in unison. It was the most terrifying sound I had ever heard, and we wondered for a moment if the camp was under attack. On listening to the chants, Rod assured me it was only soldiers in training, not a Frelimo attack. I could not stop shaking, and it was hours before I got back to sleep.

The next day we spoke to some of the villagers who told us that Renamo sometimes captured Frelimo strongholds merely by instilling fear. They make such a noise that they sound like thousands instead of hundreds, causing the Frelimo soldiers to drop everything and take off in terror. This I could believe, having experienced a taste of that terror. Then Renamo would move in and capture all the artillery without even firing a shot. It reminded us of Gideon's 300 men and how the Lord won the battle for them through the trumpets and torches. In the same way, we as the army of God, even when we are small in number, can disperse the hordes of darkness through the power of praise, worship and intercession.

We did not know it, but all this was simply the beginning for us. It would be almost ten years before we spent our last night in a Renamo camp.❖

FLEE YOUR HOMELAND

In October 1987, as we were preparing to head home through Malawi after one of our river-crossing trips, we received a call from friends in America who had seen a report which exposed our travels in Renamo zones. The article, published in a Roman Catholic political journal would likely appear in Africa as well, if it hadn't already. We were shaken!

Returning to Zimbabwe was a risk, but we had no choice, as our children were there. Would we get through Mozambique? What about the roadblocks? Perhaps officials would be waiting to take us at the border post? We prayed and felt the reassurance of God's hand upon us. By this time it was forbidden to travel the Mozambique "hell run", as it was called, without military escort. We were racing against time; it might take just a few days for the report to appear in Zimbabwe, and we did not want to be delayed by long, slow convoys.

The presence of God was tangibly with us, and we experienced miracle after miracle as He supernaturally intervened on our behalf. We drove as fast as the road would allow without seeing a single other vehicle. The Frelimo roadblock – a barbed wire strung across the road surrounded by armed soldiers loomed into view. As I was wondering what Rod was going to do, he screeched the truck to a halt just in front of the wire and shouted to the soldiers, "Open up, I have orders from the highest authority to proceed with speed!" Immediately, they jumped into action and opened the road to us. We drove off laughing, excited about God. At the Zimbabwe border we sailed through the formalities without any problem, and headed home. **We did not know it was for the last time.** Arriving in the middle of the night, we collapsed into exhausted sleep.

We awoke early the next morning to be told by one of our workers that the police had been around three days in a row asking for us. This was bad news, and we knew they would return. I worked around the house, filling the rooms with treats for our children who were scheduled to arrive in a couple of hours. Tammy and Dustin were at boarding school in South Africa. Rod and I prayed that if we were to be hauled off to prison, we would at least have some time with the children first. I was so worried, I even packed an overnight bag to take to jail in spite of Rod pointing out that I would not be allowed to take it with me anyway.

The kids arrived, and we had a great time. As we laughed and talked together, entertaining our usual stream of guests, we noticed two police cars driving slowly past the house. This continued at intervals throughout the day; only Rod and I noticed as we were on the lookout. A couple of times the cars stopped and a policeman would get out, but then they would drive off again. We guessed that they had no real evidence and were reluctant to confront us with so many visitors around. Loath to allow our visitors to leave, we kept them all day, flooding them with cups of tea.

The next three days were a political holiday, and nobody was on active duty to bother us. The last day before taking Tammy and Dustin back to school, we went on a picnic. We returned from a beautiful day at the Bridal Veil Falls at Chimanimani, to find a police jeep parked at our gate. Rod greeted the policemen cheerily, "What can I do for you?" They had some lame excuse about hearing that Rodney was soon going to South Africa and would it be possible for Rod to buy one of them a watch while there?" Rod said perhaps. That was it, they left.

Saying goodbye to Tammy and Dustin and Rod was very hard. How serious was this threat and what lay in store? The night before his return from South Africa Rod phoned me and told me to pack whatever I valued most without letting on that I was packing. He felt from God that we were to leave Zimbabwe immediately. This was confirmed by a secret warning message from a friend in the CIA. The days with our children and other family members had been God's special gift to us.

The last night was taken up with the regular weekly church meeting in our house; members of our very precious fellowship gathered. We looked at the beloved faces of my mother, my sisters and friends. We had told them we were off on another mission to Malawi. It was the truth, but not the whole truth. I could not tell them that we were to be separated possibly for years. But we could tell them that there is nothing on this earth that can separate us from the love of God.

"For I am persuaded that neither death nor life, nor angels nor principalities nor powers nor things present nor things to come, nor height nor depth, nor any other created thing, shall be able to separate us from the love of God, which is in Christ Jesus our Lord." Romans 8:38,39

BY THE SKIN OF OUR TEETH

We pulled out early in the morning, stopping to take one last picture of our home. The jacaranda trees and flowering shrubs were in full bloom, and I fought back the tears. Uncertainty weighed heavily on us; we had to leave for Malawi through separate routes. Rod wanted to get the car out and the few things we could fit in it so he would drive through Mozambique on the road we always traveled. He insisted that Deborah and I were to fly from Harare airport, as it was much safer. I remember Rod holding me very tight as we kissed goodbye. "Don't worry, tomorrow night we will celebrate our wedding anniversary together in Malawi, you'll see. When your plane lands, I'll be there to meet you."

It was a long day. Our plane was delayed three hours and

then I sat with four-year-old Deborah for a further two hours after boarding. I had been relieved to find we were not yet black-listed at the airport customs, but the wait on board was nerve racking. What were they waiting for? The answer came in the form of a group of government officials who walked on board and started looking around. I recognized one of them as the Minister of State Security at the time, Ushiwokunze. He had to be looking for us! He wasn't; he chatted cordially to a passenger in a black suit, and then the officials walked off the plane. The plane had been delayed for a late government official. At last we took off but were delayed again in Lilongwe.

Meanwhile, Rod had a reasonably uneventful trip through Mozambique and was waiting to meet us at the airport on schedule. But no plane came. Finally, he was allowed to see the passenger list, but to his dismay Deborah and I were not listed. Did they intercept us at airport customs? He had no way of knowing. He waited in the hopes that we would be on board despite not being on the list, and was rewarded when peering in through the door of immigration, he spotted us in line. Ignoring the "Entry Prohibited" sign, he charged through and grabbed us both, one in each arm. The security guards came over to tell him he was in a prohibited area. "You don't know how happy I am to see my wife and child!" Rod exclaimed happily. They laughed and told him not to do it again. We did celebrate our anniversary together, in a tiny little mission house. There was nothing but bread for dinner, we had had no opportunity to buy gifts for each other, but to be safely together was the most precious gift in the world.

Four days later, we received a call from friends in Zimbabwe saying reports about us had been published in "Moto" Magazine, a Zimbabwe political update. The report told about missionaries that had been collaborating with the enemy, Renamo. **God had perfectly engineered the timing;** we had gotten out by the skin of our teeth! Some days later we became the subject of both radio and television news in Zimbabwe as the public was requested to report our whereabouts if they knew. The die had been cast, we could not return to Zimbabwe, or we would be imprisoned and tried for treason.

My family had a difficult time with the CIA questioning them strongly about us and our activities, especially my poor mother. There was no way they would believe that she did not know about the activities of her children. She didn't, but CIA and some Army officials returned again and again, to find out if she had anything at all to tell. My sister, Lorraine, and her husband, Don, were questioned too. We were in disgrace and certainly caused a lot of problems for them all. It was embarrassing for them to try and answer questions of the local community too. "What's going on? Why did Rod and Ellie have to run away with their children? Is it true that they're involved with the bandits in Mozambique? We were in disrepute with the government and with those who did not understand our commission. Some said, tongue-in-cheek, "We knew those Happy Clappys would get themselves into trouble one day!" To this day our family has not complained, and have faithfully stood by us in love. (Thank you, Ma, Don & Lo, Richard and Sannie; we appreciate you!)

Taken from our October 1987 newsletter written shortly after we arrived in Malawi:

We escaped from Zimbabwe to Malawi covered by the mighty hand of the Lord. It is truly a miracle that we made the crossing in safety. We know we will be able to do a more effective work for God from here. Just as the children of Israel must have had trepidations about crossing the Red Sea, and then decided it was the only thing to do as the Egyptians were after them, so have we been pushed into making the crossing. We are excited, having been baptized anew into our calling; we have been immersed into the river that separates the new way from the old. We can do a far more effective work into Mozambique from Malawi than we could from Zimbabwe. God is good!

Right now the new land is rather lean: we have no home, no furniture, but we have each other and we have Jesus. Our prayer is that when the test of the bitter waters comes, we will drink without grumbling and complaint. If we can learn to drink willingly from the cup, even though it be bitter at times, we will be spared much heartache and fruitless wandering in the wilderness. God has given us many wonderful opportunities, let us press on to know Him, that we may accomplish that which He has sent us for.

SHELTER IN THE WARM HEART OF AFRICA

"For in the day of trouble He will keep me safe in His dwelling; He will hide me in the shelter of His tabernacle." Psalm 27:5 (NIV)

Our frequent river crossings, prior to our flight from Zimbabwe, had not gone unnoticed by the Malawi police. The "Young Pioneers" trained by Dr. Hastings Banda's government to be the eyes of the nation were quick to report any unusual activity. There had never been any attempt to stop our trips, and we could only conclude that the Malawi government was not concerned enough by our preaching expeditions to raise any objections. However, they were watching more closely than we realized, and on one of our trips prior to our escape from Zimbabwe Rod had received a message that the Special Branch wanted to ask him some questions. We drove to Lilongwe to meet for the first time with William Lunguzi, who was at that time Deputy Chief of Security for the Southern Region. Not knowing what to expect, Rodney was shown into the office by a smartly dressed officer. Lunguzi, an impressive man in his dark suit, stood up from behind his desk, stretching out his hand.

"Mr. Hein, I have been wanting to meet with you for some time."

Relieved at the friendly tone, Rod shook the hand of the man that unbeknown to any of us, was to play a vital role in the destiny of Mozambique, as well as our own lives. Sadly, he was to die long before his time, in one of Malawi's famous car accidents; one of those where you never know for sure whether or not it actually was an accident.

"I must speak to you on a matter of extreme delicacy," ventured Mr. Lunguzi. "I am aware that you have made contact with and frequently visit with Renamo in Mozambique." Rodney said nothing. "Don't worry, I am not about to make things difficult for you. In fact, I am in need of your assistance." Lunguzi explained. "We all know this war in Mozambique has dragged on too long and is affecting not only the economy of Mozambique, but of all her neighbors, especially Malawi. The Nacala railway line, our only link to the ocean, which is closed because of the war, must be reopened. This cannot be done without speaking with the Renamo leader, as his troops control that region. You know our own forces have been sent in there to defend the railroad, but Renamo is strong. We have no way of making contact with President Dhlakama, but I have been informed that you have a good relationship with him. Can you get a message to him, a request for him to meet with me for discussions? If he agrees, I can arrange for him to come secretly to Malawi."

Rod agreed to try. Lunguzi was clearly intrigued by this missionary's association with Renamo. "We visit Mozambique to preach the Gospel; our motive is Christ Jesus." Rod told him. "No, we are not in any way involved militarily."

"But you are a Zimbabwean, and Zimbabwe is at war with Renamo. What does your government think of your friendship with them?"

"They must not know, or it will be over for us." Rod told him. "While we are on the subject, I too have a request to make of you. If we should run into any trouble in Zimbabwe, would you be willing to give us refuge in Malawi?"

Lunguzi thought briefly then said, "If you have to leave Zimbabwe, yes, you can come here. But do it quietly. Then come to my office, and I will try to work something out..."

A silver tea tray with matching silver accessories was brought in. The bearer laid it reverently on the low coffee table and bowed from the waist down to Lunguzi. "Ah, coffee for you?" Rod accepted; "I prefer to drink Milo," said the Deputy Chief, rising from his desk to do the honors. This meeting held more significance than we could ever have imagined. **The Holy Spirit was making sure that when He led us out of**

Zimbabwe, we would have a safe haven in Malawi. God makes plans and prepares the way for us long before we know we are going to need them.

REFUGEE STATUS

By the last quarter of 1987, Malawi already had thousands of Mozambican refugees within her borders. Now we were here too, in a slightly different category, but refugees nevertheless. Would we really be allowed to stay, and if not, where would we go?

Sometimes called "the little Switzerland of Africa", Malawi is known for her friendliness and acceptance of foreign visitors. Travel brochures boast beautiful beaches on the azure shores of Lake Malawi, which holds a magnificent variety of fresh water tropical fish as well as the famous "Chambo," one of the most delicious fish in creation. Palm trees and sunsets, beautiful mountains and nature reserves call out from glossy brochures with the slogan "Malawi, the Warm Heart of Africa." A few days after our arrival, Rod made an appointment to see Lunguzi. The time had come for us to seek refuge in the warm heart of this small nation.

Lunguzi had not thought his tentative acquiescence to receive us in Malawi would be put to the test so quickly. Malawi, at that time under the rule of Kamuzu Banda was the odd one out in African politics. She felt the squeeze from all sides as the Socialist and Communist bullies of Tanzania, Zambia, Mozambique and Zimbabwe put the pressure on. Trapped in this cocoon of unfriendly neighbors, Malawi had to tread softly; she was small and vulnerable. The consequences of rattling the bear's cage by harboring missionaries whose names appeared on Zimbabwe and Mozambique's "wanted" list could mean big trouble. Being in a top security position gave Lunguzi a fair amount of authority. In helping us, he had a good chance of contact with Renamo. On the other hand, he could overstep the mark within his own country as well as in the neighboring states. Trying to strike the right balance became from that day a major preoccupation in Lunguzi's career.

"Here's what we will do." he told Rod. "You and your family can stay here in Malawi. If you have trouble from immigration or any other quarter, phone me at this, my personal secure number. I will inform certain of my fellows to turn a blind eye on your activities across the border. However, if your Renamo contact is exposed and you become an embarrassment to Malawi, we will have to ask you to leave. Let us say that you have unofficial permission to remain here, but if anything goes wrong, you're on your own."

This was good enough for Rod, who understood Lunguzi's position. "We are very, very grateful for your assistance, Sir. God bless you!"

The news that we could stay was very welcome. We did not think too far ahead about things that could go wrong. We had a call on our lives to Mozambique, and at this time it could only be fulfilled through living in Malawi and operating into Mozambique from her borders. It was our appointed time to live in this nation for as long as God saw fit. Our children would attend St. Andrew's, a good English-speaking school. God was answering our prayers in more ways than one. We had agonized over Tammy and Dustin being at boarding school for a year now, coming home only during school holidays. Chipinge, our hometown did not have a high school, so we had no choice but to send them off. "Oh, God. Please make a way for us to have the children home with us," I had prayed. Now this prayer was answered!

The mission house we were staying in was too small for a family plus visiting missionaries. We needed a home and set off in search of one after asking God for something good. Rents in Malawi were astronomical, the cost of living much higher than in Zimbabwe. Our minimal income was already stretched in keeping us fed. We were mainly eating rice, cheaper than other foods, and the paw paws that grew free in the mission garden.

The third house we viewed said to us "I'm what you

want." It was spacious and airy with a large fenced garden. The rent was surprisingly lower than the other houses, but the problem was that we had to pay six months in advance. This was another of Malawi's unusual customs we were rapidly learning about. Six months in advance! We didn't even have enough for one month. However, Rodney said "We'll take it. I'll have the money for you within a week." My head spun.

Back at the mission house I lay on the bed, migraine in process. "I can't move. Just leave me here to rest" I moaned. The truth was, I was miserable and depressed and homesick, so full of despair and sorry for myself. Where did Rod think he was going to get the money from anyway?

A while later he returned with a letter from our mailbox. "It's addressed to you, from the States" he said. "Just put it down, my head's too sore to read." I replied, but my curiosity overcame my self-pity and I opened it. The contents blew me away. Any trace of migraine fled from my head. Inside was a letter signed "from the Women of Grace." This was a women's group from Grace Church in St. Louis. They had been on a retreat and had taken up an offering. "We asked God to whom we should send this offering, and He impressed you upon our hearts, Ellie." A check sufficient for the six months rent was enclosed. Oh praise be to God! How faithful are His ways. We were thrilled beyond description. Not only was our need provided for, God had confirmed our move. There was no way the Women of Grace could have known of our need a month before it occurred!

We lived in that house for eight years. It was a refuge to us and a shelter to many in need. Literally hundreds of guests entered through our doors, some just visiting, others in hiding. Some folk dubbed it "The Railway Station." It seemed as some took off, others arrived. There was scarcely a day that our dinner table was not surrounded with extras, some expected, some not. It was a challenge to keep meals flowing, but God gave me an assurance, "As long as you have guests around your table, you will never lack provision."

Our life in Malawi was uncertain, we never knew when we might have to leave at a moment's notice, or what lay in store for tomorrow. So, we never got the dog we wanted to get, in case we had to suddenly leave, but we did get a cat. Sam, a ginger and white cat died a short while before we finally left Malawi. During all that time, God filled our home with His peace, though there were many storms. We were very happy in that house, and God miraculously provided the rent each time we had to pay. The time of persecution in Malawi and the time to leave did come, but only after we had fulfilled the mission for which we were sent. Thankfully, we couldn't see what some of those tomorrows would bring.❖

Part Two

A VOICE FOR
THE VOICELESS

*Speak up for those
who cannot speak for themselves,
for the rights of all who are destitute.
Speak up and judge fairly;
Defend the rights of the poor and needy.
Proverbs 31:8-9 (NIV)*

"All it takes for evil to prevail
is for good men to do nothing."

Edmund Burke

One

MISSION MALAWI

FEED MY SHEEP

God not only provided us a home, but a place where His sheep could come and feed upon His Word and learn to feed other sheep. Leadership remains one of the greatest needs of the African church. We called them in from the bush; pastors and leaders who had suffered for Christ, men who had hazarded their very lives for the Gospel. Some walked for several days through Mozambique; others came from southern Malawi.

Excerpts taken from our March 1988 newsletter:

The men arrived at our rented premises in Limbe in ragged clothes but with great expectancy. Most of them walked long distances to Nsanje and caught the train to Limbe. We showed them their rooms and they stared in amazement — real mattresses? They had never slept on one before; wouldn't they fall off? A switch on the wall that flooded the room with light when touched. A miracle! Then there was a shiny pipe object - when you turned it water gushed out into a big bowl. This was as incredible as Moses getting water out of a rock! As for the strange seat over a hole, when you pulled that handle water roared around with a terrifying noise! Very strange.

Best of all, the good food. Imagine eating three times a day! They later told us it was the first time in years that they had gone to bed with full stomachs night after night. "Truly, God is blessing us!"

As well as the famine for food and thirst for water in Mozambique, there is also a famine and thirst for the Word of God. Many of the pastors have received little or no Bible instruction, often not even owning a Bible. One pastor testified of having only one Bible among a group of churches. They tore it into sections and circulated them among the churches, literally breaking the Bread of Life into portions so all could partake.

Some of these men had gone to neighboring countries to seek work and received Jesus as Savior. They subsequently returned to their villages where they witnessed to their friends and families. When these also believed, the man automatically became the pastor of the flock. A church would be born, and it usually took on the name of the church where the pastor was saved. Consequently, because of lack of teaching, ancestral worship and witchcraft is frequently incorporated into the church beliefs. Some of the churches have a Pentecostal name but have never heard of the baptism of the Holy Spirit. In the midst of this confusion, God in His mercy has drawn out men and women with a sincere love for Him and a desire for truth. He has kept them, nurtured them, and has brought them to a place where the cry of their heart has been answered. "O Father. Send someone to teach us your Word, to bring us Bibles and to teach us about You." We in turn have been crying out to God to lead us to key men and women, whom we can teach, train and work with and send out to possess the land for Christ. These people are able to reach places we cannot go and thereby accomplish much more than we can."

We covered many subjects but found praise, worship and intercession of utmost importance. These men lived in difficult, dangerous situations. They needed to understand spiritual warfare and how to exercise the power given by the Holy Spirit. They were amazed to see what the Bible says about witchcraft and curses. They had thought that only in Africa do these things exist. Many of them have had loved ones die or become ill after being cursed. We showed them from the Word how to deal with curses, to pray for one another and break the power of the devil in their lives.

The training seminars in Blantyre continued for a few years. Two faithful servants from the USA, Jane Crane and Bonnie Gloth, gave their very hearts to the success of the short-term training school. Others came out for shorter periods of time. We later transferred the training seminars to Nsanje for a season. Always we knew that no matter how far and to how many places we ventured with the Gospel, equipping leaders was one of the most important aspects of our ministry.

Now that we were living in Malawi, we had opportunity to do a more effective work in this small but highly populated country. Various visiting teams, mostly from the USA spent time with us. They were a great encouragement and the Malawians loved having them minister at conferences. We took them out to the villages and refugee camps where they could experience the real Africa and personally touch the lives of the villagers for Christ.

BOMBARDING THE DEVIL'S DOMAIN

Witchcraft is rampant in Malawi and we had some hair-raising experiences. In one of our attempts to bombard the devil's domain, we were bombarded ourselves. While driving to Mankhokwe refugee camp for our scheduled meetings, we slowed down at a village called Sorjin where we saw a large crowd gathered. We were curious to see what the attraction was. Suddenly, the centre of the group broke away, running and screaming in terror. A witch doctor – clothed in animal skins, with ringlets of dried tree bark around his head and a wooden mask of a most hideous design—leaped and danced to the rhythm of the drum played by his counterpart. He was brandishing two long daggers and chased after the people as if to kill them. The terrified people fell into the road as they ran, causing us to stop for fear of running over anyone. Abruptly, the witch doctor returned to his arena, placing the daggers back in their sheaths. Drawn by the power of evil, the people returned to march around him again in fascination, keeping time with the drum.

We started handing out tracts through the window. In seconds, frenzied bodies were climbing all over the truck, sticking their arms through the window to grab tracts and anything else within their reach, including my arm. Fingers clutched into my wrist; pulling with amazing strength I couldn't pry them off. More bodies leaped onto our trailer, which was loaded with Bibles and bags of food for the seminar. We thought they would surely steal everything if we didn't get away fast; so though we could not see the road for the sea of black faces, Rod started driving slowly to shake them off. A few held on for some distance. One man had firmly seated himself on the trailer with a never-to-be moved expression. Rod speeded up and as we hit a big bump, he flew into the air. When he landed again, the trailer was no longer beneath him, and he fell into the road to be trodden underfoot by the yelling mob. He was not hurt and stood up as if nothing had happened. Such a crowd can be dangerous. Filled with demons they were ready to tear the truck to pieces. We were thankful to get away safely. Devil worship and public rituals are quite legal in Malawi. Witch doctors control the lives of thousands. When people disappear mysteriously, serious inquiry is seldom made. Frequently the missing person is used for ritualistic purposes and sacrifices.

In Refugee Camps

We arrived at Mankhokwe camp just in time to put up our tents before the first meeting and nightfall. The usual crowd of children swarmed around us to watch in amazement as the strange object they call "Nyumba Azungu" (white man's house) was erected. We found many old friends. They had walked from far and wide to learn from God's Word. The refugee camps, though hardly endurable, gave us opportunity to live amid the people, partaking of their very lives. This makes for a veritable entrance into their hearts. Jesus could always be found among the people, living with them, eating and sharing with them. This knowledge gives us strength when the going gets tough, and we are tempted to pack up and leave. There were only a few pit latrines among thousands of people, and most would find their present area quite acceptable to use. This, plus the goats, chickens and pigs that roam around the huts and our tent, did not make for good hygiene. Each time we ventured towards a pit latrine we were followed by a stream of children who stood around the thatch enclosure till we came out. The same with taking a bucket shower. Little hands would rustle in the thatch to make a peek hole. One child was heard to exclaim, about one of our visitors, "She really is white all over." This was not from naughtiness but from sheer curiosity. Many Mozambican children had never seen a white person before fleeing to Malawi as refugees.

At night, as in most African villages, the pigs, goats and chickens are put into small pens; some simply sleep with the owners in their huts. The animals bleat, snort and grunt all night while dogs howl and bark. Cat fights add to the concerto. Roosters start crowing from 2:00 a.m. Sleep is a rare treasure pursued in vain by most visitors unaccustomed to the assorted noises. A particularly bad night for us was when a nearby hut was being used for brewing beer and partying all week. A family in the hut beside our tent was much involved in the business and were tormented by demons day and night. They screamed and writhed, ran out and wailed. The devil gives no peace even to his own. Though they are dedicated to serve him, he makes their lives miserable; yet they often choose to remain in his service rather than to accept Jesus and receive deliverance and eternal life. It was terrible to hear them, impossible to sleep. The roosters heralded the dawn long before its arrival and our last chance of sleep was gone. One rooster attempted to crow from the top of our tent, but unable to find a firm perch, tumbled down the side, screeching and flapping his wings. With that, we got up to put the kettle on the fire. Tea was the answer!

One of the hardest trials was the total lack of privacy. Not for one moment was there respite from someone staring into your face from close range. They do not consider this rude; they are simply taking every chance to see something very unusual. White skin, hair like chicken feathers, and if you have blue eyes, well, what can you expect? All Africans have dark brown eyes, never any other color. The first day or two it was bearable, but after several days I was so tired of being stared at I wanted to scream. "I must find a place to hide my face before I lose my grace!" Every move was watched by a constantly changing audience. As one group satisfied their curiosity, another crowd moved in. It was too hot to sit in the tent; our seating space was outside and had no boundaries. When we ate, the journey of fork to mouth was followed like a puppy watches its master eating cookies. Then down to the plate again, then a row of eyes lifting up to follow the fork to the mouth again. Day in, day out. It was no use turning our chair around because the people formed a circle around us. Finally I had an idea. I hung my shawl of very light cloth over my face for half an hour a day. This gave me a chance to relax, to unwind, and be by myself. We spent time in between meetings talking, laughing and playing with the children. We had a lot of fun and had to laugh at ourselves too. This is often the true test of a missionary. Not the good preaching, but how you behave in trying circumstances. Our success can only be measured by how much we become like Jesus. We didn't always pass the test!

The meetings were glorious from the start and the people hungry and responsive to the teachings. Some shared their testimonies, how they had fled for their lives from guns and fighting, losing family members on the way. Some were reunited while others continued the search for loved ones. They had lost everything they owned and did not know how many years they would be living as refugees. Strangers in a strange land. We prayed for broken hearts, we prayed for sick bodies. We answered multitudes of questions and encouraged them continually with the words of Jesus. *"I will never leave you nor forsake you."* and *"Fear not, little flock. For it is your Father's good pleasure to give you the Kingdom."*

The fighting in Mozambique intensified and the numbers of refugees increased alarmingly. It was heartbreaking to find a group of small boys sleeping in the dirt under a tree. "Why are you sleeping here? Where are your parents?"

"We don't know where our parents are. When we heard

the shooting we started running. Now we are here."

A little girl told us, "when the guns were shooting, my mother told me to start running and not to stop running until I was out of Mozambique. I ran for three days. Alone. I don't know what happened to my mother."

Some children wandered around from point to point, wailing for mothers and family they had become separated from while on the run. New camps mushroomed overnight as refugees flooded in. People assembled together by the hundreds of thousands. It was an opportunity for the Gospel we must not miss. For many, it was their first time to hear of Jesus. Churches sprang up in the camps; many pastors were also refugees and had fled together with their flocks. It was the day of salvation for all who would listen. When the time came for them to go home in peace, they would carry the flame of the Holy Spirit with them to ignite the fire of God's love in their own remote regions. We were amazed. Suddenly, Mozambique was at our feet in a greater way than our feet were able to take us to in Mozambique.

Our trips across the river continued. There were those who did not flee, determined to stay in their own country. God spoke to some pastors and Christians to remain and uphold the standard of the Cross in a nation that was getting darker by the hour. To these we had a mission of encouragement and support. We visited when we could, taking Bibles and clothes, teaching and preaching as we went. Strong relationships developed between us, as happens when people share together in hardship and danger. We could not forget their suffering and were compelled to go to them, again and again.❖

*"The Gospel must be communicated
not just by our lips, but by our lives."*
— Billy Graham

Two

MASSACRE OF THE INNOCENT

Unaware of the tragedy and trauma ahead of them, it was a cheerful group of men that set off for home after one of the training seminars. They were excited, full of the Word, of renewed vision and hope. Each carried a bag of clothes, gifts for their wives and children. They were barely recognizable themselves; having arrived in rags, they were returning in good clothes with shoes on their feet. It was a full day's train ride to Nsanje where most of them planned to cross the border into Mozambique and foot the rest of the way home.

It was not to be. Before they got to the border, they met masses of refugees streaming in from Mozambique. Canoes were ferrying grey-faced people, some shocked into silence, unable to speak of the things they had seen and experienced. Others told of killings, rape, house-burning and other acts of terror. "Where is my family? Are they safe?" – questions flooded the minds of the men who had returned from the seminar with such great expectations. Some found their families in the refugee camp, others on the riverbanks. Some never saw their families again.

We arrived early on Sunday to find a heavy quietness hanging like a cloud over the camp. We had come for a Sunday service, knowing nothing of what had happened. The Christians greeted us solemnly at the car. "What is the matter?"

we asked. In accordance to African custom, they did not immediately tell us. First they walked us to the meeting point and sat us down on chairs, which they had carried out of the huts. Only after inquiring about our journey and our health, and matters at home, did they begin to tell us of the recent events of horror.

MiGs Rain Death

Early one morning as the villagers started about their daily business of cooking food, carrying water and working their fields, MiG jets started bombing the villages. Helicopter gunships followed, dropping in Frelimo troops as well as Zimbabwean and Tanzanian soldiers. The gunships proceeded to move in on the villages, mowing down at close range people running for their lives. They fired into huts, setting the thatch ablaze. Those who were able to kept running. They headed toward the Malawi border where they could find refuge from this insane attack on civilians. Some ran for five days, stopping only to rest when they could go no further. There was no food on the way and only a little water till they reached the river. Mothers fled with babies tied to their backs, dragging other children by the hand. Fathers tried to find a safe passage for the family through the bush where they could be as obscure as possible. The sick and old got left behind.

More troops were dropped in. They combed through the villages, killing and maiming with bullet and bayonet, showing no mercy to man, woman or child. They set afire food stores, huts, fields ready for harvest – this to ensure that the people would have nothing to come back to. This scorched-earth-policy was aimed at killing and destroying everything possible to make the land uninhabitable. They did not want people living in the Renamo zones, for as long as Renamo had people living around their camps, feeding and supporting them, they could not be defeated.

The Communist troops carried out their wicked deeds with evil precision. The villagers who managed to hide watched as terrified women were raped. Pregnant women were sliced open, their babies tumbling from their bellies to the ground to be spiked through with bayonets. Huts were set alight and children thrown on top of the blazing thatch, their little bodies consumed by the roaring flames as they sobbed and screamed for their mothers. Others witnessed several families herded into a church, which was subsequently set alight, burning them to death. Indescribable deeds of villainous brutality would forever scar the lives and minds of innocent people as their eyes saw hell loosed upon the earth.

At the refugee camp, under the big tree we used as an outdoor cathedral, the Christians were worshipping God, uplifted hands reaching out to the "One" who knew all things. They did not understand what had happened, but they knew that only in Him would they find comfort. After a while they sat down, waiting for the Word. We looked at their faces, strained and grief-stricken, and knew we were hopelessly unprepared and unequipped for a situation such as this. What can one human say to another whose mind and spirit are drowning in a sudden bloody rain of horror and death?

The Lord spoke to our hearts. "Let them see My beauty, My glory – and the power and majesty of My throne room." We opened our Bibles to Revelation and read aloud the scriptures, proclaiming the power and glory of God. *"Then I looked, and heard the voice of many angels around the throne, the living creatures and the elders; and the number of them was ten thousand times ten thousand, and thousands of thousands, saying with a loud voice: 'Worthy is the Lamb who was slain to receive power and riches and wisdom, and strength and honour and glory and blessing.'" (Rev. 5:11-12)*

We led them in a hymn, and as they worshipped the Lamb, and poured out their hearts, they encountered Jesus. In His mercy, the Lord met them and led them to fountains of refreshment and wiped away their tears. Knowing we had no way of ministering to these exhausted, despairing people, it was wonderful to see the touch of the Comforter upon their lives bringing the first stage of healing.

Reports came daily of further killings as the madness continued, stretching in a 30-mile-wide belt along the border. The camps grew fuller by the day. Unprepared for the insurgency, the Malawi government did their best to facilitate the needs, but it was impossible. Aid organizations could not cope. How grateful we were for the container of clothes that had arrived from the USA a while ago. Surely God had sent it for such a time as this. We took blankets, clothes, cooking pots, water pails, and food by the trailer-loads to our friends and church members who had been so hospitable to us on our walking missions. It was a joy and privilege to return kindness to them in their time of need. But it was tragic to see so many going without. The most heartbreaking sight was the small children huddled together in the cold without warm clothes or blankets. Their flight had been in the winter, and an African winter is surprisingly cold at night. The children constantly watched the sea of faces, hoping to spot parents, relatives or friends. Many were now orphans.

The attack raged for days. Standing at the river's edge we watched helicopters, heard the explosions and saw the smoke from the burning villages rise into the sky. Anger filled our hearts; and **agony**. We wept and prayed for Mozambique, for the innocents trapped in the pit of war.

NEWS - FALSE AND FRUSTRATING

The media carried reports of the massive refugee influx into countries bordering Mozambique. Brutalities committed against the civilian population were reported. The problem was that **they were incorrectly reported**. The propaganda machine had the channels well oiled to keep the lies rolling. The refugees testified that it was the **Mozambique government troops** assisted by Zimbabwe and Tanzania committing the atrocities. They had seen them, heard them and fled from them. We knew who it was and others knew, but **the news media reported that it was Renamo**, the Mozambique Resistance Forces who were responsible.

It was the most frustrating experience, hearing the false reports over the BBC and other mainline news stations. We had recently seen an article in Newsweek magazine that carried horrific reports of atrocities committed against civilians. **Renamo was accused of it all**. The Frelimo government was getting away with murder, literally. Mozambique was in crisis; the terror of the civil war would intensify while being fueled with more lies. The only hope for peace was in **truth**. But the propaganda pipeline blocked access for the truth to come through. Renamo had no means of getting their own reports out to the world. Who would help to get the truth out? Who would help bring about the change that Mozambique so desperately needed? Finally we knew **it was to be us!** We had to do what we could, no matter how difficult or what the personal cost. A nation depended on it.

There are some things one would not normally choose to do or get involved in, but the need in a situation changes one's heart and mind. The need here was for **a radio link with the Renamo headquarters**. Rodney agreed to the request put to him by President Dhlakama. "Please, my friend. You must help us. We have no way to contact anybody or get messages to the news media and friends that we have in other countries. Please, will you put a radio at your house?"

This would be very tricky as Malawi had very strict laws about civilians operating HF radios. We would have to keep the operation hidden, as discovery could mean **big** trouble. We were already in so deep, what difference would a few more feet make? Anyway, it would also be of great benefit to us to have this link with the bush. We would be able to arrange for bush ministry from home rather than having to do the river crossing to make our plans. Also, when either of us was in the bush, we would have a link with home at least some of the time. This was sounding better and better, and we did not need much persuasion. It proved to be a venture with multiple advantages not only to us, but to many others, including the Red Cross, the release of prisoners and the Mozambique Peace Process. Most of all, we were able to spread our evangelism net through this network in a way we never had thought possible.

A Portuguese-speaking radio operator was needed, one who knew and understood the Mozambique situation and could be trusted with security. There was no such person in Malawi so we bent again to the need, bringing a young Renamo soldier from the bush to live with us. Gostode lived with us for three years. At 18 years of age, he looked no more than 14. His woolly hair was long and twirled into spikes that stuck straight up all over his head. This, combined with his wide eyes, gave him a look of constant surprise and wonder. From the moment Rod collected him from the canoes by night, his every move reflected astonishment. Never before had he traveled in a car, and the land cruiser was fast and furious around the potholes in the road. The steep climb from the Shire Valley up to Blantyre where we lived and the sudden appearance of a small city lit up with electricity was mind-blowing. Here was a young man who was accustomed to firelight and the moon by night. Yes, it was a life of wonder that lay ahead.

Gostode could not speak English or "Chewa", and Portuguese is not spoken in Malawi. We communicated well enough in Shona. For him to blend in as a Malawian was very difficult. He looked different and moved with the alert, cautious rhythm of a bush soldier. He was as unlike the unhurried, easy-going Malawian as he could be. First things first, Rod got the scissors out and Gostode submitted to having his twirls cut off. This left him feeling naked but helped his appearance, as did the clothes we gave him.

A few meters from our house, within our garden fence, was a tiny cottage which became the Secret Service operating room, and Gostode's house. The experience of running water on tap, a flush toilet and a gas stove was brand new. Gone were the days of digging for roots to eat in the Gorongosa forest, trapping mice and trying to keep warm and dry over a smoky fire. Gostode had hit the good times.

To work at once, but where can we put the radio antenna so it cannot be detected? Rod, as always, flowing with ingenuity, put his ideas to practice. Onto the roof went a toilet vent with the antenna base and cord concealed inside. The stays holding the tube were the antenna wires. It looked good and worked wonderfully. We were now daily in touch with the heartbeat of Mozambique at war and the plight of the suffering people. Thousands of messages would be transmitted through our little station before the war finally came to an end.

To the President of Renamo from "Joseph":

Are you safe? My wife and I visited the Refugee Camp the people are running to. They told us that Frelimo are bombing their villages. We watched helicopters and planes fly along the river and we saw the smoke of villages burning. There is also a Frelimo boat on the Shire River. We deeply regret the atrocities and deaths that have come to your people. We pray every day for peace to come to Mozambique. I trust Psalm 91 will encourage you today. It is only Jesus who can help us through these troubles, if we accept Him into our hearts.

From the President of Renamo to "Joseph":

I am well, together with my family and the soldiers on the ground. Only the civilians, they are being killed. My friend, you must telephone to the news medias and inform them what is happening in Mozambique.

We had to do something, but who would listen to us? We were nobodies with no claim to fame except for being on the "wanted" list. The last thing we needed was publicity. Should we risk blowing our cover by speaking out? After much deliberation we decided yes, we had to speak for those who could not speak. But where to start?

We made telephone calls to ABC and other networks, telling them what was going on. "Yes, but who are you? Who do you work for?" "If you don't believe us, send someone to come and see for himself." we said. They were all too busy on

other assignments. We phoned Newsweek and lodged a complaint about their report on Mozambique and requested they
send someone out to review the present situation. We were
pleased when they agreed, but it was more than a week before
they sent anyone. A photographer and journalist from
Newsweek, reporters from The New York Times and
Washington Post all came together. The photographer would
walk with us through the killing fields and the others would fly
into Gorongosa Headquarters to interview President
Dhlakama. This was a major breakthrough; for the first time
major newspapers were prepared to come and see first-hand
rather than gullibly print the lies expertly churned out by
Noticias, AIM, and other Frelimo communist propaganda
machines.

From Joseph to the President of Renamo:
**I have contacted some journalists who are ready to
come to Shire to take pictures of the victims and to your
Gorongosa Base to interview you.**

From the President of Renamo to Joseph:
**Thank you for finding journalists to come to our zones.
However for security reasons you cannot travel to Shire
now because there are combats along the border between
our forces and the enemy forces that have been dropped by
parachute. You must come when the situation improves.**

INDESCRIBABLE HORROR

It is terrible to feel so helpless in a situation where friends
and Christians are dying. One of the African pastors wrote to
us, "The people woke up to their village being bombed.
Soldiers were dropped by parachute, and they killed many people. Some were caught and locked in a house, which was set on
fire. They were burned alive. The names of these were Zuzee,
Watchman, Aruveshita, Arinesto, Esther, Izabel, Nsayu,
Zhuwao, Tangwe, Antonio and Nsiku. Dead bodies are lying
around in other villages also. Frelimo soldiers have set on fire
nearly every house. All the food and crops have been burned.

Pastors Rozario, Joaquine and Manuel have been killed and the children are fatherless. Our church elder has been killed by a bayonet and his wife and children are in Malawi now in the refugee camp."

Three weeks after the attacks began we received a message that the fighting on the border had stopped, and we were free to cross. We were warned to be very careful, as there were still enemy troops about. The journalists had agreed to come; we had to find a way to organize the trip. It was not an easy task to find a pilot to fly the team to Gorongosa. Rod was not yet trained, and we had no plane. Finally, after numerous messages back and forth across the Mozambique Bush Airwaves, the operation was set in motion.

THE KILLING FIELDS

We had crossed the river to the Mozambican side many times, but this time circumstances were very different. It was not a happy preaching trip, but a very sober entry into a familiar place that had become the unknown. Like our other trips, this one was illegal. It is possible to do something that is illegal, yet not immoral. A time comes when we have to obey God rather than man, or obey our conscience rather than the laws of man.

We did not know what we would find, and though the killing had stopped, there was no telling whether all enemy troops had gone. Crossing the river at night is precarious because of the hippos, which are active night-feeders. The wide river has narrow channels between islands and floating vegetation that has to be maneuvered with care. Using a flashlight is not a good idea as it attracts the hippos, but how else were we to see where we were going? It was imperative that we disembark at exactly the right spot on the other side; we did not want to fall into the wrong hands.

Anthony, the Newsweek photographer was a nice guy. He was a bit nervous about getting into the canoe. Who wouldn't be? The boatmen expertly negotiated the channels, fighting against the strong current. As we swerved into yet another channel, the boatmen gasped Ah! Ah! Ah! The reason: the hulks of at least eight hippos right in the middle of the channel. There was no going back, the channel being too narrow for the canoe to turn, and the current too strongly taking us ahead. There was only one thing for us to do; we rebuked the hippos in the Name of Jesus. Uninhibited at the best of times, I made my supplications loudly in the prayer language of the Holy Spirit. It all happened very quickly! The hippos came toward us and dived underwater as we rode over their backs, thud, thud, thud. They swayed and moved beneath us and we held on, trying to balance the wobbly canoe, which was threatening to tip over. Then all was still again as the canoe steadied. Praise God for His deliverance.

The canoe bumped against the riverbank and several pairs of hands reached out to steady and help us get out. We recognized faces of the Renamo soldiers in the guarded light of the flashlight. Never had we seen them so heavily armed. Bands of ammunition strapped around their waists and chests, grenades attached to belts, bazookas and machine-guns in hand. Absent was the relaxed, friendly banter we were accustomed to when meeting with them. Instead, whispered orders were quickly issued in a somber atmosphere. We fell into single file and walked silently through tall grass, wet with dew. It was dark, and at times we couldn't even see each other. It was dawn when we stopped at Shire Base, the place where we had spent our days under hut arrest earlier. We rested for a short while. The glowing embers of a fire, heated water in a bucket to wash away some of the strains of the night, followed by a cup of tea, did much to restore us.

Patches of misty drizzle periodically hid the rays of the weak morning sun. Anthony of Newsweek was concerned that if the weather did not lift he would not be able to use his video camera. "We'll pray." We prayed right there, and God was faithful to clear the skies sufficiently. We had to walk a couple of hours to Candiero Village, which had suffered worst in the attack. Along the paths we saw shattered clay water jars littered around where unsuspecting women were going to fetch water for the household, when death came out of the skies. Dropping their water jars they ran for their lives. Warheads fired from the choppers had atomized bodies, leaving only bones and scorched bits of clothing, flesh totally disintegrated. The paths were devoid of any sign of life. We experienced the meaning of the words, "a deathly silence."

Almost every hut had been burned down. Inside we found the skeletons of families who had died a horrifying death together. The little skulls of children and babies were heart-rending. I picked up a small clay bowl filled with ashes... the ashes of destruction, broken dreams and shattered lives. *"Beauty for ashes, the oil of joy for mourning."* This was a promise of God; yet standing amidst the ashes and sorrow, it was hard to picture joy and beauty. I picked up the bowl, dusted off the ashes and put it sadly in my bag. Outside, a pot stood over the ashes of a cooking fire long since gone out, breakfast porridge crusted inside. Hungry little faces would have been eagerly watching mother cook, never realizing that it was a breakfast they would never eat.

Littered around were pamphlets of Communist propaganda as well as empty food supply cans. The cans were army issue, labeled, "Tuna, made in Russia" – "Zimbabwe Corned Beef"–"Pineapple, Tanzania." The marauding soldiers had built their own cooking fires and eaten their meals in the midst of their destruction. They hadn't bothered to hide the evidence. Who would come out here to see what had been perpetrated? The world would have no problem believing this was the work of Renamo. Frelimo would see to that. We made sure Newsweek's Anthony took note of these items, though he was unaccountably reticent to take photographs.

BODIES IN THE BUSH

Beside the huts in a small field we found the remains of people bayoneted to death. Empty sockets stared at us. Hyenas and starving dogs had eaten most of the flesh, but the stench of what remained was awful. It was a gut-wrenching experience one can never, never forget.

We felt the Lord's grief at this senseless massacre of innocent civilians. Often we had ministered in this village. Our friends and fellow Christians were among the dead. It was horrible. We were grateful we'd had the chance to bring the Gospel to these souls before this happened. The determination to preach the Gospel further afield welled up inside us. There were thousands who had never heard; they had to be reached before this insane war claimed them. Here was another landmark in our lives. The unbearable sights, and the blood crying out from the ground, gripped our souls. *"Whom shall I send, and who will go for me?"* Rod and I looked at each other, hung on to each other, and silently heard our hearts answer.

"NEWSWEEK" PROVES WEAK

Anthony was strangely quiet.

"What do you think? Why aren't you taking pictures?" Rod asked him.

"These bodies are too old, they won't mean anything. To make impact your news has to be up to the minute."

"It was up to the minute, you just took so long in deciding to come." Rod replied.

"But look at the evidence," I interjected with tears on my face. "You can see from the evidence who is responsible for this." I couldn't believe that we had risked so much only to find that the reporter wouldn't do his job and that there would be no pressure to stop further genocide. Anthony's face was pale. He was shaken by the experience of the whole trip, and he was embarrassed.

"Look. This is off the record, but I have to tell you. I came here expecting that I would be able **to prove that Renamo was responsible for all this. But I can't.** All evidence points to Frelimo."

"Well, tell your magazine the **whole** truth, then!"

"It's no use. There's no way they would print it; it's too soon after the report we put in attributing all atrocities to Renamo. The magazine would lose credibility."

I cried. It was one of the many lessons concerning the news media we were yet to learn. Today, that small clay bowl I had picked up is in our home, an evergreen plant growing out of it. True to His Word, God gave beauty for ashes. The killing in Mozambique has stopped. There is hope in the land. But it was a long road to freedom, a road full of death and despair, hopelessness and pain. If we had known what a rough, tortuous road was ahead of us, would we have had the courage to continue? Probably not. So God shows us just enough to keep us going, and He gives enough strength and grace for each task as we need it.

We returned to Malawi so Rod could accompany the rest of the journalists who were waiting to fly into Gorongosa. Rod knew the landmarks and the way to get to the unmarked airstrip. For the pilot it was truly a venture into the unknown. For an hour, all he could see was bush and forest; he had to rely totally on Rod's navigation. When Rod said, "The airstrip is in sight," the pilot said "Where?" He could not recognize the small clearing as an airstrip. Sweating profusely, he landed the aircraft and exclaimed. "You call this an airstrip? If you think I'm coming back to pick you guys up, you can think again. I'm out of here, and you'll have to find some other way of getting home." He was supposed to be back in three days. Would he really not come back?

It was an informative three days; the journalists spending long hours interviewing President Dhlakama and others in the camp. There was some teasing about the pilot not returning and the guys having to walk back, a three-week journey on foot. Nobody took the pilot seriously, and all were confident he would return for them. Unfortunately, the pilot had been dead-serious, as I was soon to learn. Our phone rang and I was informed, "You tell them I am not coming back. They will have to find some other way to return." Off I went with the message to Gostode. For two days frantic messages went back and forth with phone calls to the pilot in between. At last I was able to persuade him to return, only after Mr. Dhlakama promised to level off some of the bumps in the airstrip (which were actually not dangerous).

On the day the pilot was scheduled to return he was three hours late. Eyes desperately scanned the skies in vain. No sight of the plane. It was hot, the journalists were thirsty and very worried. Finally one of them we called "Old Cowboy" said to a soldier, "Give me your pistol. I'd rather shoot myself and die on the spot than die walking back over those mountains." "Old Cowboy" was an overweight alcoholic over sixty in age. He heaved and panted even on short stretches of flat ground. "No, don't give him your pistol. Give him a rope," said Joseph. "We can't let him waste a bullet!" This brought roars of laughter from the soldiers. The journalist smiled and spirits were lifted. "Don't worry. The pilot will come," Rod encouraged them. He did eventually, but never again.

WASHINGTON POST, NEW YORK TIMES FAITHFUL

The journalists from The Washington Post and New York Times wrote positively about what they had seen and heard. **It was the beginning of a breakthrough for truth. They were faithful to keep their promise not to disclose their route of passage or our names.**

To The President of Renamo from Joseph:

The plane journey back was safe, and all is well. The journalists are impressed with their visit to Gorongosa. Today Renamo received front page plus photographs in both New York Times and Washington Post, also a full inside page in each paper. Washington Post tells us the coverage is very good indeed. We will get copies.

We were pleased with the success of this venture, which

had not been easy to put together and make happen. We felt that in some measure at least, the cry of the people of Mozambique was at last being heard. Our efforts in taking various journalists into Mozambique, where they could see what was really happening, played a large part in ultimately bringing an end to the suffering of the people. A voice for the voiceless was being lifted up, and little by little it was being heard.❖

BEYOND THE
GREAT ZAMBEZI

MOLIMA

A young man leaned against the rough bark of the tree. The sweltering heat of the Lower Shire Valley in the southern tip of Malawi lay like a thick blanket over the group of people seeking shade outside the house of Pastor Chakanza. The young man was silent. His thin, tired body streaked with the sweat and dirt of many weeks of walking through the Mozambique bush, trembled as tears coursed slowly down his face. "I have seen much death, I have seen great suffering. I have walked these weeks from Quelimane where the mighty waters thunder onto the sand. I have come because we have heard that you have the words of eternal life. My people have nobody to tell them about this Jesus, nobody to give them hope. Please come to my village with your message of life and hope."

Our hearts were stirred as Pastor Chakanza related this incident to us. We burned with a fire to GO. "Oh God, you have seen the grief of this young man. Put his tears in your bottle, bring forth a harvest from the price he has paid to come and ask for your Word." *"Thou tellest my wanderings: Put Thou my tears into Thy bottle: are they not recorded in Thy book?" Psalm 56:8 (KJV)*

Walk to Quelimane? If it took the young man three weeks to cross the rivers, swamps and mountains, it would probably take us more. Calculating a month to get there, a month to get back and at least a month there to do anything effective, we realized the impossibility of the situation at this time. With three children in school, we could not do it. Yet the fire continued to burn in our hearts. In our waking and sleeping we heard the young man's voice with a multitude of other voices. "Please come to our land and tell us about Jesus."

We spent hours poring over the map of Mozambique. If we could not reach Quelimane, there must be other places closer by we could get to. We had one month free. My mother, who had come from Zimbabwe to visit us for a few months, would stay and take care of the children while we were gone. One month: how can we best use it for Jesus? Our attention was drawn to a certain place across the Zambezi River. The name "Molima" stood out like a beacon.

There was much to organize. First we needed clearance from Renamo to move through the region. There were thousands of Renamo soldiers who did not know us and if we as strangers walked their routes they could mistake us for spies. We also needed a good team of native Christians to walk with us. Interpreters, as well as a team of counsellors to work individually with the people, are of utmost importance. We also needed porters to carry provisions and the boxes of Bibles.

After two weeks of preparation we were ready to leave. Renamo agreed to our proposed visit on condition that a group of armed soldiers stay with us at all times. This was for our own protection as the area was periodically attacked by Frelimo and Zimbabwe forces. Our national team would be waiting at the footpath where the clandestine crossing into Mozambique would be made. Some of the team were Mozambican, and they would be waiting on the other side.

Now for the hardest part: saying good-bye to our children. Together with my mother we joined hands as a family and prayed, asking God's protection upon each one, His love and strength and courage to fill us and to unite us safely again. The children smiled bravely; I was closer to tears than anyone else. Just a week ago I had wavered and declared I just could not go; the price of leaving the children was too great. It was Deborah, just six years old who put me right. "Mommy, if you don't obey God you will be like Jonah. You don't want to be like Jonah running away, do you?" Out of the mouths of babes! One final hug and kiss all around, and we were on the road.

COMMANDER GULAI

The journey to the border took about four hours. It was a very dark night; we couldn't see a thing. This was exactly what we wanted; we were not likely to be seen crossing in this blackness. It did pose a problem though. Behind which bushes are our team and guides hiding? We stood staring blankly into the darkness when a faint rustle followed by whispers announced the presence of our team, accompanied by a Renamo army commander. His enormous shape seemed vaguely familiar. It was Gulai! – a man we met just weeks ago. We felt a surge of excitement as we recognized the hand of God in choosing which Commander was to lead us through the bush. We were concerned, however, that Pastor Domi was nowhere to be seen. We were accustomed to working with him and had been delighted when he wanted to join us on this trip. It would make things a lot easier for us. Oh well, perhaps he had been delayed and would catch up with us. Quickly our motorbike was pushed across the path where it would remain hidden in a hut until we returned. The owner of the hut promised to let nobody in and not to tell a soul the bike was there lest it be stolen. Rod cautioned him not to light the customary cooking fire in the hut as the tank was full of petrol! We wondered if the man really understood. Nodding his woolly head furiously and grinning toothlessly he said, "She understand." We hoped he did.

It was 1:00 a.m. and we walked for an hour to the nearest Renamo camp before we could bed down for the night. We had to remain out of sight till we could get a ways inland before showing our faces, lest anyone too close to the border reported our presence, and we were retrieved. Walking in the dark on a rough path is not easy, and we frequently stumbled. Our yellow suitcase was dimly detectable as it bounced along on top of Commander Gulai's head. It gave something to set my sights on in this blackness. On reaching the small outpost camp all our provisions, plus the boxes of Bibles, were set neatly in order. We opted to get to sleep immediately, not wanting to start our day tired, and rolled out a groundsheet under the awning of the thatch hut. I felt strangely exposed sleeping without shelter and realized there would not be much privacy for the next month. A shadow fell across us; it was Gulai's. Deftly he tied an army ground sheet to the awning forming a wall and providing a screen and shelter for us. The ground sheet and kind gesture brought a warmth and security to my heart. "Good night." Gulai spoke softly as he disappeared into the darkness.

Dawn! Groaning, Rodney and I tried to sit up as a chicken squawked, frantically flapping its wings. The hard ground left us stiff and sore, the first three nights always being the worst. "Wamuka?" Gulai cheerfully greets us. This is a customary Shona morning greeting, which translated literally means, "Did you wake up?" We watched him busy himself around the camp giving orders, and we marveled again at the way God had brought us into contact with this man. It had happened some weeks back when we were conducting meetings right at the path that separates the border between Malawi and Mozambique. The big shady tree which we used for a church shelter actually grows in the middle of the path. We sat in the shade on the Malawi side. About two hundred people were in attendance, Malawians and Mozambicans together. Some of the Mozambicans had walked a long way to come; this was a chance not to be missed.

While sharing the Word, we had noticed a big, bearded man sitting half hidden behind the tree on the Mozambique side. He listened very intently, but when he noticed us looking at him, he withdrew out of sight behind the tree only to reappear curiously again a few minutes later. The moment the meetings were over, he quickly walked away. Intrigued by this man whose presence was very commanding, we inquired about him. The people told us he was a Renamo commanding officer in charge of the surrounding area. He had heard there was to be a meeting and had come to hear what would be said. Though many had responded to the appeal, this man had sat quietly without making a move. The message had been about Barabbas, and how Jesus had been delivered up to be crucified while Barabbas, who was the one deserving of death, had gone free. Certainly this big man had heard that Jesus has given His life for him. With our natural love for soldiers, we were quickened by this encounter. Would he come back for the evening meeting? When nightfall came we could not see whether or not he was there; it was too dark. As Rodney got up to speak a scorpion which had climbed into his shirt, stung him on his stomach. Had it been me, all would have had a very dramatic start to the evening meeting, but being Rod, he simply caught his breath, grabbed the offending creature between his fingers and killed it. Scorpions inflict severe pain; I was sure Rod was pale in the dark, but he carried on and brought forth his message very well.

As we were getting ready to climb into our bedrolls a message came that someone wanted to see us. We walked into the night and found the big man waiting. Not knowing that we had been many times into Mozambique and were very familiar with Renamo soldiers, he told us not to be afraid. Please would we give him a Bible? We asked him about his stand with Christ, and he admitted that he had not received Jesus as Savior. No, he did not want to do so now, but he would like to have a Bible to read. We gave him one and did not expect to see him again; thus our surprise when now he's the one to escort us on this trip through Mozambique.

We were eager to start off. There were more boxes of Bibles than our team could carry. "No matter, soldiers carry", said Gulai. We were disappointed that Pastor Domi had still not shown up. A trip like this was not without risk. Pastor Domi had suffered much in Mozambique; a number of his direct family having been killed in the war. If his courage had failed, who could blame him?

The bright morning sun promised a very hot day. We started the steep descent down the mountain and walked for several hours. How thrilling to be out in the wilds again. It was just five hours to the nearest village, and we arrived well before dark. The people welcomed us with hallelujahs and hand-clapping. This was our first visit to Chaka Village, but a number of the Christians knew us, having attended our meetings at other villages. We noted a man and woman, both crippled, walking on hands and knees. They had strength only in their arms, their legs dragged along. Both had polio when they were small babies. Marriage would normally be out of the question for them. Who would want to marry a cripple in this land where physical strength was so important for survival? The man told us how his uncle, the Chief, had heard of a crippled lady from another village and had arranged their marriage. Now they were the proud parents of lovely children, a boy of two and a baby girl. The boy they named "Strength" and the girl, "Replenish." "These children will be what we never can be," they said. Already the little boy was a great help, fetching and carrying. In the morning when all the people set out for the fields with their hoes, this couple set off too. Crawling through the bush, unable to see over the long grass, they made their way to their own piece of land where they dug and planted from a sitting position. They have dignity and a place of respect in the village; they are not beggars but work for their own living.

Three days of hard walking stretched between us and the Zambezi River. The mornings were bright and fresh, but it was not long before we were sweating and thirsty. October is such an incredibly hot month in Africa. After several hours of walking I felt faint with fatigue. The water in our bottles was lukewarm, and we dared not drink much as it had to last the whole day. My mind began to wander, and in my imagination I could hear the sound of tinkling ice in a glass of soda. Tripping over a rock I woke up with a start. I had actually dozed off on my feet!

The terrain in Zambezi Valley was rough and dry. We had long since left the beautiful mountain greenery. The thorny scrub was steadily eating away at my skirt, the strong thorns catching and ripping pieces off. Mopani flies buzzed around us, seeking moisture from our eyes, ears, mouth and nose. The common housefly thrives in the bush, and these infuriating insects almost drove us crazy. We worked out a good method of relieving the worst of the pressure. Walking in single file, each one of us carried a small branch to flick flies off the person in front of us. This line of mercy stopped at the soldiers carrying boxes of Bibles and supplies on their heads. Having to use both hands to balance the heavy weights, they had no hands free for swatting. The further we walked the more desolate the surroundings. For a whole day we did not see a single other person. Miles and miles of emptiness, except for a prolific array of birds which delighted us with their color, call and song. Duiker (small deer) bounded across our path, and a large troop of baboons moved close to watch us pass by. These hairy creatures grow quite large and sitting on the rocks can be mistaken for people from a distance.

Night fell as we approached a small village of about five huts. The headman came out to meet us – a gray-headed old man looking quaint in a full-length ladies' coat, the only article of clothing he owned. He welcomed us cordially and bade us sit on deck chairs of animal hide. What a relief to get off our feet. We were introduced to the headman's wives, three of them, each with their own hut, which they share with their own children. The headman sleeps in whichever hut he has chosen for the night. Here the women are all bare-breasted, wearing just a cloth around their hips. Custom does not require them to cover their breasts as these are purely functional, made for feeding babies and have no sexual connotation. But, if a woman were to wear trousers, that would be unforgivably indecent.

A fire was lit to boil our water for tea; my tongue was positively hanging out for tea. There were two chickens in the village: one skinny and undergrown and another skinnier and more undergrown. The headman gave orders for the less skinny one to be killed for supper. We protested, saying we did not desire meat, but he insisted. We know how valuable chickens are in these parts. Many people don't have any at all; they are considered a great luxury. African hospitality is generous and sincere. "I still have another chicken," he said, pointing at the scrawny bundle of feathers that more closely resembled a sparrow. Roasted over the fire the chicken tasted delicious – even more so when the headman's son took up a hoe and started digging up crickets. These are considered a great delicacy, and we sacrificially declined saying, "Oh no, we are so blessed by having the chicken; we want to bless you all by giving you the crickets!" After supper our team gathered to sing and worship around the fire. Our hosts were not Christians, but they listened and joined in the songs. The Gospel was simply explained to them, and they assured us they would carefully consider the matter during the night. "Please may we have another meeting in the morning before you depart?" We replied we'd be happy to and made our way to a reed mat placed on a level piece of ground for us. We were more than ready for sleep.

HIDDEN TREASURE

Morning broke in a beautiful pink African dawn streaked with gold. We gathered for prayer and another short meeting. The headman told us he had decided to accept Christ as his Savior, and two of his wives followed suit. The third decided she did not wish to change her life. There was a young man among them who could read, so we left a Bible with him, instructing him which passages to read first. They promised to gather daily to read the Word and pray and would wait for us to come again on our return. The Renamo soldiers stood to the side, watching. Already they were hearing a lot about Jesus as we walked and talked, all the while sowing seeds in their hearts.

MISTAKEN FOR CUBAN SOLDIERS

We had little time to stop for a rest as the Renamo camp where we were to sleep was a long way off and must be reached by nightfall. After several hours a cluster of huts came into view; we were surprised to see a group of women run away in fear. Gulai asked us to stay where we were while he moved ahead, calling to the people. Shyly, six women and some little children came out of hiding. With eyes downcast in the traditional manner of respect they extended their hands to touch ours, bobbing a little curtsy. They turned to Gulai and rattled off in their own language. "You are welcome to our home. We ran away when we saw the white people. White people do not come here; we thought they had come to do us harm." They went on to say that three seasons ago some Cuban soldiers had come here with Frelimo, killed many people and burned the crops. "The people ran away and are refugees in Malawi, but we returned to our own home. There are no other people living here now. When we saw the pale faces coming towards us we thought they were Cubans." All six spoke at once with much waving of arms. This was confirmation of what we already knew. What had happened at Candiero Village was happening all over Mozambique. Gulai asked where their men were. "They have walked to Malawi to trade mealie meal (corn-meal) for soap, sugar and salt."

Glad for a reason to rest ourselves, we gratefully accepted water served in calabash gourds. The women ranged from ages 16 to 80 years of age. The younger ones served us, kneeling with the gourd clasped in both hands. It is customary for the women to kneel before visitors and **always** before their own men. It is their way of showing respect. "Where does your journey take you to?" They are curious to know the reason for our presence in this war-torn, desolate land. "We are servants of the Most High God, and we've come to tell about Jesus, the only begotten Son of the living God. He is the Way, the Truth and the Life." With shining eyes they exclaim, "We know of Jesus. Before all the people ran away we gathered many times for prayer and singing every Sunday and sometimes other days. Now we do not have church anymore because our Pastor is gone." "You can meet together without a pastor and without a church. If you believe, you are the church." This was new to them. Could they really pray without a priest? Roman Catholicism had left many wrong concepts in the hearts of the people. We assured them they could. Sharing from the Word with them we challenged them to rededicate their lives to Christ, which they did gladly. We all felt the thrill and excitement of the moment. They had many questions, and we answered as quickly and clearly as possible.

Three of the younger girls asked if they should remove all their jewelry now that they were once more serving Jesus. Most of the people rely on the witch doctors for every need they have. To ward off evil spirits they tie bits of string around their necks, waists, ankles and wrists. When a soul is converted, these need to be removed and burned, being witchcraft fetishes. So missionary influence had forbidden any decorative bracelets and any form of outward adornment. We looked intently at the girls. They possessed only the cloth wrapped around their hips for clothing. There were no well-stocked wardrobes in the huts. Barefooted, there was nothing of beauty to enjoy or make themselves attractive with. Nothing except the jewelry carefully made by hand. Bracelets made of wire, a valuable material not easily found. The combs in their hair were a work of art. Out of big chunks of hard rubber they cut comb teeth. Tiny bits of colored plastic cut into different shapes had been melted into the rubber over a fire. "We will burn it all if you say we must," they solemnly declared. "Did you get that jewelry from the witch-doctor?" "No, no! We like it because it is pretty," they replied. Defying all missionary tradition I said, "As long as Jesus is more important in your life than these ornaments, you may wear them." They were very happy.

The little group escorted us for some way, chattering and laughing. This day God had smiled upon them in sending people to encourage and call them back to Himself. "God loves us," they said. "When you return our husbands will be here; they will want to hear your words, too." Two of the girls were still unmarried; the other four shared two husbands between them.

(This was always a tricky one. I wondered if King Solomon would have ordered the husbands to be chopped up into pieces and evenly distributed around? No, of course not; he had more wives and concubines than anyone else.) Not even Solomon's wisdom avails for this one!

THE LONG MARCH

On and on we tramped. Commander Gulai marching in front swayed from side to side like a big tree in the wind. José carried my sling-bag of necessities, such as Bible, water bottle and a candy bar at the bottom that I was about to retrieve. Reaching into the bag my hand clasped something unfamiliar. Pulling out my hand I shrieked as I threw out a handful of crickets. José, not having a bag of his own to put his crickets saved from last night's dinner, thought it a good idea to use my bag. All enjoyed themselves at my expense. José apologized, and I graciously assured him of my forgiveness, but please next time to wrap the crickets in a banana leaf and tie them up with string so they would not crawl around in my bag. He and Afonso were our two leaders in place of Pastor Domi. They lacked experience but were of willing hearts.

It was miserably hot. No trees here, the sun blazed mercilessly down on us. Tying a thin scarf over my straw hat, I pulled it over my face. It was thin enough to see through and kept out the worst of the scorching rays as well as keeping flies and bugs out of my face. "So this is why the early missionaries dressed so weird," I thought to myself, remembering some of the pictures I had seen in a missionary book. The women wore cloths over their faces just like this, but they were being carried in a sedan chair, not tramping like this. **Oh, for the wings of a bird!** The dream of an aeroplane had long been in our hearts. Would we ever see it fulfilled? Ahead we saw a green belt of trees winding like a snake through the dry brown grass. This could only mean there was a stream of water in the wilderness.

"Yes," said Gulai. "There is good water; we can fill our bottles and cool down." With renewed energy at the thought of

perhaps even a quick dip, we speeded up. Very near the greenery now, just another hundred yards, but oh my, what was that
awful smell? Thick green and yellow fermenting slime awaited
us in place of the cool, clear stream of water we had been
expecting. What a disappointment! We had to cross, but no
way was I stepping into that cesspool. The lack of rain caused
the river to cease flowing, and it had become a stagnant death
trap. Further down we found a place where we could leap from
rock to rock without touching the water. Not unless one of us
slipped, of course.

Commander Gulai had become very quiet. A loud cheery
man, always heard at a distance, he now walked in silence. He
was suffering acutely from the lack of nicotine. The further we
traveled from the Malawi border, the further we distanced ourselves from any comforts, luxuries and supplies.

Though Rod had frequently spoken to Gulai about
Jesus, he was convinced that he could not be saved because he
couldn't stop smoking. "If you receive Jesus into your heart,
you will also receive power to resist temptation. You don't have
to give up smoking to be saved, you only have to put your trust
in Christ." Gulai remained doubtful. Now Rod teasingly told
him Salvation must be near, as Gulai had no choice but to give
up smoking, seeing there was no tobacco around. Gulai smiled
knowingly, and we wondered what he had up his sleeve. We
found out later in the day when a runner arrived with a good
supply of "LIFE!" He had been sent to Malawi the day of our
departure to buy the supply and ordered to catch up with
utmost speed. Here was a man with foresight. In fact, Gulai's
leadership qualities and good rapport with his men made him
excellent potential for the army of God! We determined to
intensify our pursuit of his soul. "That which you have just
received is not LIFE, but DEATH, wrapped up in paper to
make it look good. It will make you happy for a moment, but
you will be left unsatisfied in a short time. Only Jesus can satisfy your soul." Gulai politely acknowledged Rod's statement
and disappeared behind some bushes where he lit up and

pulled on the long awaited cigarette. He emerged again with a mixed expression of guilt and delight.

On and on we trudged, our feet dragging. Gulai dashed off into the bush. Surely not another cigarette? No, out he came from behind a shrub triumphantly waving a large red tumbleweed type of flower. With a flourish he presented it to me. "For you, Madam." I was amazed. Who would ever expect a wild Renamo commander to present a lady with a flower far out in the wilderness. Gulai was so pleased with my obvious delight, he found a whole heap further along. This was too much. These giant blooms were too heavy to carry; I was finding it hard enough carrying myself. Receiving heavenly inspiration, I handed a bloom out to each of the team and some of the soldiers who had a free hand. We began to march, holding the flaming red flowers up like blazing torches. Explaining spiritual warfare to them, I quoted some scriptures and told them we were fighting as we marched. "Mozambique shall be set free from the grip of Satan through our prayers and intercession. War, famine, sickness and disease is trodden down by the high praises of God in our mouth!" We sang, we shouted, declaring the Kingdom of God in our midst. A victorious army, doing battle against the work of the evil one, tearing down powers and principalities and wickedness in high places, we put to flight the hordes of darkness. What a glorious time, what a victory. Strengthened and renewed, mounting up with wings as eagles, we no longer felt weary. *Hallelujah!*

Shampoo in the Wilds

As if to assure us of a battle won, a running stream of clear, cool water came into sight. Packs, boxes of Bibles and all loads were hastily flung down while we all headed for the water with a shout. Rodney and I walked upstream to a sheltered place where we could enjoy a real bath. This was luxury in its extreme. With shampooed hair and soothed limbs we were a new creation. Returning to join the others we found a fire had been made and the kettle boiling for tea. What more could anybody ever want?

Just three hours later we arrived at the next Renamo camp where we spent the night. This, like so many others, was very much a "transit" camp. Soldiers came in and out all the time, stopping for food, rest and orders before going on to fulfill various missions. Though we were offered a good hut to sleep in, we preferred to pitch our tent. We surely needed it here where armies of mosquitoes launched all-night attacks from the nearby marshland, making life miserable for humanity.

Our team of native Christians had left us for the night to sleep in a nearby village where they ministered to the people. Gulai was happy to be with fellow commanders, and we chuckled as they shared incredible tales around the fire. The Africans are wonderful storytellers, and a story that has not been stretched in several directions with great elasticity is hardly worth telling. They slapped their legs, throwing back their heads and laughing. Suddenly the storyteller would turn deadly serious, get up, and prowl around, dramatizing his story. A good time was had by all. After a while as they lowered their voices we guessed they were talking about us. Gulai had to explain again what we were up to. "This is hard to believe. Are these white people truly walking through Mozambique just to tell the people about Jesus? Do they not know that there is war, and they could be captured or killed?" We enjoyed immensely hearing Gulai give all the answers that he had heard us give when questioned. "Yes, they do know, but they love God and want to serve Him. The Bible says, *'Go into all the world and preach the gospel to every creature.'* They obey God because Jesus obeyed Him. Jesus gave His life on the Cross so that man can be saved. He died so whoever believes on Him can be saved." Gulai, without realizing it, was preaching the Gospel. He had heard us enough times to be able to answer the many questions fired at him. We knew it wouldn't be long! God's army needs new recruits – always!

There was no sight of the African dawn to greet us as we awoke. The Renamo camp was hidden under a thick growth of trees so troop planes and helicopters would not detect the whereabouts of the camp. I understood now why we had left the footpath and trailed through the bush to reach the camp in the night. Footpaths are often followed from the air, and thickets which they lead into are then bombed. This way, there was no visible path leading into the thicket. We were much aware that from this point trouble was not unlikely. Frelimo and Zimbabwe forces frequently flew along the Zambezi River and surrounding areas to attempt to pinpoint Renamo positions. We were near the Zambezi River now. We found Gulai reading his Bible beside the cold ashes of last night's fire. He told us that we would rest for the day and depart in the afternoon. Some of the soldiers who had carried the Bibles and supplies would return to their own base-camps, and others would take their place. Seizing the opportunity Rodney asked him to gather all the soldiers in the camp so we could share the Gospel with them.

In the straightest of lines they stood: shoulders back with heads held high, soldiers alert and ready to act upon the first order. Standing before them with open Bibles in our hand we couldn't help but compare this natural army with many modern-day saints from the western world. How often a pastor faces a congregation of lethargic, disinterested and unresponsive people.

These bush soldiers wore no uniform. Ragged and mostly barefooted, some of the clothes were comical. Shirts barely covering the stomachs; some so ragged they were no more than strips of cloth tied across the shoulders. Not one pair of pants that actually reached to the ankles. As for shoes, so torn and tattered, some pairs not matching, and even one soldier with two left shoes. It was all they had.

We greeted them in the name of Jesus. I stamped my foot and tried to give a smart Renamo salute. This made them laugh and helped put them at ease. Sharing the Word with them was not easy, as we had to go through two interpreters. These men come from different parts of Mozambique where varying dialects are spoken. However, they listened intently and seemed to comprehend.

FREEDOM ISN'T FREE

"You are fighting a war in Mozambique to overthrow communism and oppression of the people. You want to live peacefully in your villages without being robbed of your crops or taken by force to slave labor camps to work on state farms for the Frelimo government. You think that if you win this war you will be able to make your own decisions about how you live your lives. You are deceived. We tell you that there is no true freedom without Christ. Even if you win the war and are free from communism, you are still a captive of an enemy unless you allow Jesus to set you free. The devil will direct your life, tell you what to do and you will obey him because you are chained to him. He marches you around and compels you to follow his orders. If Jesus is not your Lord and Master, then Satan is. Jesus has a wonderful plan for you. He has power to break the chains of the devil if you will confess your sins and give your life to Him. He has prepared a place in heaven for you, He wants to enlist you in His army, the army of God which cannot lose."

Rodney continued with the message of the Cross. These men know the meaning of blood and death. They discovered that Jesus voluntarily laid down His life to defeat sin and death, that He rose after three days, leading captivity captive unto Himself. (*Ephesians 4:8*) To be captured by Jesus is true liberty.

The men were given the opportunity to choose whom they wanted for their Commander-in-Chief, Satan or Jesus? We did not make it easy for them. They must not make this choice lightly. Anything of true value costs a price, but it is surely worth it!

After praying with several soldiers to receive Christ, we prayed for the sick. One man lay on the ground beside a hut. He was one of the new carriers but at this stage could not even sit up. Groaning with pain, it looked like he had appendicitis. Only one thing could we do, pray. A number of men had wounds that have never healed properly. We administered whatever medication we could from our First Aid bag and prayed for them all. For us it was a great joy and honor to be there, sharing the love of Jesus. We spent the rest of the day getting to know some of the men individually. They had many questions. The kettle was never far from the fire, and we enjoyed the luxury of lots and lots of tea drunk at leisure, even allowing ourselves some of the chocolate cookies packed in our rucksack.

CROSSING THE GREAT ZAMBEZI RIVER

This mighty river carries with it centuries-old African myths and legends, powerful enough to terrify the life out of any but the most lion-hearted. Traditions and superstitions control the thoughts and actions of most tribes along the Zambezi, and the river-god is feared and respected. In times of drought and trouble the greedy river-god demands the sacrifice of human lives. They believe it is a very fierce and angry demigod, and when displeased, commands the heavens to shut up life-giving rain, thus controlling the people and enslaving them to the impossible task of satisfying its craving to swallow up human bodies. It can be appeased for a short time, but at great cost. Whatever the cost, it must be paid, for without rain all will die anyway.

Times of drought are very profitable for the witch doctors, who enjoy the extra attention and adulation shown to them, not to mention the gifts and treasures of the people in exchange for their prayers and incantations for rain. It is not uncommon for a village to be awakened in the night by the yells and whoops of the witch doctor and his helpers as they raid the huts of little children. The river-god has a particular appetite for small children! The villagers are powerless to do anything as their children are carried off to be thrown into the swirling depths that suck them down to feed the hungry crocodiles. The mothers are left wailing and mourning, throwing themselves on the ground and rolling in the dust, heartbroken. Such a grip Satan has upon these lives. "Beware you evil hordes of darkness. The redeeming blood of Christ reaches even to the shores of the Zambezi River!"

Our spirits thrilled as we headed for the group of carriers and escorts who would take us across the Zambezi. Beaming from ear to ear the suspected appendicitis case stood with a load on his head. No more pain! We spent a few moments talking to the carriers, thanking them for their kind help. "These loads are very heavy, we know. It is difficult to carry them but we pray a special blessing on you for you are carrying the Bread of Life, the Word of God that will never pass away." One man was not looking very happy. Afonso sheepishly complained of not feeling well and said he did not think he could make the journey across the Zambezi river. His knees felt weak and his body was aching all over. I immediately offered my sympathy but Rodney, with his usual practical perception, eyed Afonso knowingly. "You are sick only with fear, Afonso. There is nothing wrong with you. You are afraid to cross the great river." If Afonso could have blushed he would have. "No no. Me sick! If you cross that river you will die. You not come back. Please not cross river." Afonso pleaded.

"We shall not die and if you don't come you will miss a very great chance to do something for Jesus. You may go back if you wish, but I tell you, you are very foolish if you do so. Jesus has commanded us to GO. He will take care of us." Afonso was not to be persuaded. Looking very guilty and ashamed, he turned away and in apparent pain walked slowly off to a reed mat where he laid himself down with much groaning and effort, declaring he could truly go no further. The fear of the unknown was too much. After all, he had never crossed the Zambezi River before. We were disappointed to lose Afonso, especially as Pastor Domi had never caught up with us, suffering from the same disease as Afonso, no doubt. Perhaps it was better that the fearful turn back lest they inspire fear in the others.

Feeling the need to cheer up, I took out my Walkman for the first time to listen to some good praise music. What a stir this created. These soldiers had seen radios before but what is this I wore over my ears? So much for my escape into solitude. Gulai begged to try it and others peered eagerly across his shoulder. How could I deny them? Gulai swung along the path, his huge frame moving in time with the music. I followed on behind hoping that the batteries would last long enough for me to enjoy at least a few turns on the tape. Before long we met up with the rest of the team who spent the night in the village. Excitedly they told us of the tremendous reception of the Word. "There are many wanting to be baptized." José told us. We promised that on our way back we would stop over and hold more meetings, baptizing those who had repented. The enthusiasm of the team was catchy, and we all sang together and clapped as we walked.

Suddenly, above the sound of our singing we heard the drone of an aeroplane. Commander Zachariah, of higher rank than Gulai, was now leading us. Zachariah held up his hand, motioning us to stop. He listened intently then motioned for us to continue. "Nao probleme," he said in Portuguese, adding that the aircraft was heading away from us. We breathed a sigh of relief, as it would be most inconvenient to have to hide in the bushes right now.

Too many crocodiles

We could see the tall reeds growing beside the Zimira River in the distance, a tributary of the Zambezi. Soon we were walking alongside the river to the crossing point. The sharp pointed reeds stood taller than we did. At the crossing point we were met by a fisherman standing beside his canoe, a hollowed out tree-trunk. He grinned broadly and with a shout of joy rushed up to Pastor José. They were old acquaintances and had not seen each other for a long time. The fisherman would take us across in his canoe. The Zimira River is not wide but deep and fast flowing. "Many, too many crocodiles." the fisherman told us with rolling eyes. The river is full of fish, too, and a small fishing village is situated right on the banks on the other side. We climbed into the wobbly canoe and were quickly rowed to the other side. With wet shoes we slipped and slid as we tried to get up the steep bank. The villagers stared in silent amazement as we made our way to the nearest tree. It is very strange to see white people here; what could be the meaning of this? The women gathered around curiously watching from a short distance. They returned our greetings. The children were more unsure and hid behind the huts. Perhaps they thought we worked for the river-god! Every village seems to have at least two deck chairs made of solid wood and animal hide. They are very comfortable, and I sank gratefully into one. Rodney took a look at my muddy sneakers, laces thick with mud, and kneeling down before me proceeded to take them off. Shrieks, squeals and loud laughter followed this act of kindness. The women were rocking with laughter, slapping each other on the back; slapping their hands together they guffawed and carried on as if they had never seen anything so funny. They hadn't. In African custom it is unthinkable that a man should kneel before a woman. Secondly, it is outrageous that he should stoop to remove her shoes. This event would be related over the cooking pots for many moons.

Jesus frequently drew His illustrations and stories from situations that the people were familiar with. This is part of the art of being a good missionary: to see in small events the opportunity to bring forth spiritual truths. Waiting for the hilarity to subside we told the women about Jesus, how He who is GOD came in the form of man to serve, making Himself of no reputation. The men crept up behind the women to listen, too. "If you want to be great in God's kingdom, learn to be the servant of all. Jesus girded Himself with a towel and washed the disciples' feet. By this shall all men know that you are my disciples, if you have love one for another. Humble yourself in the sight of the Lord and He will exalt you." The women were suitably impressed and the men looked thoughtful. We told the women how they too are required to serve their husbands with love and a willing heart. These people love a story. They do not have television, videos, the movies or books to feed their minds and imaginations. Stories, whether truth or fiction are of great worth to them. They will not forget what we told them. Now added to the strange event of the white man removing his wife's shoes, would be all the illustrations of a Christ-filled life we had given them. And of course, every good Bible story includes the message of the Cross. Not only did Jesus serve, but He gave His very life-blood to save us and wash away our sins. *"Greater love hath no man than this, that a man lay down his life for his friends." John 15:13 (KJV)*

The fisherman had given us his catch of the day, a tiger-fish eighteen inches long. Though it was rather course and boney, it made a welcome change in our diet, which had not been very exciting. Fish were drying on racks all around the village. The smell was awful and flies more prolific than usual. After a meal we were happy to move on. Our new friends were sad to see us leave and begged that we should stay. "We still have a long way to go," we said, giving the usual promise to see them on our return, which satisfied them to some degree. We marvelled at the grace of God, which had given us souls in this place, too. The harvest is so incredibly ripe, just like Jesus said. It seems all one has to do is stretch forth a hand and pick the fruit off the trees.

"I WILL DIE WITH YOU"

At last! The Zambezi River, 1,700 miles long, lay like a gleaming snake ahead of us. Though most of the Zambezi valley is very dry, here we had to walk through marshland before we reached the banks. The scenery was beautiful. The silvery river flanked by green marshland on one side, blue mountains reaching into a dark grey sky on the other. With a start we realized the dark grey was storm clouds that had quickly gathered.

It was three clock in the afternoon, and we would have to cross very quickly to make it before dark. On reaching the marsh we were enthusiastically greeted by clouds of mosquitoes. For half an hour we sloshed and waded through black mud and water, some places thigh deep. Sharp reeds pricked and cut, squelchy clay gulped at our feet as we placed them into the dark depths. We saw some canoes dragged from the river into the marsh, but no boatmen. The answer came after two hours of searching and calling; the canoe owners had gone on a journey, all except one who had spent the day drinking palm wine. With his hat pulled over his eyes he stood unsteadily to his feet and told us we could not cross today because the rain was coming, and it would be dangerous. Looking around us we decided we must indeed cross as there was no place to sleep. The canoe owner's hut was visible in the distance, built on stilts to keep out of the wet, and though it may be dry we do not relish the thought of sleeping in it. If it was to be judged by the owner, it had to be dirty and smelly. The only alternative to crossing the river was to head back to the village we just came from. Remembering the words of David Livingstone "Anywhere, as long as it be forward," we made up our minds to cross. The canoe owner prophesied our doom, but we assured him it would not rain until we were safely across. Gathering our team we asked God to hold back the rain. Much to our amazement Afonso's face peered out from the group. "What are you doing here? You said we will die if we cross." "Yes, you will die," he said, then very earnestly, "But I have decided I will die with you!" We laughingly assured him that none of us were going to die. Climbing into our unsure vessel we settled ourselves on the wet bottom in preparation for a cruise. The strong rowers started our race against the sunset and the rain. Light drizzle caused us to huddle close, but the storm was a way off. Lightning flashed across the sky to the left of us, and great peals of thunder boomed through the heavens. Preoccupied with the skies we were distracted from worrying about the hippos. It was chilly; mosquitoes rode with us. Our arms, legs and any visible patch of skin were covered with big red bite welts. I did not feel very heroic nor happy at all.

The boatmen maneuvered the canoe first downstream then upstream, around numerous islands. Natural landmarks and a life of fishing on the river had given these men a keen instinct and sense of direction. They told us it was good that we were crossing in the late afternoon because often in the mornings helicopters flew along the river and buzzed canoes, causing them to tip over. Our white skins would stick out like neon lights from a low flying helicopter. The deep grunt of hippos in the distance rolled across the water. They were too far off to be interested in us, and hopefully the crocodiles as well.

The peoples along the Zambezi River in Mozambique are very much unreached. Years and years of war prevented the influence of civilization, and these people are of the most primitive in Africa. We felt very privileged to be there, our discomforts quickly forgotten. It was good to feel the canoe slide onto a sandy bank. At last we had landed, there was no rain and it was still light enough to see. The crunchy sand felt like a gold paved road after the mud we had left behind. An excited jabber of voices from women who had come to collect water floated through the hazy late afternoon air. Hallelujah! Hallelujah! we greeted them with the universal declaration of "Praise the Lord." This greeting immediately identifies us as Christians. Often we have no time to stop and talk to all the people we pass, but in greeting them thus, they know we are believers. It is beautiful to see a smile of Christian recognition break out on a sun-parched face decorated with tribal markings. Though these areas are largely unreached with the Gospel, one can find scattered about in the most unlikely places, those who have received Jesus into their hearts. Some have travelled to far places where they have heard the Gospel, and others have received visits from friends and relatives from afar who have told them about this Christ.

As we walked by, our team chatted to the women briefly telling them our purpose and announcing that there would be two weeks of meetings at Molima, and we would very much like them to come. From this side of the river some would come to the meetings. After all, this was the familiar side of the river to them; to cross to the other side was very dangerous; anything might happen to them there!

Night settled over the land but the moon was out early, casting a pale light on the stony path under our feet. The boatmen would sleep at the river. They were happy that our prayers had been answered, and the weight of the reward for their efforts felt good in their pockets. Early in the morning they would return and declare that the power of Jesus is real because the river-god was kept away! Its roars could be heard in the distance of the black sky, and even though its fire did split the sky, it could do us no harm.

The rugged path became quite steep. Gulai explained that we would sleep at another Renamo camp at the top of the mountain. Though the air was chilly, we were perspiring from the exertion. We arrived at the camp where we set up our tent and gathered around the fire for tea and roasted sweet potatoes.

LONE WITCH

Set on a small hill was the tiniest hut with someone standing a few feet from it. The place had a desolate, dead look about it. Tall and thin, the figure of a woman stood very still. She wore necklaces, long and heavy, made up of bits of bone, seashells and small pouches filled with dried potions. She stared coldly at us - no welcome for us here - this was her domain, and she did not like us walking through it. We greeted her; no response. Inquiring after her health we endeavored to converse with her, but she was hard as stone. There was only one thing left to do: Tell her about the saving power of Jesus. His love for her. His desire that she should enter the kingdom of heaven. But she told us that she was not interested. We went on, seeing that her heart was seared. It felt strange to us, that we should make no further effort, but in our hearts we knew it would be a waste of time. There were others who would listen. On reaching the bottom of the hill again we looked around. There she was, still standing in the same hostile position.

There was a tangible change in the spiritual atmosphere from this point on. The air seemed heavy and dark even though the sun shone brightly. Though Rodney and I continued to chat, the team was growing very quiet. We noticed that the people working in their fields did not greet us as enthusiastically as usual. There was a dark reserve in their manner. On entering the village where we would sleep that night, we noticed again the quietness of the people. Our welcome was not with the traditional African warmth.

With furtive glances we were shown a place to pitch our tent, but my heart said, "No, I do not want to sleep in this village." Gulai said we could not go further, as it was too far to the next stop, which would be Molima. After some persuasion he agreed to let us put our tent just outside the village. Waking early in the morning we decided to take a look around. Following a narrow path toward some trees, there, in front of an old tree stump we found the root of the problem of hostility.

THE REASON

A smooth mound had been formed out of clay, making a little hill with the tree stump directly behind. A hole 8 inches in diameter was in the center of the mound, a tunnel going straight down. In front of the hole lay a clay bowl filled with meal and bits of dried food. We had stumbled upon an altar of sacrifice. Calling José, our interpreter, to come and join us, we pretended we had no idea what was before us. We wanted to know just how much he would tell us. He told us that this was simply African tradition. He looked a little pale. "No José. This is not just tradition. This is witchcraft." "Yes." He hung his head slightly. "What do the people do here, José?" "They just pray to the spirits." "No, José. They offer sacrifices here. They kill chickens, and let the blood flow down the hole." "Yes." He looked surprised that we should know such things, and his head hung a little lower. This revealed that though he had accepted Jesus, he was not entirely free from the fears of witchcraft. These customs are embedded very deeply in the people, and many find it extremely difficult to shake loose of the fears and superstitions.

It is no wonder there was such spiritual bondage in this place. We prayed and interceded, tearing down powers and principalities seated in high places. Fear of evil spirits here was far greater than any fear of war. Fighting comes and goes, bombs are dropped and planes leave, but the spirits stay around forever, haunting and mocking, controlling and demanding, terrorizing by night. The lone witch doctor was angry to see us come into her territory. We walked back to the village where a handful of people had come to see us from near-by huts. We shared the Gospel with them, and only one man responded. He would not find it easy to grow in this place, and we exhorted him to seek out other Christians and share fellow-ship with them.

We were eager to be on our way. Surely tonight we would reach Molima and set up camp for 2 weeks. We walked all day, our mood contemplative. The seriousness of the responsibility in bringing teaching to the people was sobering. No other missionaries visited here. What we didn't share with the people they might never hear from anyone else. We had to give our best.

Our team talked quietly in their native language, not as exuberant as usual. Picking up a few words relating to witch-craft, the devil's power and witch doctors, we inquired about their conversation. "There is a witch doctor at Molima, not an ordinary witch doctor, but a very powerful one. The people we met along the road have been telling us things." Eyes rolling, hands tightly clasped together, our mighty men of valor began to extol the powers of this witch doctor. Taking a deep breath, José blurted out the worst of it. "They tell us this witch doctor is a woman so powerful she can cut a stick from a bush, throw it down and it becomes a snake." We fully know the fear the African people have of snakes. This was the worst news our team could receive concerning the power of witch doctors, whom they are about to meet. "Then she picks up that snake by its tail, and it turns back into a stick!" The strain of relating such dark sayings to us was almost too much for José. Rodney put a hand on his trembling shoulder. "Have you not heard of such a thing before? This is spoken of in the Old Testament when Moses did the very same thing before Pharaoh. Even Pharaoh's magicians performed this act. This is nothing new, it is nothing to fear for God is greater than the devil." Relief lit up the faces. How could they forget? Of course they knew the story of Moses; of course they knew that the children of God have more power than the children of the devil. I said nothing, but inwardly I prayed that we should not be put to such a test.

Now that the team felt encouraged normal chatter broke out, and we walked throughout the rest of the day without incident. Late afternoon found us in the Molima district but quite a way from the main village where we were to camp. Night fell and still we were not at our destination. We determined not to stop until we had reached the appointed place, even if it meant walking all night. Mechanically we trudged on and were finally rewarded with the glow of a small fire outside a Renamo post. We looked for a level piece of ground – anywhere would do; then we could select a good site to make our home in the morning. All we wanted now was to lay our weary bones on the ground.

ELENA'S TEN-YEAR PRAYER ANSWERED

We fell immediately into a deep sleep, only to hear within the far recesses of our minds the sound of joyful singing and clapping of hands outside our tent. It couldn't be true. Surely they were not having a meeting now. "Oh Lord, spare us; give us the night off," I prayed. The singing group seated itself outside our tent. José shook the side flap. "Mother, Father! These Christians have come to welcome you. They want to see your faces." I buried my face deeper under the blanket. I did not want my face to be seen. I did not want to lift my heavy bones. Even the hard ground felt comforting, and it was heaven just to lie down. Rod unzipped the tent and putting his face out to be seen said, "Thank you for welcoming us. It is dark now so you cannot see our faces well. We are very tired, but in the morning we will show you our faces clearly." "Amen, hallelujah!" Quite satisfied, the Christians rose with this universal salutation and walked back to their huts. In the morning they would come again. In the morning they would bring gifts of meal and sweet potatoes and look upon our faces.

Early morning heralded another scorching hot day. We

determined to find a shady place to set up camp. As we would be there for two weeks, we might as well be as comfortable as possible with good shade cover. Sitting on a fallen tree trunk we were reading our Bibles and sipping our morning coffee when singing and clapping and shuffling feet made their way down the path, stopping right before us. Expectant faces gazed into ours. With shy giggles the women lightly touched our hands in greeting; the men followed with their traditional hand-shake, lightly gripping the hand in three different squeezes. José was positively bursting to tell us something, but good manners forced him to stand aside while the long ritual of greeting was carried out with hallelujahs and amens in between. José and the team had not retired to bed like we had. Oh no, no chance of that; the people would not let them go, nor did they want to go. They stayed up most of the night talking and sharing. At last José had a turn to speak. "This lady is the leader of the church here." He indicated a woman standing with her ten-year-old daughter beside her. The leader of the church a woman? This was most unusual.

The woman began to talk with José interpreting for her. She told an incredible story of how for ten years she had been praying for God to send missionaries to this place. When she arrived here she found there were no Christians. Through her witness and exhortation a few of the villagers received Jesus as Saviour. The number grew slowly over the years, and she got a little church going. Now there were forty members meeting regularly to pray, sing and learn what little the woman could teach them. Her great difficulty was that she had no Bible and found it difficult to teach the people about God, her own knowledge being limited. The only answer to the problem was that God should send some missionaries to teach them and bring them Bibles. Villages from miles around knew of this ridiculous prayer. It was a time of war. Missionaries never came into these remote areas even in the time of peace; to think they would come in the time of war showed lack of intelligence. Still the woman kept on praying and believing. She had even been telling the people the time of the visit would be soon now, and here we were. No wonder the excitement, and no wonder the special interest to see our faces! We felt stunned by the account, remembering how we had pored over the map of Mozambique asking God to show us His appointed place for this time.

"My name is Elena," she said. Her story grew more and more fascinating. Ten years ago she had left her home, walking for weeks with her small baby in order to visit her family whom she had not seen in years. During the first month of her visit there was a big escalation in the civil war. Renamo forces were gaining vast territory in their fight against the Communist Frelimo government. Now, anyone trying to enter the cities from Renamo zones was more than likely to be imprisoned or killed by Frelimo who were still in the main towns and cities. The woman was trapped in the village area of her birth, as it was under the control of Renamo. She dared not return back to her husband and four children for fear of the consequences. Now after all this time, she was not sure if they were still alive or if they were still living in Chimoio. She had received no news in spite of sending various messages. She put her arm on the shoulder of her daughter. The baby was now a ten-year-old girl. "One day we will return and look for our family," she said. "I know that God is great and knows all things. He has sent you to help us with the Gospel. Our days are in His hands."

CAMP GRAVEYARD

Commander Zachariah agreed for us to camp outside of the Renamo base but only at a spot he approved. "For security reasons," he told us. With the group of Christians in tow as well as an entourage of curious children we set off looking for a temporary home. A large lone tree looked ideal, its thick leaves promising shade most of the day. "Not good." We were disappointed at the rejection of Commander Zachariah. He explained that one tree on its own could not hide us from enemy aircraft. We must find a group of trees. We walked another twenty minutes and found a wooded place. "No, this also is not good." The Christians agreed with Commander

Zachariah. "But this is perfect. It will hide us well and give good shade," we argued. Puzzled, we followed the soldiers to a thorny patch of ropy trees. "This good," we are told. We did not agree. The shade was slight and thorns were on the ground. "No. We do not want to camp here," we said. After fruitless pleading and arguing we decided we would not be intimidated and to the horror of all bystanders, military and civilian alike, we picked up our rucksacks and moved to the inviting greenery of the wooded spot. We found a level place; some small branches needed chopping out; if we cleared away a bit of brush we'd have a beautiful home. Our friends having quietly followed us stood a little distance away. We beckoned for them to come and help clear the ground but solemnly they shook their heads. "Why not? What is wrong with this place?" we inquired, but got no reply. Feeling more than a little impatient we began to clear the place ourselves. It was difficult as we had no tools and had to use bits of wood to clear with. We felt sure our friends would feel sorry for us and come and help. It was hot; we perspired as we worked, dust flying in our faces. Pausing to see who was coming closer to give a hand, we saw the mournful faces had not moved an inch. This was very strange. African custom is to be helpful to strangers, and we were after all not really strangers, but part of the family of God. The thought of spending two weeks camped in the thorns and sun strengthened our resolve to keep on with the work of clearing. As we scratched and dug we found several pieces of broken pottery which we threw aside. I heard Rod chuckle as he threw something into the bushes. "What was that?" "Oh, nothing much, just some junk," he replied. At last we had cleared a big enough spot. We drank thirstily from our water bottle and set up our tent. Before long we were seated outside our house on logs, looking quite civilized and relaxed. Our audience was still watching. Rod walked over to them and asked José to invite all to come to our first meeting which would be at 4:00 p.m. The Christians told of a good place to meet about half an hour's walk away; the people would gather there. José and our team went with them to get to know the people. We were very puzzled as we watched them walking off in single file along the path, casting worried glances our way. Oh well, we'd get to the bottom of it all before too long.

Our first meeting was not a roaring success. About 50 people were present, and though they were obviously happy to have us with them, there was a strange hesitancy. We wondered if it was because of the soldiers who were never far away and insisted on escorting us every time we moved down the path. However, the people chatted to them in a relaxed manner and seemed perfectly at ease with them.

We were based in the middle of a large population scattered around in numerous small villages. Our strategy was to visit different villages each day in a small group and to return late afternoon each day for joint meetings with people walking to the meeting place from their villages. The meetings had to be late afternoon into the evening as large groups seen from the sky invited bombing. Before we headed for home (home is always where bed and tea and coffee is), a contingency approached us with a special invitation. The local witch doctor wished us to visit her village in the morning. We accepted the invitation with thanks. We should be delighted to meet her as we had some important things to tell her. Several people escorted us back; this is the polite thing to do. A scorpion on the path stung one of the soldiers. He yelped and rubbed his foot. Scorpion stings are very painful and the fiery darts burn for ages. "Ambush!" yelled Rod. The soldiers dissolved into hysterical laughter. They were supposed to be protecting us, and now they had been attacked by a scorpion – their guns of no use against this enemy.

Our followers stopped just outside our camp. Instead of returning to their homes they sat down at the edge of the trees and watched. They made a fire and roasted some sweet potatoes for us. This was a real treat, sweet potatoes making a welcome change from the red/brown coarse porridge cooked from ground sorghum, which was our staple diet in this area.

FILTHY LITTLE WITCH DOCTOR

The village lay ahead of us, huts clustered on a bare hill of red earth. Three mangy dogs barked shrilly; flies feasted on their ragged sore-infested ears. These are the veritable 'tick taxis' of Africa, scrounging for food, kicked by all mankind. Someone threw a handful of stones at them and howling like a pack of wolves, they fled with long skinny tails tucked under arched backs.

We moved through the usual preliminaries of greeting. A man stepped forward to inform us that the witch doctor and her co-worker, a lesser witch doctor, requested us to enter their special hut where they were waiting with their husbands to show us the tools of their trade. Word of our coming had gone ahead of us. Feeling the caution of the Holy Ghost we declined the invitation to the hut and said we would meet outside. The messenger returned to tell us "No", the contingency wanted us inside their hut. Remaining firm we replied we would wait outside.

The team launched into a cheerful chorus. People gathered to see what was going on. Most of the people had never heard the song before, but this does not pose a problem in Africa. Songs are repetitive in word as well as melody. A lead singer sings out the words while the rest pick up in an echo, different voices harmonizing beautifully together. It is customary to state one's purpose when entering a village. We decided on this occasion to do so with an evangelistic meeting. We entered into the joy of praising our wonderful Lord. Dust flew as we clapped and danced. After some time we noticed a foursome had come out of their hut and were standing at the edge of the small crowd. It was now time for the Word of God.

"For God so loved the world, that He gave His only begotten Son, that whoever believes in Him should not perish, but have everlasting life." John 3:16. "This Son of God is Jesus Christ, who gave Himself as a living sacrifice, laying down His life and shedding His blood to cleanse us from all our sin. He will forgive you if you repent of your sins, turn from your old ways and follow Him."

All listened intently, but I felt as if I were preaching to one soul. The wizened face of the witch doctor gazed up into mine, taking in every word. She was not much more than four feet tall, dressed in a dirty piece of cloth tied round the waist, reaching to just above the knees. Necklaces of shells, beads and bones and who knows what else draped around her neck, some tied around her waist and tails of various animals as well as small pouches filled with potions hung from her hip.

She had a most interesting face – almost jolly. There was none of the usual contempt, hatred or mockery which most witch doctors reflected. Was this really the notorious witch doctor? Standing behind her was her associate – a tall thin woman with sly expression and furtive eyes. Directly behind them, two men, nondescript and insignificant-looking. These must be the husbands, very much in awe of their wives. In African custom a man is much mocked if his wife appears to be the boss; but these men were to be excused. After all, who wants to argue with this kind of power?

A WITCH DOCTOR'S SINCERE QUESTION

"I have a question." The crowd tangibly stiffened as the chief witch doctor speaks. What kind of trickery or challenge is about to come forth? The woman walked slowly towards me, gazing earnestly into my face. I have heard many stories of witch doctors challenging the power of missionaries in the style of Moses versus the magicians. I did not feel ready to act the part of Moses. "Please," she spoke respectfully. "**Please, who IS this Jesus?** I have never heard of this man before. Who is He?"

The sincerity of her question touched me deep inside, and I experienced something in a way I never had before. Love welled up in my heart and surged through my being. A holy anointing coursed through me, and I felt more than a little dazed. It was a baptism of love. The love of God was being supernaturally shed abroad in my heart by the Holy Spirit: God's love for this little witch doctor! I felt a smile spreading over my burning face as I reached out my arms and drew the woman into an embrace. A gasp rose from the people. I knew what they were thinking, particularly the Christians. "Does not this missionary know what manner of woman she is embracing? If she were truly of God she would know that this was a woman of sin, demons and evil. She would not touch her." Turning to the people I spoke, "This woman and I are going to become friends." Carefully I explained to her again the story of Jesus, His love for her and for all mankind. She was most interested in the bit about the blood. Her profession was in shedding blood to help the sick get well, to cast out evil spirits, etc. Multitudes of chickens and pigeons have been sacrificed at her hand. Goats, too. "Jesus is the sacrifice Lamb of God, the only sacrifice that can save us. He died to save YOU. Will you choose Him today and give your life to Him?" She thought for a while then replied, "No." Such a decision could not be made suddenly and without first consulting with others of her trade; but yes, she would come to the meetings every evening and hear more about this Jesus, Son of God.

Day by day our ministry at Molima gained momentum as we walked out to nearby villages and visited the people. Talking about Jesus, we talked also about their daily lives. Food was scarce, but they fed us sorghum grits, an occasional bit of chicken and sometimes sweet potatoes. There were no vegetables or fruit in the region; it was arid and dry and water was carried from a long way off for drinking, cooking and washing. Each night attendance grew at our meetings. People were receiving Christ, healing and deliverance. We found out a few days after our arrival what the concern about our choice of campground was. We had set up camp in the middle of a burial ground. There was no way we could sleep there and live, or so the people thought. How relieved they were when they saw we woke up perfectly well after our first night, then the second and third as well, with no trace of sickness. It must be true then, that our God was more powerful than the dark spirits of the region. Word spread quickly that the missionaries were living in the graveyard and suffering no ill effects. People came from all around to see for themselves. "Did you know it was a graveyard?" I asked Rod. "Not at first, but when I dug up a hip bone next to a broken pot, I realized what we were into." "A hip bone?" "Yes, that's what I threw into the bushes while we were clearing," Rod grinned at me. "I wasn't going to tell you in case you, too, thought we should rather sleep in the thorn grove."

Every night the witch doctor came with her group to our meetings, and every night we longed that they should receive Jesus. Though they listened with interest, there was no real indication of a change of heart. Sometimes Nanga Wakuru (Big Witch Doctor), which was the name given to the little witch doctor on account of her power and not her size, sent us gifts. Two bananas, once a mango, a couple of eggs. Where she got hold of fruit in this place we could not imagine. "You must not eat those things," we were advised. We thanked God for His provision, blessed the food and ate with relish. Again, the people were impressed by the power of God. We should surely have become ill or perhaps even died from eating Nanga Wakuru's food. It was great developing relationships with some of the people and watching them grow spiritually; the soldiers too.

Our teachings focused largely on the life of Jesus and the power of His blood, as well as on the Holy Spirit. We also spent much time answering questions using Bible verses to back up our explanations. In answering questions, we found we covered the subjects that were most pertinent, as the questions came out of their own needs and situations. Worship time was special and the presence of God beautiful under the starlit skies.

Our time at Molima was drawing to a close. We had one more evening meeting and still Nanga Wakuru was not saved. "Oh God," I prayed. "I have felt so sure that you would give us this soul. Please don't let us return leaving her like this." The baptism of love I had experienced for her would not allow me to accept that she would reject Christ. That night we totally poured out our hearts in our messages and worship. People were weeping and moaning as they yielded to God, and many who had been unwilling to make a final decision did so freely and openly. Surely, Nanga Wakuru would do so, too. But no, she sat unmoving as a rock. We could not believe it; we had been so certain that tonight would be the night for her.

After the meeting we said goodbye to the people; we would be leaving Molima at dawn. As we touched hands with individuals in farewell, we looked out for our friend, the witch doctor, but she had evaporated into the night. Later, lying on our mats, sleep evaded us. The success of the visit was undeniable, but there was this empty space for Nanga Wakuru. We felt sad.

MOST WELCOME NIGHT-VISITOR

Unexpectedly there was a tugging at our tent flap. José spoke urgently, "Pastor, Mai (mother). Nanga Wakuru is here; she wants to say goodbye to you." We got up quickly and someone rekindled the fire which was burning low. She laughed, showing the gaps in her teeth. "Tomorrow you are going, and I have not yet given my heart to Jesus!" "Do you wish to do so?" "Oh yes. That is why I have come to see you. I want you to pray for me." Her associate and the husbands stood a little way behind her. She had heard the Gospel message many times now, and she had watched as souls accepted Jesus night after night. There was not much we needed to tell her on how to do it, but plenty to tell her about her new life. As we talked, we heard voices singing down the path. It was a group from the meeting who had stayed on to pray. We called them over. It was important that those living here should witness the conversion of the chief witch doctor.

"You will have to publicly renounce your trade and all witchcraft practices you have been involved in and practice them no more," we told her. "You will need to join with these Christians so you can learn more about God and walk in His ways. Very important, you must burn all your fetishes and witchcraft tools." She unhesitatingly said she would do so. This was, after all, not a sudden decision. One of the greatest joys of our ministry life was to lead Nanga Wakuru to Jesus. With the night breeze blowing cool and fresh, the stars peeped through the trees in the burial ground. There, where the bones of the dead lay in shallow graves, the powerful witch doctor died to her

old life and was born again. New life in the midst of the graveyard. Oh, what a victory! In this very place where they thought
we should surely die, the villagers witnessed a great miracle of
life as Nanga Wakuru prayed the sinner's prayer and invited
Jesus into her life. As I hugged her in congratulation, I was
reminded that she needed more than a spiritual cleansing. In my
back pack was a brand new fragrant bar of soap still in its wrap-
ping. This was my gift to her. Her associate and the two husbands also prayed to receive Christ. They were now free to do
so; the "boss" had led the way. We were not convinced of the sincerity of the tall, thin witch doctor, but who were we to judge?

We briefed the Christians thoroughly on what to do concerning Nanga Wakuru. For a start, that would no longer be her
name. She must publicly testify of her salvation and publicly burn
her witchcraft material. She did so. We received word months
later from a group we sent in to do follow up, that this woman was
serving Christ and was well and happy. The other one, however,
had not turned from her ways and had died three months later.

Baptizing in the Zambezi River

The journey home was highlighted by a great victory on
the banks of the Zambezi River. We baptized ten soldiers.
Among them was Commander Zachariah and several other soldiers in leadership positions. Gulai was included. He had at last
surrendered to Christ; how happy that made us. The banks of the
river were steep and the water deep at the edge. The canoe was
pushed a little way out and two soldiers stood in it, **eyes alert and
guns at the ready in case of crocodiles!** One by one they went
in and under as Rodney baptized them on the confession of their
faith. Afterwards we danced and sang for a long time on the river
banks. The river god must have trembled at the pounding feet of
the army of God with the high praises of God in their mouth!

Slave-Traders?

Some of the Christians had escorted us to the river and
said farewell there. We had tried to persuade four of the men to
return all the way to Malawi with us for training at the Bible

School. They would not hear of crossing the Zambezi River, never having been that far away from home before. "We have heard that when you cross that river, you are in danger of being captured as slaves and sent far away to other lands." Was it really possible that these people living in the remote recesses of Mozambique believed the slave trade was still operating? Apparently so. We realized that though these were truly committed to Christ, and had been with us for some weeks, we had only scratched the surface of breaking through mindset and traditional beliefs. Again the necessity of a Bible School in Mozambique was impressed on us. Here were pastors and leaders with little or no knowledge of the Word of God.

On the north side of the riverbank after our canoe crossing, we were again escorted by other Christians who joined us as we passed through their villages. They would go all the way to the Malawi border and wait there for us to return home and collect a land cruiser full of Bibles and clothes for them to carry back with them.

By the time we reached home, having stopped at all the same villages on our return journey, it felt like we had been gone for months and months, so much had happened. It was heaven to be with our children again; we had missed them terribly. We arrived while they were still asleep in bed. Rod had a special way of waking the kids by jumping on their beds. We had plenty to tell them, and they loved the adventure stories. I had picked up some white quartz stones, which had been lying in the path while walking through one of the rocky areas. These were for Deborah. Still young enough to find great treasure in a pocketful of stones, she convinced herself they were diamonds, and she carefully guarded them for years. Rod had collected some empty bullet shells for Dustin. He polished them and proudly added them to his collection on the shelf. We had hunted in vain for something that would interest our teenage Tammy. She was too smart to be fooled with fake diamonds.❖

SOS

FOR THOSE IN DISTRESS

Bush telegraph is the amazing communication system of Africa that traverses over hundreds of miles through jungles and grasslands, across rivers and mountains by the fleet foot of man and the call of his mouth. With no vehicles operating in most of rural Mozambique, there is no way to get anywhere or receive anything but by foot.

Word was getting out further afield that there were missionaries living in Malawi who travelled the war zones preaching the Gospel. We received notes and letters from afar, begging us to come to them, to bring Bibles and to teach the Word of God. How we wished we could respond to each one, but it was impossible. As much as we could, we sent teams of national pastors to various locations, but still this could not begin to answer the cry. The letters pulled deep at our soul.

We developed relationships with people we had never met and began to carry them on our hearts. None moved us as deeply as two Italian priests whom we were privileged to assist in a small way. These two men lived in a remote part of the Zambezia province, not far from the ocean. This zone was a liberated Renamo area. It had been under the control of the Frelimo government, but during the battle that ensued leaving Renamo the victors, the Communists had fled. The priests continued to live here by choice and were free to carry out their work though without supplies other than what was grown in the ground.

The priests had heard about us and sent some letters by courier, requesting us to mail them to Italy. They had no way of buying stamps and Malawi, two to three weeks walk away, was their nearest hope of a Post Office. We were delighted to help and sent them some literature as well as some small gifts. We had received a large consignment of Bible Studies in Portuguese, printed by Christ For The Nations. A box of these was carried on the head of the courier who had brought the letter.

This small gesture was to grow into a major courier service. Several times a year up to twenty large cartons of supplies came from Italy for us to get to the priests. This meant clearing them at customs, and taking them in our land cruiser down to the Shire River at night under cover of darkness. There we would be met by a group of Renamo soldiers, who loaded the boxes onto canoes and carried them on their heads in relays all the way to the Catholic Mission near Mocubela. This involved quite a bit of work, loss of night hours as the journey to the river was three hours there and three back, and not a little risk. It would be bad news for us to be found handing over large boxes to Renamo soldiers.

It was a joy to be able to bless these faithful men. They were the Unknown Soldiers on the spiritual battlefield. They lived full time in a war situation without a break. No getting away for a few days, no visit to a restaurant once in a while, no touch with civilization, year after year. They did not know our names, they knew only that we were missionaries. The material we had sent revealed our beliefs; we were obviously Charismatic. These books included among others, The Baptism of the Holy Spirit; Prayer that Moves Mountains; and How You Can Be Healed. They addressed their letters to us in a rather singular way.

11 June, 1989
To The Reverend Priests of Pentecost,
We have received the goods you sent. We thank you with thankful heart for your help and generosity in this context through difficulty and danger of war.
Please, we would like to have a letter to know you, if possible. We ask a favour of Reverend Priests, please to send more Bibles and books in Portuguese and English. Thanks very much. We are Italian Priests.

----

19 August, 1989
To Reverend Priests Pentecostals,
We received with great fun and wonder your letter and so we know your work and mission. The Peace of our Lord be with you always. We have great pleasure to meet with you one day if God likes.
We always pray to Jesus for you. Your work and help to us is a great signal of love and unity with Jesus in middle of us. We would like to do some prayers together in this zone with you. We think there is no Pentecostal churches here. Thank you for Bible studies, cassettes in English and paper of guidance. Our students were much enthusiasmed. We hope and pray there will be no damage and danger of yourselves for you to continue helping us during this time of war.
In Jesus Christ our Saviour, Padre G. & P.

----

1 January, 1990
Reverend Missionaries Pentecostal,
The Peace of Jesus, Son of God be always with you. We received this day your congratulations of Christmas and boxes of Bibles, books, teas, coffees, sugars, gifts of flour and cooking oil and many other things. Thank you sirs, missionaries, for your kind heart. We are waiting for this year 1990 to be peace, no more war and a time to meet with you.
With hard hugs from Priests Roman Catholic.

----

15 April, 1990
To Mr.'s English, Miss Pentecostal.
You have been helping us a long time. You stir a deep emotion in us. Thank you, thank you, thank you. May our mutual Christ bless you and give you more than you do. We are happy to know your photograph. I will not add more for fear of dropping on this paper tears of joy and gratitude. We kiss you all. I can use no other language than this word. Italian Priests.

We send SOS to you. We think there have died 30% of children. Please, we need medicines for the sick urgent. We have many sick here, malaria, cholera. We have no medicine, people are dying.

To The Reverend Pastors of Pentecost,

The Peace of Jesus be with all your Christians. We thank you for your gift of food, Bibles and books. We want very much some medicines if possible. We have no treatments, disinfectants, pomade, tablets, anti-biotic etc. The Frelimo that govern, think only on killing and oppressing the poor and God's people, and those that they make to live on state farms. BLESSED BE HE THAT CRY FOR HE WILL BE CONSOLED. Here the people spend a week burying the dead because of sicknesses and lack of medicine. Now measles epidemic has arrived here. Please send us more Bibles and Bible studies for our students to learn in school.

Always in unity with Jesus we love and pray for you. The measles is giving of extremity to many children who are dying. We ask your help of anti-biotic. Thanking you

We increased our efforts to obtain medicines, a difficult and expensive task. At last we had a good load of medicines as well as clothing and various other supplies. We made the long journey to the river and delivered them to couriers. In response, we received the following heartbreaking letter.

To Pastors of Pentecost,

Grace to you, peace in Jesus. On 5 November Frelimo assaulted our station. 300 men attacked, destroyed the chapel and tried to liquidate us. We are 12 nuns, novices and learner priests. We ran away and became lost in two groups for thirteen days until we found each other. We met large colonnade of hundreds of Renamo soldiers. We marched with them in safety for 20 days or more, 450 kilometre to a place near M. where we now are.

Frelimo arrived same day as boxes you sent. They took everything. Medicines and supplies but not desiring Bibles. These men are anti Christ. We have only clothes we are wearing. Jesus is our comfort, we escaped with our lives. In heaven we can talk about these things and understand. Please may you send once more Bibles and supplies, which are possible. We thank you, praying God will do you much good. We wish you happy felicitations for Christmas and for 1991.

Padres Giovanni & Pedro

We were able to collect more supplies and in January 1991 sent 25 large boxes across the river and 29 in February. These priests were bravely starting out from scratch, carving out a new Mission with nothing. When the Peace Accord was signed in 1992 they were able to move about freely again. They went back to Italy for a period of time and returned again to Mozambique to continue their work. We never did get to meet them, but we shall see them in heaven.

Attacks on Distribution Centers

Our radio link became of importance to the International Convention of the Red Cross Society, ICRC. This organization was carrying out relief operations in the Communist Frelimo zones, delivering food, medicines, blankets and clothing to the population. They were not, however, helping the people in Renamo zones. The majority of the poorest and neediest of the population was in Renamo controlled areas, but the ICRC as well as other aid organizations ignored them for political reasons. The West was supporting the Communists and would operate only in Communist areas. This was a mystery to us, until as time went by, we began to comprehend to some extent the workings of the World System.

In order for the ICRC to reach the areas they wanted to work in, they had to fly over Renamo airspace. How could they be guaranteed safety? Renamo was disenchanted with the ICRC for favoring one side only. Also, Communist military planes had been flying with the Red Cross emblem attached to their aircraft, then bombing and shooting Renamo targets as well as civilians living in Renamo zones.

We had already approached the ICRC for assistance with medicines but when they realized we were in Renamo territory, they politely told us it was impossible for them to help us. Now that they wanted clearance from Renamo, but no way to contact them they remembered us.

One of the ICRC representatives requested a meeting. Could we get messages to Dhlakama and could we assist in procuring security for them? We said yes, though we told them nothing of our radio link. They thought we would simply send messages across the river. The reply from Dhlakama was conditionally affirmative. Certainly he would guarantee safety for ICRC. Renamo does not shoot down Red Cross aircraft. But because Frelimo and Zimbabwean forces were abusing the emblem, it was necessary for Renamo to know the flight schedules and airstrips Red Cross would be landing on ahead of time. This way there would be no confusion about who was really flying the plane. Another thing, the ICRC should also start relief work in the Renamo areas. These were after all also the people of Mozambique. Renamo was not asking for help for their **forces**, but for the **population** living in their zones.

We were happy with this. For too long the people had been suffering without assistance from those that should have been giving it. The ICRC office in Blantyre telephoned when they had the flight schedules. We would go and pick it up, and then Gostode would radio the information through to Renamo Headquarters. Help was slow in coming. Word would be sent out for the villagers to gather at a certain point where ICRC was to land with supplies. People would walk for days and wait at the airstrip day after day, with no plane coming in. In the meantime the Frelimo airstrips were busy with tons of supplies coming from the Red Cross. Dhlakama was not pleased.

Tragically, this situation developed into something far more ugly than favoring one side above the other. **Frelimo planes saw the crowds of people gathered at the airstrips and began bombing the crowds waiting for relief aid from Red Cross.** It was devastating. Men, women and children lay shattered in the bush, dying without medical assistance. Dhlakama sent us an urgent message.

"You must telephone ICRC to inform them that Frelimo and other Foreign troops working with Frelimo are bombing the population concentrated at the airstrips where these people were awaiting the ICRC aircraft for supplies. The enemy deployed helicopters, MiGS and Antonovs against the civilian population in Molumbo, Derre and Mulevala, then later at Lugela Township. All these are in Zambezia Province. The enemy has also used helicopters against the population in Tambara, Manica Province. Many civilians have been killed and wounded. You must therefore tell ICRC they are responsible because they have left the population waiting there for weeks, people staying there and waiting for their promise of supplies but they never landed there. They were landing on Frelimo side while the population was languishing with no food, waiting for them."

We relayed this message to the Red Cross agents, who simply did not believe it... until one day, when they finally did make a flight into an appointed area, the airstrip where they had landed came under attack. The attackers did not at first see the Red Cross plane tucked away at the end of the runway. The population began to run for their lives as the first bomb was dropped. When the Communists saw the Red Cross plane at the end of the runway, they quickly withdrew. The truth was now known but **it did not change matters much**. The ICRC was politically controlled and remained generally unresponsive to our appeals for help. There were at least two individuals, who being disillusioned with the system, genuinely tried to help. They managed to get some Red Cross emergency packs to us, but what they gave was quickly used; there were not enough of them.

BETRAYED AND BOMBED - THE WAY IT WAS

In these remote areas people have been cut off from civilization for years. With no access to basic commodities such as soap, clothing, blankets, sugar, salt or anything other than what they are able to produce from their fields, they survive from hand to mouth. Imagine their joy and excitement when news comes that they are to gather at a certain airstrip to receive goods to be distributed by the Red Cross.

"What do you think they'll bring us? Soap? What luxury! For years we've not felt the lather of soap clean our bodies. Perhaps a cloth wrap to cover ourselves in place of our coarse sacks and tree bark. And maybe, just maybe, a blanket to keep out the winter cold at night."

Word spreads like wildfire from village to village. Women chatter excitedly over their cooking pots. Men talk importantly about the prospects of obtaining provisions for their families. Children laugh and jump. Sugar? A few had tasted sugar before, but most had not. "They say it is very sweet, sweeter than honey but it comes in a packet with no bees to sting you." It would be fun to try some. Yes, certainly they must all make the journey to the appointed place, though it would be hard walking all that distance with no place to sleep on the way. They could not carry much food with them and better to leave the cooking pots behind because they would need to carry the supplies back on their heads. This was an opportunity not to be missed.

The great day arrived. "Today the big bird will come from the skies with gifts." People gathered from various places. Old friends were rediscovered, news exchanged. There was grief over reports of friends and loved ones having died and rejoicing over others who had been given up for dead, but now arriving at the distribution point. "This terrible war has been going on for so long. When will it end?"

"Ah, listen. That is surely the sound of a plane? The engines sounded big and deep. They must be carrying lots and lots of goods for us!" "Yes, yes. It is big. But it is coming fast, not circling to land. It is behaving strangely."

"Run, Run! Run for your lives!" Someone had recognized the plane. It was not a Red Cross distribution plane, but a Russian Antonov bomber. The kind that Frelimo Forces used when they bombed the villages. "Run and lie flat, everybody!"

Women wailed as they grabbed at little children; anybody's child. With babies on their backs hampering their speed, they ran as fast as they could. Men shouted instructions while bigger children yelled and shrieked. As the plane flew overhead the people threw themselves on the ground. The deafening explosion filled the air and the plane flew on. Next would come the helicopter gunships. Those that were able got up to run into the bushes, others dragged themselves painfully. Some didn't move at all. Gone were the hopes and dreams of soap, clothes and other wonderful things. Wiped out, lives that had come here so full of hope.

A Doctor's Dilemma

One night, shortly after one of the bombings, we had an unexpected visitor. Dr. Soares, the Renamo doctor from the Gorongosa bush camp had come all the way to find us in the hopes of getting medical supplies. He had been deployed to Tambara to try and help the wounded civilians there, but was unable to do much as he had so little to work with.

"People are lying wounded under the bushes, and some are dying because we cannot treat these wounds," he told us. "I need a proper amputation saw and some anesthetic. We have been taking off limbs with an ordinary hacksaw, with no anesthetic or pain killers."

As we sat in our office at home listening to this report, we felt sick. Who would help these people? The responsibility was ours. I remembered an article in a magazine I had seen a few days previously. It was about the war in Eritrea. I had observed the similarities between the Eritrean Rebels' stand against the rule of their Communist government and that of Renamo against Communist Frelimo. The article featured a secular medical organization which prided itself on the fact that the group knew no borders and offered assistance to all, regardless of political affiliations. Full page photographs showed land rovers filled with medical staff and equipment in the rough terrain where the rebels were in control. The personnel treated all those in need in these areas. This was it! This group had a branch in Blantyre and would surely help in this desperate hour.

We had to proceed with caution; we were, after all, supposed to remain hidden. The desperate situation demanded that we take risks. Looking again through the article, our hopes were built up. We were confident that at last here was an organization that would not be hindered by borders, whether physical or political. They were committed to transcend red tape in order to help all in need, regardless of religious or political affiliations. In anticipation we entered their office and asked to speak to the man in charge. He was not available; would we please state our case to the secretary. We replied that we would prefer to wait for the manager. We waited for a couple of hours, then he came. In the privacy of his office, we made the situation known to him.

"Please, will you help these people? Please, will you send a team to Mutarara to give medical assistance to these wounded civilians?" The man had listened with sympathy but shook his head at our request for help. "It is impossible." "But why? Is this not what your organization is for?" He had the grace to blush and look very embarrassed. "We cannot risk upsetting the Frelimo government."

We couldn't believe our ears. I took out the magazine article and showed him the pictures that boasted the good work of their organization. The front page sported a picture of the land rovers taking supplies into the Eritrean Rebel territory. Medical personnel could be seen treating wounded people. The man blushed deeper as he said, "Yes, but you don't understand. Mozambique is different."

We were so tired of hearing that Mozambique was different. So very tired of help being refused to people in Mozambique Rebel areas when it was given everywhere else in the world. Fighting back tears I looked at the man and said. "How can you do this? Your organization is living a lie!" He looked guilty, but would not budge. Rod suggested that as they would not go and help the people themselves, they could give us the medical supplies needed and we would go ourselves. (Rod is a very ably trained medic.) This too was denied and we left that office deeply disappointed and disgusted.

No supplies went in to help the people so most of the

wounded died from infections. We appealed to private sources, and what joy when medicines eventually started coming in. They made a great difference though we always needed more. We even received an amputation saw and some anesthetic from a single donor. God was hearing the cries of the people and preparing hearts of individuals to help medically on the field.

LITTLE PADRE

"He has sent me to proclaim liberty to the captives and the opening of the prison to those who are bound." Isaiah 61:1

There is no song so joyous as the song of a soul set free. To see someone brought out of darkness into light is a wonderful privilege. Ours was the added joy in not only bringing liberty to those in bondage to Satan, but in being instrumental also in releasing several prisoners into physical freedom.

Father Gioconde Pagliara was at his desk at Inhassunge when the peaceful Easter Sunday morning was shattered by automatic gunfire and exploding bazookas. A battle had erupted between Frelimo and Renamo troops. The former fled in the direction of the Catholic Mission Station pursued by Renamo. Three of Padre Giocondo's fellow priests were out in the vegetable garden on the edge of the mission vicinity. They had no time to run out of the way and tragically were caught in the crossfire of the battle that continued. Two of the Italian priests were killed and the third seriously wounded.

Renamo prevailed in the battle, killing most of the Frelimo soldiers, the remainder managing to run away. The Renamo soldiers entered the mission building and found Father Gioconde. "You must come with us," they said. "It is not safe for you to stay here. Frelimo will be back and if they find you they will kill you."

Father Gioconde begged to be allowed to take some of his belongings and was given time to quickly pack a few clothes, supplies and papers. He also requested that he should be allowed to give the priests a proper burial. Though they treated the injured priest as best they could he had died also. The Renamo soldiers took up the bodies, placed them in coffins and buried them after a service in the chapel. This traumatic ordeal and the weeks that were to follow was related to us by Father Gioconde himself and later recorded in his book written in Italian, "Bazooka e sangue Quando era Pasqua a Inhassunge" (Bazookas and Blood during Passover at Inhassunge.)

The fact that the Renamo soldiers had not only allowed the time for the burial, but had also helped in the funeral procedure made a profound impression on Father Gioconde. "These men showed compassion and care towards us. I could not believe it could be so in the midst of war with danger all around. The people had run away to hide, but the Christians came out from where they had run to, and they came with flowers. The chapel was filled with singing; my brothers were buried with dignity."

Then started the six-week journey, which proved to be an ordeal that several times almost cost the life of the 73-year-old priest who was growing more frail with each harrowing day. Inhassunge is a small village near the coast of the Zambezia province. Father Gioconde could not remain where battles may continue for control of the town. For him to remain in Mozambique at all would be dangerous; the best thing would be to return to Italy. But how, and from where? All major airports were in the cities controlled by Frelimo. It was not safe for the priest to enter into those zones from the hands of Renamo. Previous tragic incidents had taught Renamo not to give over to Frelimo any people needing to get out of Mozambique. Dhlakama told us of a particular instance when a group of nuns who had been held by Renamo during a battle were released to Frelimo. The nuns were killed and the blame for their deaths pinned on Renamo. The involvement of a third party was needed for the safe release of this man. Using humanitarian organizations had not proved to be the answer either, as confidential information about dates and locations frequently leaked out, causing the transaction to be compromised.

Through coded radio communication, Renamo HQ requested that we should help in the operation of getting Father Gioconde safely to Italy. We were to collect him at a certain point on the border during the cover of darkness and keep him hidden in our home until we could safely hand him over to the Red Cross in Malawi. Of course we wanted to help and set into motion the plans, contacting various parties. We used non de plume names, did not give our address to anybody and our telephone number only to a few. Nobody was to know the details of how Father Gioconde would get to Malawi or who would be the ones to carry through his release into the civilized world. We were also given the name of an Italian journalist to contact. Once he knew Father Gioconde was safely with us, he would fly out to Malawi to interview him. Previous news reports had carried fabricated stories about Renamo brutally murdering four priests at Inhassunge. It would be a scoop for the journalist to interview and film one of the supposedly dead priests and get the true story.

All these clandestine arrangements took a certain amount of ingenuity. We did make some mistakes, but God intervened each time and the plans worked out without any serious threat to us. We were trying to live like a normal family with three children going back and forth to school daily and people popping in at odd times. The phone was constantly ringing with family calls, ministry calls, prisoner-release calls. Many calls came in the middle of the night, and we rarely had an uninterrupted night of sleep.

Each time we answered we had to quickly guess which hat to wear. The kids were great; they would call to us, "It's for you Mom," or "Somebody wants to speak to either Mr. or Mrs. Joseph," whatever the need was. We had our moments of fun, like when someone rang asking to speak to "Father Joseph". This one was new to us; we were accustomed to Rod being called Joseph, or Mr. Joseph, but not Father Joseph. I took the call and said, "He's not in at the moment; may I take a message?" "Oh no! I can speak only to Father Joseph," was the reply. I tried to persuade him that it was safe to talk to me. Finally I said, "You can trust me; I am his wife." There was shocked silence and then some stammering as the person said he would prefer to call back later. Feeling a bit embarrassed I assumed they may be under the false impression that Rod was a Catholic priest and were thinking something like, "Not only does this priest collaborate with the Mozambican rebels, he even keeps a wife!" Once, someone said to me on the phone, "You must be Mary." "Mary?" I inquired. "Yes, Joseph's counterpart." We had our own names for people too, sometimes taken from literal translations that were nothing like the real name. There was "The Buffalo," "The Elephant," "The Lion," "The Boss," "The Prof.," "The Thinman," "Poppet," "Bedbug," and many others. I fancied the name of Esther Hadassah, (my own initials), but it never stuck, I was always returned to being Mrs. Joseph. I didn't mind; I was proud to belong to Joseph.

We did not know much about Father Gioconde except for the fact that he spoke no English at all – only Italian and Portuguese. At that time, we had no knowledge of Portuguese whatsoever. We tried to think of ways that we could assure him of his safety with us and of his welcome in our home. We wrote a warm letter explaining everything to him, telling him how happy we were to have him with us and that he would be on his way to Italy in a few days. A friend translated this into Portuguese. We placed it in a new Portuguese Bible and left it beside his bed together with a bag of toiletries. We knew that a toothbrush, toothpaste and soap would be very welcome, as it was unlikely that he had access to these since leaving the mission. Deborah had vacated her room for him and we placed a vase of flowers on the dresser and made everything as nice as we could.

Armed with a basket packed with food and loads of coffee we set off late in the afternoon on a journey that would see us back with the rising of the sun, hopefully with our guest safely in our custody. We had no trouble on the road and arrived at our meeting place in good time. Out of the bushes surrounded by a group of men walked an old man. A bald forehead and long white beard hanging to the waist glistened in the moonlight. Rodney walked up to him and hugged him tenderly speaking the universal word of praise to God, "Hallelujah." A little shaky, with throat constricted with emotion and eyes brimming with tears of relief, the dear man responded, "Hallelujah!"

We beheld a moving scene as Father Gioconde turned to the Renamo soldiers who had escorted him. "Gracia, gracia," he thanked them over and over again, falling upon the neck of each one with tears. We were yet to learn of how these men had cared for him on the extremely difficult six-week journey through the wilds, nursing him through sickness, carrying him on a pole and bark stretcher when he was sick or too tired to walk. He owed his life to them.

When at last they had made their farewells, the soldiers carried his belongings to our land cruiser. "Non, non, non!" protested the priest. He would not think of taking anything with him other than the clothes he wore and his papers. All his other clothes and personal articles were to be shared among them. We were touched by the genuine love displayed from both the soldiers and the priest. "Adeus amigos," and they replied, "Adeus Padre." They looked forlorn as he turned away; they were losing someone they had grown to love.

We needed to be on our way; delay at this point could mean trouble. Rod helped the old man into the vehicle with a "Bem Vindo! Welcome." "Oh, oooh," the priest groaned as he climbed into the high vehicle. He was weary, stiff and sore. With a sigh of relief he sank into the seat, tears slowly rolling down his cheeks while he thanked Rod and God again and again.

The land cruiser started to roll and sway along the rough mountain track and we waved to the faces dully reflected in the moonlight. Conversation was difficult because of the language barrier and the priest was so overcome he could scarcely talk anyway. But there is no barrier in the language of love, and as he whispered, "Jesus, Jesus," we echoed, "Jesus, Jesus," in response.

Once we reached what we considered to be a safe spot we stopped on the side of the road and offered him some coffee, cold chicken, rolls and fruit. He took only water. We had expected him to be very hungry, but he pointed to his stomach and shook his head. He had suffered much from diarrhea and had pain in his stomach. We drove on with the cassette recorder playing. Every now and then we'd hear him join in a chorus that he knew in Italian. "There's some charismatic influence here!" we chuckled to ourselves.

From the Bush to the Pope

Dawn was about to break when we stopped outside our gate. Rod showed the padre to the bathroom and to his room. Again, with tear-filled eyes he hugged Rod and said, "Gracia, gracia!" We felt excited. It was truly an honor to be thus employed and we had a very real assurance of "being about our Father's business" on this strange mission. It was too late to go to bed, or was it too early? Anyhow, we would soon need to get our children off to school. We chatted and planned after making a call to Italy to inform the journalist that Padre Gioconde was well and safe in our home. The journalist would board the first plane from Rome to Malawi and after spending some time with the priest, would accompany him when we hand him over to the Red Cross and fly back to Italy with him.

To our surprise Little Padre was up and about in just a couple of hours. He looked refreshed and far more confident in daylight. His expressive face wrinkled with smiles as he saw Rod who was wearing his "Jesus is Lord" T-shirt. "Jesus is Lord!" he said in heavily accented English and hugged Rod. From that moment on, each time he saw Rod this expression and action was repeated. What a very precious soul he was.

At the breakfast table he ate very little. It would take him a while to build his strength and all we could do was offer him a place of comfort, love and security. When we rose from the table he pointed to my keyboard with a smile. He wanted me to play. I played a few notes then waited for him. He started to sing a hymn and I picked up on the universal melodies of some of the most famous and beautiful hymns. Little Padre sat on the steps and worshipped God in song as tears wet his beard. I cried as I played and Rod tried to sing with a very choked-up throat. We realized the significance of this moment. Little Padre needed the healing that flowed through the worship. His heart was still grieving for those who had not lived to make the journey with him, and the suffering of long years of war was very near the surface. The Holy Spirit was present with us and we experienced an amazing unity and bond in Christian love. In our home for four days he spent much time walking up and down the veranda praying and actually started his book on our old typewriter. He wrote about his stay with us, specially noting the times spent worshipping at the keyboard. His gentleness endeared him to us all and though our religious persuasions are different, we were one in Jesus.

The journalist arrived and interviewed him under the banana trees. We were all very moved at his story. He could not give enough credit to the Renamo soldiers in whose care he had been for six weeks. The journey had been perilous and very taxing. Long distances on foot over rough terrain. Part of the journey had been as a passenger on a motor bike. Though this took him off his feet, riding all day where there is no road is back-breaking. He had come down with malaria, then with diarrhea and vomiting, many times despairing of his life. It was amazing to him that his life had been spared while the younger priests had died. He shook his head over and over at the tragedy of their deaths.

Radio messages came daily from Dhlakama. "Father Gioconde, how is he? Is he happy; is he strong? Have you made contact with the Red Cross?" We assured the HQ that all was well. Little Padre's flight to Italy was booked and the day for his handover dawned. Rod telephoned the Red Cross, "I will meet you in the Mount Soche Car Park; be ready there at 3' o clock."

Little Padre turned to thank me again. This time he took

my hand and kissed my wedding ring. I have been thanked in many ways but this was the most unusual. I realized that he had expressed his deepest thanks in the best way he knew how and I was touched. Rod helped him into the car and off they went. The proceedings were carried out smoothly. The Red Cross car was waiting and with a final hug for Rod and a heartfelt "Jesus is Lord", this servant-leader left his field for the last time. We never saw him again though we did receive a letter and later a copy of his book. The central page holds several photographs, one of the coffins of his fellow priests in the chapel on that fateful day. Another was of Padre Gioconde receiving an award from the Pope.

The journalist wrote a good report, relating the stories and experiences as told him by Father Gioconde. **The world was beginning to hear reports about the Rebel Movement in Mozambique that they had never heard before. Could it be true that Renamo was not as bad as the press had painted them for years?** We were delighted. Truth makes the way for the light to shine in the darkness. The more we could get the truth out, the greater the possibility of the war in Mozambique coming to an end.

PRISONER OF GORONGOSA

A British reporter who walked into Renamo-administered areas of Mozambique was detained and held captive by Renamo, as a suspected spy, for some eighteen months.

"Can you help us find any information concerning a British journalist who has disappeared in Mozambique?" A telephone call from the Red Cross requested our help in locating the missing Mr. Della Casa.

Following our coded radio message of enquiry, Renamo disclosed that Della Casa was being held for questioning. He had blatantly walked into their territory without making contact through the correct channels. The Red Cross requested that we mediate for his release, but Renamo were not about to let him go without finding out what his mission was.

Understanding the concern of Della Casa's family, we requested that he should be allowed to send a message home that he
was safe. This was granted and we forwarded Della Casa's
message word for word. During the months that followed the
British postal service and the jungle HQ worked together,
keeping the almost impossible connection alive.

Della Casa was frequently in our minds. Remembering
the difficulty and uncertainty of our own captivity, we endeavored to do what we could to encourage the man. We had never
met him and knew nothing about him. Though we knew that
Renamo would not harm him, there were other dangers, such
as malaria and air raids. He was in a hot spot; there was no certainty that he would come out of there alive.

I packed a box of supplies to make life a little more pleasant for the prisoner. What would an Englishman be missing
most of all? Why, tea, of course. Into the box went a substantial supply of tea, sugar, milk powder, soap, toothpaste and various other basics. Also a Bible and some Bible studies. For
security reasons, I did not reveal our names; only Renamo and
the Red Cross knew that we were the ones playing postman. I
enclosed a letter, part of which read,

*".........you probably have more time for reflection than you have ever had
in your life. You must know that your situation is precarious. While we are
happy to send you a few things for your comfort, the most important is to make
known to you Jesus Christ, and your need to know Him. We hope you enjoy
reading the literature we are sending.*

*I am also sending some flour, baking powder and strawberry jam, every-
thing you need for making English scones. Ask the soldiers to show you how to
bake them on a metal sheet over the open fire. And then of course, you cannot
enjoy the tea half as much out of a plastic mug, so I am sending a china mug.
From two friends who care."*

We corresponded several times. When Rod took some
journalists in to interview President Dhlakama, they were
allowed to interview Della Casa, also. Rod stayed in the background as Joseph, not disclosing his identity. Soon after that,

Renamo decided to release their prisoner. His release was to be transacted in the following manner. Della Casa would make the long journey to the Malawi border under escort of the Renamo soldiers where he would be handed over to someone who would drive him to Blantyre from where he would fly to the UK. That someone would be us. We worked out a strategy. It so happened that we had some friends joining us for ministry in Mozambique; Rod would already be there with them at the time of Della Casa's release. He could not, however, leave our friends there and drive Della Casa back. I would have to make the four-hour journey in the evening, collect Della Casa at midnight when nobody was about, and get home again before sunrise. I looked forward to an interesting ride back, talking to a man for whom we had been praying much.

I was a bit uneasy, waiting alone at night on the border. The silence was occasionally broken by the hoot of an owl or the call of small night animals. I strained to see in the darkness; the soldiers would approach silently and I would most likely see them before hearing them. It was not long before the grass swished and there they were, dark shapes in a dark night. I opened the door for Rod; a quick kiss and instructions to leave immediately, no time to talk. Della Casa got in front with me and two Americans who had been in to interview Dhlakama got in the back. Without talking, we drove along the mountain trail. I searched keenly for possible roadblocks of logs or rocks set in the road, negotiated the precarious little bridge, then breathed a sigh of relief as we turned onto the main road. No ambushes were likely now.

Sensing the tension ease up, my passenger spoke.

"Hello, I'm Nicholas Della Casa. I don't know how to thank you for what you are doing."

"You're welcome, Nicholas, I'm glad to be of help," I replied without introducing myself. We started chatting and I asked him some questions about his experiences in Mozambique.

"Fascinating, I saw and learned things I would never

have dreamt were happening."

He told me how he had journeyed on foot to different places with the soldiers, visiting and talking with the local population in their villages, how he had narrowly escaped death during a couple of air raids, having to run for his life.

"I wish I'd had a video camera with me. These helicopters came right over the camp. I was sitting by the campfire, roasting a small chicken. My tea kettle was on the boil and I was looking forward to a good lunch. The next thing, choppers were flying right above me; I could have filmed the men inside. I ran for the trees as they started shooting. It was close! I was unhurt, but my chicken was nonexistent and my tea kettle was smashed."

I laughed. Nicholas was clearly elated. After eighteen months in the bush, he was coming out into safety and civilization; he was going home! He chattered on.

"I was really upset about that chicken. One of the locals gave it to me when it was still very small. I fed it and watched in anticipation as it grew. At last I decided it was ready for Sunday lunch, and though it was actually still too small, I couldn't wait any more. Then it got blasted to smithereens!"

I laughed again, picking up his excitement at being safe and free.

"I was really sad about the tea kettle. I never got another one. My mug was shattered too."

I picked up on the tea kettle story. "A tea kettle? Where did you find a tea kettle in the bush?"

Nicholas proceeded to tell me of two people who had written to him and sent him packages. "I wish I knew who they were so I could thank them," he said.

How I enjoyed myself as we continued to talk. The time passed quickly and soon the land cruiser started the steep climb up the escarpment and we reached the police post near the top. I always held my breath at this point, but the police simply asked where we were going, no other questions. Nicholas became silent for the rest of the way. He had not seen a town, streetlights or a neighborhood in a long time. I stopped at our gate to unlock it and drove into the yard. It was 4:00 a.m.; soon dawn would break. Beds had been prepared for all three guests but we were all too wound up to sleep. I made coffee and cheese sandwiches while the others freshened up in the bathroom.

Identity Exposed

Nicholas sat down at the kitchen table. He was in shock. "Electric lights, water coming out of a tap! I've just seen myself in the mirror for the first time in eighteen months. My beard!"

He was clearly overwhelmed and starting to thank me again. As he sat down I passed him his coffee. He stared at it, a strange look on his face. I reminded myself that this man had been through a lot. Now his sudden release and the culture shock of civilization were almost too much for him. He stared from the coffee mug to my face, then back to the mug and back to me again. I felt a bit uneasy; what was going on?

"This mug!" Nicholas said. "It's exactly the same as the one those people sent me when I was in the bush." Silence. "It was you, wasn't it?"

My face turned red. Nicholas jumped up and again started thanking me. "No, no, you don't have to keep thanking us," I said. "Really, you don't know how glad we were to help and how we wished we could do more. Don't thank us. If we've been able to show you God loves you, that's enough."

I decided I was not very good at keeping our identity secret and Nicholas was quite a good detective. He promised not to disclose who we were. He kept his promise. It was time to get our three children up for breakfast and school. The guests would sleep for a few hours while I made arrangements for flights out to the UK. It was a quietly happy and thoughtful Nicholas who said goodbye. He promised to be in touch.

Nicholas returned safely to England and to quite a bit of publicity. He appeared on television and several of his articles were printed in the top newspapers. He wrote positively about his time with Renamo, disclaiming many of the lies that were constantly pumped out of the Frelimo propaganda machine. He also spoke about the air raids, many of which were targeted at innocent villagers by Frelimo and Zimbabwean forces. It felt good to have our own reports verified. He did not forget Mozambique once he was back home, but came out again several months later to make the journalistic report that he had intended to make the first time he entered into Renamo territory. This time he used the correct channels. We took him across the border and he gathered valuable information, this time not as a prisoner, but as a free man. Clearly this writer was an adventurer. He told us amazing stories about months in the Sahara desert and other isolated and difficult places.

"You should use your sense of adventure for God," we told him. "You enjoy doing crazy things that few other people will do. Why don't you preach the gospel everywhere you go, then you'll be achieving something that will last through eternity? You're going through all these hardships for things that will come to nothing in the end."

"I suppose you're right," he said, but did not commit himself. We were sad to receive news that Nicholas died during the Gulf War. Newly married, he went to Iraq on a journalist mission with his wife. They disappeared. Later, reports confirmed that they were both dead.

We remembered all the words we had spoken to him about Christ. Nicholas had promised to seriously think it all over. Our hope is that in his time of trouble, he remembered the only One who can save us.❖

WINGS

LEARN TO FLY!

I am by nature a home person. There's nothing I love more than to be at home with the family. Before we accepted Christ, Rodney could hardly pry me away. I love homemaking, cooking, gardening, just being a wife and mom. On family vacation I would sit on the beach and wonder how many eggs the chickens were laying. How God changes us!

Now it seemed we were always planning another trip for one or both of us to go. This was hard, as I still loved being home and it was awful having to say goodbye to Rod or the children. We were no longer our own. God had placed a burden on our hearts for Mozambique and we could not shake it. In my sleep I would hear the crying of children, the weeping of women. Sometimes I woke up with the stench of death in my nostrils; I could not forget the massacres and suffering of the people. So again, I would pack a bag and go.

This time it would be to the Gorongosa mountain region. We had heard much about the people there, the frequent bomb attacks and their poverty and isolation. Our hearts yearned to take the gospel and the love of Christ to them. Renamo were not keen to let us in to this region. "It's too dangerous. You could easily be killed," we were told. We persisted, we insisted. "We are helping you with communications. You must help us with our work. You must allow us in to this region."

Finally they conceded and we made plans to go. The week before our departure, bombing raids started. There was no way we could go in. The population was scattered, abandoning huts and fields to hide in the jungle and live like animals in a lair. We were devastated. How many were dying without Christ? We should have gone sooner; now it was too late for many. We prayed, we wept. We had six blank weeks ahead of us; our agenda had been wiped out with the lives of many of the Gorongosa people.

I was praying beside our bed, "God what do we do now? How do you want us to use this time we had thought was for Gorongosa?" The answer came to me so plainly – a clear voice in my heart. "Rod must learn to fly." I jumped up and ran to the office to tell Rod what I had heard. "I've heard exactly the same thing," he said and picked up the phone to call the Chileka Flying Club. "How soon can I come for my first flying lesson?" "You can come first thing in the morning," was the reply.

We had no idea how we would pay for the lessons. Rod had only enough money for the first lesson, but as he stepped out in faith and obedience God provided. We had no idea what he would fly once he qualified. The thought of owning our own plane was far from our minds. We had faith, yes, but our faith had mostly been exercised in staying alive in war zones. We did not know how to believe God for an airplane while we were struggling to pay the rent, put food on the table and pay our children's school fees.

If God had revealed His plans for us, we would not have been able to take it in. **"Learn to fly."** He didn't say, **"Learn to fly and I'll use you to help bring peace to Mozambique; I will give you an airplane; you will make over eight hundred flights into war zones; you will save lives in time of famine and disease; you'll be shot at; men will seek your lives more than ever before; you will be arrested; they will speak lies about you and falsely accuse you; you will be** disgraced and hated; you will spread the gospel into the regions beyond as you have never thought possible" etc. etc. No, that would have been too much for us to comprehend. He simply said, "Learn to fly," so Rod did.

During the course of his training, Rod observed a Piper Aztec that had been sitting on the apron for three and a half years without moving. It looked rather shabby and forlorn. "There's a plane just waiting for someone to pick it up," he told me. While conversing with someone, he mentioned that he was interested in the Aztec. "It belongs to my uncle," the man replied. "He loves that thing and will never sell it. Lots of people have tried to buy it from him but though he doesn't fly anymore, he won't let it go."

Rod phoned the owner, telling him he didn't have the money yet, but would get it, and was ready to put down a small deposit. "Sure, come out and see me," was the reply. Everyone was amazed when Rod moved the plane to the workshops where the engineer and mechanic stripped the engine and airframe. It took a while to build it again and a while to pay the last installment but it was all done in time for Rod to make a historic flight into Mozambique that almost cost him his life, but changed the course of our work into a wider field than we ever dreamed.❖

"They that wait upon the Lord shall renew their strength; they shall mount up with wings as eagles; they shall run, and not be weary; and they shall walk, and not faint."

Isaiah 40:31 (KJV)

FLIGHT INTO THE HORNETS' NEST

WE PLEDGE FOR PEACE

Long years of war have tortured Mozambique and her people. Thousands have never known any life other than war. How long would the devastation continue? Was there any hope for peace? The question of peace in Mozambique was hanging heavily on international minds. Obviously this was not one of those bad mistakes that could forever be covered up, and certainly it was not going to just go away. The manipulating and meddling from external powers had only worsened the situation. The wounds and infections of this nation were so very deep; the hope for healing of this open sore could only come from within.

It was imperative that Renamo and Frelimo should meet and talk, that a platform should be built, upon which the process for peace could be laid. With strong hostilities and abject mistrust between the two parties, such negotiations would be difficult to bring about. The government of Kenya offered to host preliminary peace talks. Malawi agreed to secretly allow Renamo passage through her borders in order to catch a flight to Kenya. If both Renamo and Frelimo would send representatives to Kenya, they could meet in a neutral situation and express their views to one another and to the world.

The practicalities of such a venture held enormous complications for Renamo, whose leader, Afonso Dhlakama, was based at the Gorongosa Headquarters in the Sofala province together with the men that would need to accompany him on such a visit. With no vehicles and no roads to Malawi, it would take ten days or more to walk to the Malawi border. Not a very practical means of travel. The sensible thing would be to send a plane to airlift the delegation out of Mozambique. Simple. This task, however, was more than either Kenya or Malawi was prepared to take on. Though Frelimo, together with her warring partner, Zimbabwe, had sanctioned the movement of the Renamo delegation through Malawi to Kenya, the assistance that the latter two nations offered did not include transport through Mozambique. Neither was prepared to risk their pilot or aircraft over the killing fields of Mozambique. Renamo did not own an aircraft. To hire one was extremely difficult and expensive, as previous attempts had proved. In addition, Renamo held strong suspicions against Frelimo concerning a safe exit from the country. Previous air attacks to prevent Renamo from travelling to the outside world where they could make their voice heard, were fresh in the memory of Dhlakama and his men. Nor did they trust just anyone to fly them out; it would be too easy for someone to dispose of them in the wilds without having to answer for them.

Before any peace proceedings could begin, a trusted friend was needed to fly into Gorongosa and pick up the delegation. The flight would have to be carried out in utmost secrecy, and there would be risk involved. Who would do it? Rodney knew that his recently completed flying lessons and our miracle plane was for such a time as this. Joseph was ready to fly in to Gorongosa, collect and deliver the Renamo delegation to the Kenyan and Malawian authorities awaiting them in Malawi.

The carefully made plans would allow Rodney to fly into Mozambique on the 12th of July 1989 and land on the tiny airstrip hacked out of the forest. This date was to be known to very few. The Permanent Secretary to the Minister of Foreign Affairs, Kenya, would receive the delegation from Rodney in

Malawi and personally escort them to Kenya to ensure their safety. A momentous occasion! Never had African states offered any such hospitality to Renamo. We were thrilled to be instruments in the mission, believing it to be the beginning of a sure path to peace in Mozambique. We knew we were in God's perfect plan and working according to His timetable.

"Blessed are the peacemakers, for they shall be called the children of God." Matthew 5:9

Waking early on that beautifully clear morning I was intensely aware of the precious gift of life and the priceless value of Rod as husband and father to me and our children. **"Father, please bring him safely back to us today,"** I prayed. How blessed we are to have our faith and confidence in God. I did not underestimate the potential dangers ahead but the assurance that God was in control flooded my heart. We spent some time praying in our room, breaking bread together and sharing the cup of communion in the presence of God. Just as the children of Israel had applied the blood of the lamb on the doorposts of their houses to stay the hand of the angel of death, we applied the blood of Jesus spiritually over the plane and over Rod. On departing for the airport we checked with the Gorongosa base by radio to make sure everything was in order. "All clear," came the reply. "We are waiting for you; have a good journey."

We had loaded the plane the previous night with as many boxes of Bibles as we could fit in. There were thousands of soldiers who needed Bibles; not one opportunity for the Gospel was to be missed. Normally the boxes would be carried in on the heads of couriers; it was exciting to load the plane with "air mail from God!" As Rodney went through all the routine plane checks I placed his suit and tie over one of the seats. He grimaced at me and I grinned in return, pleased with the battle I had won. Rodney is comfortable only in shorts, T-shirt and flip flops. I had remonstrated with him about being properly dressed when flying the President of Renamo around. "Don't get it all creased!" I said. Also knowing the president's intense love for chocolate cake I had baked a masterpiece for him to enjoy. It was iced in the Renamo colors with three arrows and "PAZ" (peace) written across. Rod promised to defend the cake with his life and present it to the president intact and in perfect shape. The last one I had sent to the bush had been bounced upside down on a courier's head for a two-hour walk before it appeared on the table. "Don't worry, I'll take care of this one myself," Rodney assured me.

One more hug and kiss and Rod slammed the plane door shut. He started first one engine and then the other and taxied onto the runway. He had filed a flight plan with the control tower to a nearby town. He would fly over it without landing. The air traffic controllers in the tower **did not know this;** the mission was top secret and hopefully leakproof.

"STOP JOSEPH!"

I stayed just long enough to watch the plane lift off before driving home where the radio was crackling frantically with an urgent message: **"Joseph must not come. He must not fly into Mozambique!"** I replied that it was too late, he had already taken off. "Stop him quickly. You must call him back!" I heard the desperate note in the voice and rushed to the telephone to ask the control tower to recall the plane. The line was out of order. The phone was working when we left home half an hour ago; now it was totally dead. I ran across the road to our nearest neighbor but their phone was not working either. I knew that by the time I drove to a telephone, it would be too late to call Rod back. He would have already crossed the escarpment, where all radio contact ceased due to the range of mountains that blocked air communication. Obviously something was wrong, but I did not know what. On return to the radio, I could get no contact with the base at Gorongosa. The radio was silent.

THE TRAP

As the Piper Aztec rose into the air, Rodney's heart soared with a great joy. This flight was a fulfilment of God's promise to him and he was in awe of the magnitude of His ways and plans. From childhood he had harbored the desire to fly. To own an aircraft was the impossible dream, but now God had done this wonderful thing. This was Rod's first mission and flight in a twin-engine plane since obtaining his license. The airstrip he was to land on was more suited to stunt pilots than beginners. However, with God, we do not function in the natural only.

The craft dropped over the escarpment across the rift valley. There would be no further communication with Chileka airport. Half an hour later it swept across the border, dropping low just over treetop level. Rod headed for Gorongosa. There were few landmarks to go by and with no navigation equipment it was difficult to fly low and navigate with the eye at the same time. He had studied the aerial maps thoroughly and knew from his marks on the map where the Frelimo observation posts were. The Zambezi River came into sight and after another half-hour Rod knew he was close to the airstrip. Careful not to overfly into Frelimo territory, he circled and spotted the bush strip nestled in the forest. To his surprise, the strip was deserted. Where were the welcoming soldiers and where was the white flag to show the all-clear for landing? Obviously something was wrong! Previous discussions had clarified that if there was no white flag laid out on the strip the plane should return immediately without landing. It is imperative during a time of war for orders to be obeyed, yet Rodney felt in his heart that he should not turn around. Obeying the voice of the heart, he dipped the plane into a precision landing onto the short, narrow clearing. Nobody came from the trees to meet him and again he heard the voice of the Holy Spirit speak to his heart, this time to get off the strip quickly. There was no help around to push the plane under the cover of the trees; he would have to offload the heavy Bibles before he could move the plane. Suddenly, a Renamo commander burst through the thicket. Putting all his weight against the plane he began to push. Of course he could not move it, though he continued to try. Abruptly he stopped. Staring at Rod but saying nothing, he appeared to be listening for something.

"Helicoptoro!" he panted. Rod heard the thud thud of helicopter blades beating the air. Out of the bushes leaped fifteen more soldiers. They had been outrun by their commander but had now caught up. They scurried around like ants in a frenzy, attempting to move the plane while Rod tried to communicate to them to offload the cargo first. They did not speak English nor did Rod speak Portuguese but they understood. Hastily the boxes of Bibles were passed hand to hand from plane to bush cover, while the choppers orbited closer and closer. At any moment the plane might be seen. Not a moment too soon it was pushed off the strip and under the trees where the soldiers covered it with brushwood and branches for good camouflage. Rod carefully took out his suit, briefcase and the cake. The choppers were close now. If they flew directly in line with the strip the plane would be spotted and undoubtedly the gunships would open fire on the area. Miraculously, the choppers circled just 300 meters short.

The soldiers started digging holes to bury the Bibles and supplies Rod had brought in for a future extensive mission, when we would walk through the area for some weeks, preaching the Gospel to soldiers and civilians alike. Having hidden all as best they could, each man found a tree to hide behind as the choppers were coming closer now. As they came overhead, each man moved around his tree, pressed close to the trunk. There were eight helicopters altogether. Six French Allouettes and two deadly Russian Hind 47's, cannons mounted and ready for destruction. The helicopters circled purposefully. It was obvious they had seen something to zero in on. A dry riverbed clearly showed the tracks of motorcycles, which only Renamo soldiers could have been using. The tell-tale signs in the sand showed them they were close to the needle in the haystack.

Unbeknown to Rod, the choppers had been over just five minutes before he landed. They had crossed over and returned again, leaving just that short space of time during which he landed and hid the plane. Perfect timing. The hunt focused on that particular spot for an hour. When one chopper came straight towards Rod he was sure he had been seen. The thud of the blades changed to a whine as happens when a chopper comes directly towards one. "Lord, hide me from the enemy," he prayed. He was not seen and the choppers moved on to continue their scouring in another direction.

Using the respite, the commander ordered two soldiers to take Rod to a safer place away from the airstrip while he himself stayed with the rest of the group to protect the plane. This was a valiant decision on their part. If the choppers saw the plane the soldiers would attempt to keep the "vicious dogs at bay" with hopelessly inadequate weapons, but protect the plane they would.

The soldiers urgently led Rod on a three-kilometer run through the forest. One of them ran with the suit while Rod deftly balanced the precious chocolate cake on one hand and held the briefcase full of important documents in the other. He held the cake aloft, maneuvering it among the branches as if his life depended on the safety of that peace-decorated delicacy. As they ran, they heard the explosions of cannon fire some way off. The choppers had found a target; the runners had no way of knowing for sure what that target was. The plane? The people?

Branches and vines snatched at the three men as they ran, protruding roots catching at their feet as they pushed on. Panting and sweating, they tumbled into a clearing hacked out of the forest. The clearing was full of the belongings of Renamo soldiers who had hastily evacuated their camps at the start of the attack which had begun minutes after Rod had been given the all-clear message at the airport. Ducks and chickens were tied together by their legs to stop them from running away. Personal belongings of the soldiers were stacked in piles against the trees. A deck chair was brought out and opened with a flourish for Rod to sit on under a thickly-leafed tree. Hospitality was not to be neglected, no matter what the circumstances. Whilst untying the chickens for the purpose of selecting the choicest one to barbecue for Joseph, the distinguished guest, the chosen chicken cut loose and darted with flapping wings and squawks into the thicket. With AK-47 rifles slung over their shoulders the two soldiers launched into heavy pursuit. In a remarkably short space of time "Operation Chicken" was victoriously concluded as the fat offender was brought into line and duly dealt with. A cooking fire crackled to life over which the chicken was hung on a spit. Some maize meal was brought out of a bag, water out of a jar and a good heap of sadza was cooked in a pot balanced on rocks over the fire. Rodney was surprised to find himself suddenly very hungry, and when the meal was ready the three men shared it together with relish. It was the first meal of the day for all of them and with events being as they were, who could tell when next they would have a chance to eat? The cake was safely tucked away in a shady branch out of reach of marauding ants. It was being saved for someone else!

The hours passed by. Rod was greatly distressed at the sound of the 20-millimeter explosive-head cannons. The surrounding area shuddered with the repeated firing. He felt no immediate danger to himself but he knew well the village that was under attack. Three months back he had visited the place with two of our Christian friends. The president had called the people together for the visit. Four thousand had gathered. Poor, half-naked, they had listened with dignity to the address of their president, followed by the Gospel message brought by the missionary team. Rodney had promised that we would be back to share further about Jesus and that we would return also with medicines and clothes which were being sent by Christians from the USA. The people had whooped and rejoiced at the news and were looking forward to our forthcoming visit. And now this!

How many were being killed at this moment? How many innocent men, women and children were being massacred or wounded? Rod cried out to God, moved in his innermost being for the plight of the people. This was what so often happened. Frelimo, aided by Zimbabwean troops and Air Force, attacked villages, killing hundreds of civilians and then claimed that they had won tremendous victories over Renamo soldiers, eradicating military camps. We had seen all this happen before. After an hour of continuous attack, the choppers would move on to yet another area to carry out the same heinous crimes on other villages. The pattern was that troops were parachuted in after the choppers had done their work. These troops used bayonets and guns to hunt out and kill any survivors, frequently herding them into their huts and burning them alive. How helpless Rod felt – the sounds of war bringing horrific mental pictures to mind. He could do nothing physically to help, but he could pray.

HOMEFRONT BATTLE

Meanwhile, back at our home, Gostode, the Renamo radio operator we kept hidden for three years, tried again and again to make communication with the Gorongosa base. Other than extreme expressions of alarm at Gostode's news that we had been unable to prevent Rod from flying into Gorongosa, there was nothing further from the base. The radio crackled and became totally silent. They had gone off the air. I kept reassuring myself that we would soon receive some explanation for the irregular actions, but my hopes were in vain. The ashen face of Gostode told me he knew more than he was letting on. He was hiding something out of concern for me.

"What is it?" I demanded. "Is there fighting?"

"I not know the problem." he answered with a dazed expression, tears brimming in his eyes.

"Yes you do know, tell me!" Dropping his eyes, his voice barely audible, he said flatly, "It is war."

My heart sank into my feet. A cold chill spread through my body. "Oh Jesus, please protect Rodney."

Gostode looked like death. He was a 19-year-old Renamo soldier sent to us straight out of the bush, to take on the communication system which we kept hidden on our premises. He had accepted Jesus as Saviour soon after arrival and Rodney had baptized him in Lake Malawi during a family camping weekend. Unaccustomed to life out of the bush, every day was full of new experiences and he learned quickly. What fun we had introducing him to the strange ways of a city. Blantyre can hardly be called a city but for someone who has been for so many years in some of the most primitive parts of Africa, it is a metropolis. His exclamations of delight and surprise were very amusing. "Aaaaiii!" he would exclaim at the town lights. He was accustomed only to the light of the moon and of cooking fires. When Rod took him to a store, he walked in amazement around the plaster figure modeling clothes. "Wantu, wantu?" meaning "A person, a person?" Now he was saying "Aaaiii" for a different reason. Gostode was devoted to Rod. There was nothing he would not do for him. "You are now my family," he would say. "I think all my own family are dead because of war. You are now my father." His smile would be fixed on Rod. Now he sat lamely before the radio, despair written all over him. "You must trust Jesus," I said. "Pray. You cannot just sit there like that. You must fight the battle in the spirit. Fight for your father."

In our room where we had broken bread and prayed together a few hours earlier, I fell to my knees and poured out my heart before the Lord. I held on to the promise of deliverance though I felt sick inside. I had no idea what was happening to my husband. Had he been shot out of the sky? Was he lying wounded somewhere far away in the bush where there would be nobody to help him? Or had the worst happened? No! Unthinkable! I opened my Bible to Psalm 34. "*The eyes of the Lord are on the righteous, and His ears are open to their cry. The righteous cry out, and the Lord hears, and delivers them out of all their troubles. Many are the afflictions of the righteous, but the Lord delivers him out of them all. He guards all his bones; not one of them is broken."(Psalm 34:15,17,19,20)* Who can explain the voice of God, the way He speaks through His Word and makes it real, alive and valid to the situation of the hour? I **knew** God had spoken to me and this was His Word to me. I believed Rod was safe. He was not dead, he was not wounded and not even one of his bones was broken. Through the rest of the day I clung to that Word, though I confess there were times when doubt crept in and I despaired, but that Word saw me through. I ran to the radio room to share the promise with Gostode. He was still in the same limp position, defeat written all over him from head to toe.

"It's all right. God is taking care of him; we must keep praying and believing," I exhorted him.

" 'Stoo late, 'stoo late!" he wailed. "Ees dead, ees dead!"

"No, he is not; it is not too late." I reached for his Portuguese Bible, found and marked the scriptures for him. I prayed and then made him pray. "Now you read these scriptures over and over again until you believe them," I ordered. I could see this little soldier needed a general around and God's general I would be.

Eighteen months back Gostode had not been able to speak one word of English. Through Rod and Dustin's conversations, my teaching, and Deborah's tireless efforts to read with him and teach him after she came home from school, he could now converse, read and write without difficulty. "Tank you." he said. We had battled to teach him to say the "th" in thank you and he had finally mastered it but now in the time of distress he lost it again. I did not correct him this time. I left him at the radio reading his Bible. I had work to do.

DIPLOMATS, STATESMEN AND RULERS

The honorable Mr. Bethuel Kiplagat, Permanent Secretary to the Minister of Foreign Affairs, Kenya, sat in a Blantyre hotel room waiting to receive a call from me that everything was in order and moving according to schedule. This tall, stately gentleman had worked hard against a multitude of odds to bring negotiations to this point. He had entered Renamo areas several times to talk with various generals and commanders of the movement. His goal had been to convince them of the sincerity of President Daniel Arap Moi of Kenya to assist in maneuvers for peace negotiations. He had braved the Shire River and swamps by night in a dugout canoe through herds of hippos. He had sloshed for miles through the thick black mud while being eaten alive by clouds of blood-thirsty mosquitoes. After gaining the confidence of Renamo he had flown several times from Kenya in anticipation of meeting President Afonso Dhlakama in Malawi and escorting him back to Kenya. Each time, the trip was foiled due to some security leak or other problem and he had to return without success. Mr. Dhlakama was considered too suspicious and touchy, but events to follow would prove that his suspicions were not unfounded. This time, Mr. Kiplagat was certain all plans would flow according to pattern and he would not return empty-handed. Frelimo had given their word that there would be no interference with the exit of Dhlakama and his delegation. Frelimo had actually requested for the delegation to come out of Gorongosa and meet them in Kenya. Mr. Kiplagat smiled to himself. No, he did not expect to be disappointed this time. He had every confidence in Joseph though he did find him to be a bit of a puzzle. Why would he and his wife care so much about the people of Mozambique that they were prepared to risk their lives time and again to preach the Gospel to them? And now here was Joseph, a new, inexperienced pilot, willing to fulfill the mission in his own plane for no pay at all! Oh well, missionaries were known to do strange things. The important thing was that he could trust Joseph and that was all that mattered right now.

I waited for the receptionist to put me through to Mr. Kiplagat's room. He answered at the first sound of the ring. "Well, good morning my dear. Is everything going well?" Having studied abroad for many years, his accent was more English than African. "No, sir." My voice stuck in my throat though I tried hard to sound sane and in my right mind. "Joseph has flown into a battle. An air attack is being launched on Gorongosa." "Ooooh, my Loord! What can we do?" "Pray," I said, then, "and it would be good if you could use your influence and position in this operation to protest against the attack."

"But this cannot be true, my dear. You must be mistaken. They wouldn't do such a thing. Why, they have given their word!" Mr. Kiplagat was incredulous.

"I am not mistaken, sir. I am convinced this was deliberately planned. They are trying to prevent Mr. Dhlakama from
coming out to the free world." I spoke what I knew was true.
Poor Mr. Kiplagat was shattered. He immediately offered to
come around to the house and stay with me. I assured him it
was not necessary and that I would be all right, but soon a vehicle pulled up at the gate; he came anyway. He still looked a bit
doubtful, but the moment he saw Gostode's mournful expression, he knew the situation was indeed very serious. He paced
up and down the living room carpet, hands held behind his
back saying, "Oh, my Lord." Then to me, "Oh, my dear." This
carried on for some time, then suddenly he made a decision for
action. With fervor he set about making a series of phone calls,
the first straight to President Chissano of Mozambique.
Though he tried repeatedly, the appalling telephone systems in
Mozambique could not connect him to Maputo. Finally, he got
hold of one of Chissano's representatives who assured him
there was no such attack taking place; how could there be
when they were wanting to speak to Dhlakama direct? Mr.
Kiplagat spoke at length and finally told the man in no uncertain terms that he would not be deceived and that the attack
had better be called off immediately. "I know what is going on,"
he said. "My pilot is in there and he is in great danger. This is a
violation of your promise to allow safe passage."

At last the man on the other end promised to do what he
could. He got through to the chief of the Frelimo military in
Maputo, who denied any such attack. The attack carried on for
three weeks of successive raids on Gorongosa and the surrounding area. Hundreds of innocent civilians were killed and
wounded as their villages agonized under the cruel air attacks,
followed up by ground troop assault. Frelimo claimed massive
success in eradicating Renamo camps. The truth was that very
few Renamo soldiers were killed. Frelimo news announced that
though President Chissano of Mozambique had shown himself
willing to speak with the rebel leader, Dhlakama and his dele-

gation had once more failed to show up for talks. Lies, lies!

TOP BRASS PRAYER

In the office of the Malawi Commissioner of Police in Lilongwe, Mr William Lunguzi, alias Marcos, was feeling very satisfied about the immediate visit of the President of Renamo. Marcos had his hands overfull with the many incidents that adversely affected Malawi through the war being waged in Mozambique. Malawi found herself in a tight and uncomfortable position. Wedged like a finger into the heart of Mozambique, she could not remain untouched by the war that was sending over a million refugees fleeing across her borders for food and safety. Her economy was badly affected because of the successful attempts of Renamo to bring the Frelimo government to its knees through attacks on road and rail transport routes. Marcos was determined to speak to Mr. Dhlakama about the reopening of the Nacala rail route that connected Malawi to the Mozambique ocean port of Nacala. The route had ceased to function due to the war and if it could become operative again, Malawi, a land-locked country, would once more have vital and valuable access to the ocean. Imports and exports could be handled speedily and efficiently, saving Malawi a great deal of currency. Ironically, in spite of Chissano's forceful claims that the government was in control of Mozambique, Dhlakama was the one to speak to concerning this. Renamo, administering 85% of Mozambique through enjoying the popular support of the people, were the ones to determine whether or not the Nacala rail route should be opened. Chissano's claims that Renamo was nothing but a "bunch of bandits" with no direction or leadership was fast losing credibility.

Yes, it was a stroke of luck that had brought Joseph across his path. For some time he had wanted to make contact with Renamo but to do so was a very tricky business and would not have the approval of the Mozambique government. The latter had on numerous occasions breathed threats down Malawi's narrow neck, and their planned invasion of Malawi that was foiled by the death of Samora Machel in October,

1986 - the then President of Mozambique, was fresh in the minds of Malawians. Now he would get to meet Dhlakama and it would be done the "right way." He could receive the Renamo delegation without fear of intimidation by the Frelimo government. Marcos had set plans for a rousing welcome. A contingency of top security men would be waiting at the airport, ready to whisk the delegation away the moment Joseph landed his plane. The receiving vehicle would drive right up to the plane so Dhlakama would not have to walk anywhere. Joseph was also invited to the luncheon; Dhlakama would not have him leave his side at this stage anyway. When Joseph had mentioned that Dhlakama was very partial to fish, Marcos had immediately called the caterers and told them to ensure there would be plenty of the famous Malawi Chambo (a delicious fresh water fish native to Malawi) on the menu. "But sir, there is a shortage of Chambo right now. There is none to be found in the shops or in the market." "Then get in the jeep and drive to the lake and get some." he had ordered in response to the caterer's despair. The lake was a three-hour drive away but orders were orders. This was an important occasion and Mr. Dhlakama must be shown that Malawi was taking him seriously.

Marcos was a busy man. We had on occasion sat with him in his office and watched while he held conversations with three parties at once via three telephone lines. He would hold a telephone in each hand and have another on hold on the desk while he chatted and gave instructions, at the same time not losing communication with us. With this picture in mind, I rang Police Headquarters in Lilongwe wondering how the news would affect the busy office. Marcos would have to be informed of the change of program. I had never called him at this office before; this was Rod's job and I was not sure what procedure to take. "May I speak to Mr. Lunguzi please?" " 'Old on please." Very few people in security knew about the meetings to take place. It was all being kept very hush-hush. I had to be careful not to give anything away. Mr. Lunguzi came on the line and I told him the news as briefly and calmly as I could. (Later he would tell Rod, "As soon as I had finished speaking to your wife, I stood up at my desk and said a prayer for you." We could well imagine all the telephones being put on hold while this man in his much decorated uniform stood up to pray a solemn prayer in his Roman Catholic way for Joseph. We were touched.) Shocked at the news, he begged me to keep him informed. The Chambo and special luncheon was not to be. Not this time around, anyway. The receiving contingencies were recalled from the airport. A hope had died.

I brewed tea for myself and Mr. Kiplagat, who was fast wearing out the carpet with his endless pacing back and forth. I brought out some home-baked cookies but neither of us could eat anything. I kept assuring him that all would be well. I shared with him portions of Psalm 91. *"For He shall give His angels charge over thee, to keep thee in all thy ways. Surely He shall deliver thee and under His wings shalt thou trust."* Mr. Kiplagat said, "Yes, yes," and looked at me with deep sympathy. However, in trying to convince him, my own faith was greatly built up and I felt much encouraged. It was good to have Mr. Kiplagat for company and I thought I was coping very well with the situation. Fact is, I looked a wreck and tears were never far away. I kept disappearing into the bedroom to pray and at one time in particular entered into a fierce spiritual battle during which I saw in my mind the plane explode in the sky, then blood obliterated the picture. I prayed and fought, wept, pleaded, believed and doubted and believed again. At last I knew I had done all I could and there was nothing left but to leave Rodney in the hands of God. I had exhausted every prayer I could utter. It was time simply to trust. It was not easy. To live without Rod was an unthinkable nightmare. My peace came at last, not in the sure knowledge that I had won that spiritual battle through intercession, but in the sure knowledge that God is God. He knows the path we take and if we can trust Him in life, we can surely trust Him in death. Our life is in His hands and that must be enough.

MEANWHILE, BACK IN THE JUNGLE

After several attempts to get to Kenya via Malawi had been thwarted, Afonso Dhlakama, President of Renamo, was not too surprised at this latest attempt by Frelimo to stop progress. He was, however, very disappointed. It was a good thing that Joseph had been stopped from coming; he was very glad of that. His radio operators had sent a message of warning at the sound of the first choppers; at least Joseph would be safe. His great concern was not only for his soldiers; they melted into the forest and found places of refuge quite easily. His concern was for his people, the local population who loved him and supported him. Their huts, fields and villages were easily detected from the sky, being outside the forest. They would be the ones to suffer most. There would be no going to Kenya now; this was going to be a busy time. He was needed right here to fulfill his role of Supreme Commander of the Armed Forces. Troops must be deployed for a counter-attack against the ground forces that would be parachuted in.

The roar of a light aircraft flying low overhead brought Dhlakama to his feet. "Oh, no!" It was Joseph's plane. He must not have received the message in time. His heart tumbled to his feet. "My friend Joseph," he groaned. They watched the plane disappear in the direction of the airstrip, **in the direction also of the enemy helicopters.**

Joseph was well-known among the Renamo forces. His name had become something of a byword and he was loved and respected. He had become a close personal friend of President Dhlakama and they had met together many times in the bush to work on strategies for evangelism. Dhlakama was fully supportive of our Gospel work and his interest and assistance made many an impossible mission possible. Joseph's faith was smiled at by some of the Renamo officials but several of them received the message and gave their lives to Christ. At meals the president would always turn to Joseph and ask him to pray before the meal commenced. Many a Foreign Diplomat or journalist found themselves having to wait for the blessing before they could partake of the food. It was a strange thing for them to have to take part in a Christian principle out here in the bush, when at home in the Western world they never gave Christianity a thought.

Sometimes after dinner the president would ask Joseph to bring out his Bible and share a Word with him and his men. A favorite portion was the deliverance of king Jehoshaphat and his army. The odds against Jehoshaphat were overwhelming – three armies against one, but God delivered them. They worshipped the Lord, humbled themselves, putting their trust in Him rather than in their own strength. They acknowledged that without God's help they could not win the battle, and because they humbled themselves, God delivered them.

It is not an easy thing for soldiers to humble themselves. These Renamo soldiers were fierce fighters, brave and skilled in battle. Certainly they had enough success to their name to think themselves very able. The air attacks were difficult to combat, however. Especially when the villages where nobody had any weapons were attacked. Certainly, verse 12 was apt for the moment. *"O God, we have no power to face this vast army that is attacking us. We do not know what to do, but our eyes are on You."* II *Chronicles 20:12 (NIV)*

Joseph was flying around like a small bird among vultures. Everyone knows the work of vultures; they peck, and strip, attack and tear, until only a shell remains of the victim. Would the God of Joseph deliver him today in the manner of which Joseph had so often spoken? *"Do not be afraid nor dismayed because of this great multitude; for the battle is not yours, but God's. You will not need to fight in this battle; position yourselves, stand still and see the salvation of the Lord, who is with you."* II *Chron. 20:15,17*

Yes, Joseph was a special man. He had not allowed even the President of Renamo to escape his pointed questioning concerning his stand before God. A Roman Catholic, Dhlakama was not ignorant of religion. It was not religion, however, in which Joseph was interested. He spoke of a life transformed by the power of the Spirit on accepting Jesus as personal Saviour. Dhlakama had to admit that though he knew about Christ, he did not know Christ; he had not received Jesus into his heart and life. It took two years before he could finally tell Joseph with a broad smile, "I have something to tell you. I have received Jesus as my personal Saviour. I know He is in my heart." Rod had been overjoyed at the news. A number of generals and top military and political men also received Christ, along with many soldiers. They knew Joseph loved them and carried their cause upon his heart, but they also knew that his prime cause was Christ. If Joseph died today, it would be for both causes.

Rodney smiled as he looked at his two protectors. The sounds of war quiet now, they had fallen asleep in the lower branches of a tree. Totally relaxed, they were taking rest while they could. Chances of sleep would be little enough in the days ahead. Suddenly a group of runners burst through the thicket. The president had sent them with a message for Joseph. Having run a long distance they were out of breath. Joseph was to fly out at the first opportunity for his own safety. "Oh, no," replied Joseph. "I have come to collect the president and his delegation and I am not leaving without them." In dismay the runners stared at each other. What was to be done with this stubborn White man? They were secretly impressed, however, that he did not jump at the opportunity to get to safety leaving the others in danger. They could not move him.

Surrounded by Paratroopers

Some time later two more runners appeared. Five had set out, only two came the whole way; the others lay in ambush in case they were pursued by enemy troops who had already been dropped in by air. "This whole area including the airstrip has been surrounded by ground troops who are moving in closer. Soon they will be here. They are also calling in the MiG fighter planes. You must leave now!" The runners spoke urgently, and Rod knew it was indeed time to go. Renamo radio operators had intercepted the Frelimo communications, thus they knew the ploy being used against them. They started the three-kilometer run back to the plane. The choppers were still around but not too close. There should be time to get the plane onto the runway, and take off before they returned. Each minute was vital. On reaching the plane they stripped off the brush camouflage and tried pushing the plane onto the runway but it kept sinking into the sand. Time ticked by, movement was difficult but at last the plane was positioned on the runway ready for takeoff. What was that noise? The dreaded thud-thud of the chopper blades in the distance! They were return-ing! Panting and straining, the men got the plane off the run-way and hidden under the brush again. As in the morning, the choppers circled just short of the airstrip, moving off after a while. The same procedure for takeoff was again carried out but unbelievably, the choppers returned again. Sweating and struggling, Rod and the soldiers managed to get the plane off the strip again just in time. This was too much! After the chop-pers disappeared once more, the attempt was again made. This time surely the choppers would move on and not return to the same spot. The plane was once more heaved through the sand and vulnerably sitting exposed on the cleared space. Rodney stepped up and opened the door to get in, waving good-bye to his friends; he was arrested by a cry of alarm.

"Helicoptoro, helicoptoro!"

"It can't be true," Rod thought out loud, but it was. For the third time the soldiers pushed the plane under cover yet again, nerve-racking and hard work, to say the least. This was serious. Time was moving by and soon it would be too late to get home before dark. When the choppers moved off once more, Rod made a snap decision. He would start up the plane still half in the bushes, drive onto the strip and take off as fast as possible. Unorthodox as this may be, it was now or never. Starting up the propellers still half under the trees, Rod taxied up the sandy bank and with a knot in his stomach and a prayer in his heart, revved the engines and took off. The plane seemed incredibly slow; he really thought two engines could push harder than this but it felt he was hardly moving at all. At any moment the choppers could reappear. They would either shoot him down or escort him to some place of landing of their choice – either Beira or Tete – neither a desirable place to visit as he was on the "wanted" list in both Mozambique and Zimbabwe because of his activities with Renamo. Anxiety caused Rod to make a wrong decision. In his eagerness to increase speed, he lifted the plane high above the trees. Flying would be much easier and faster this way and was he in a hurry! As soon as he gained height, he knew he had moved in error. He could now be clearly seen for miles around. The choppers had far greater speed than the Aztec and they could catch up with him in no time at all. There was only one thing to do: correct the mistake in hope he had not been detected. The new pilot put the plane into a daring nosedive, straight down, levelling just above the top of the trees. Disappearing from view, it looked as if he had crashed. Good move!

It was July, midwinter, when the sun sets early and rapidly in Africa. Rod realized there was another equally urgent need for speed now. Soon it would be too dark to see where he was going and he was not instrument-rated on the aircraft, all navigation having to be done by sight. Already long shadows darkened the landscape. To his intense relief no shadows from choppers flying overhead or alongside him cast their threatening image on him. Though the light was failing fast, God did not fail him. The Malawi border was not far; he lifted up and over into friendly territory with release and thankfulness in his heart. The sun was already down, its last rays briefly illuminating the sky. There was no possibility of getting back to Blantyre, but he could make it to an unmanned airstrip en route. The deepening red and gold rays held back the veil of night just long enough for Rod to dimly make out the Sucoma airstrip and to touch down. Of course they did not know he had just flown in from Mozambique. By the time he stopped, locked up the plane and started walking down the road to the nearby village of Nchalo, it was already dark.

HIS FAITHFULNESS REACHES TO THE SKIES

Meanwhile, back at the house, when we saw night fall around us, Mr. Kiplagat got up to go. "My dear, I hate to leave you like this. Will you be all right?" "Don't worry, I'll be fine." It was obvious that hope of news had gone with daylight. Gostode had sat in vain in front of the radio all day; there would be no communication during the night and of course Rod could not fly back in the dark. I saw a sad and worried Mr. Kiplagat off at the gate and made my way to the bedroom where I planned to spend the night on my knees. As I knelt down, I was glad for the hundredth time that the children were away visiting friends. They would have been frantic and badly affected by the events of the day. How often hope fades with the light. Darkness emphasizes doubt and gloom. By now I had forgotten all my faith promises and was convinced I was a widow and my children fatherless. And they do so love their dad! I was no longer brave and strong and proceeded to cry an enormous wet patch onto the carpet.

The phone rang shrilly, cutting through my tormented mind. I did not want to answer it. It could not be news of Rod anyway; there were no phones in the bush. I did not want to speak to anyone and not being able to hide the crying in my voice it would be awkward trying to explain the reason for the state I was in. It kept ringing, however, and at last I reluctantly lifted the receiver.

"Hello, darling." It was Rodney's voice! "Where are you? Are you all right?" I howled my relief. "I'm fine, no problem. I'm at Nchalo." "I'm coming to get you now," I said, crying even louder at the sound of his beloved voice. "You'd better not. You don't sound like you're in any fit state to drive," he answered. I immediately stopped crying, assuring him there was nothing the matter with me and said I was on my way. I ran to Gostode's rooms and shouted, "It's O.K. Everything is O.K. God has heard our prayers. Joseph is all right!" He gaped at me and then his face lit up in wonder. "Ees O.K. ees O.K.?" "Yes, try and get on the radio and tell our friends he has arrived safely." With a huge grin stretching from ear to ear and tears of joy in his eyes Gostode pressed the radio button to pass on the good news. Shouts crackling from the other side told us they had understood the coded message. I made a hurried call to Mr. Kiplagat who listened in stunned amazement as I excitedly told him Rod was safe. He promised to let Marcos know so I could be on my way immediately. A more excited Foreign Affairs diplomat I have never heard. Trying not to drive too fast down the escarpment in eagerness to get to Rod, and with Gostode chattering non-stop all the way I made the one-hour journey to where Rod was waiting. As we approached the small town our eyes eagerly scanned the side of the road where he would be standing. There he was! Patiently standing with his briefcase in one hand and his suit wadded up in the other, leaves and twigs caught in his hair, he literally looked like he had been dragged through a bush backwards. In a sense, he had. To me, he had never looked more wonderful! (It didn't even occur to me to ask about the chocolate cake.)

One week later the phone started ringing at 6:00 a.m. and continued ringing for most of the day. Friends and associates were anxiously inquiring about a disturbing news release from Maputo. A great victory for Frelimo against Renamo in the Gorongosa headquarters area was announced. Large military camps had allegedly been wiped out and hundreds of Renamo soldiers killed. To crown the so-called success, the plane of Renamo's president, flown by his personal aide had been shot down. This was victory indeed for Frelimo if it had been true and they blew their trumpet very loud.

Of course it was false, typical of the propaganda used to cause Mozambicans to believe Renamo had been defeated. Some smaller camps of Renamo had been reached, yes, but the Renamo soldiers had evacuated them! There was no great loss to Renamo as an army, but the loss of hundreds of civilians and the destruction of their villages was real. It was not Renamo soldiers but innocent civilians who had been slaughtered. As for the plane, we can only surmise that Rod had been seen when he nosedived it and they thought he had crashed, and they took opportunity to claim the victory: an incredible achievement of downing the plane of the President of Renamo. They had no idea that the President of Renamo did not even own a plane; and even less idea that the plane had been flown by a private pilot using his own aircraft, with the simple aim of promoting peace while they were clearly still at war.

What a joy to have Rodney safely at home. "Sorry about the cake." he apologized. "What cake? Who cares about a cake!" It would not have gone to waste and was probably being enjoyed by two soldiers sitting in a tree.

Mr. Kiplagat returned emptyhanded to Kenya with much to tell President Daniel Arap Moi about the fraudulent behavior of the Frelimo Government and forces. Before taking off he spent some time with Rod trying to work out a new strategy for getting the President of Renamo and his delegation to Kenya. It would not be easy and Dhlakama might be very reluctant now, but they would not give up trying. We were not to know that in spite of many efforts and after finally getting Dhlakama out of Mozambique, it would be three years before the actual signing of the Rome Peace Accord and another two years before the first democratic elections in Mozambique were to be held. A lifetime of experiences, good, wonderful, bad and terrible, lay between us and that time.

Taken from the book "Mozambique, Resistance and Freedom" by David Hoile.

After a decade of denying both the existence and legitimacy of the democratic opposition movement in Mozambique, the Mozambique government eventually started to explore avenues towards a negotiated settlement. The Mozambican churches, both Protestant and Catholic had been advocating dialogue between Frelimo and Renamo for some years. It must be noted that these calls for dialogue were harshly dismissed by the government at the time, Catholic bishops being labeled "apostles of treason." Frelimo sincerity in the negotiation process was seen as somewhat treacherous by an overt attempt to kill Renamo leader Dhlakama and Renamo's peace team as they were waiting to leave Mozambique for the Nairobi peace meetings. (This was the attack Rodney was caught in when flying in to collect the peace team.)❖

Adullam's Cave

The cave of Adullam was a place in the wilderness where David hid with his men when King Saul was pursuing them. In I Samuel 22:2, we read how those who were in distress or trouble gathered themselves around David. Our home was becoming more of a hideout and rendezvous point with each passing week. We named the office in our home, "The Cave of Adullam."

Dhlakama had to be brought out of Mozambique another way. Flying in to Mozambique was an absolute no for some time. Dhlakama moved from his Gorongosa base to a hideout very near the Malawi border. If anyone wanted to talk with him, they would have to go to him. Several times a week Rod made the long night-time journey down the escarpment to the Shire valley then up the mountain to Chididi. From here it was a short walk across the border, then about an hour's walk into Mozambique to the camp. When there was no moonlight, this was not an easy walk.

Mozambique was becoming an increasingly hot news issue. We no longer had to try and persuade journalists or political representatives to visit Renamo zones, they were asking to come. They came from the USA, UK, Italy, Portugal, Germany, Kenya and South Africa. We were busy and operations were still difficult. Certain sectors of the army and police made it their business to put a stop to the activity they were hearing rumors about. Some officials were friendly with Frelimo and committed themselves to eradicate any Renamo influence in Malawi. This made matters not only difficult, but dangerous.

The newly-located base camp had only maize meal to offer for food. We were planning to bring quite a large group and Dhlakama, who liked to give his visitors a decent meal, sent a message, "Please, my friend. You know we have no good food to offer these visitors. You must bring us some chickens so we can offer good hospitality." Off to the market we went to buy 24 squawking chickens. These were put on the back of the trailer, and started out into the night with Rod, British reporters from The Times, The Independent and The Guardian as well as a few others.

The crew returned at dawn, mission unaccomplished. When they had reached the rendezvous point, there was no guide to meet them. They waited a while, then had to turn back. We radioed the base for an explanation. "Sorry, my friend," came the reply. "We had some problems – please try again tonight." The group went to their hotel to catch up on the sleep they had missed during the night, and Rod spent the day doing his work with only a couple of hours of sleep in the after-noon. That night, off went the group with the chickens again. I couldn't believe it when they returned again at dawn. "Our man was there, but you did not see him. Please, my friend, you must try again tonight," came the message. Needless to say, the journalists were not very pleased, but agreed to try again. They started off for the third time, everyone getting a bit weary and the chickens a lot quieter than on the first attempt.

On arrival at the border, Rod felt uneasy and turned the land cruiser around ready for a quick takeoff. Suddenly, about twenty men came running onto the road armed with clubs and knives, shouting at the top of their voices. They took hold of the vehicle, brandished their weapons at the faces at the windows and tried to pull the doors open. The shocked group began rolling up windows and locking doors. Rod put his foot on the accelerator and the men jumped out of the road. It was a frightening experience for the visitors.

When I heard them all arrive back at dawn again, I groaned. A pleading message came from Dhlakama. "My friend Joseph. You must convince the journalists to come one more time. I have some important statements to make to the media. Last night, our guide was caught and beaten by some of the Malawians who have been told to catch people crossing the border. That is why he was not there to meet you. We now have another meeting place." We were given new instructions and a new place of rendezvous.

"Not again. Not with those wild men about. We didn't know savages like that still existed in Africa!" The journalists had had enough.

"You might as well finish your mission," Rod said. "If you go back now, you'll just be sent back another time."

"We'll try one more time... just leave those wretched chickens behind."

The fourth attempt was smooth as butter. The guide was there to meet them. It was Gulai. He showed Rod the marks where he had been beaten. "No problem!" he said with a grin. The big man had managed to break free of the attackers before too much damage was done. Rod crossed over with the group and left them all in the safety of the camp where they were received with an enthusiastic welcome. At dawn, I was relieved to see only Rod get out of the vehicle. Mission accomplished.

After several days Rod collected the group again, this time without incident. On reading the newspaper reports later on, **we were disappointed to read more about the difficulties and personal adventures of the journalists and the marauding Malawians with clubs and knives, than of the important issues that needed to be publicized!**

AMBUSH

Shortly after those escapades, we were ambushed four times on the same road. Rod and our friend, Tim Salmon, were in Mozambique with a group for a few days and I had been given the job of picking them up. Being an early-to-bed, early-to-rise person by nature, missing a night of sleep was a major thing for me. I had to time the trip so I would arrive there at midnight. Rod and Tim would be waiting, so I would not be parked there all alone. The four-hour drive was slow; I was a bit nervous about negotiating the narrow little bridge over the eight-foot drop. It was not even a proper bridge; just two poles with a few planks loosely nailed on. "Just aim straight at it, put your foot down and go," Rod had said. It was a short bridge so this wasn't really difficult. With the headlights picking up the planks, I was over in a flash. Realizing I was early, I parked beside a thicket and locked the doors. My ears picked up the sound of running feet and loud voices. Rod and Tim would not arrive with such a noise; what was this? Faces appeared at the windows, hands grasped at the doors, trying to wrench them open, the car began to rock. "Get away from there!" I heard Rod's voice in the African language. Surprised, the men turned around long enough for Rod to jump in as I unlocked the door for him. Rod had felt uneasy about me and had run ahead of the group by himself to make sure I was OK. How glad I was to see him. We drove a short distance and picked up Tim and the others and started for home as quickly as we could.

Unbeknown to me, as I had been driving up the mountain trail, ambushes were being set behind me for our return journey. The first one was just around the corner: big rocks across the road. Praise God for a good 4X4 vehicle. Rod drove right over them. The next was logs across the road. The Toyota climbed over that too. Next a big, leafy tree with branches sticking up; somehow we sailed through that one; I was praying out loud in tongues all the way. Then right after the tree was the bridge. The planks had been removed off one half of it. How could we possibly cross over that? "Hold on tight!" said Rod, "we're going over." I would have liked to protest, but there was no time. Rod aimed the right wheel at the pole with no planks, the left wheel at the pole with planks. It was a tightrope trick, but by the grace of God we made it. Big nails had also been laid in the road to puncture our tires, but one of the pastors from a nearby church where we preached, had seen this being done and had gone quickly to pick them up when the ambushers moved on to their next task. We lost count of how many night trips we made to the border in that land cruiser.

Messages and visits from Kenya and others continued to try and persuade Dhlakama to visit Kenya for talks. The answer was "No," but it was agreed to send out two top Renamo representatives, Vincent Ululu and Raul Domingos. They would travel to Kenya to meet with representatives of parties wishing to assist in steering Mozambique towards peace. Today, Raul Domingos and Vincent Ululu are both Members of Parliament. At the time they were hiding in our home this was hard to imagine. Rod brought them in during the night and we housed them in our guest room. Vincent spoke English; Raul, not a word. He was determined to learn, however, and amazed us at his rapid mastering of the English language. They stayed with us on transit many times. They played board games with the children and we had a lot of fun. Raul was one of the keenest learners we had ever met. He was always asking about the English culture and how to do things correctly. For someone who had been living in the bush so long and serving as a top general, this could be a daunting task, but he was all eagerness and absorbed as much as he could as quickly as possible. Rod had sat with them around a fire in the bush many a time while they joked how one day they would eat with Joseph and his family around his table. They also joked that some day we would all eat together in Maputo, the capital city. This dream was wilder than the first, but they both came to pass.

We gave up counting how many Mozambicans of all rank and description stayed in our home. Some messengers were as uncivil as you could get them, never having sat at a table to eat or slept in a bed before. We would find the beds unslept in, but the cover all crumpled as they would roll themselves like a sausage into the cover and sleep on the floor, like they did back home. The bed was too high - they might fall off and hurt themselves! I never knew who or how many Rod would bring home in the night or at dawn. When friends popped in unexpectedly, there was always a scurry to get people out of the way. How would we explain the presence of these African/Portuguese-speaking people in a country where Portuguese is not spoken? Some were from the regions that we had not yet been able to penetrate with the Gospel. It was fascinating talking with them and asking questions about the life and customs of their people. "Jesus?" "No, they did not know about Jesus." Using Gostode as a translator and evangelist, we shared the Gospel with all who came through our doors. At night we put the *JESUS* video on for them to watch.

As the momentum of the talks and journeys out of Malawi increased, some of the female Renamo members started traveling too. They were the secretaries for Raul, Vincent and others. Tammy would wake up in the morning to find a girl or two sleeping in the room with her. She was sweet about it and generously shared her clothes and shoes with these girls who had to board the plane from an international airport with so very little to wear. It was an interesting few years, which we would not have chosen to miss.

KENYA AT LAST!

Mr. Kiplagat returned with new proposals from the Kenyan government. President Arap Moi urged Dhlakama not to delay in coming to Kenya himself. Rod and I both accompanied him on the visit to Dhlakama. By now Lunguzi had managed to call off some of the dogs and we were able to cross the border without difficulty. People were friendly and waved as we passed by. It felt good. This was an exciting time; history was in the making and we were part of it, preaching Jesus at every opportunity. Mr. Kiplagat was a wonderful statesman and we learned much from him during personal discussions as well as official talks with Dhlakama. He was grateful for our assistance and for our commitment to the peace process. After several visits, Dhlakama finally agreed to make the journey to

Blantyre, and to fly on to Nairobi. We were all delighted.

Malawi security agreed to help transport Mr. Dhlakama, his wife and three children as well as a full delegation to Blantyre. This would be at night, just like the trips we had done, but with added security. Two police land rovers took to the border trail, with Rod following in the land cruiser at Dhlakama's insistence. This was just as well, as both land rovers broke down and Rod ended up fixing them on the way. In the end, the Dhlakama family was transferred to our vehicle, and finally taken to a safe house in Blantyre. The next day, a special committee welcomed us all at the police resort on Lake Malawi, right next door to Club Makacola. This was incongruous! A fence separated us from the holiday makers on the beach of Club Makacola. We had several times been on the other side of that fence during a weekend break, but who ever thought we'd be entertained with dignitaries on this closed-to-the-public side. We all got to eat Chambo, after all.

When the Renamo delegation finally landed in Kenya, we were elated. How long we'd all been working towards this and at what considerable cost! It would surely not be long now before the end of the terrible Mozambique war. It was in fact two more years before the Rome Peace Accord would be signed and a cease-fire called.

FAMILY BLESSING

We had a wonderful family surprise waiting for us. In appreciation for our work and sacrifices to facilitate preliminary peace talks, President Moi of Kenya wished to show his appreciation in a special way. We were given a fortnight's five-star vacation in Kenya, all costs plus spending money covered by the Kenyan government. It was amazing. I called my Mum in Zimbabwe, "Get on the first plane to Blantyre, you're coming with us to Kenya!" She couldn't believe her ears but got ready quickly. The children were over the moon. We hadn't had a vacation in years. It was everything we could have hoped for.

On arrival at Nairobi airport, we were ushered through

the VIP section, all formalities cleared for us, and shown into the VIP lounge. Dustin was very funny. Though the quietest member of the family, he knew a good thing when he saw one. He stretched himself out on the sofa, helped himself to the mints on the table, ordered coffee and turned on the TV. We did not have TV at home, but he put on like this was everyday stuff for him. After a while we were escorted out to a waiting black limousine. Now Dustin's eyes sparkled even more. The chauffeur dropped us off at the Pan Africa Hotel while someone from Foreign Affairs saw us to the door of our suite. The following morning the tours would start. We visited the Amboseli and Nankuru Game sanctuaries. They were magnificent. Then we spent ten days at the Two Fishes Hotel on the Mombasa coast. We were given a special card, which enabled us to call for a vehicle to take us to any tourist spot we wished to visit. We didn't pay for a single thing. How we enjoyed our family time on the beach, sightseeing, eating, playing, swimming and lazing. We ate seafood and all the specials we could never afford at home. "This is your reward for having to live on macaroni for so long," we told the kids. It was a far cry from the hardships and discomfort of bush trips, and the scrimping that we had to do so often at home.

At the end of the vacation we went back to Nairobi and met with Mr. Kiplagat, Dhlakama, Raul, Vincent and others. We ate with them in the hotel restaurant, quite different from the campfire of the bush. It made the children feel so important to be fussed over by these smartly dressed men... some we had hidden in Adullam's Cave. Back in Malawi, Adullam's Cave was empty for a time while we enjoyed the luxuries of five-star living for a season. It was God's gift to us, especially to our children, who did not have it easy living with missionary parents, and such strange ones at that!❖

FAR FORBIDDEN REGIONS

GORONGOSA FOREST

My tightly packed backpack, boxes of Bibles and Christian literature stood stashed against the veranda wall together with the bags of clothing, soap and other gifts for the Christians in rural Mozambique.

"Ready?" Rodney put his arm on my shoulder. My luggage was ready, but was I? I felt more than a little unsure as we loaded the truck and drove off to the airport. "It must be because of the experience Rod had the other day at the Zambezi River," I told myself. The most difficult part of a mission trip into dangerous areas is often the leaving home bit, always a struggle for me, and today I felt it more than usual. The children were at school; Rodney would collect them in the afternoon after flying me into Gorongosa. For a long time the children were unaware that we were ministering in Mozambique. The whole mission was so delicate, the less they knew the better for them. They thought we were flying to one of the refugee camps in the south of Malawi and that I would remain behind there, as we had often done in the past. In time we told them. Dustin responded with, "When can I go, Dad?" We did not speak about the danger but simply told them who to phone if we were delayed and did not get back at any time. These were contingency plans made with a friend, in case something went wrong and we did not return. Horrible thought.

Parking the truck next to our plane to make loading easier, and while the plane was being refueled, I read through Psalm 91. This psalm has become our watchword and I was in need of reassurance. When the ground staff had departed I said "Show me the bullet hole." We bent low under the belly and there it was. A neat little round hole. "Let me see where it came through on the inside." Rod pulled back the mat and exposed the small hole, not so neat this side, shiny metal gleaming on the jagged edges. A knot tightened in my stomach and I wished I had not asked to see the hole, which was right behind my seat.

The engine roared and we gathered speed for take-off. "Oh God, bring Rod safely back to this runway today." Fifteen minutes later we were indeed back at the same runway. A heavy bank of clouds along the escarpment had totally blocked our passage making the trip impossible. I didn't know whether to be relieved or disappointed; having got through the worst part of leaving, I'd just have to go through it all again the next day!

Morning dawned bright and clear. I was excited, and wondered why on earth I had allowed fear to cloud my mind before. We soared over the escarpment and on across the border. The difference between Malawi and Mozambique is distinctly clear from the air; one can follow the border line with the naked eye just by the diversity in terrain. Malawi, a small but heavily-populated country cultivates almost every inch of ground. Mozambique is vast, miles and miles of sparsely-populated grass, tree savannah and forested areas. Once across the border, Rodney dropped the plane low, 15 - 20 feet above tree-top level, to avoid being seen and heard a long way off. This way, any patrol that may be on the ground would be caught unawares and by the time anyone tried to shoot, we'd be long gone. Not so easy at the Zambezi River, however, as the long stretch of sand banks and water give an uninterrupted view for anyone who knows what they are looking and waiting for. Rodney pointed out certain landmarks and we marvelled to see some of the places we had visited on foot. To think we actually walked across that mountain range. No wonder my big toes lost their nails from pressing down so hard into my shoes for hours on end down the steep incline. There was the place where we walked through the tree savannah without seeing a single hut or person the whole day and where we finally found a village late at night where we could obtain water and roll out our sleeping mats. Memories flooded our minds but there was no time to dwell on them. The present is far more important than the past. How we had dreamed back then laughing and joking about one day having our own plane instead of having to walk. It was an impossible dream that had gloriously come true. What a joy to turn two weeks of foot-slogging into an hour and fifteen minute flight!

As we approached the Zambezi River we remembered the dugout canoes in which we had crossed some months ago. Today, instead of paddling the Bibles over and dodging hippos we were flying Bibles across, ready to dodge another kind of danger, the possibility of bullets. The hippos looked content and perfectly harmless from a few feet above. Not very far from the river was the village area where "my friend, the witch doctor" lives. We waved at the people standing under the trees. Some of them waved back, having become accustomed to the blue plane; Rodney had flown over so many times now. Initially the people had all scattered into hiding at the first sound of the plane, wary of Frelimo and Zimbabwean bombers. Though they had no idea who was in the blue plane, they had learned that it posed no threat and freely returned our wave at the window. As we flew deeper into the interior, emotion filled my heart. What a love God had planted in our innermost being for these people. We prayed and interceded for souls to be saved, for the glory of God to be revealed in the villages, that men may know Jesus. We prayed for the villages below us that we would in the near future visit by motorcycle and on foot, from the closer central position of the forest airstrip near Gorongosa Mountain. **Prayer prepares the way before us**. The kingdom of God is within us. Spiritual forces of wickedness fled before our intercession as we scattered the enemy and shattered their ranks, breaking the strongholds of the forces of darkness. Watch out, devil, here we come!

"We're here." Rod skillfully brought the plane around in a tight circle. "Here? I can't see anything." I strained to see the airstrip but saw nothing other than forest beneath us. If Rod missed the airstrip and flew a little too far we could find ourselves over a Frelimo stronghold. Timing and accuracy was of utmost importance. With no sophisticated navigation equipment, an amazing sense of direction and meticulous calculation was required. Rodney has both and as he swooped down, I could make out a brown strip of cleared ground. It looked more like a motorcycle track through the forest than an airstrip. With no windsock, the wind direction had to be gauged by the fluttering of the leaves on the trees. I held my breath, screwed my eyes closed as my stomach fell into my shoes. The plane dropped over the edge of the trees, touching the ground with only a couple of feet spare on either side of the wings, so narrow was the strip.

The Renamo soldiers enthusiastically welcomed us. In order not to waste time and unnecessarily leave the plane exposed on the strip, they immediately unloaded the baggage, carrying it into the bushes. Rod had left the propellers running and we barely had time to say goodbye. It was as well for I was feeling a little desolate. The twin engines powerfully lifted the plane on a short takeoff in a cloud of dust for the one-hour-fifteen-minute-flight home. "Godspeed my beloved. Carry him safely home!"

LONE LADY AND SOLDIERS

The soldiers spread out an old parachute on the ground for me to sit on. Zimbabwean soldiers had used this parachute during one of their many air attacks when troops were parachuted in after the bombings. Renamo managed to capture many things that come in with foreign troops. It was ironic; a Zimbabwean sitting with a bunch of Renamo soldiers on a parachute provided by President Mugabe.

The Gorongosa forest is incredibly beautiful with a large

variety of magnificent trees. This valuable timber found protection in the war that prevented lumber companies from coming in and exploiting the natural forest. Birds call and fly from tree to tree. Dark red squirrels with thick bushy tails leap in the branches. I relished the beauty and wildness of the surroundings of this other world.

Voices over the radio transmitter linked to the main camp informed the soldiers that a motorcycle was on its way to collect me. I read my pocket Bible while waiting and it was not long before I heard the sound of one of the Renamo fleet. I could not ascertain which side it was coming from as the paths wound in all directions. At one moment the sound came from ahead of me, then disappeared only to be heard again behind me. A final roar and there it was before me. A smartly uniformed soldier, obviously of superior rank, disembarked to the foot-stomping and salutes of the lesser soldiers on the ground. He gave orders for all my goods to be carried to Main Camp immediately and walked formally towards me, greeting me with a regimented handshake. I had just met General Mateus Nyangomo whose life we would be instrumental in saving in the near future. He was also to become one of the most well-known names in Mozambique. Of course we didn't know any of that at the time.

General Mateus indicated that I was to ride with him. He started the shiny red Honda 200 and leaned it over slightly to make it easier for me to get on. The ride through the forest was fast, to say the least. Trees were negotiated and narrowly missed. The path made up of sharp turns was anything but level. Up and down, turn to the left, then the right, down and up and over and up again. I held on for dear life. General Mateus paused only long enough to enquire over his shoulder if I was OK. "Zakanaka!" (Everything is good), I answered him in Shona.

Was there no stretch of straight path anywhere in this forest? Only the dry riverbed proved flat. With sand so loose and thick I was sure we would fall; I was actually relieved to be back on the path again. I wondered at the reason for this speed. The enemy was not pursuing us but if they were, there would be no chance of their catching up with us. Nor were we late; after all this was Africa where there is never any need to hurry. At least there was no other traffic on the road. I chuckled at the incongruity of the situation. Here we were in the middle of Mozambique, riding like we were on the Kyalami racetrack, the nearest petrol station being in Malawi, two weeks' walk away. There was no road or passage for the bikes to get to the border, couriers having to walk cans of petrol in on their heads. My toes were locked in a cramp from gripping the footrests, every muscle in my body doing its part to keep me on this bucking bronco. When I knew I must surely submit to falling off, the driver threw some quick gear changes and slowed down as we approached a contingency of soldiers being drilled along a short stretch of straight path. They stepped deftly out of the way as they continued to carry out their exercises at the shrill whistle of the commander in charge. We passed through the middle of them, and I was amazed to see they hardly turned a hair in spite of the fact that a white woman on the back of a motorbike was a very rare sight. This was discipline in its highest form. Training is serious business and they dare not be distracted! Suddenly, General Mateus lurched into some more gear changes and we were in the middle of the Renamo Gorongosa Headquarters.

THE PRESIDENT'S PALACE

The clay-and-thatch houses neatly laid out were hardly detectable from a few meters away, so effective was the camouflage of the forest. As the bike came to a halt with a sweep and a flourish and the fanfare of one final roar of the engine, the reason for the speed and drama of the ride dawned on me. Fetching visitors from the airstrip to this important base where the President of Renamo, Mr. Afonso Dhlakama himself was in residence, could be done in only one way; with the style and alacrity singular to the make up of the Renamo Forces! I climbed off unsteadily, trying my best to look dignified while I picked pieces of scrub and leaves from my hair. I could feel a layer of dust on my face and wondered what color I was. To think I had actually put makeup on that morning! Almeida, a member of the political wing who showed me into the "reifato-rio" (dining and living room), cordially welcomed and intro-duced me. Several men rose to greet me and I marvelled at their immaculate appearance. Their clothes were smartly pressed, some in uniforms with stripes and shiny badges depicting their rank, others in civilian clothes. A number of the men I already knew, and they inquired with interest about the family and var-ious friends. The conversation being in Portuguese, I appreciat-ed Almeida's good English as he translated. Lunch was soon to be served; the fact that it was 3:00 p.m. made it lunch. Nevertheless, I was invited to first take a bath that had been pre-pared for me. A pretty girl with a round dimpled face stood nearby, ready to play the hostess and show me the way.

Smiling shyly she led me first to my sleeping quarters, a large oblong hut beautifully woven out of cane and reeds. She swept aside a curtain hanging at the entrance to reveal a cozy room. The walls were hung with sheets of colored cloth, total-ly hiding the reeds, giving a wallpaper effect. Four beds and two tables were planted into the ground. The furniture had all been made on the spot with only a machete and knives for tools. The headboards make the beds look quite attractive. I was happy to note a foam rubber mattress, sheets and blankets, all scrupulously clean. A four-inch layer of clean river sand served as a thick carpet, thus the need to plant the furniture, as underneath there was no level floor – only the bare ground. I would be very comfortable here, though only for a night or two before going out to the villages where luxury is not to be found. I enjoyed a refreshing wash from a large dish of hot water standing on the table of the shower room. Soap and clean tow-els were laid out, the reed walls serving as pegs for hanging clothes on. A few rays of sunlight filtered through the canopy of shady trees, making the shower room most picturesque.

The toilet facility was a little farther on. I was curious to investigate, remembering the story Rodney told me of one of his experiences in a Gorongosa toilet. It was night time and a slight rain was falling when Rodney visited the "little house." The deep pit with small wooden seat complete with a lid on hinges - a masterpiece of bush hygiene. On his way out again, Rodney sensed a movement behind him and shone the torch into the hole. There, curled up inside the seat was an Egyptian cobra, its eyes shining in the light. It had been there all the time! It was a miracle it had not struck out and bitten! Rodney called for one of the soldiers who deftly took his pistol from his holster and fired one shot. Thud. The snake landed in the bottom of the pit. I could picture it all exactly as Rod told me, the small wooden seat and lid being just as he had described. I determined to shine my torch into the hole to make sure there were no snakes lurking about **before** using it at night.

The reifatorio had been transformed during my brief absence. Three tablecloths covered the long table surrounded by twenty chairs. Cutlery and crockery were laid out complete with serviettes and all that goes with the promise of a good meal. At the head of the table stood a singular carved chair, which just had to be for His Excellency, the President of Renamo. My theory was proved correct as the President appeared in the doorway, escorted by some of his men. Those already seated at the table stood up as he entered. He greeted me with his cheerful smile and warm handshake. "I am very happy to see you, Madame. Welcome, most welcome to Gorongosa. How is your family? What about the children?" With his natural charm and personal communication he set me at ease, insisting I take the chair on his right.

Six serving girls busied themselves with carrying in the food. In African custom, a girl takes a bowl of water around so the diners have the opportunity to wash their hands before dining. I followed the custom while the girl peered shyly at me from under her lashes. She wanted to see me close up but tried to do so unobtrusively. I winked quickly at her and if her skin were not such a dark brown she would have blushed.

The girls served the food in the typical Portuguese style. From the left side, portions of each dish were placed on each plate while the servers moved around the table. Water was poured into each glass. Nobody touched their food but waited for a sign from the President. Turning to face me he said, "Please play for us." Being accustomed to the interchanging of the 'L' and 'R' in many African languages, I realized he meant pray. I prayed. "Thank you, Bom Apetite!" he smiled his appreciation and as he picked up his knife and fork, all followed suit.

The chef had produced an excellent meal. Vegetable soup with delicious home-made bread was followed by locally grown rice and buffalo stew. There was also a chicken casserole but I found the buffalo stew so good, and knowing chicken would be the only meat out in the villages for the next couple of weeks, I decided to give it a skip. We talked about the night trips to the border, the visit to Kenya, what was currently happening in Mozambique and about our respective families.

The serving girls were quick to replace any food as soon as it was eaten. When each individual was finished, a bowl of water was brought around again for a final wash. Coffee added the finishing touch and so relaxed was the atmosphere, it was easy to forget this was a rebel army camp in the far-off bush. With the meal at an end, the men prepared to go on with their different tasks of work. The president was to continue with lectures and discussions with his cabinet and military unit. There was a war going on and much to be done. "Feel well, feel well." (Feel welcome) "This is your home. Go any place you like." The president's broken English added charm and sincerity to his efforts to make me feel welcome.

I roamed around the camp and was warmly received by the different members of staff. Rodney is well known and much loved. Because of this I was treated with the same warmth, though they did not as yet know me. "You are the wife of Mr. Joseph? We are happy, very happy to see you." Being the wife of Mr. Joseph was obviously quite a claim to fame around here!

The kitchen intrigued me. A hut with walls built half way up to allow the smoke to escape from the fire placed in the middle, made up the main cooking room. Adjoining was a room with shelves from top to bottom whereon pots, crockery and cutlery were stacked. No modern conveniences here, yet the meals produced were very tasty. Chibonde, the chef proudly showed me his oven. An igloo-shaped room built out of termite heap mud produced the delicious home-baked bread. A fire is made on a metal sheet and pushed inside. When the igloo oven is hot enough, the metal sheet with the fire is withdrawn. The bread dough which has risen near the warmth of the cooking fire is placed inside an old drum, which has been cut in half to serve as a pan, and is placed in the oven. At the appointed time the bread is removed, hot and crusty; there is nothing to beat it. The aroma floated through the camp. Who needs a bakery when Chibonde and his termite oven are at hand?

Chibonde proudly wore a striped pair of trousers with matching jacket, a white apron and a chef's hat; remarkable attire for a bush chef. The girls all looked very smart too. Their dresses were unique, not the typical shop dress and yet with tailor-made effect. On inquiry as to where they got their clothes, one of the girls motioned me to follow her. We walked a short distance along one of the many paths, coming to a small clearing in the jungle. Four old-fashioned treadle machines stood under the trees. Pieces of cloth hung over poles and branches. At each machine a tailor sewed busily. Who would have ever expected to find a tailoring factory out here in the jungle? The tailors, three men and a woman showed me their work. I admired their ingenious craftsmanship. They informed me they had learned tailoring in the towns but because of the war they were now living in the bush with Renamo, not wanting to live in the Frelimo Communist-controlled towns. "When the war is over, we will return to the towns and set up our businesses again."

ROSA'S STORY

Rosa, a young girl dressed in olive green battle dress had been assigned to me as a companion. She spoke only a little Shona but we were able to converse fairly well through a mixture of several languages and a good deal of sign language. She had the cutest round face with a sweet smile. What was an attractive young girl like this doing in a Renamo army camp dressed as a soldier? What story lay behind this expressive and sensitive face?

"I was born in the capital city of Maputo and went to school there. I was lucky to be in school as there are not enough schools for all the children to attend. I did well in my studies and advanced quickly. There were many things we did not understand about our country. We learnt that Frelimo had fought to liberate our country from the oppressive colonial rule of the Portuguese and we were taught that Mozambicans are now prosperous and free under the rule of the Frelimo government. What we did not understand was why so many people in the cities were starving and homeless if this was prosperity? Why were people not allowed to travel freely from place to place if this was freedom? Why are people imprisoned and killed for speaking their minds if they have been liberated and why do so many of our friends and acquaintances disappear, never to be heard of again? There were some things that frightened us, like children being taken away from their parents because they are the property of the state and have been selected for 'special' training. We also knew about the slave trade with East Bloc countries. Thousands of Mozambicans were being sent as cheap labour to East Germany, Romania and Cuba in exchange for arms and ammunition and money. Why would a free country need arms? To fight Renamo who was fighting to free this free country? We began to question many things and we learnt about Renamo through some of our friends though we had to be very careful not to be found showing an interest in them. We knew some of our friends had already gone to join Renamo and we began to seriously consider doing the same. After some time, five of my girl friends and I made the move. Through meeting with some contacts we arranged to run away from school and join Renamo. We understood how we the people of Mozambique have been robbed and destroyed by Communism. We wanted to be part of building a new Mozambique, a Mozambique that is truly free. My friends and I walked to Gorongosa from Maputo with the Renamo soldiers. It was very difficult. It took three months to get here. To some places we had to walk for three days without water. Sometimes we had very little food. We have been here for six months now. We know that the time will come when our country will be free."

The earnestness and conviction in Rosa made me wonder about myself. Am I as committed to my cause as she and her friends are to theirs? Am I as willing to give my life to see people set free from the spiritual kingdom of darkness and brought into the joy and liberty of knowing Jesus? These girls had left home, family and all that is familiar for an indefinite period of time. There was no assurance of a safe return. "Oh God, give us soldiers of the Cross such as these. Men and women who are not in the fight for personal gain and glory, but who reach out for the reward of seeing life, peace and liberty given in exchange for the chains and misery of Satan."

As night fell Rosa expressed concern about me sleeping in the hut by myself, offering to sleep with me so I would not be alone and afraid. I assured her this was not necessary, and I do not mind sleeping on my own as Jesus is always with me. She told me how afraid she was of the dark and how she would never sleep alone if she could help it.

"What is it you are afraid of?" I asked. "You have told me you have learned to shoot and fight. You are a good soldier."

With eyes large and round she lowered her voice. "It's the evil spirits that I fear. They come in the hut and move around, I can feel their presence. My friends fear them too but when we are together it is not so bad."

This is the bondage of Africa; more powerful than the physical forces, the spiritual forces of the devil rule and reign in too many lives. "When you are free from Communism and oppressive rule, will you be free from the spirits?" I challenged her.

"Oh no! These spirits are from our ancestors, we cannot get away from them. They will always be with us."

"Rosa, listen to me." Taking her by the arm I led her into the hut. Sitting side by side with her on one of the beds I told of the One who could set her free from fear, the One great Spirit who is love, goodness, joy and peace, in whose presence no evil spirit can abide. "You need to ask Jesus to come into your heart, to control your life. When Jesus rules in your heart and mind, there is no place for the devil." She listened, receiving my words but unsure that this could work for her. I realized it was going to take some time for her to understand the reality of Christ. She had prayed the rosary for years, putting her trust in crucifixes. Religious objects and rituals were all she knew about, and it had brought no relief. She said she wanted to bring her friends to see me, then slipped through the door into the night.

"Excuse me!" Almeida's voice entered my sleep-befuddled mind, announcing that it was dinnertime. "Dinner time?" My watch showed 11:00 p.m. but if lunch was at 3:00 p.m. then this must indeed be dinner time. I had fallen into an exhausted sleep and felt anything but hungry. On Almeida's assurance that everyone was waiting for me, I realized I should put in an appearance. The same routine as for lunch was carried out and a hearty meal was served. I managed to look half-awake and was soon fully awake as the president relaxed and told some very funny stories. When he laughs his whole body shakes and he so thoroughly enjoys himself that one cannot help but laugh with him. He has a keen sense of humor and every now and then he wiped tears of laughter from his eyes. His men joined in and I was treated to several hilarious accounts of various amusing incidents that have taken place during the history of Renamo.

Chirping crickets and singing tree frogs filled the night with their melody. The lights strung from hut to hut through the trees had gone out with the generator now silenced. Thankful that there were no rats in the "Presidential Suite", I fell into a deep sleep only to be rudely awakened by three shrieks and what I thought was automatic gunfire. My heart leaped into my throat as I sat up. Three shrieks ripped through the night again and I realized that it was the noise of some animal or bird. The rat-a-tat-tat following puzzled me. It was not gunfire but surely there is no animal on this earth that can make such a noise? Whatever it was continued for some time.

Swish, swish, swish. I woke up to the sound of sweeping all around me. Ah yes. It is customary in Africa for villages to be swept clean at the earliest traces of first light. The Renamo camps strictly adhere to this rule of cleanliness and neatness. I opened my eyes to behold six pairs of eyes fastened upon me. "Bom dia. I have brought my friends to see you." Rosa had kept her word. Three girls sat on the bed beside mine while three others stood at the end. They smiled shyly in unison. "Bom dia." I replied. With gritty eyes and muggy head I stared at the eager expressions on the six faces. I smiled in return as I spied the tea tray they had brought. The girls were eager for contact with the outside world. We chatted away and before long they were each in possession of a Bible. Turning to the Gospel of John they began to read in turn. These girls were educated and I realized the unique opportunity for the Word of God right here in the main base camp. Most village girls in these parts cannot read. God had brought these girls walking all the way from Maputo, not only for Renamo, but for such a time as this, a time for the Gospel.

Breakfast was served in the reifatorio, the president taking time to join us. Drop scones, scrambled eggs, baked pumpkin and loads of coffee enhanced the lovely morning. A bodyguard stood discreetly several feet behind the president under an exceptionally tall tree. Stamping his foot he moved towards the President making a low-voiced request. The president smiled, nodding assent. A shot and a thud caused me to sit upright. "Nao probleme" I was reassured. "Some small animal." The largest rock rabbit or hyrax I have ever seen, with teeth half an inch long was proudly displayed. Unbelievably, this was the animal that made the queer noise in the night. I was amazed, not knowing that some species of rock rabbit made such a dreadful noise and that they also live high in trees. The body guard gave orders for the animal to be taken off to his own hut in the forest. A feast of stew would welcome him home at the end of the day.

MARCHING INTO ENEMY TERRITORY

Fourteen Renamo soldiers stood in line. Some wore olive green uniforms, some tattered shorts and shirts. Several had army boots and others were barefooted. One thing they had in common, an A-K rifle slung over the left shoulder. My boxes and bags were stashed under the trees, ready for an important mission. We planned to march into enemy territory, rout the enemy and set men, women and children free. Our war was spiritual.

At the command, soldiers picked up the boxes and bags, placing them on their heads. Some carried two boxes of Bibles, 40 copies in each box as well as a rucksack filled with clothes, cloth wraps, soap and various gifts for the local people. I was introduced to David, who had been assigned to me as interpreter. He carried my personal bag, two water bottles with which he would not leave my side. He also carried an A-K rifle.

"Avanco!" The soldiers started single file down the path. I held back to allow them to get ahead a bit, and to ask myself if this was real, or was I dreaming again? As always, the incongruity of the situation struck me. How can it be that we missionaries walk through the bush escorted by a troop of armed soldiers, as if we were some kind of high officials? This was wild! I was the only born again person in the cavalcade. The stranger I had just met for the first time, who would interpret my preaching, did not know Jesus. It was at the insistence of the president that these men were sent to protect and assist me in my jungle evangelism. I realized a new wonder and miracle of our work in Mozambique. Jesus had broken down every wall of partition that hindered us from bringing the Gospel to the uttermost parts. Through these strange and unprecedented ways we were given access into the heart of this poor nation.

After three hours of walking we were out of the forest. The magnificent trees with their high canopy of shade were behind us; the dry grass savannah with a few scrubby bushes stretched out to draw us into its thirsty territory. We approached the dry river bed, its sand baked hot by the sun. The streams had stopped flowing some time ago; no surface water to splash onto sunburned skin or soothe parched throats. No water pumps or pipes in this desolate region. Through the heat mirage we spied a group of women standing in the riverbed with clay water pitchers. Could this dry riverbed yield water, the source of life? Yes! If one is prepared to dig deep enough, if one is thirsty enough, if one desires to live! This spiritual principle was enacted before our eyes. A cavity three meters deep and three meters wide had been dug into the riverbed. No spades being available, the hole had been gouged out of the sand with pieces of wood and broken pot shards. At the bottom of the pit, another smaller hole had been dug. Two young girls climbed into the large hole. One stood at the bottom, dipping a calabash gourd tied onto a stick into the small hole. Drawing it up, she trickled the precious liquid into a clay jar. After dipping and pouring many times, the jar was finally full. It was passed up to the other girl standing midway down the big hole, who in turn passed it to the top where it was placed on the head of a woman and carried several miles to the home village. Thus the process of transporting treasure in earthen vessels continued all day, every day. Water drawn from deep within, passed along to others who carry it to bring life and hope to others. Shyly the women offered water to each of us. The soldiers having no water bottles drank thirstily while they had the opportunity. I drank and filled my water bottle. "Oh Father. Just as these people have freely given valuable water to us, let multitudes in this nation receive the Living Water as we share your love."

Faces peered inquisitively at us as we passed through a small village. The people were poorly clad with shredded garments tied around their bodies. In the natural, these people are of the poorest we have ever seen; but what's that written on one of the mud huts? *"Take no thought for your life, what you shall eat, neither for the body, what you shall wear. Consider the birds, consider the lilies. Fear not, little flock, for it is the Father's good pleasure to give you the kingdom."* I was amazed. How wonderful that the name of Jesus had already found entrance into some hearts in this wild place. These people who are so poor in the natural are actually wealthier than many who own houses and land and big bank accounts, for they have found eternal treasure in Christ Jesus.

It was a strange feeling being here in the area where

Rodney witnessed a massive air attack almost two years previously when Frelimo forces had killed hundreds of civilians. Rodney had stood for hours against tall trees, moving around them cautiously as low-flying helicopters searched the ground. Several people had made coverings for their bodies out of the parachutes that were abandoned by the soldiers. The olive green cloth was a grim reminder that death stalks and strikes unexpectedly in these places. One can never be sure how the day will end. For me, it was a great honor to be there, carrying gifts and the words of eternal life to a people so ravaged by war. The main path was quite wide and easy to walk along. Smaller paths wound off to various small villages. On some of the entrances to these paths lay bowls of grain and offerings of food. The people, superstitious and ruled by their fear of the spirit world are ever on the alert, looking out for evil spirits and seeking to please "kindly spirits" or "not so wicked" spirits, in hopes of assistance and protection. Appreciation and respect must be shown to kindly spirits to ensure their support. Evil spirits must be appeased. Thus food and sometimes even money is put out for either or both. A gift could well prevent evil spirits from coming down the path to visit hut, hearth and home. In the same manner, a gift may encourage kindly spirits to stick around and be of some help. These people understand the difference between good and evil and because God has set eternity within their hearts they recognize and accept Christ's death upon the Cross as payment for sin. The difficulty comes in allowing Jesus to be the only way. It is so much easier for them to simply incorporate Him into their beliefs rather than turn away from other gods and serve only the Living God. The tradition of ancestral worship is powerful. Satan robs the people by giving them a counterfeit. Great is our rejoicing when souls not only accept Jesus as Saviour, but renounce their old ways of bondage and idolatry. God will share His glory with no other.

15 WIVES AND SO MANY CHILDREN

Golden rays streaked across the pink-tinged sky. My leg muscles were beginning to protest against continued exercise and I scolded myself for never getting into good shape before a trip. The first two days of walking were agony but by the third day I traveled well. Soon it was too dark to follow the path. We stopped at a cluster of huts where the people received us with the usual African hospitality and prepared a meal of chicken and nsima (dry grits) for us. The chief of the village spoke a little English and was happy to chat with me. He had learned to speak English many years ago when he went to Rhodesia and worked as a chef in a hotel. Who would ever have thought a man living so far from any sign of civilization ever lived in a city and cooked in a grand hotel kitchen! The chief proudly informed me he had 15 wives. A very rich man indeed! In our culture one wife costs a man significantly but in Africa, the more wives you have, the richer you are. These days even in Africa, wives are becoming rather expensive. In Mozambique a wife can cost a man several goats whereas in the good old days a wife could be bought for a handful of mice. How many children do you have, Chief?" "I cannot count the number. I don't remember how many have died by disease and war."

The fire gave light and warmth and it was hard to drag myself up again to continue the journey, the moon having risen to shine sufficient light onto the path. Strange how Africa can be so hot during the day and frequently cold at night. The terrain had again changed and to me it looked like lion country. I asked the soldiers if there were lions about. "Not many. Some." Feeling that just one was too many, I strained my eyes to peer as far ahead as possible. We walked for several hours. By 11:00 p.m. I was beginning to fall asleep on my feet when the sound of distant drums floated through the still African night. At last, there must be a village nearby; I breathed a hopeful sigh. Half an hour later we arrived at the place where we were to sleep. I was shown to a hut and in spite of a warning voice in my head, I accepted to sleep in it. Village huts are not my favorite places of abode, especially old ones like this as they are invariably inhabited by rats and other creeping things. Tired and unwilling to sleep outside in the wintry night, I disregarded the warning voice. With bones and feet aching, I retired onto the reed bed only to experience a strange fluttering next to my head. "Oh please, not a rat already!" It was a half-grown chicken looking for a warm place to sleep. It squawked its protest as I threw it out by its feathers. There was also a hen sitting on eggs in the corner. She would not be moved and growled threateningly at my approach. At least she could be trusted to remain in her corner, protecting her eggs. Ten minutes later the real thing leaped from the thatch roof onto my pillow, landing with a thud. I slapped the bed and it scurried off. There was only one way to sleep; blanket pulled right over the head. No matter if breathing became difficult, at least the whining mosquitoes were forbidden entrance along with the rats. I questioned my sanity! How often have I prayed, "Here am I Lord, send me? I'll do anything for You Lord, etc. etc." God is faithful to answer our prayers!

Dawn was heralded by the usual crowing of roosters. Eager to see my surroundings I ventured out of the hut. Most of the soldiers were still huddled in sleep, some on reed mats, others on plastic fertilizer bags. Very few had blankets, and tried in vain to cover themselves with a bag. Packing together like sardines lent some body warmth but the ground was cold and hard. The winter nights are dreaded. The days, however, are usually sunny and warm, even hot by midday. I spied three soldiers blowing life onto the embers of last night's fire and joined them. It took a while for any heat to be generated but my tea kettle began to hum of good things to come. Several more soldiers crept up to the fire. "Wamuka?" they asked me. This literal translation of "Did you wake up?" never ceases to amuse me. I reply in Shona, "Yes, I have woken up. Are you awake?" They assured me that they had indeed woken up.

Sipping scalding tea, I contemplated the promises of the day. The Renamo headquarters had sent word to the Administrator some days ago to inform the people of the forthcoming missionary visit. David, my interpreter, could not speak Sena, the local language of the people in this region. His English and Portuguese were good but many of the villagers do not speak Portuguese. This meant that David had to translate my English words into Portuguese to a local man who could speak Portuguese and Sena but no English. We have often had to preach this way and it is very restricting. I had specially requested an English/Sena man and had been assured there would be one available. Though I was very disappointed, I realized that in a time of war I must accept whomever the Renamo forces could spare. Certainly we were privileged to be working in their zones at all, taking the time of soldiers, administrators and many others. Is there any other resistance movement in the world who gives so much time and energy to helping missionaries spread the gospel of Jesus Christ? Not that we've heard of, nor is there any government at all with a special department to assist missionaries and carry Bibles for miles through peaceful countryside, let alone through war zones.

THE MAPOSTORO CULT

"Tendere Mapostoro!" (Peace to you, Apostles.) The religious leader in long white robes, walked up and down the ten-foot-wide gap that separated the men from the women. He chanted and wailed, 1,000 people responding in reply in the same manner. The "chief apostle" strode to and fro with a long staff shaped into a shepherd's crook. Sweat glistened upon his brow-shaved head. His long grey-flecked beard reached almost to his chest. Most of the men were of the same appearance, though few sported such a marvelous beard. Africans do not easily grow prolific beards; many men have no facial hair at all. A good beard commands great respect because of this coveted sign of manhood and wisdom.

"Tendere!" the rumble of male voices vibrated through the air as they raised their staffs in agreement to each sentence spoken by their "priest." I was in shock. Were these the Christians that had gathered for the meetings from many different villages? We knew this cult; it has an enormous following throughout southern Africa. Women have no part in the religious ceremonies, except to sit some way off at the side and keep silent. These guys would never let a woman preach, least of all a white woman.

I considered my choices. Either I could walk away from this place of cultish practice, shake the dust off my feet and lose an opportunity to share the Truth with them. Or I could accept these people, identify with them, and win a place in their hearts for the Gospel.

I didn't have to think twice. The latter was the course I would take though it was not without its problems. Other religious or Christian groups in the area could reject us because we showed kindness to these people they avoided, misinterpreting the chance to speak to them of Jesus as acceptance of their cultish practices. If the group did allow me (a mere woman, and a stranger at that) to speak, I would have to be very careful not to offend them lest we lose an inroad into their lives forever. At the same time, I could never compromise the Gospel. Trying to look perfectly at home and at ease, I walked over to the women's section and sat down on the dirt among them. This created a small stir but I looked straight ahead at the priest as **I silently began to intercede.**

These people are full of religious zeal. Like the scribes and Pharisees they believe they have all the answers. They do not know that their laws and traditions are chains of bondage keeping them from life and truth. Religion is not Christianity; Jesus came to set us free from dead traditions. The laws and traditions of these people can be seen on their very appearance. The flowing white robes set them apart from the local people who are dressed in rags. Where do they get the cloth for their robes? Well, when something as important as religious tradition is at stake, it is nothing to send some of the younger men by foot across 200 kilometres to sell grain, so they can buy white cloth in neighboring countries. All must be able to recognize the "Mapostoro" as religious men.

The Mapostoro consider only the Old Testament to be of value – not that they obey the law in all instances. All that is forbidden in Deuteronomy 18 is freely practiced. While in a trance, they walk through fire, protected from the red-hot coals by demonic powers. They practice divination, consult with familiar spirits, converse with the so-called spirits of their ancestors, receiving advice and guidance. They also speak in tongues, by demons, not by the Holy Spirit. They forbid the use of medicine but have great faith in sea water as a cure for any ill.

So, "Here I am, Lord. You have sent me," I said to God. After some time of continued chanting the leader stopped and told the interpreter they were ready to hear the white lady speak. The phenomenon of the presence of a white woman in these uttermost parts was enough to push aside all normal resistance to allowing a woman to address them.

John 3:16 "For God so loved the world that He gave His only begotten Son, that whoever believes in Him, should not perish, but have everlasting life."

What greater message than this? The message had to be extremely clear and simple. Going through two interpreters was difficult at the best of times and this was one of the worst of times. After each sentence the leader insisted on raising his staff and shouting "Tendere Mapostoro" after which all Mapostoro in turn raised their staffs and thundered, "Tendere!" There is no Bible school that can train and equip a missionary to preach well under such circumstances. I wondered what I was doing there, being even less qualified, never having been to Bible school or received any formal training. The leader directed the interpretation of my message to the men only, totally ignoring the women. After all, they are of no importance, particularly when it comes to important matters such as religion. I wondered if perhaps they thought salvation was not for women, so I made a point of turning towards the women as I spoke, saying, "This good news is for the women and children too!"

Emphasizing Jesus as the only one that can set men free, I challenged them to accept Jesus as Lord and Saviour. To my amazement, the men raised their staffs – "Tifunani" (We want

Him.) I turned to the women and urged them to accept Jesus into their hearts, to repent of their sin. There was a faint rumble from the men but no real objection. The women responded enthusiastically. They too wanted Jesus. All stood to their feet to pray the sinner's prayer. Did this mean they all desired to be born again? Sadly, no. These people are essentially polite and eager to please. To show no response to the message would be impolite. Many would not change but seeds had been planted and hearts touched. Something very real had taken place and I truly believed there would be fruit from this meeting. There was, as we were to discover in later years. How I praised God for this unique opportunity to speak the whole truth to these souls who so diligently followed half-truths for lack of knowledge.

A second meeting was arranged. This time Roman Catholics and a few Protestant groups came together. Joy and liberty was evident and the singing had life. It was a welcome change and I enjoyed myself, joining in the dancing and clapping, happy to notice that about twenty-five Mapostoro men had joined the meeting and several of their women were also present. They would not be here if the Holy Spirit had not done a real work in their hearts.

BATTLE STRATEGY

Without doubt, God had done great things during this one day of unique meetings. However, a flash-in-the-pan ministry is not what we are pursuing. A vital work that shows forth fruit that will remain is the least we can be satisfied with. For this to come about, a battle strategy must be carefully planned and carried out. Already we had much to our advantage. The fact that these areas have never been visited by missionaries, and that we came in spite of the dangers of war gave us an inroad into the hearts of the people. Through this alone we gained a place of acceptance. We preached a God of love. A God of love? Who has ever heard of such a God? Their own are merciless and demanding. This acceptance did not mean however, that we could neglect to fulfill the moral code of the people or the ethics of good manners and respect of their customs that are so important to them. A successful strategy must be worked out with the approval of the local chief, headmen and leaders as well as the religious leaders. Already we had the approval and support of the Renamo forces – this first battle having been won several years ago during our time of captivity.

THE MIXED MULTITUDE

As everywhere else in the world, the age-old question was asked: "To what church do you belong?" Competition between churches is strong and all wanted to lay claim to the one and only missionary around. We tell the folk we preach only what is written in the Bible. The "Christians" are made up of many different beliefs; many not Christian at all. Of course each group is convinced that they are right and other groups are wrong. Bibles are non-existent or very scarce. Pastors preach from hearsay; much of it inaccurate. Some leaders have Bibles but read and use only the parts that appeal to them. However, there is a genuine desire to learn and few will not jump at the chance to be taught the Word of God. They are hungry for the truth and plead for spiritual food.

We arranged to have a church leaders' meeting the following afternoon. The group of leaders that assembled under the large acacia tree represented the mixed multitude of the region. The Mapostoro were there in full force; undoubtedly the largest following. The MaZion were there, the Roman Catholics, Seventh Day Adventists, Methodists, Assemblies of God Africa, and several lesser known groups. The MaZion are the wildest, even wilder than the Mapostoro. They are the tongue-babblers conversing with "departed spirits" and the most vocal in animal noises, while supposedly bringing forth messages from God. Many is the time in the early days of inexperience that we've looked around for the snake or leopard that has found its way into the meeting only to discover it is a MaZion hissing and growling.

The men stood up respectfully at our approach; the Mapostoro looking very "reverend" with their beards, shaved heads and crooks. The Roman Catholics wore a solemn "holy" expression. The MaZion looked brazenly confident or perhaps "a little wicked". The various Protestant groups had expectant but rather timid expressions. The Pentecostals could not hide their obvious joy and delight, the smiles they tried hard to contain to a respectable size, kept stretching wider and wider. It is hard to look "reverent" when one is so happy. Our arrival was an answer to their years of praying; how could they be expected to look serious?

This meeting with the leaders was of crucial importance. Should they in any way be offended or disappointed, our work in this region would be restricted. If their approval and respect was gained, the door of utterance opened to us would be unlimited. How frequently we have prayed and requested others to pray for us the words of the Apostle Paul recorded in *Colossians 4:3,4. "And pray for us, too, that God may open a door for our message, so that we may proclaim the mystery of Christ, for which I am in chains. Pray that I might proclaim it clearly, as I should." (NIV)*

We had been in bonds for the sake of Christ. Our door of utterance was gained through our capture and temporary hut arrest by Renamo some years ago. However, this in itself is not enough and counts for nothing unless we speak as we ought to speak by the anointing and guidance of the Holy Spirit.

"Come, let us pray to the Living God." All adopted their respective traditional poses and I began to pray. "Father God. In the name of Your only begotten Son Jesus, Who died and shed His blood to cleanse us from our sins, we stand before You today. Please open the understanding of each person here, open ears to hear Your truth and open eyes to see You for who and what You really are. We know it is only because of Your great love that we are together here under this tree. We know that You have a mighty plan and purpose through this meeting and we are excited to be part of Your plan for Mozambique. Come, Holy Spirit, and reveal JESUS."

A rumble of "Amen" followed the end of my prayer, which

had been interpreted into Portuguese and then into Sena. The men shuffled themselves into position on the ground, all eyes riveted on me. Somehow I had to convince them that we had not come to present yet another cult, but the truth. I held up my Bible. "Friends, this is the Word of God. Do you believe what is written in these pages is the truth?"

"It is truth!" they responded unanimously. I marvelled at the certainty in their voices. Most of them had read very little from the Bible. I wondered if there was any person who had read all of it; yet they recognized it as a book of authority and believed all its contents to be true. This would be our greatest point of advantage. I promised we would teach them nothing that we could not show them from the Word of God. If there was any doubt in their minds concerning what I taught, would they believe if they saw it written? "Yes, we will believe." If there was anything they did that the Bible tells us is wrong, would they be willing to stop doing it if I could show them where it was forbidden in the Word? "We will stop." This was all too easy. Either they genuinely believed all they did was right, or they did not think I could prove any of their practices to be contrary to the Word of God. Whatever, they had given me permission to question their practices, to show them a more excellent way. Their consent was what I was after; it would give me freedom of speech and they would be obliged to hear me out on every subject.

The African people love dialogue and it is their custom to give a hearing to whichever party wishes to speak. It was decided that as the next day was Sunday and each group wanted to have the visiting missionary at their own church, all churches should meet together in one place so the missionary could be shared equally among them. I hoped the days of putting the visiting missionary in a pot and sharing him/her literally with all was truly over. This would be the first time in history that the different churches would gather together on a Sunday. After all, each group considered the other to be sadly in error. Of course most of them were right on that assumption, even though they themselves have lacked a lot of the truth in their own beliefs. Again, the most difficult part of the meeting was in conversing through two interpreters. Each question, answer and sentence was an exhausting process and I was becoming irritated with David, who was trying so hard that he was beginning to stutter and forget what I had just said. **"Oh Lord. It's hard enough just being here in these circumstances with such a mixed group. Spare me the agony of two interpreters who appear to be deaf half the time, dumb the other half and without understanding in between!"** I suddenly felt weary but was encouraged when one of the bush apostles stood up to speak on behalf of the gathering. "We thank God for your coming. We pray God's blessing upon you. We want to learn about God. This is a great thing you have done, to come here because of the love of God. We hope you will be happy with us here. We want to meet each day for lessons from the Bible. Thank you, thank you very much for coming to visit us here in the bush." I was deeply touched by his sincerity.

"Oh Lord, PLEASE, work a miracle for a Sena/English interpreter to come and help!" I prayed. Back at the camp I revived myself with a cup of tea and wrote out a message to the Military HQ.

"We are facing a serious problem here at K. as the interpreter cannot speak Sena. This means we speak English, our interpreter in Portuguese, and a local man in Sena. This makes things complicated. Please, if it is possible, send a man who can speak English as well as Sena. The people are very happy to have us here and are sending many gifts of mealie meal, pumpkins and chickens."

God Bless you. Because of Jesus we are here.

The message was given to the radio operator at the radio station under the same mango tree. The set comprised of a hand-wound generator tied to a tree and was connected to a telephone-type radio. This had all been arranged for my benefit in case of emergency, giving us contact with the military HQ. The message was sent in code and would be decoded on the receiving end in case it was picked up by Frelimo radios. This was as much as I could do; the miracle would be in finding the right man and for the general to be willing to take that man from his present job. Would this missionary endeavor be considered more important than some military need?

PREACHING IN A STRANGE LAND

Sunday found us an hour's walk from camp in a strange enclosure of poles planted in the ground with strips of bark lashed in and out. The enclosure resembled a cattle kraal or pen. It had two entrances, each with a cross made out of two sticks above it.

These crosses were unlike the Christian cross we are accustomed to seeing in churches, but more like the medical cross, sticks of equal length. I was led to a small wooden table with a few chairs behind it at the side of the enclosure. It all felt a bit weird but I sat down and tried to look at ease. This must be the place where they were planning to "share" me. People began to file in through the entrances and when it seemed the kraal was full, no more were allowed in and the rest were told to gather outside the pole-and-bark fence. It was stiflingly hot; no fresh air finding its way to where we sat on the seats of dubious honor, right in the thick of sweating humanity. I was amazed that with so many people in the enclosure there was still a fairly large open space in the centre. A man stood in the clearing and began to speak while David relayed bits of the speech to me. Each group represented would have a chance to sing and say a few words before the missionary was shared among the people.

The Roman Catholics started off with a song, crossing themselves as they walked towards the center. Some of them had crucifixes, a rare treasure in these parts, obviously the envy of those who had none. Already some had come asking if we had brought crucifixes along with the Bibles. The crucifixes are thought to have special powers to ward off evil spirits and are in demand by some of the soldiers who believe they will be pro-tected from bullets if they wear such a "holy" object around their neck. The explanation on why we do not need crucifixes to protect us is a Gospel message in itself.

After their two songs the leader thanked the "holy mother" for bringing the visitors. The legalistic side of me struggled with this. The Mapostoro chanted and sang their way into the circle as the Roman Catholics made their exit. What I could understand sounded OK but as my Sena was very limited, they may have been calling up their ancestors, for all I knew. These are the bush Pharisees with their long white robes and shepherd's crooks and their "Mtendere Mapostoro!" Though these people are in deep error they have a sincerity and genuine desire to please God. We are not advocates of Inter-Faith, but in a situation like this, one must know how to be flexible if a real and lasting work is to be achieved. While we allow others to express their beliefs, we never compromise the Word of God. **"Holy Spirit. Lead them into all truth,"** I prayed. They made their address, which was lengthy because of the repetition, then moved away to make room for the next group.

The Protestant groups followed in turn, each singing two songs and giving a short address. Amazing that so many denominational names have found entrance into these remote parts. Somebody heard about Jesus from a Seventh-Day Adventist, Baptist or whatever, then told others the same message and thus is a church group born. They may not know much about the group after whom they call themselves, but a name they do have.

With wild whoops the MaZion burst into the circle and began a dance similar to an Indian war dance around the table. One of the members carried in a bucket of water. What now? I was sure the bucket must have something to do with some ritual about to be carried out, but was relieved to see it was for sprinkling around to prevent the dust being kicked up and choking us. The MaZion let rip with total abandonment, unfortunately to the wrong spirit. This was after all, their territory, their enclosure; they could take as long as they wanted and do whatever they liked. They took full advantage of the situation, their leaping and stomping interjected with whistles and howls.

We are accustomed to liberty in worship and are ourselves very free. But this! How would I ever manage to preach after this display? Every demon within a hundred miles must already be hanging in the trees with gleeful anticipation. There was only one thing to do; I lifted my own voice in intercession and while the sweating bodies leaped and somersaulted around the table, eyes glinting and teeth flashing, I was involved in my own bit of warfare. The water on the ground was long since trodden underfoot; dust hung heavily in the air but finally the mad throng stopped. The leader looked intensely pleased with himself and smiled happily at me with a "Did you like that?" expression. I smiled back and stepped into the center of the dust bowl at his invitation to proceed. It was now my turn.

Every face was turned towards me; sweat trickling through dust leaving little mud trails across eager expressions. I did not know where to start. The MaZion exhibition had left me a little lame. Catching the eye of the Assemblies of God Africa pastor, I indicated for him to stand beside me. "Lead the people in worship for a while before I speak." He complied and a few worship songs prepared the way for me. I did my very best. I poured out my heart and soul in an attempt to convey to these precious people the love that God has for them and His desire for them to know, love and serve Jesus. I used illustrations, scriptures, stories, whatever I could think of. Though all listened very politely and tried hard to follow, I knew much was being lost. The three-way translating was catastrophic. Finally an invitation to receive Christ as Saviour was given. A few responded. Thank God for these, but greater fruit than this **must** be seen.

I urged the people to pray for a Sena/English interpreter so we could enjoy a free flow of the Word. They agreed and prayed right there. The meeting was closed by one of the leaders, with profuse thanks for my coming. As had been previously discussed, it was announced that Bible studies would be held at the camp every afternoon for church leaders, that is pastors, elders, deacons or anyone who played an active role in sharing the Gospel. The approval of this news rumbled through the crowd. What will the new week bring? I wondered.

THE BUSH RECTORY

My study consisted of a small square table and folding chair under the mango tree. Here I did most of my reading and preparation of lessons. Privacy is not a word that is understood or even known in the African bush, and we have learned to work and concentrate in spite of numerous little faces fastened in fascination to our every move and expression. The entrance to this outdoor study was from the front, the back, the sides and in between. A commotion that registered more than that of inquisitive children caused me to look up. Whop, whop, whop! Three of the soldiers gave a triumphant cry as a one-meter-long snake was decimated with a heavy stick a few feet from my chair. This snake had used yet another entrance into my study, from above, out of the branches of the mango tree. The bright green color and unusually large round eyes identified it as a Boomslang, one of the most feared snakes in Africa. A group had gathered around the hated thing, exclamations and shudders of disgust conveying their feelings. "Remember, this one has a wife somewhere around and perhaps a large family of children too!" My words brought forth a volley of further exclamations and shudders. I was uncomfortably aware that there was a large possibility of truth in my teasing.

Snakes were a daily part of life in the bush. Not a day passed that we did not see one, or several. Mostly, snakes are more afraid of humans than we are of them, but they are dangerous, nevertheless. Without any antidote, people die or lose limbs due to gangrene setting in after a poisonous bite. No wonder snakes are hated and feared, and even the most harmless is annihilated on sight. We watched one of the pastors stomp a snake to death with his bare feet. Sitting around the camp fire during a cold night, a snake wriggled out of a log that had just been thrown on. "Nyoka!" (Snake!) the man shouted, and without thinking twice, crushed the head beneath his bare heel.

One night, anxious voices called us to come and pray for

a soldier who had been bitten by a snake. "You must come quickly and pray, or this man will die," they told me. It had been raining and it was quite a long walk on a slippery footpath. The flashlight cast long shadows and images of snakes filled our imaginations. Finally we reached the man sitting on the edge of the path. Two holes trickling blood were evident on an already swollen leg. We prayed and encouraged him to believe for his healing. He had not seen the snake as it was dark, but he had heard the unmistakable slithering rustle and felt the strike of the head. In the morning we received word that the swelling had gone down and he was almost back to normal.

We had our own encounters with snakes. Rod had felt something rubbery under the tent doorway early one morning and put his bare foot under to feel what it was. His toes curled halfway around a black Egyptian Cobra. It had come seeking the warmth of our bodies but had not been able to enter through the zipper. I never saw Rod get going so fast before. He grabbed a stick and after a few good whacks the cobra was no more. The snakes seem to love living in the thatch walls of the roofless shower rooms. An eyeball to eyeball encounter with one twined around the poles just inches from my face was not a good start to the morning.

Sitting in under the trees was so peaceful, it was easy to forget there was a war - until one of the Antonov bombers flew over. We could not know where the bombs would be dropped. The slow drone of the plane sent everyone scurrying for shelter under the trees, away from the village huts. On impact, the echoing blast could be heard up to twenty kilometres away. Generally, the Antonov did not do much damage; it was the MiG fighters that were feared, and most of all, the helicopter gun ships. These guns mounted on a craft that circled the trees and sought you out like a huge bird after a rabbit, chill the blood like nothing else. There are few sounds as ominous as the thud and whine of a chopper homing in on its prey.

Our contact with the Base Camp was reassuring only in that hopefully we could let them know if something had happened to us. Because we covered large distances only on foot, there was little chance of any reinforcement arriving in time to help us if in danger. And really, there was no chance of medical assistance in case of serious injury or snake bite. There was no chance at all for the millions of people being born into the bush, living there and hazarding their lives daily in the wilds and war.

THE CENTURION WHO GAVE HIS LIFE TO JESUS

The answer to our prayers and reply to the message sent to General Mateus was announced at the perimeter of my study by a stamp of a foot. (There was no door to knock on, after all.) I looked up to a smart salute from a tall, lanky soldier in bush green uniform, new army boots and a pistol at the hip. The man smiled shyly as he came forward with Commander Manuel, the leader of the troop that was escorting me. "I am Commander Luis Jose Goba. I have been sent by General Mateus to help you," he said in good English.

"Do you speak Sena?" "Yes, I am from the Sena tribe. These are my people. I speak also Portuguese and Shona and Chichewa as well. I hope I can be of good help to you."

"**Hallelujah!**" This was reason indeed to rejoice. Here was a mouthpiece that could speak many tongues!

"Do you know Jesus? Have you given your heart to Him?" This was a vital part that must be settled. "I am not sure of this thing," Luis replied. "I am a Roman Catholic, but if Jesus is in my heart, can I know such a thing?"

"Indeed you can. Sit down and I will tell you." There was no other chair, but my tea box being an old ammunition box of metal served as an adequate chair for Luis and he sat attentively while the Gospel was expounded to him. The Holy Spirit had been speaking to his heart non-stop ever since he had been sent for by the general. The ground was well-tilled and ready for the seed of life to be planted. Luis comprehended fully. He asked Jesus to come into his heart and was born again. His face was aglow and the shy smile spread a little wider as he related his story.

"I have been in the Renamo Forces for many years and am now a commander. I was working on a special job a long way from here when I received a message from General Mateus saying I must leave everything and come very quickly. Ah! I became very worried. I have one hundred men under my command, I cannot just leave them. Another commander was sent to take my place. I was told to report to the general who was some hours away. I did not even pick up my blanket. I left everything to be able to walk very fast. I was thinking 'What have I done wrong? I am in trouble now. The general is an important man, why does he send for me like this?' I was remembering all the things I have been doing, even some mistakes, anything I could think of. Is it because of this thing? Or that? Ah! I could not know, but I started to pray very much. I was walking very fast to reach the general. I was praying, 'O God, please help me. This day I am in trouble.' Then when I saw the general there was no trouble. He told me I was to keep moving without stopping till I reached this place where I was to help the Nzungu lady. Now I am here and you are telling me very wonderful things. Surely and truly, God has answered my prayers!"

"Tea for me? These biscuits for me? Thank you, thank you very much. I have not tasted biscuits in years. These taste very sweet to me." Luis enjoyed the lemon creams I had packed away in the bottom of my rucksack. Those were very special weeks: to us, to Luis, to the local people and to the soldiers who escorted us and carried our supplies. The teachings came across clearly and lives were daily being added to the Church of Jesus Christ. To see the rapid spiritual growth in Luis was a wonderful experience. While in the midst of interpreting he would suddenly stop, amazement imprinted on his face, forgetting to interpret, so intent was he on the Word being opened up to him.

There is a question that plagues the soldier. "I am a man with a gun. I have been in many battles. How can I be a Christian when I have killed?" Many a time we have counselled with a soul in deep anguish, longing for the cleansing flow of Jesus' blood, but struggling to believe it is available for him. The scriptures are the only means of bringing across the truth. We read of the thief on the Cross, who at the last hour put trust in Jesus. He was a robber, a murderer, a wicked man, but as he gave his heart to Christ, he was forgiven and set free from guilt and fear. In the book of Acts 10, we read of Cornelius, a centurion, the captain of one hundred men. (Just like you, Luis) He was a man of authority, a man in military leadership who is described in verse 22 as a just man, a man who feared God, a man of good report. Jesus chose one of His disciples from a rebel group. Simon Zelotes (Simon the zealot) was a member of the Jewish party that rebelled against the cruel rule of the Romans. Nobody is denied Jesus.

"But I am in the army. I cannot stop being a soldier. It is my job!" came the reply. John the Baptist answered this so well in *Luke 3:14. "Never demand or enforce by terrifying people or by accusing wrongfully, and always be satisfied with your rations and with your allowance."* (Amplified Bible) It is possible to be an honorable soldier, not oppressing or showing cruelty.

The afternoon Bible studies were the greatest success. At least 200 men came daily. They listened intently, asking questions afterwards and clearing up many things that had long puzzled them. There was a genuine cooperation and a bond of togetherness in spite of the diverse beliefs. When people have suffered together, much of the animosities of life are laid aside. It was sad, however, to see so much religious bondage. Men heap up to themselves rules and regulations, always thinking they have to in some way earn the approval of God or follow rigid laws to make themselves holy and acceptable. The message of Grace often seems just too simple. Jesus fulfilled the law in love. *"A new commandment I give unto you, that you love one another as I have loved you." "You shall love the Lord your God with all your heart, mind and strength."* These are the issues that matter, yet many of the major concerns inquired about are on subjects such as, "Is it a sin to eat pork? Which day is the day of worship, Saturday or

Sunday? Are we allowed to take medicine when we are sick?" The latter has to be answered carefully so as not to advocate visits to the witch doctor. The Word of God is the only measuring rod used, and Romans 14 answers these questions clearly.

The lesson on baptism caused the greatest stir (pardon the pun). Some have been sprinkled, some had received "John's baptism." (Amazing what they find in the Word of God, the problem being that they base doctrines on portions, not the whole.) Some have been baptized in the name of a dead Mapostoro. Whatever their baptism, they believe it is the real thing. The entrance of God's Word gives light, however, and they were eager to learn and many grasped the truth once it was revealed to them.

"Today is a great day for me. I am asking you to baptize me." It took only three days since his conversion for Commander Luis to make this request. A happy time was experienced at the water-hole when the Centurion, followed by Commander Manuel and several of the soldiers stacked their guns against a tree, stripping off rank and uniform to enter the muddy water. Humbling themselves with joy, they gained authority in spiritual places. The symbolic cleansing and burying of the old life, being resurrected into a new life with Jesus in obedience to His command, was a powerful testimony to the local people watching. "Can this be?" The evidence was before their eyes and many were challenged to obey the scriptures in the same manner. As often happens during baptism, demons made their protest. As one of the women went under the water, a demon shrieked, causing her to flail her arms and legs. The Assemblies of God pastor and his assistant could barely keep her head above the water. Several men rushed in to help and carried out the woman, now as stiff as a plank. The crowd shuddered and exclaimed excitedly. The agony and contortions on the woman's face made me very angry at the devil. **"Come out of her, in the Name of Jesus. Loose her, I command you by the power and Blood of Jesus Christ!"** With a final demonstration of growls and snarls, the demon left the woman. Her stiff body grew limp, the glazed eyes returned to normal as she sat up looking rather bewildered. We counselled with her for a while and on our instruction she verbally renounced Satan's hold on her life, confessing her sin, forbidding him to return into her life. Then she entered the waters again to be baptized. This time there was no problem and she came out of the water smiling, free and victorious. The people marvelled. Never before had they seen demons conquered thus in the Name of Jesus. Day and night the Word was discussed. Underneath the mango tree, around the campfire at night, along the paths while walking from village to village.

Luis was appointed to be our official interpreter any time we needed him. We were delighted, this made our work far easier and more efficient. Luis shared the Gospel with soldiers and the local population at every opportunity, even when we were not around. News of the centurion turned Christian spread all around. Messages requesting him to bring the missionaries "to our village also" poured in.

"My Backbone, It is Laughing"

On return to main camp we spent several days preaching in the army barracks. The centurion had returned a changed man. We saw a phenomenal move of the Holy Spirit during that week. Luis was well-known in the barracks. His obvious joy at knowing Jesus and learning more and more about the Bible was contagious. We were gathered in the forest where the soldiers had their meals. The moon filtered through the trees, casting long shadows across the bamboo tables. We spent some time in worship; the presence of the Lord was tangible. I taught on the Baptism of the Holy Spirit and invited those who wanted to receive to come forward. We began to pray. Luis, though naturally shy and reserved, was the first to begin speaking in a spiritual language. The words flowed like a river from his innermost being. Then suddenly he began to laugh and laugh and laugh. Everyone looked rather surprised at first, but then ignored him as they too began to speak in new languages. Afterwards I asked Luis to explain what had happened to him.

Luis testified, "My backbone, it was laughing. My backbone, it could not stand up straight because it was laughing so much. All over me, I was laughing. I do not know what happened, but I am feeling very happy, and I was speaking in new languages."

The time came for me to go home. It had been a wonderful mission, but I was missing Rod and the children very much. At the "Palace", I sat talking with the girls, listening for the sound of the Aztec. At last I heard the engines right above the trees we were sitting under. Within thirty minutes, Rod would come roaring into camp on a motorcycle. He would visit for a while and then take me on the back to the airstrip. As we took off and flew over some villages where we had ministered, my heart was full of thanks to God for the privilege of teaching His Word in this region. That night we sat around the dining table at home, once more a complete family. How rich we were, to have each other, to share bush experiences and school stories and be a family.❖

Nine

The Power of the Pen

You are One of Them!

It was never our intention to become entangled in anything but the Gospel. Our desire was to reach the rural people living in remote areas where Christ had seldom if ever been preached. Though we tried, we could not get to these regions without moving through the forbidden Renamo zones. Once we entered there, we were captured by Renamo, **then released with a request to preach throughout their zones, which meant 85% of Mozambique.** We saw this as a door opened by God. Today, we still see it as that.

The deeper we got into Mozambique, the more distressed we were at the plight of the people. No hospitals or access to medical supplies. No shops where they could buy clothes or food, no money, no schools. They dressed in animal skins and the beaten bark of the Baobab tree. All this in peace time would be hard to cope with, but this was a time of war. Wounds and injuries that could have been healed with a bit of medicine, caused the loss of limbs or death. Only a cessation of fighting could usher in a new era, where once more they would be able to live in peace and begin to believe in a future for their children. Sickened by the atrocities and lies, and ongoing propaganda of the Frelimo Marxist Regime, we determined to give ourselves to the **cause of peace** in Mozambique, as well as the **cause of the Gospel.**

Sometimes it was hard to know how far to go. To the best of our ability we followed the Lord's leading. We broke through the bounds of acceptability. We were despised and cut off from those who could not understand our vision and purpose. When you cross an international border illegally you are breaking the law. The penalty in our case could mean imprisonment in a Communist cell or death. When the army of your own nation is fighting against the rebel soldiers among whom you are moving, it is considered treason, punishable by death. We could choose not to enter through the opened door, and continue in conventional missions, living normal lives; or we could choose to step through into a place of service which would mean being hated, misunderstood and in frequent danger. We chose the latter, knowing that we would pay a price for it, but confident that we would also reap a reward worthy of the cost. If we had turned back, we could have saved ourselves much heartache, but we would also have missed the joy of the harvest that we have seen in fields where few others would go. It has been a short-term price to pay for a long-term reward.

Renamo was a national movement. We loved the people of Mozambique, and the majority of the people were Renamo supporters. We were well aware that atrocities were being committed by both sides, as happens in any war. However, the misrepresentation of the Renamo Resistance forces by the Communist government was tragic. Even more tragic was the way the West bought the lies of Frelimo, backing the Communists and opposing those who stood for freedom and democracy. It was a mystery to us, that the West should support Communism. In our struggle to find a balance between mission work, journalism and involvement in the peace process, we continued to make our decisions using the same measuring rod we had used from the beginning. It may be illegal, but it must never be immoral. There are times when we need to make a decision as did the disciples in the book of *Acts 5:29*, *"Peter and the other apostles answered and said, 'We ought to obey God rather than men.'"*

A team, an army, any group, is made up of individuals.

We enjoyed getting to know many of the individuals that made up this intrepid army that seemingly could exist on nothing and advance and grow with nothing. We learned a lot from them and were constantly amazed at their tenacity in the face of adversity, their determination, perseverance and refusal to give up no matter what the odds were against them. They stood together, committed to a common goal, helping each other and giving their lives for each other.

Gostode was now able to converse fluently in English. He was a reliable little worker and had become one of the family. Renamo had set up an official office in Nairobi. They wanted someone who could receive telephone calls from English speaking countries as well as Portuguese, and relay back to the Gorongosa HQ. We were unhappy when they decided Gostode was the best candidate. He did not want to go to Kenya; he wanted to stay with us and begged us to speak to Dhlakama on his behalf. We did, but Gostode was needed in Nairobi. So after three years with us, Gostode mournfully said goodbye and left for Nairobi. He was there for three years and did very well. We were proud of the way this young man, who had come to us a wild little bush man with sticking-up hair, conducted himself. Meticulously dressed, he was able to hold his own with the many he had to speak with and translate for, as they passed through the Nairobi offices. We saw many changes in the lives of those caught up in the bush war. They were civilians become soldiers, some by choice, some against their will; just ordinary men and women who longed for peace and freedom and a normal family life.

A Praying President

You cannot spend a lot of time with people in a war situation without becoming personally entangled in their lives. We felt a genuine love for the soldiers and came to know many of them closely. When love is shown, confidence is won, and President Dhlakama would say to Rod, "My friend Joseph, you are one of us." It really seemed so. We were missionaries; we were not supposed to become politically involved. Several times through the years we were accused by Zimbabwean and Frelimo soldiers at gunpoint, "You're one of them!" We did not carry guns, but we did feel we were "one of them." The fact that we had the same Communist enemies after us formed a bond with which only those who have been in that position can fully identify. And so my husband had fingers pointed at him and was labeled by some as a bandit. I am very proud of him, my Beloved Bandit.

We spent long hours in conversation with Dhlakama, the Rebel leader who had become a dear friend. His warmth and sincerity is evident to those who had opportunity to spend time talking with him. His passion for his people and desire to see peace and justice is obvious. A devoted family man, his face would soften as he spoke about his children. He told of his mother and father living at Chibabawa, and his relatives there. He sadly spoke about a brother who was a commanding officer in the Frelimo Air Force. Civil war is one of the greatest tragedies of mankind.

When we first met Dhlakama, he stated that he believed in God and was a Roman Catholic. He did not understand what it meant to be born again or to receive Jesus as personal Savior. Being a Catholic meant being a Christian, he thought. Rod explained that there is no church label that can guarantee salvation, one must personally accept and walk with Jesus. Dhlakama promised to think it over. Rod had given him a Bible and some literature. He also told him about the responsibility of leaders, that he needed to be guided by the Holy Spirit. It was a great day when Rod's friend finally accepted Jesus as Lord and Savior. He asked frequently for prayer. "I believe God answers prayer." On an occasion when Rod was very ill with malaria in the camp while visiting with Tim Salmon, it was Dhlakama who gathered together his men, some of them officers as well as a few visitors from outside the country. He said to Tim, "Come, we must pray for our friend." Led in prayer by Tim, they joined hands together around Rod and asked God to heal Him. God answered their prayer.

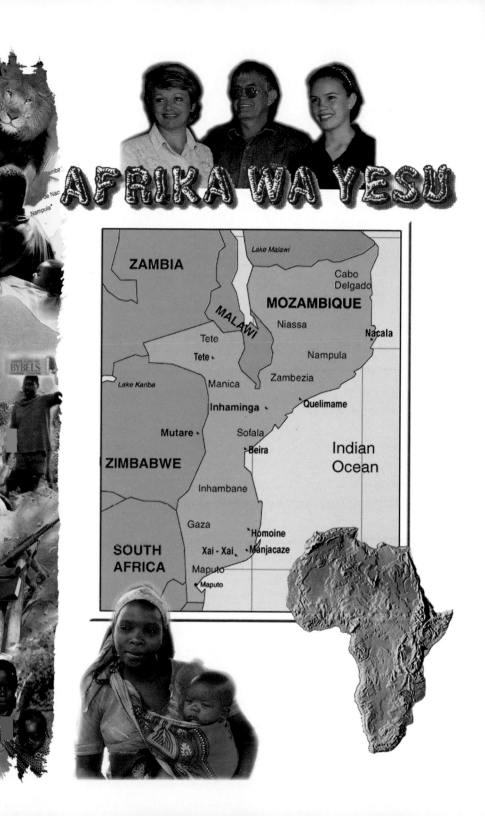

AFRIKA WA YESU

ZAMBIA

Lake Malawi

MALAWI

MOZAMBIQUE

Cabo Delgado

Niassa

Nacala

Tete

Tete

Nampula

Manica

Zambezia

Lake Kariba

Inhaminga

Quelimame

Mutare

Sofala

Beira

ZIMBABWE

Indian Ocean

Inhambane

Gaza

Homoine

SOUTH AFRICA

Xai - Xai

Manjacaze

Maputo

Maputo

BYBELS

Rod, Ellie, Tammy, Deborah and Dustin in the early years of our ministry.

Dustin (14) and Deborah (8) on a family mission trip in the Gorongosa Forest.

Ellie, Rodney and Deborah Hein, 2000

One of our many homes out on the trail.

Rodney, Dustin & Deborah view an abandoned Russian personnel carrier.

Dustin loved to accompany his Dad on flying missions.

Clad in rags and tree-bark, the homeless and helpless come seeking hope.

Children of Mozambique scraping the empty pots in time of famine.

Receiving food and vitamins

People of Mozambique

A family in the remote areas of Mozambique. The father was killed and the young boy with the bow and arrow hunts to keep the family alive.

Pushing the Piper Aztec from out of bush camouflage
onto a clearing in the forest to take off.

The Cessna 206 parked at Inhaminga airstrip, just
500 meters from the Africa wa Yesu Bible School.

Unloading food for the hungry. Ground maize is the common staple food.

Women bring their gifts of meals as we arrive in their village to share the Gospel.

A water hole on the out-skirts of Beira City; Mozambique.

Fishermen in Northern Mozambique.

Delivered at bush airfield with food and the Word of God.

Together we will learn to read. Together we will learn about God.

Preaching the Gospel with boldness.

Crossing the crocodile-infested Zimira river, a tributary of the Zambezi.

Baptizing the Renamo commanders in the Zambezi River. One soldier standing by with a rifle in case of crocodiles.

Another river resident, the hippopotamus.

Bibles are taken into Mozambique, using the vehicle donated by donations to Christ For The Nations.

Evangelism on foot through the bush and war zones with clothes, Bibles and medicine.

Bush pastors receive Bibles.

Preaching the Gospel
and sharing the love
of Christ with people
of Pango.

Baptizing
believers in the
water tank.

A typical thatch church
in a remote part of
Mozambique.

Gathering for
worship in a
local church.

From
War to
Peace!

During the Peace
Process. Standing
with Rodney from
left to right, Raul
Domingos, Afonso
Dhlakama
(Renamo leader),
Vincent Ululu.
These three are
currently members
of Parliament in
the Mozambique
Government.

Renamo
president
Afonso
Dhlakama,
encourages
his stricken
villagers.

Handing out
Bible studies
in Portuguese,
to Renamo
soldiers who
were fighting
against the
Communist
Government in
Mozambique.

Renamo soldiers
holding up the
literature written
in Portuguese,
which they
gladly read and
learn much from.

Jane, the
nurse who
worked with us
for two years,
with some of
her medical
team.

"Big Foot," the DAF truck donated by Wayne Myers, stuck in the mud.

Braving the infamous Inhaminga road in our Toyota Land Cruiser.

Big Foot carries ministry teams and supplies through Mozambique. Camping alongside the road where lions sleep at night.

Rebuilding the war-torn ruins to house the Bible School.

Reconstruction starts on Inhaminga Bible School in 1994.

Armando (front) and Bambo, faculty members working in the office.

Teacher Lindalva with
Batsie Snyders
(Ellie's mum).

Teachers Gilda, Arnaldo and
Patricia, from CFN Brazil.

Singing with
marimba at
baptismal
service.

Staff and students in front of the main building entrance of the
Africa wa Yesu Bible School.

BUSH CORRESPONDENT

The Mozambican conflict was characterized by a particularly vigorous propaganda war in which Frelimo enjoyed considerable advantages. Firstly, Frelimo was the government in power, with all the resources available to the sole party of the one-party state. Trained by Marxist-Leninists whose skill in media management was considerable, they continued to control all media outlets with their massive misinformation campaign. Most outside media networks drew their information from these sources.

Renamo on the other hand, had minimal equipment and little access to the news media and were largely powerless to counterattack the media war. Their HQ was in the bush, they had no means of a constant flow of information and they lacked trained personnel who could communicate with the media. They did not have the means to issue statements or repute false allegations, particularly in the English language. It was important also that they should be able to keep heads of states informed, and when Dhlakama traveled abroad, he needed some literature with him to give to those he met. It was the Kenyan representative who came up with the idea that there was indeed someone who was able to fill this need. None other than Mrs. Joseph. After all, she had already written a book, "Mozambique, The Cross and the Crown," which he had read. He spoke to Dhlakama, who thought it was a great idea, called me from Kenya and asked if I would be willing to assist in this matter. At first I did not take the suggestion very seriously, but continued requests got me thinking. Our book, "The Cross and the Crown," had already been used in unexpected ways. Though a very simple little book, lives have been touched by it, some to take up the missions call; our book found its way into departments of various organizations. At that time there was little information on Mozambique other than the usual propaganda line; this was something very different and was written from first-hand experience. Dhlakama carried our books with him and gave them to various people with whom he met. It is amazing what God will do and use to get His Word to people who will ordinarily not read the Bible or go to church.

We received an embossed letter from the Parliament of Australia, which greatly encouraged us.

> *Dear Mr. and Mrs. Hein,*
> *"I was delighted to receive your book and thoroughly enjoyed reading it.*
> *I enclose, for your information, a copy of a speech I made in Parliament in which I made reference to your book. Thank you for taking the time to write to me.*
> *Kind regards,*
> *Yours sincerely,*
> *Michael R.Cobb, B.V. Sc., MP.*

I agreed to be a correspondent from the bush. Rod periodically flew me in to the Gorongosa HQ where he would leave me for a few days at a time. Here they were already using their office, a neatly built pole-and-thatch hut newly equipped with typewriter and copy machine run by a diesel generator. At a table under the trees, I sat taking notes while Dhlakama made his statements and Vincent Ululu translated. It was my task to make it all plain and type it out on official paper. Only occasionally did I need to stop and ask them to repeat or explain a point more clearly. It was an experience I shall never forget, sitting in the forest, sometimes hearing the Antonov bomber, while making headlines on a piece of paper. We were fighting a war with the power of the pen. On returning home, I would fax the material to various locations. Rod particularly enjoyed faxing articles to President Mugabe's office in Zimbabwe and President Chissano in Maputo. The material also went to the White House, British House of Parliament and many other strategic offices. It was rewarding to receive acknowledgment and thanks for my work from some, though they did not know who I was. It was also great to hear some of it being read over World News stations; at last, some of the truth was being broadcast.

While still a schoolgirl, I had dreams of becoming a writer but never followed this course. Now I was actually doing more than the job of a journalist and had access to opportunities that many journalists would jump at.

It all sounds so simple and easy, but really, it was not. While I was in the camp taking notes and typing, the war continued to devastate the nation. Radio messages would come in and Dhlakama would share some of them with me. They told of villages bombed, people massacred, as at Candiero. I saw him in tears as he spoke of his sorrow. "My people, they are dying. Women and children, they are being killed. My country is being destroyed by suffering."

Dhlakama launched retaliation attacks. When Zimbabwean or Frelimo camps were overrun by Renamo, they had the added advantage of capturing needed supplies of weaponry and food.

While in the base camp I was acutely aware of the war situation throughout the nation. It seemed there was action somewhere all the time, and it all was reported to the main camp. Sessions with Dhlakama and meals were constantly interrupted by an urgent message that needed his direction.

Sometimes I could hear Rod's plane fly overhead as he worked ceaselessly on the famine relief project. With my heart in my throat I would pray for God to protect him. One afternoon, the camp began to vibrate with action as messengers scurried from the radio station to Dhlakama's office and back to the radio station again. I was writing at a table under a tree and sensed the urgent uneasiness in the camp. Furtive glances were thrown my way as bits of paper were hurriedly carried back and forth. "What's going on?" I asked suspiciously. It was obvious that these people were hiding something from me. "Nothing, everything is OK," was the answer. I could see there was a problem, but didn't know what. Were we soon to come under attack? Had something happened to Rodney? Much later I was told that a light aircraft had crashed further south and they had thought it was Rod's plane and didn't want to tell me.

In 1992 we were invited to visit a few churches in England. Rod had too much going on at the time to be able to leave the field, and one of us had to be near the children, so it was decided that I would go. London was quite a shock after Mozambique and Malawi, but I loved England and the people received me warmly. On my first night there, while watching BBC news on television, Mozambique flashed onto the screen. The footage of atrocities that had been committed on civilians and the commentary that went with it attributed the crimes to Renamo. "How do they know it was Renamo who did it?" I asked myself, remembering the many times that Frelimo carried out atrocities, called in the press and blamed Renamo for it. I voiced my doubts to my hosts who said, "We should look into this." They did. Rachel Tingle, who was running the Christian Studies Center invited Baroness Caroline Cox from the House of Lords to meet me. We shared together and prayed together. This resulted in Baroness Cox contacting the BBC and asking them if they could verify that Renamo was responsible for the atrocities that they had shown. The answer was that they could not. They were simply quoting what the Frelimo Officers had told the cameraman. On hearing that there was someone in London who had recently been in the war zones of Mozambique, the BBC spoke to me at length on the phone, then asked if I would be willing to come to Bush House for an interview. I said I'd think it over. Personally I did not want to do it. I was in England for ministry, not for political interviews. We were trying to keep a low profile in Africa, and to be heard live on BBC could only put us in high profile. I phoned home and spoke to Rod. "I think you should do it," he said. "I'm seeing Dhlakama today, I'll ask him for an update on the situation." Rod wrote down the particulars of names and places and events that had been reported so he could verify the details with Dhlakama.

That afternoon I walked through the lush green fields of a small farm where I was staying with friends at Worcester. The yellow buttercups peeping through the bright green carpet were a stark contrast to the parched ground of a drought-stricken

Mozambique back home. In my mind I saw the scattered scarlet flowers that push through the soil when the first rains come in Africa. On long hard walks, they always remind me of the Blood of Jesus shed for the nations. I had come outside to pray about whether or not I should do the interview. It wasn't necessary to wait for an answer. "Lord," I said, "You really are going to make me do it, aren't you?" I could feel His smile of encouragement.

Some hours later Rod called. "Dhlakama confirms that his troops have not been in any of those areas; Renamo is not responsible for the atrocities." He gave me a few more details, then said, "We really feel that you should do this interview." "I know, God has already told me," I replied.

Speaking on BBC had not been on my agenda and I was more than a little nervous. It was strange walking down the corridors and into the recording room. However, I recognized that God was giving me an opportunity to speak for the nation I loved. "I'll do it, Lord, but only if I also get the chance to give glory to Your name." Having spent much time with Dhlakama, I knew the way he thought and had first-hand experience of a nation at war, so was able to speak clearly and answer questions with confidence. Then came the personal questions; how was it that we were working in the midst of such dangers? It was the opening I needed and I was able to tell of the call of God to preach the good news of Jesus Christ. I told about our walking missions, preaching, healing the sick and of the rebel soldiers carrying loads and loads of Bibles for us across the mountains. All glory was given to God.

The final question was, "Mozambique has been at war for so many years. There is no sign of the possibility of the war ending. Do you think there is any hope for peace in the near future?" "Yes, there is hope. We are praying and believing for peace. The leader of Renamo wants peace, but he is given no opportunity to state his cause to the world. Last week the British government received the President of Mozambique, Mr. Chissano for talks. You try to negotiate for peace but you talk only to one side. You refuse to acknowledge or talk to Renamo. If the West is serious about peace for Mozambique, the Renamo leader must be acknowledged and consulted also. You cannot speak to one side and ignore the other."

Within two weeks, Dhlakama was in London, by invitation of the British government. We like to think my interview on BBC made a difference. Certainly, things began to change for the better.

Back in Africa, family members and friends were astonished to turn on the news and hear my name by introduction and then hear my voice on BBC World Service. Deborah's teacher asked her, "Was that your mother I heard on BBC?" "I don't know," said nine-year-old Deborah, but I know she's in London!" Our well-kept secret was not so well-kept any more.

On my return I wrote to Dhlakama:

The President of Renamo
Mr. Afonso Dhlakama,
Gorongosa.

Dear Sir,
Greetings to you in the Name of our Lord Jesus.
I returned this week from the UK where I met with a few aid organizations and individuals who are interested in helping the suffering population of Mozambique. We hope to get food and medicines into some of the villages soon.
The BBC interviewed me first by telephone for half an hour. During this time I was given the opportunity to speak freely to the interviewer. I challenged them about their biased reports, favoring Frelimo, never reporting anything from Renamo. They told me that they do not have access to Renamo. I replied that they should visit Gorongosa and meet with you there, and see for themselves what is going on. They have agreed to do so. If you can give us a date when you will be available, we can work on a program for a BBC team to visit Gorongosa.
Enclosed are the tapes of the interviews. Two were broadcast on

World Service, the other on a Christian News Station. These interviews were possible only because God made the way. It is not easy to get on BBC, but it all happened without effort because God planned it. We have had more coverage in a short space of time than most of the professional journalists that visited Mozambique have had. The BBC asked me to continue reporting and to be on call should they need more information. I am ready to visit you at Gorongosa for your next press release and information update such as we put out a few months ago.

In the meantime we continue to pray for peace and justice for Mozambique, for wisdom and Divine guidance for those who speak for her, especially for you, Sir. Many Christians in England are praying for you, and for the suffering people.

Sincerely in Christ Jesus,
Ellie Hein

Our perseverance helped bring change. There were some that responded positively and gave a lot of themselves for the cause of truth and justice in Mozambique. We admire those who had the courage to speak out and act in the face of so much opposition. Some of these were Christians who got involved through knowing us, others were from the secular world, people of principle and integrity who care when the world goes mad and determine to do what they can to restore sanity and perspective.

Baroness Caroline Cox, a deputy speaker of the House of Lords, is an intrepid lady who travels all over the world for Christian Solidarity Worldwide. Together with Rachel Tingle from the Christian Studies Center in London, the two traveled extensively with us through Mozambique on fact-finding missions. Both these ladies put a lot of effort into their work and were able to both speak and send their written material to places of influence. How well I remember going for a walk with Caroline up the mountain behind our house in Malawi, talking about the sorrows of ostracized peoples, the call of God to take responsibility for the oppressed. The term, "A Voice for the Voiceless" cropped up frequently in our conversations and I felt that here was someone who truly understood my passion to speak for those who could not speak for themselves.

Baroness Cox can periodically be seen on TV hot spots as she continues in her relentless efforts to help the suffering peoples of the world. Her remarkable life and work is portrayed in a masterly biography, *"A Voice for the Voiceless,"* written by British author Andrew Boyd who refers to Caroline as "The Battling Baroness."

David Hoile of the London-based Mozambique Institute wrote several books on Mozambique and visited many times.

Andrew Hunter, MP, also flew into Gorongosa with us to meet Dhlakama and others in rebel-held zones. Others, not named here, risked much to enter the forbidden territories. We feel a personal gratitude to each one. It was a fascinating time for us, meeting so many interesting people and watching as God touched the lives of many.

Professor Andre Thomashaussen, of the Institute of Foreign and Comparative Law, became a special friend of ours. His commitment to Mozambique was incredible. He probably did more on the long and treacherous road towards peace and freedom than anyone else. He labored tirelessly, writing document after document, giving his time and energy unreservedly; arguing, pleading, persuading and convincing until the fight was won. He paid a great price for what he believed in. There are few, if any, in the secular world whom we admire more.

Many in the body of Christ stood with us. Various church leaders visited to preach, encourage, and share. None gave himself so totally to being our rear guard and helper as Pastor Tim Salmon, a graduate of Christ For The Nations. He flew in emergency supplies for us in his own plane, and many times with Rod in the Aztec. He was never concerned with what people would think. He believed in what we were doing, and that was enough for him. When we were criticized he stood up for us; nobody could speak a word against us within a hundred miles of Tim. Living as precariously as we were, who can know what it meant to us when Tim said many times, "If ever you need me, no matter where you are or what trouble you're in, call for me. I'll drop everything and come get you." We knew he meant it.❖

Ten

THE TIME OF THE
GREAT HUNGER

URGENT HARVEST

The increasing turmoil of the nation intensified our sense of urgency to reap before it was too late. It was like looking across fields of ripe corn, ready for harvest, with dark clouds gathering. We needed harvesters to help us reap. God saw the need and provided some wonderful people. Tim and Sally continued in their support and backup. Wik and Sue came from England to take on the load of the Malawi work. Chris and Fernanda spent eight months with us helping in many ways in Malawi and Mozambique. Various pastors came for short visits, bringing life and encouragement to us on the field. Dr. Harold Harder of Blessings International brought in loads of vital medicines. We organized seminars in different locations and flew our visitors in to teach and preach where large crowds gathered to hear the foreigners speak. Each visitor that came suffered the discomforts of rough living. We cannot mention each person by name, but God has seen the sacrifice and giving of each one. There are those who were never able to come, but through whose prayers and financial support we were able to accomplish the work of the ministry. These have equal share in the reward of the harvest, for without them it could never have been done. We're forever grateful.

Jane and Claire, the two nurses who gave so much of

themselves, left an indelible imprint on many hearts. Jane had heard Rod speak in a church in South Africa. As she listened, she knew that Mozambique was the place of her calling and we were the people she was to work with. In a short time, she was ready to join us. The first time I met Jane, was when Rod flew her in to the Gorongosa forest to join me where I had been teaching the Word in outlying villages. I was looking forward to receiving the help of a nurse who could give some medical assistance to the people I was preaching to. Jane was the right person. As we started out on our mission together, her typically long nurse's strides had me running to keep up with her. She was great. Not only did she dress wounds and teach village health care, she also taught the Word of God to adults and told stories to the children. Jane was everything and more than we could have hoped for.

During that first mission, after a particularly long walk, we prepared for the night at the new thatch mission base the people had built for us. It was lovely; the huts being new, we did not anticipate rats or any creepy-crawlies. We had some rules about ministering in war zones, and I had briefed Jane as best I could. "We don't expect to have to run from anything in the middle of the night, but in case we do, this is how to be prepared. Always have your flashlight beside your bed. Your kit bag must be ready and packed, shoes and socks ready to put on, your water-bottle filled. Nothing must be lying around the camp. If the enemy comes, you must be able to get away quickly without leaving any trace of who you are." We always followed these rules, but on this particular night, as I prepared to lie down on my reed bed, I thought to myself, "I'm so tired I can't keep my eyes open another minute. I'm not going to pack up; nothing is going to happen tonight." I felt a whispered warning, but ignored the Holy Spirit. "I'm just too tired and that's just my conscience reminding me of a habit I keep." Again I heard the still, small voice speak to me, but was in a deep sleep before I could answer Him.

It happened at 3:00 am. Several bursts of automatic gunfire echoed through the night air. I was up in a flash. "Oh Holy Spirit, I'm so sorry I didn't listen to you. Please help me to pack quickly and not leave anything behind. Please help Jane get organized too."

"Ellie, Ellie!" Jane's voice was at the hut entrance. "What's that noise?" "It's gunfire and it's close, Jane. Don't worry, I'm sure everything will be all right. Just get ready quickly, we've got to go." "I am ready. My stuff was packed up before I went to sleep." The moment was too urgent to worry about what a bad example I was, I threw my things together, while Luis said, "You must hurry, Mai. Frelimo are coming!"

We hurried down the dirt path in the moonlight. Occasionally someone stumbled over a root or hole. Luis kept telling me to go faster. Jane had no problem keeping pace with him. Almost two hours later we reached a cluster of huts where a runner had gone on ahead to ask the people to receive us. It was winter, and though we were warm from exertion, we nestled around the comfort of the coals where a low fire was burning. Pastor Branco and his family welcomed us. They had even heated some water so we could have a wash, and had put sweet potatoes and corn on the coals to cook.

"What happens now?" Jane asked. "Well, it depends. If this is a serious attack, we may hear the helicopters at first light. Then we know we're in deep trouble, because after the helicopters come the bombers, then after that, troops are parachuted in. If nothing further transpires, we'll stay here until we get further instructions." Luis had gone back in the direction where we had come from to find out what was happening. Though he was on this mission as our guide and interpreter, he was still an army commander and after seeing us to a safe place he returned to the place of action.

Some hours later Luis returned to say that all was clear. We were relieved that nothing further had transpired. We did not return to our mission base, but set up Jane's clinic under a tree on a borrowed table. The medical supplies had been carried forward during the night. We would do our job right here. But nobody came. The report of the night's shooting spread like wildfire and sent everyone into hiding. The following morning when it was obvious that there was no follow-up fighting, a few people began to bring their sick to the clinic. Jane was incredible. With no examination table, she lay patients down on a sheet under a tree. She was practical, purposeful and compassionate in all her administrations. I was not much help to her, though I tried. While she cleaned and treated wounds and sores I hugged the patients and cried.

We stayed just two days. Nobody was at ease so it was difficult to work. When Rod and I returned some time later, we saw that the entire mission base had been burned to the ground. We didn't know the full story of what had happened. A couple of years later we were told by some of the local population that yes, a platoon of Frelimo soldiers had attacked and burned down the place. Nobody wanted us to know at the time in case we were frightened off from doing mission work in the area.

That was the beginning of Jane's work with us. Some months later Claire joined her for a season. Together they made a great team and Rod flew them into different areas where they stayed for weeks at a time, preaching the Gospel and healing through medicine as well as prayer. Jane put a lot of emphasis on village hygiene and preventative health care. She had her own little team of Mozambicans whom she schooled and trained in health care. It was a tremendous time of learning and seeing lives changed. When the famine and cholera epidemics hit Mozambique, these girls were invaluable to the people. Both Jane and Claire are fair-skinned, beautiful girls with long blonde hair. We couldn't imagine why in their late twenties both should still be single. "We'd love to be married, just haven't met the right person yet," they said. "Not likely to meet anyone out here in the bush either!" I shared with them the scriptures about Ruth, who faithfully gleaned in the fields, then ended up in a rewarding marriage to Boaz. "You are faithfully gleaning in the harvest fields of Jesus; you wait and see. He will send the right man to find you, no matter where you are." Just over two years later, Jane and Claire left us, both to be married. We were sorry to lose them but delighted for them. It is as the psalmist says in *Psalm 37:4*, *"Delight yourself in the Lord, and He shall give you the desires of your heart."* They each have families of their own now.

Having Jane and Claire and others on team helped us achieve so much more. Sometimes we worked together but mostly we could leave them to get on with it while Rod dropped me off to continue in other places on my own. They also helped us care for our children when one of us was away. God had brought us extra helpers in preparation for a very difficult time. Famine like we had never seen before was about to devour the nation.

HUNGER

The African winter's night blanket covered the land, keeping out not the cold, but only the light. I fought the twinge of anxiety that gnawed at my stomach. Rodney must land the plane before dark and he was not yet home. "It's just as well that Dad is not night-rated on the plane, or he would fly all night as well as all day," Tammy had remarked. I suspected she was right, though it would not be from choice, but the urgency of the famine. All over Mozambique people were starving. Rodney was making two, sometimes three trips a day into some of the worst affected areas, taking food, life and hope to a desperate people. I breathed a sigh of relief when a sound at the gate announced his arrival. All three children leaped up to be the first to welcome Dad home. They would race to the door like bullets trying to pass each other to be the first to leap onto their Dad. As Rod climbed out of the truck, I searched his face for the signs that would tell what kind of a day it had been. Through the smile he always has for us all, I detected more than the shadow of weariness and strain. There was a reflection of sadness, deeper than sadness; it was grief.

While Tammy made the coffee Rod told the story that

was outlined on his face. "I circled Senga-Senga but could not find the new airstrip they have cut out of the bush. I didn't want to return home with the food, so I decided to try and land at Madzuire, though I knew they would not be expecting me, as they were not on the schedule. As I came in, I saw a crowd of at least 300 people at the airstrip. The Renamo Commander came running to greet me, thanking me over and over for coming as if they were expecting me." "These people have been waiting here for three days with nothing to eat," he said. "They have heard your plane flying over many times and stories are reaching us about your taking food to the people in different places. They have come here to the airstrip hoping you will come here too. Now you have come!"

Rod had unloaded the bags and come back for more. On his second round some hours later, there were 2,000 people waiting. They had come running out of their huts and the bush after the first flight. Never had he felt more helpless. The women stood with empty baskets on their heads. The 20 bags of food were not even enough for a handful of maize meal for each basket. Yet he was sure it was by the leading of the Lord that he was there; that's why he couldn't find the other airstrip. He promised to return with more in the morning. I felt my own heart constrict with the weight of the need of these people. What could we do to effectively help? Our limited resources could never meet the need. The plane could only carry ten by fifty kilograms of meal at a time. "I'll come with you tomorrow," I said to Rod. You can leave me on the ground to minister to the people while you ferry food loads. I can share the love of God along with the little bit of food."

At the first ray of morning light Rod collected Jane and Joanne, another lovely girl who had come to help out for some months. They stood ready with all their equipment for one month's stay in the bush. Boxes of medicines, blankets, clothes and soya protein food made up the first load. More food to follow tomorrow. The three flights planned for the day would keep Rod flying from dawn till dusk. As we prayed together I was overwhelmed with thankfulness for these two women, willing to enter the difficulties and dangers of a war-torn, famine-stricken land. After two weeks we would join them for evangelism and a leaders conference for bush pastors. I waved them off; Rod would return to pick me up for Madzuire on the second trip.

We lifted off from Chileka airport, loaded to capacity with food. We flew in silence for most of the way; I prayed for the land as we flew low over villages and shriveled fields that had yielded no harvest. As we neared Madzuire, Rod pointed out some landmarks. We had to shout above the noise of the engines. "Do you see that white spot? That's a Frelimo base." I wished I had not seen it; it reminded me that we already had one bullet hole in the belly of the plane. The land was barren and dry and I marveled that anyone managed to survive there at all. We crossed the Zambezi River; its strength had been swallowed up by sand and in places it was so shallow we could see the sand at the bottom. Never in living memory had the great river been so low. Rod leveled the plane to land. "Hold on – this is a 'kangaroo' strip," he shouted. We bounced over the dips and mounds, finally coming to a stop after lifting off and landing several times. It seemed to me a miracle that the plane was still intact.

All these people! I lost sight of the surroundings as the massive cloud of dust we had created enveloped us. As it settled, Rod opened the door and we climbed out to the grinning faces of the soldiers. "Bom dia, Bem Vindo!" they happily welcomed us. Quickly they unloaded the meal, stacking it at the side of the strip. I half expected the people to mob for the food, but they stood still along the side of the field, their chatter resounding like the drone of a far-off plane. A few minutes later Rod took off again; he would collect me at the end of the third trip.

Skin and Bones

The bleak, colorless scene jarred my senses with the shock of desolation. Madzuire was a ghost town. Derelict from the ravages of war, gutted buildings with no roofs stood starkly against the background of leafless trees and dry brush. The walls, broken and pockmarked from bullets, gave testimony of the effects of war; what once was, no longer is. In the forefront of this nothingness is a scene even more desolate. It's the scene of nakedness, sickness, hunger and impending death etched upon living humanity. Not a shred of color. The dark-skinned people clothed in brown sacks fade into the horizon of a brown sea of endless waiting.

"Oh God! Where and how do we start?" I prayed. José, one of the Renamo commanders appointed to be my guide explained the procedure to me. "The people will be divided into village groups. Each village has a headman or chief who knows the people. There is not nearly enough food but the headman knows who is the most in need. One bag will be distributed amongst each group." General Pascaul gave instructions for people to assemble into their respective groups. Before long they were seated, their baskets beside them. The distribution took all day, one group at a time. I was amazed at the patience of the people – or was it hopeless resignation? They could see the supply was inadequate, but they sat quietly, waiting.

If from afar the people looked dismal, close up they were devastating. There was an old lady who had walked the whole day to get there – not an easy thing for an old person. Bleeding feet stuck out from under her worn wrap. Even more difficult was the journey for another old woman who was blind. I took her hand. Many of these people had never seen a white person before; this woman had not seen a face of any color for years. A nursing mother held a small infant. "This must be a newborn baby," I said. She shook her head. "My baby is two months old; I have no milk." I gasped as she unwrapped the bundle. Tiny limbs protruded from a skeletal body, ribs stuck out from under feverishly hot skin. The mother's eyes were shallow pools without hope. "I am so sorry, so very sorry," was all I could say. Empty gazes followed me as I moved around. Such thin, emaciated people I had never seen except on TV. The children were the most heartrending.

I tried to instill hope, telling them to put their trust in Jesus. Easy words to say. To my own ears I sounded like an empty vessel with empty words speaking to empty stomachs. How easy it is to believe God for the impossible when we are in the comfort and security of our own homes, and in the midst of positive confession people. And yet, even here, surrounded by hopelessness I was intensely aware of God's presence. He cared. I knew it. He could meet the need and I knew He wanted to. That was why we were there, to see with our own eyes, to hear with our own ears and to speak on their behalf, making their need known.

When everyone was gathered to hear the Word of God I urged the people to seek the living God. "We are going to die. There is no hope for us," they said. "Christ is your only hope," I told them. "Seek God and you shall live." Steeped in witchcraft and idolatry, these people were praying to any god or idol in any name they thought might help. The key was for them to know Jesus, to become children of the living God. We told them that the food had come because of the love of God. We expressed our regret at the short supply and challenged them to put their faith in Him, to pray in Jesus' Name for more food to come. We too would extend our faith, we would trust and believe on their behalf and do what we could to see they did not die for lack of food.

José had called the Christian leaders together to receive the few Bibles we had brought with the food. We always gave out the Bread of life, together with food. As we talked with the leaders I was greatly encouraged. These men looked different, they were different. Though ragged, they were clean and alert; not without hope. Excited at the events taking place around them they said, "Truly God has heard our prayers. He is faithful. Thank you for coming. We are very happy to receive the Bibles." A wide cross-section of denominations was represented in the group. Seventh Day Adventists, Roman Catholics, Protestants and Pentecostals joined together as one. If ever we have seen persecution and suffering do a good thing, it is in breaking down the barriers that men erect around themselves.

In this hour of desperation brothers and sisters in Christ put aside their differences; they needed one another!

José took me to the shade of one of the broken-down stores. Stepping over the machine gun, we found a place to sit on the rubble. "What must I do to be filled with the Holy Spirit?" he asked. "First of all, have you given your life to Jesus?" "Oh yes, a long time ago. Your husband, Joseph, gave me some literature about the Holy Spirit when he was here yesterday. I have read it through, now I want to be baptized in the Holy Spirit." Removing his pistol from its holster, he laid it on the cracked cement floor saying "Please pray for me." I found the scriptures in my English Bible and he read the same in his Portuguese Bible. Satisfied that he understood, I placed my hands on his head and began to pray in the Spirit. In no time at all Jose began to pray in a new language as he was gloriously filled. It was wonderful. No matter how dark and difficult the situation, the light of God shines through.

I stood on a large termite mound to see if the overflying plane was Rod's. It was! His third load was for the people at Senga-Senga where he had not made it the day before. In just a short while he would land to pick me up.

"Please, Mai. My children are sick and we have received nothing today." The pleading eyes of a young mother met mine. She had a small child by the hand and a smaller one tied on her back. I thought of my lunch sandwiches packed in my bag. I could not eat in the face of such need, but I would have to give it to her secretly. Taking the packet out I said, "hide it in your clothes, I do not have more to give anyone else." *"What clothes?"* I thought to myself as she removed her torn sack and placed the meager package beside the baby, retying the sack. Reaching again into my pack I pulled out a two-meter length of bright pink design fabric. Her eyes widened as she slowly took it with the traditional curtsy of thanks. Rolling it as small as possible, she stuffed it under the sack. Later on, in the privacy of her hut she would unwrap it. Clapping her cupped hands together she thanked me in a husky voice. How I wished I could provide for her every need! Lack of space in the plane prevented us from bringing a load of clothes. In this time of famine, food had the highest priority.

I looked up into the sky at the sound of a plane to see if it was Rod. It was. He was flying on further with a load and would soon pick me up on his return journey. I thought of how many of us depended on that plane. If something happened to Rod, Jane and Joanne would have a two-week walk home from where they were, almost the same for me. The food flights would stop. God had many reasons for keeping Rod safe.

The chatter of the people heralded the sound of the returning plane as they ran off the airstrip to make way for the big bird, which came bounding over the termite mounds as it landed. Rod jumped out and triumphantly pulled out a small deer by the hind legs. "God has provided!" he laughed. As he had dropped for landing at Senga-Senga, the duiker had run across the field into the path of the plane. To avoid hitting it with the propellers, Rod had lifted the plane just in time, but unable to avoid it completely, hit the duiker with one wheel. "Take it to the people at Madzuire," the Renamo commander there had said. "They are in a worse situation than we are. Take it as a gift from us."

We learned much about giving during the time of the great hunger. We saw how those who themselves were without, gave to those who had less. God bless them.

Though I had been at Madzuire for only a day, I had seen and felt so much, it was as if I had been there for a week. I was emotionally drained and exhausted, but so glad I had made the trip. We said goodbye, promising to return again with more food and the *JESUS* film. They cheered as they waved us off. The fact that they showed such appreciation even though many had received nothing, touched us deeply. We determined to do our best to get word of their plight out and to work hard at getting help to them. We arrived home to hug our three children and to hear the accounts of their day at school. It was another world.

DODGING THE ENEMY

Rod continued his daily flights, even on Sundays. If he didn't fly, people didn't eat. He had made a few more trips to Madzuire and now we were on our way to show the *JESUS* film, as we had promised. It seemed as if the plane, loaded with food and film equipment, had to fight its way through the thick haze and heat. Every year most of Africa burns as runaway fires devour the parched earth, filling the sky with smoke and almost obliterating the horizon. The plane dropped several feet and rose suddenly as it hit air pockets caused by the heat. It was not a pleasant flight; we could hardly see the ground even though we were fairly low.

The people were excited about the film. We would hide the plane under brushwood and camp overnight. On approach, we both felt uneasy. Was there a problem or was it simply the flying conditions that made us feel this way? As Rod brought the plane in for landing, we saw 10 men standing abreast across the runway wildly waving us away. Behind them stood a soldier in uniform, clearly indicating with his arms in traffic-police manner that we should not land but leave the region. We looked at each other in disbelief. These people were expecting us; why should they be waving us off? By now we were almost touching the ground but seeing the desperate waving, Rod lifted the plane and turned sharply around and up. We deplored the idea of returning home with food on board while people were starving below, but obedience is vital to survival, not only to ourselves but to those on the ground. We scanned the skies and the ground for signs of Communist enemies, but saw nothing. We headed straight for home where we were met by an anxious family greatly relieved to see us. My mum had come to visit for a while to help with the children and while we were gone, an urgent message had been sent to Gostode to stop us leaving for Madzuire. It had come too late though; we had already left.

Later in the week we discovered the cause for alarm. The local population had reported seeing a group of Frelimo soldiers moving in during the night. At the time of our approach,

Frelimo and Renamo were engaged in ground contact behind the hill at the airstrip. Shooting could be heard from the airstrip but we couldn't hear it above the noise of the engines. We were glad we had returned home!

It was time for us to join Jane and Joanne at Ndoro for the conference. From our place of landing we rode three hours on motorcycle. Our visitors, Keir and a friend of his, would be doing most of the teaching. It was always fun to watch the response of our visitors. It has to be a shock when one comes tearing down the path on a motorcycle, almost colliding with a group of armed soldiers walking in single file. The hardest to handle though, was to see starving people with empty baskets walking from village to village in search of food. To see painfully thin mothers carrying scraggly children on their backs and leading others, barely able to walk, by the hand, is to have the heart pierced in places never touched before. This was as another era, an existence of which the world was not even aware. How often I thought of the tons of food wasted every day in faraway flourishing cities.

The team waiting at Ndoro was relieved to see us. They now had contact with the outside world. It had been a difficult time, now reinforcement would share the load. Pastor Time, who could be counted on for his cheerfulness, was subdued. His smile was half the normal width, but he was trying. "Because of famine, people not come to conference," he said in his broken English. "They eating nothing." Three months ago his joy had been full when we planned for the conference; he had expected a minimum of 500 leaders to walk in from other villages. Now he hung his head in shame to say there were only 60 men present. "No matter," we replied. "We will still have a good time in the Word."

In the morning Jane set off for her clinic with her team of helpers whom she was training in basic first aid and health care. Jane bravely took on the cares of a nation. She could not change the world, but she changed the world of many. Mothers brought their malnourished children who were given vitamin syrup, and health-building food from the pot bubbling on the open fire. Some of the children, though starving, were too lethargic to eat. The mothers battled to get food down a little one too starved to care, the mind having given up the will to live. Sores, wounds and skin diseases were cleansed and treated.

Death pulled at young Pedro's life. Could this hideous condition truly be the result of mouth ulcers? Where there is famine, the body has no resistance against infection. Swollen gums had loosened and displaced his teeth. Eating and drinking was an ordeal; his face was swollen like a balloon. The witch doctor's potions, rubbed into incisions made by dirty instruments, showed painful results. Without proper treatment, Pedro could not live. Fatima's life too could be saved by the medical team. A small scratch had become a wound all the way to the bone on her leg. Intense pain racked her life. She had no medicine at all; now she was being treated with penicillin injections and ointments. As Jane tried to clean the wound Fatima wept with pain. I sat behind her holding her, crying also. I was not much use to Jane, but my tears comforted Fatima.

While the clinic was in operation, Keir and the others taught the Word daily to the men. Sunday was a day of celebration and the thatch church was packed out. The cooking fires outside promised a meal along with the spiritual food being received inside the church. Both kinds of food had been brought at a price. The couriers had panted and sweated carrying 50 kilograms of maize meal on their heads for a long way. Our visitors had left the comforts of their homes and churches to sit on the pole seats of a dirt floor church while flies buzzed and sweat trickled down layers of dust. Nobody complained. We were here on commission.

What a good time we had with the colorful cloth wraps we had brought. We broke tradition and had each man walk up arm-in-arm with his wife. The man selected a wrap, which he presented as a gift to his wife. Joy and laughter filled the house as unity and love was expressed. Traditionally, the men sit on one side and the women the other. Affection is not publicly displayed, but today was different. Outside was poverty and fear, inside the church, families received new hope and vision. With God, all things are possible. He who had sought them out and brought visitors to Ndoro, could keep them through the worst of the famine and bring them home rejoicing again.

In an ocean of intense experiences, there are singular occurrences that stand out above others, leaving an indelible mark on the soul. These become landmarks in our lives, beacons from which the cries of the destitute reach into the recesses of the mind at the most unexpected time, even in sleep. They forbid that one should forget. These are as in Acts 16:9, *"And a vision appeared to Paul in the night. A man of Macedonia stood and pleaded with him, 'Come over into Macedonia and help us.'"*

In the face of such a call, can one respond in any other way than Paul describes in verse 10? *"And immediately we sought to go to Macedonia, concluding that the Lord had called us to preach the gospel to them."* It seemed our daily life was impacted by such calls that drew us again and again to the famine-stricken land where hidden from the world, families were swallowed up by the naked earth as they became one with the dust in which they were dying.

"PLEASE DON'T ROLL IN THE DUST"

As we walked down the path to visit a nearby village, the unending flatness of the Ndoro plains stretched ahead. Heatwaves shimmered where brown earth and hazy sky merged into a fuzzy horizon. Out of the obscurity, a solitary figure of a woman came weaving down the path towards us. She was dressed in the usual tattered sacking; her glazed unfocused eyes did not see us. She staggered; it seemed that she would fall and we cried out, "Mai! Can we help you?" It took a while for her to realize that we were there, talking to her. She held her stomach and feebly whimpered, "Njala." (Meaning hunger.) Months of fear and misery spoke through that single word. A supernatural wave of compassion engulfed me. We had no food with us but we told her we would take her to where our food was. I had a wrap in my bag, which I took out and hung around her half naked body. Her reaction shocked me. "Zikomo, ziko-mo," she clapped her hands feebly in thanks, then attempted to dance. (The dance is an expression of great gratitude.) She was too weak to dance and fell to the ground and began to roll in the dust. I was appalled. "No, no, Mai. Don't roll in the dust." I took her hand and pulled her up. Then I realized what she was doing. According to custom, when in the lowest state pos-sible, this is what the women do. She had nothing, she believed she was nothing. Starved, naked, degraded humanity rolled in the dust like a dog. It was heartbreaking. I embraced her and we both wept as I prayed aloud, a prayer of intercession ripping from our hearts into the heavens where God must surely hear and have mercy on this woman and multitudes more just like her. We were on our way to the chief's house where there was a large gathering of people waiting for us. I was torn between continuing the mission and taking this woman back to our camp. Joanne volunteered to take her, and slowly they went on their way. On our return from the meeting, the woman was sit-ting at the camp with a half eaten plate of food beside her. "I did not eat it all," she said. "I am taking half of it back to my friend who is too weak to walk." Her face, so drawn with grief and fear a few hours ago, was now relaxed and at peace. Joanne had led her to Jesus. She had never heard that Name before. Without husband or children to care for her, she existed by sell-ing water. This meant long walks to the water hole, the only one that had not yet dried up, carrying a heavy pitcher full of water in exchange for morsels of food. A hard way to survive, but the only one open to her. We gave her half a bag of food to carry home with her. She placed it on her head and walked off tall and straight, her new wrap flapping gently in the evening breeze. Strengthened by the food, rest and love, she was a woman transformed, inside and out. Her friends would have a hard time recognizing her when she stepped into the village later on.

Both soldiers and civilians alike amazed us at the way they shared their food with one another in a time of famine. While on a walking mission, we arrived at a small base camp

where three soldiers were sitting around a pot of indistinguish-
able cuisine. It looked more like boiled animal hide than anything else; the smell was awful. "Come and eat with us; you
must be hungry," they invited. We declined but sat and chatted
with them while two more soldiers came by. They were offered
a place around the pot. Longingly they gazed at the food, then
shook their heads. **"We ate yesterday."** The law of survival was
you ate only every third day. If you had access to food, you
gave it to someone else. This way more people would stay alive.
Instead of the fighting over food one might expect, we saw this
incredible sharing and waiting upon one another. There were
the eight children, each taking their turn one at a time to dip
one little hand into the communal pot for a morsel of sadza. No
one pushed or shoved. They patiently waited their turn. When
we arrived at a village to minister, the last chicken within miles
would be found for our dinner. Women would send their children to our hut. One would carry a single egg, another a piece
of cassava. The little they had, they gave. We learned much
from the Mozambican people during the time of famine.

THE DAY THE BIRDS CEASED TO SING

As the days grew hotter and drier, vegetation shriveled
and crops were burned by the merciless sun, we walked in
silence, conserving our energy, what was left of it. On reaching
an outcrop of trees, we stopped to rest. A strange silence hung
in the air. Not a sound, not a twig snapped, not an insect
chirped, not a bird sang. It was weird. "Why is it so quiet?" I
asked the guide. "It is the silence of drought," he replied. It was
true. Where previously bird life had been prolific, there was
now nothing. The birds had flown away in search of a place
where there was water. Here all the streams had dried up.

It was the day the birds ceased to sing. More frightening
than the lack of food was the drying up of water sources. Many
rivers in Africa are seasonal. During the dry season, the rivers
cease to run on the surface, but beneath the dry sand of the
river bed the water continues to flow. Now this deadly drought
had dried up even the rivers that normally flowed all year.

Underground water sources were very deep, and in some cases totally depleted. In the villages, women drew empty buckets from the wells. Fear gripped the land.

Thousands had fled on foot to the refugee camps in search of food. They stopped at wells and rivers to drink and continued the journey on empty stomachs. One can survive for quite some time without food, but one cannot survive without water. Now those who had waited were trapped. There was no water en route. They died along the way, right there in the dirt on the side of the path. Other villages had water but no food at all. These people could not carry enough water to drink on the long journey to a food distribution point. They too died along the footpaths or in their villages.

It was to these cut off villages that Rodney continued to fly food. He received radio messages from the Renamo HQ telling him where the villages were located. The people were told to prepare an airstrip. They did not know how to do this properly, and though they tried their best, did not do it very well. These airstrips hacked out of the bush enabled Rod to land the Aztec and prevent entire villages from perishing. The rough strips, with humps and holes and termite mounds, would make any pilot hesitate to land and take off. Rodney was not deterred by the conditions. As long as there was a need he would do his best to meet it. He had several mishaps, but each time God made the way for him to get out of the problem. Just north of Ilhe, the plane almost crashed as it swerved and bounced without direction on the badly prepared ground. One of the wheel struts broke. Here in the bush there was no telephone, no shop, nowhere to find what was needed to repair a broken wheel strut. Then Rod recalled that on a previous overflight to check progress on the strip by air, he had seen a piece of mechanism lying under some bushes. He walked into the bushes, hunting around till he found it. It was an old metal frame for a generator, left there many years ago. It had one rusty bolt on it, just one. Rod removed it and walked over to the plane; would it fit on the wheel strut? It did! One bolt hidden in the bushes, for such a time as this. If Rod had had an accident, there would have been no medical help around. Had he not been able to fix the plane, it would have taken two weeks to walk home. Ultimately we could depend on God alone, and who better to depend upon?

President Dhlakama was distraught at the effects of the famine on his people. "Please, you must tell all your Christian friends to pray. We need God's help or everyone will die." One day when Rod arrived at the HQ, Dhlakama requested a special flight. He had been told of a group of people starving on a mountain. They had not eaten for weeks and dared not venture away from their water source to go to the refugee camps, as all water sources between their village and the camps had dried up. To leave their water hole to search for food was to go in search of death; to stay where they were without food meant death also. The group of about 30 people were found by a Renamo patrol. These soldiers were so shocked at what they saw, they changed course and returned to HQ to report to Dhlakama. Now Dhlakama asked Rod to take a load of food to them and said he would like to accompany him.

Rod landed at the nearest possible clearing from where the food could be carried up the mountain. The people did not have far to walk but most of them could hardly make it to the central point of food distribution. One old lady stood swaying, her feet refusing to move. Her ribs heaved in spasms of breath. Rodney bent down to pick her up. Dhlakama turned round and seeing this told his general to carry the woman. This he did, and the old lady had a safe, gentle ride to where the food was already cooking in the pots. The picture of a general in uniform carrying an old woman, bony and weak, caked with dirt, was incongruous, but it was deeply engraved onto the hearts of the people.

Around the cooking fire the President of Renamo sat on the ground with the people while his soldiers cooked and served the food. His face reflected the pain in his heart at seeing his people so ragged, so worn and bony. He communicated with compassion, sympathized with them over the death of loved ones. He grieved with those who had buried the bodies of their little children in the hard, baked earth. He exhorted them not to give up, to believe in a better tomorrow for Mozambique. That the President of Renamo, dressed in the uniform of a four-star general should sit on the ground with the poorest of the poor, was eloquent testimony of the man's heart. His concern and encouragement brought strength to them. Their spirits were revived, their hopes were built. Today, this group of people who had no hope of life, live to tell the story. The way Dhlakama identified with the sufferings of his people reminded us of a statement made by Dietrich Bonhoeffer, who suffered many years in a German Communist prison. *"I shall have no right to participate in the reconstruction of a Christian Germany after the war if I do not share the trials of this time with my people."*

BUSH HOSPITAL

Near Pango was the Bush Hospital, built by Renamo soldiers, hidden under the shelter of a forest of trees. It was an amazing structure built out of bamboo poles, mud and thatch. The wards had neat reed beds all in a row. There was a hut for a consultation room, another for registration, another for meals. There was even an Operating Theater. Because thatch buildings have small windows, the rooms are dark. Dr. Soares had an ingenious idea. The thatch above the bed in the operating theater was divided, making a small window in the roof that was covered with clear plastic. This formed a skylight, which let the light in onto the bed, the plastic keeping out the rain. The dispensary had beautifully made shelves to hold the medicine. Everything was so well put together, but with two main missing components: medicines and patients. There were few patients, not because there were no sick and wounded, but because there were no medicines with which to treat them.

We were delighted to receive a large consignment of medicines from friends to send with Jane and Claire. The two nurses spent almost six weeks at the Bush Hospital where they ministered spiritually to the people, and also to their sick bodies.

Valuable time was given to training health care workers who would visit the villages with practical, lifesaving information.

We were thrilled with the achievements and progress made by our two coworkers, as well as those in the bush that helped so willingly. In times past, amputations were being made with a hack saw and no anesthetic. This time, because of the gifts of Christians, Dr. Soares was able to use a hypnotic drug while amputating a young girl's leg with a genuine amputation saw.

Anti-personnel mines were frequently planted around the outskirts of a village. When people went out to work in their fields they detonated these. Sometimes they died, many times they lost an arm or a leg. Imagine being in the bush and having a limb blown off. No medicine for healing, no drugs for pain. Sometimes they died months later, infection and gangrene setting in to eat away in a long and slow death process.

Jane writes... "We are a group of literate, semi-literate and illiterate, aged from seventeen to sixty, with five different language preferences between us. Luis, our interpreter flits effortlessly from one to another, addressing and answering questions to each in their native tongue. Voicing our amazement, he assures us, 'It is God. On my own I cannot do this.' The aim is to teach in such a way that even the illiterate can be effective as health workers in the villages."

Nina: A noxious odor permeates the air. The blanket pulled back reveals the nasty effect of much of Africa's ills: ignorance and the work of the witch doctor. The gangrenous leg of nine-year-old Nina hangs tortuously from her thigh, the cruel result of snakebite treated by the witch doctor. "We must amputate." "Sorry, the amputation saw is shared with another bush clinic where they have just needed it. It will arrive tomorrow."

A runner eventually arrived with the file. Dr. Soares amputated with Jane's assistance. She helped stitch up the stump and was able to give valuable instruction re gangrene and infection. The snakebite need not have resulted in amputation, but lack of care and the medication of the witch doctor caused gangrene to set in. Nina had been bitten by a puff adder that had crawled into the family hut.

Later Jane continued, "Nina is recovering well, swinging away on her home-made crutches and exercising her thigh in the hopes of a prosthesis when peace comes." So many hopes are based on when peace comes to Mozambique. Until then, there's not much hope of anything.

Carolina: "How long have you been sick?" "Over a year." "Exactly as you are?" I tried to imagine myself in her condition for so long. Her thin, emaciated limbs and body with grotesquely bloated abdomen filled with fluid lay on the bed. The fear of death had finally drawn her to the hospital. Expectant eyes were fastened on me as if I have every solution stowed in my back pocket. This is it for her, the last stop, the last flicker of dwindling hope. If her stomach is not drained she will die. I know I can do little, and head off to consult the Great Physician, "She shall not die," are the words that echo in my spirit. Luis has remained behind to share with her the Gospel. Carolina is ready to receive Jesus. My hope is fed as a surgical procedure forms in my mind – tentative consultation with Claire – "sounds possible, do it!" comes the answer from one confident in God's ability to work through anyone.

Paradoxically, the scantily equipped "theater" (operating room) contains all we require – essentials sent by Christians who shipped medication some time ago. We swabbed the stomach, pushed the tube through the skin into the abdomen, sutured it into place. Gallons of fluid gushed out before an awed audience and the swollen abdomen subsided. Sudden noise and activity as the tension breaks, shouts of joy as assistants rush for more containers. I am deeply grateful to God."

While the two nurses were at the Bush Hospital, Rod received a visit from Dr. Harold Harder who arrived with his son David, and another load of medicines and equipment. It was a wonderful encouragement for all at the hospital and surrounding villages to see this medical assistance come in. Everything was carefully packed onto those bare shelves; it looked great.

Jane put a lot of emphasis on training her assistants. They made up a good little mobile team that worked not only at the Bush Hospital, but walked to outposts where they could reach the people who could not get to the hospital. The team working with Jane and Claire was made up of Renamo soldiers who had been stood down from military duties to take on health responsibilities and help us in our work for Jesus. There were fifteen of them; we called them our Crack Unit. All except Luis were new Christians, but they were learning fast. Anna was a full-fledged commander and took efficient charge of the medical unit. Olga was baptized in the slimy, green sludge which was all that was left of the water hole. Angelina, full of bounce and life, kept everyone looking up. She and Olga made a great team in leading praise and worship. Martiniho was the male nurse and was particularly good at relating spiritual principles to the physical. He comprehended the urgent need for latrines to be dug to prevent the spreading of disease. The people were not in the habit of using toilets, but simply went anywhere at any time or place. Martiniho proudly told us that in every village they had been, there were now good toilets. Joao was the one that fetched and carried firewood and water. He washed the clothes and ironed them with a metal iron filled with hot coals. Mangani, the chef, tried his best in the kitchen. Before the famine it was always chicken and rice; now it was mostly boiled roots and leaves, very rarely a chicken; rats were not to be sneered at. Domingo, Zeka and Camouflage had the task of digging pit latrines, cleaning up camp and carrying the supplies on their heads. All these wartime soldiers were involved with evangelism, and teaching health care principles and sharing about Jesus. When we returned home they went on ahead without us, continuing the work, setting up in new locations and preparing for our next stay. It was a system that was working amazingly well in spite of the war and famine. This could not have been possible without the assistance given to us by the President of Renamo and his men.

In Mozambique, Joseph became a byword. Everywhere people were saying, "Joseph is keeping us alive." This too had been a word spoken to us in the past. "God will use you to feed many, to be a bread basket to the hungry, physically and spiritually." The cost was high; Rod was worn out and had never been so thin. We wondered where it would all end, but we could not stop. More and more people were dying; our plane was hopelessly too small. For over two years the famine continued to lay waste the ravaged nation.

There was nothing heroic in the work being done. We were a team of ordinary people with no particularly outstanding attributes. It was simply a response to the need from hearts that desired to serve God out of love for Him. Heroes are simply men and women who act on a need greater than they are.

Finally, it was the famine that contributed to forcing the two warring factions to the point of signing a peace agreement. The arguments that characterized much of the peace talks had been leading nowhere. A people dying for lack of food will reassess their priorities and bend to make concessions and compromises that they would balk at in normal circumstances. On October 4th, 1992, the Rome Peace Accord was signed between Frelimo and Renamo.

Our part in bringing the Peace Agreement to pass was small, but for us this agreement was a tremendous personal victory. Mozambique was so much a part of our lives, we felt we had conquered the world. There was still a long road ahead, and for us as a family, more trials and trouble than we could have imagined. Our own time of peace would not come for a long time yet. ❖

FAMILY STRUGGLES
AND VICTORIES

THE HEIN FAMILY HITS THE TRAIL

Dustin was not deterred by the fact that the Honda motorcycle was just a little high for his feet to securely reach the ground. A few days riding on the rough bush paths had turned him into quite a proficient track rider. Of course he had fallen off a few times, but with no serious damage. A bit of burned flesh from landing under the exhaust pipe is part of growing up. The winding, bumpy path in and out of the forest trees was any fifteen-year-old boy's dream come true. I was a little concerned, however, at Deborah precariously perched on the back. "Dustin, pleeease be very careful with your little sister," I pleaded. "Yes, Mom." Knowing Dustin's inability to resist teasing his eight-year-old sister, I implored him some more. He chuckled, but I could see by his expression that he would take care. The days in the bush had brought about a considerable change in him.

He seemed to have grown visibly taller and self-assured. With just a little wobble, he started down the track ahead of the second bike driven by our guide with me on the back. We were on our way to the bush hospital, just over an hour's ride from base camp. I had not been able to make up my mind on which bike Deborah would be safest. I was a lot heavier than she was, and that would make it harder for my son. His bike had no foot-rests and that would make it hard for Deborah. The bike I was on had some missing gears and leaped unexpectedly, making falling off a real possibility. I decided she'd be better off seated behind Dustin, and with several prayers in my heart I watched as the two children rode off. Deborah's navy and red nurse's uniform flapped in the wind. She was also wearing a comical white cap and an apron with a Red Cross on it. My Mum had made it for her at her request, as typically of a little girl, she was very serious about wearing the right clothes to the bush hospital so she could help Jane and Claire. "I've got to learn sometime, you know Mom," Deborah had informed me. After just fifteen minutes we rounded a corner to see Dustin and Deborah stopped on the side of the path. "My legs are aching; I've got pins and needles all over," Deborah whined. Lack of footrests had caused a problem. The reason that there were no footrests was that they had been knocked off long ago by stumps and logs on the overgrown paths. I decided to change places with Deborah, instructing her to hold on very tightly to the Renamo guide. "Now, Dustin, remember I'm your Mom!" I said to my grinning son. "I'm not so young and you have to treat me with respect." (Chuckle - chuckle.) "Dustin, if you drop me in the dirt you'll be in trouble!" "Just sit still, Mom, and don't wobble." My slender son kick-started the big bike and took off gently enough. With no place to balance my feet it was hard not to wobble and when he almost hit a tree, it was not his fault. What a relief it was to arrive at the hospital in one piece!

Jane and Claire and the team were delighted to see us. The two drivers had a quick drink of water before rushing back to collect Rod and Tammy who would be landing soon. Tea was made for me and Dr. Soares produced a coconut full of fresh sweet milk. We had lots of news to catch up on and Deborah felt very important making the rounds with the nurses.

In most of rural Mozambique the people have never seen a movie, video or TV. Many have not even heard of such things. Can you imagine the thrill for people like these to see the life of Jesus portrayed on a big sheet strung across the sky?

Behold, He cometh in the clouds!

Going to the movies in the bush is not as simple as in a town. First of all, runners must be sent out to the villages to invite the people to come and see a movie. "A movie? What's that?!" "Well, it's moving, talking pictures of Jesus and His disciples and other people that can be seen on a giant page in the sky." "Oh. You mean the spirits of the dead will show themselves and talk to us?" (Ancestral worship and calling up the spirits of the dead are part of daily life around here.) "No, no! This is not that. This is another way of teaching about Jesus, with moving, talking pictures. Come and see!" You bet they'll come and see. Who would miss such a phenomenon. Muslims, witch doctors, unbelievers, no matter who or what they are, will pitch up in the thousands to see the *JESUS* movie.

Time is short so motorcycles save us hours of walking. However, the generator, sound system and the rest of the equipment cannot fit on the bikes so they are carried by couriers in advance.

The screen is roped up between two trees. Somehow the equipment must be kept from being run over by excited people. They arrive by the thousands, having walked long distances for this appointed day. The ground is all that is available for seating, but the people are too excited to sit, they remain standing through the whole two-hour show. The film is a powerful witness. When Satan appears on the screen in the form of a snake when tempting Jesus in the desert, the people gasp and some of them start to run in fear. Rod stops the projector and everyone calms down. It is explained to them that they need not fear; these are talking pictures; the snake is not real. They exclaim in astonishment and marvel at the miracles.

When the crucifying of Jesus is played out, many begin to mourn and wail. Never have we heard a sound that can so move the heart; this deep mourning and weeping of people who live in sorrow and suffering, at the sight of Jesus being nailed to the Cross. It is the most astounding experience of their lives to see the *JESUS* film.

Afterwards they plead, "Please, you must bring the talking pictures again. Please, we want to see them again, and we have many friends who will come next time. Please, please, come back again with the talking pictures!"

Just before dark we set up the sheet for the film, then Rod and Tammy arrived. Our young lady looked quite at home in the bush and actually declared she was enjoying herself. Rodney had shown her the big craters caused by the bombs dropped by Zimbabwean forces during our previous visit. The size of the craters and the shrapnel lying around had a sobering effect on our 17-year-old daughter, but it does no harm to come face to face with the reality so many people have to live with.

The film made a powerful impact, then we had to ride back to base camp. Rod put Tammy on the back of his bike and Deborah in front on the petrol tank while Dustin and I rode on the other bike. The exhausted Deborah fell asleep against the comfort of her Daddy's chest. It was past midnight before we got back to camp, but we boiled water for cocoa and opened up the chocolate cookies. We listened to one another's accounts of the day, what it had meant to each one. It was a special joy to be together in the bush as a family. We prepared for bed, falling asleep to the sounds of the night animals.

Very early in the morning Rod and I woke to the sound of far-off firing. Somewhere there was fighting; would it come near? For a moment I was sorry we had brought the children, then relaxed again as I felt the assurance from God that all would be well.

Dustin enjoyed the bush and accompanied me several times on trips. He was good on the motorcycle and a great help in getting me around. We made quite a long walking trip together during which his toughest ordeal was the multitude of flies that buzzed around us, trying to suck moisture from our skin. He did not complain, but when he asked, "Mom, are the flies also bothering you?" I knew he was finding it hard. Usually a very picky eater, he started enjoying food he normally rejected. Pumpkin for breakfast became a treat. "Never knew pumpkin was so sweet," he said, eating it skin and all. Dustin and I spent some time with the team at Matombo. The young boys were delighted to have him around. He brought a soccer ball and played with them in the afternoons. It was wonderful to hear the sound of joy and laughter in the villages. It was a special joy to have our son on the field with me. He gained a far greater understanding of the suffering of others. Having walked past several dried-up water holes with his water bottle emptying rather fast, he had a new appreciation for water on tap. "But what do the people do when there's no water? How do they manage to stay alive?"

Dustin loved to fly with Rod and made several food relief trips with him. His dream was to become a pilot and to be like his Dad.

DANGER AT HOME

Our personal security in Malawi became increasingly precarious. Frelimo knew that we were in Malawi. They also knew that some person in Malawi was assisting Renamo with communications and getting reporters across the border. Marcos, our friend in Police Security called Rod in for a special meeting. "You have to take extra care," he said, showing Rod a letter from the Mozambique Government Office. The letter stated that they knew we were hiding in Malawi and requested that we be extradited to Mozambique. The last thing we wanted was to enter Mozambique Frelimo zones; it would be the end of us. "Don't worry," Marcos reassured Rod. "I have told them I do not know of your whereabouts. But there is also a group of SNASP (Frelimo agents equivalent of KGB) in Blantyre looking for information of any Renamo contacts." Marcos reminded us that if we were exposed, he would have to deny knowledge of our presence in Malawi and would not be able to help us. "Also, two Zimbabweans have been in the country asking questions and trying to locate you." Marcos had his ear to the ground through his police security workers and not much happened that he did not know about. "Keep your gate locked. Always watch for cars that might be following you and check your car for bombs." We were beginning to feel like we were part of some thriller movie, except the camera crew was not there.

It was difficult to remember to be careful always; much of the time everything seemed so normal at home with family and ministry continuing as usual. Then one day we turned on the radio to listen to the Malawi Independence Day celebrations. The guest of honor was none other than President Chissano of Mozambique, the man who we knew would like to have us for breakfast. We were outraged when with our own ears we heard him speak to the crowds, his message being carried over National Radio. He spoke of the menace of Renamo fighting against his government and how he was determined that this movement would be eradicated. He went on to say that he knew there were certain white people from Zimbabwe hiding in Malawi who were communicating with the Renamo Rebels. He gave the ministry name which we had been using. "If any of you Malawians know these people or know where they are hiding, please report to your nearest police station with the information." Our house was just one kilometer away from the stadium from which he was speaking. I remember growing cold and shivering and giggling stupidly. "Are you sure the gate is locked?" I asked Rod. The next day the speech was carried in the daily paper.

OUR THREE CHILDREN

Every day we drove our children to school and back. "The gate must be kept locked in case of thieves," we said. True enough, theft was and is very bad in Malawi. The children were not perturbed; they were used to us going on trips and frequently accompanied us on our normal mission rounds in Malawi during weekends and school holidays.

We tried to maintain as normal a life as possible for the sake of the children, and succeeded some of the time. For special treats we would go camping on the shores of Lake Malawi.

These are treasured memories of barbecues on the beach and tents pitched under the stars with hippos grunting in the night. Deborah was a true water baby and was happy to stay in the water the whole day. Dustin enjoyed paddling a canoe and on one occasion when taking Deborah for a ride on a wind surfer, was carried off out of range by the wind. Two little dots perched on a board on the horizon had to be recovered by a rescue team!

Tammy did as well as she wanted to in school. A gifted and talented girl, she would say, "I can do *anything* if I want to." This was true, just as it was true that she would do nothing if she didn't want to. Before she had turned 16 she could make her own clothes, decorate birthday and wedding cakes as beautifully as any professional, make stuffed toys to sell for pocket money, and indeed, do anything she wanted to. She was good at sports and loved drama. Loaded with character and a fun-loving, vibrant personality, she was never short of friends.

Dustin loved the intrigue of our clandestine operations and Rod shared things with him that he did not share with the girls. Dustin could keep a secret better than anyone we knew. He was always keen to go on a trip with Rod and wished he could skip school and go more often. He was not a great scholar and seemed always to be caught in some prank, and was in trouble often. He could ride the big bike at age nine – his feet not yet able to touch the ground. He unofficially drove the car around the yard when we were out. We didn't find out until we returned home to find it stuck half way up a bank. Model aeroplanes were his passion and though he did not have access to many, what he had, he built and rebuilt continuously.

Deborah started her school years in Malawi and loved her school with a passion. She always did well in her schoolwork and involved herself in as many activities as she could fit into a day. It is still typical of Deborah to select more activities than can fit into a day. She loved ballet, and danced in the Blantyre productions of *Coppelia*, *Cinderella* and *The Nutcracker Suite*. It was Deborah's dream to be "just like her Mom", as it was Dustin's to be "just like his Dad." Tammy was her own person, full of fun, with loads of character needing a bit of channeling.

We all missed Zimbabwe and our family and friends there. Our children had been growing up together with their cousins, and I was very close to my mother and sisters. We were used to visiting each other frequently and all of the children felt as at home in the other's house as their own.

DON'T PLAY WITH THE HEIN KIDS

We felt the loss of family and friends heavily and loneliness was a struggle. We did not mix much with other families in Blantyre; it was necessary to keep a low profile. Consumed by Mozambique and our mission work, we were kept very busy. One or two families who knew our involvement in Mozambique shunned us. They stopped inviting our children to birthday and swimming parties. When they saw us they turned away. We were "hot stuff", and it was not desirable to be seen with us. A lady from a local fellowship went so far as to ask us not to show any recognition should we meet with her at the school or in town. "My nerves can't take it," she said. "This cloak and dagger style is too much for me. If we were seen to be your friends we could get into trouble." I said to her, "That's fine, we'll respect your wishes; but when the day of real persecution against Christians comes, what are you going to do then? If you can't handle being seen with us in case someone thinks you're our friend, how are you going to stand as a Christian in the day of trouble?" She did not answer me, and we were careful to pretend we did not know the family when we saw them around, respecting their boundaries.

We continued to receive visiting teams of missionaries, but most of them we put on the field in Malawi only; Mozambique was becoming too tricky.

With famine comes an increase in sickness and disease. It was hard for all of us. For us as a family there was the knowledge that we were not our own, we did not belong to ourselves or even totally to each other. Sometimes it felt like we were the dispensable property of a nation at war, a people in crisis. There was often no time to tend to our own crisis, whatever it was. People were dying around us and we had to help them. Again and again we said goodbye to one another, to our children, to be swallowed up into another life where one could not be sure to see the setting sun or daybreak again. Yet, it was during weeks such as these that we learned what it was to know God, to be totally dependent on Him, not only for life, but for companionship, for friendship. It was lonely out there and we learned to lean on Jesus and to walk with Him in a way we would not have learned in any other situation.

At home, life was becoming more and more difficult. We were all under a lot of stress with the pressures of the famine making such demands on us. The children and I were very much aware of the danger Rod was in daily, flying back and forth with food and personnel for the peace talks. Sometimes he didn't come home at night, and we didn't know where he was, or why he had not returned. The first thing they said when they got home was, "Is Dad back?" Dustin's second question was always, "What's for supper, Mom?"

GOD SPEAKS THROUGH THE COMPUTER

It seemed we were always watching the skies, listening for the plane. I had to learn again and again to trust in God concerning my husband's safety. Sometimes when praying I would have clear assurance that everything was fine. Other times I would be in such a panic I could not hear the voice of God. Once when Rod was three days late in arriving home, I more than panicked. Though I know the teachings on faith and fear, still I feared the worst and had no faith. I sat at the computer and opened up the Bible program. "I need to have faith, I need to **believe**," I told myself, and punched in the word "believe." I knew the Word would build my faith, but I was not prepared for the way God was about to speak to me. "Oh Lord, is Rod safe, is he hurt, is he alive?" I had asked. The very first scripture that appeared on the screen was Genesis 45:26, *"And they told him saying, JOSEPH IS STILL ALIVE, and he is governor over all the land of Egypt."* The words "Joseph is still alive" were just for me, straight from God. I was ecstatic! Not only was I positive that Rod was safe, but God Himself had spoken to me through the computer. How could I believe anything else?

Trying to live normally was not easy. People would come for dinner and then Rod would not have arrived home. "Where's Rod? How come he's not home?" they would ask. I couldn't exactly say, "He's flown a Member of the British Parliament into the Gorongosa forest to meet with Afonso Dhlakama," or "He's crossed the border illegally with a load of food and Bibles and I think he might have run into Frelimo!" The phone would ring constantly; Gostode would be back and forth with messages. There were always questions concerning Rod's activities that we didn't know how to answer. It was like being secret agents.

During a flight into the interior, a lump in my throat at yet another parting from my family, I heard God speak these words to me. "I am capturing you to myself for this time. You shall be wholly mine. No other call, no other voice shall come before mine. You shall be wholly mine!" The inmensity of God wanting **Me** was so great, I wept. He loves us so much and longs for our fellowship. That trip was a spiritual milestone for me, He was so close every step of the way. Sometimes during those weeks as I tramped through the bush with the Mozambican Christians, we would hear an aircraft, look up and see Rod's plane. He couldn't see us among the bushes, but he knew I was somewhere down there. So near and yet so far. The fact that our hearts were knit together in the same vision and purpose and in the same love for God made it bearable. While I felt pain to see the plane but was not able to reach out and touch, my heart would flood with joy and pride at the same time. Every spare seat had been removed in order to make more room for the food he was flying to villages where people were dying of starvation. Through all those separations, we were incredibly close. Sometimes we wrote notes to each other and sent them with couriers on foot. It was so exciting getting a note from Rod and the kids, it felt as if it was Christmas. I sent notes back which were passed on to Rod when he landed on the bush strips. Sometimes our notes never got to each other due to changes in plans on where to land, but we still wrote them just in case they did.

Separations, always separations. Sometimes we wrestled and struggled with the high cost of the call of God. Was this really His will for our lives? Did He really require this of us? The sobering question was always, "What if we give up?" Unthinkable. People would die of starvation and for lack of medicines. The Peace Process would have come to a total standstill, many times, if we had stopped our involvement. There was simply nobody else who would risk flying the way Rod was doing it. Most of all, thousands would die without hearing the Gospel if we did not go. There was no turning back! We **would** finish this race.

As a married couple, we experienced many things together that enriched our lives and relationship. After all, how many couples get to celebrate birthdays in the way described in this letter written from the bush.

The Regions Beyond   *29th September*
Wild Thorn Close
Baboon Hideout
Mozambique

Dear Friends,
    Today is Rodney's birthday and we celebrate in a unique way. We are temporarily in a brand new thatch house, specially built for us by loving hands last week. It is 3 x 3.5 meters big. The new thatch grass smells fresh and sweet. The mud-packed floor is still slightly damp, a natural cooling system refreshing our bare feet, as we peer through the small door, at shimmering heat waves.
    Birthday dinner consists of a scrawny chicken, nsima (dry grits) and sweet potatoes, the latter being a special treat. Chocolates hidden in my backpack to surprise Rod - a bit squashed and melted now, but mmm - superb!
    Our location is far into the interior of Mozambique, just as the above address indicates. We covered most of the distance by motorcycle on bush paths. A rough, uncomfortable ride, but certainly better than walk-

ing. We met with two troops of baboons, about fifty a troop. They seemed to enjoy watching the spectacle of bikes loaded with humans, Bibles, water containers and backpacks bouncing over the bumpy terrain. After some distance the path became so overgrown with thorn trees and scrub we had to abandon bikes and walk the rest of the way. We were being ripped too much by the long thorns. After about a five-hour walk we reached our destination and here we are. What better place to spend a birthday? (We can think of a few!) Nevertheless, we are glad to be here, about our Father's business.

One of the young boys here has a pet baboon. He wants us to take it back to Malawi with us and cannot understand why we are unwilling to accept his gift. I tell Rod it's the most unusual birthday present he could hope to have, but he doesn't like the idea of walking the baboon for five hours and then having it sit with the two of us on the motorcycle. He says it's hard enough keeping me in line, let alone a baboon added to that!

Our meetings are blessed and the people so glad to receive us and the Word of God. Thank you for your part in making it possible for us to be here through your love, prayers and support.

In the Service of Jesus Christ our Lord,
We are co-laborers in the Gospel,

Rod & Ellie.

Though we were pulled apart for seasons as a family, we were one in our commitment to God and to the commission He had given us. Looking back, we can truly say we do not regret the choices we made that led to such an unorthodox lifestyle. It is true that it was very tough at times, but it has been worth it all.

There are many that work in difficult and dangerous circumstances for their own cause. Many who don't even know Jesus give their lives for temporal humanitarian work. We should not be behind them in any good thing. How great the privilege to give our lives and energies for the eternal cause of Christ. It is the one cause that can never be lost, but has already been won!

As Gordon Lindsay often said, and lived it:

"Only one life, 'twill soon be past;
Only what's done for Christ will last." ❖

BUSH FLYING

CHILDHOOD DREAMS COME TRUE

When Rodney was a young boy, he dreamed of being a pilot. Growing up on a farm, he loved to watch the crop-sprayers. They swooped in low, sprayed, and soared up, repeating the pattern again and again. This was flying. He wasn't interested in becoming a routine commercial pilot; he liked the style of the crop sprayers. Rod's desire to fly was a very far-off dream. He grew up to attend an agricultural college and continued in farming, which he loved. The course of our lives was changed when God called him to till, plant and harvest in some of the roughest mission fields of Africa.

The desires of a believer's heart are many times planted there by God. He watches over them and brings them to pass at the appointed time. *"Delight yourself also in the Lord, and He shall give you the desires of your heart." (Psalm 37:4).* As we walk with God, His desires and ours merge, and we discover nothing is impossible with God.

Rod's flying was far more challenging than could ever have been imagined. His regular flight training could not equip him for the experiences that lay ahead. It is said that experience is our best teacher. It was certainly the only teacher that Rod had. With the guidance of the Holy Spirit he learned quickly and well.

FAITH FLYING

The first couple of years all our flying was done without navigation equipment. Hundreds of miles of jungle and bush showed very few landmarks. Small bush runways, not marked on any map, had to be spotted visually from the air. Flying just above treetop level much of the way did not give much time to pick them out. It was often difficult to know where we were. In later years we were given a Global Positioning System. It made an incredible difference and doubtless saved our lives on more than a few occasions.

The runways were chopped out of the bush with machetes. They were rough and sometimes had rocks or soft sand spots that we could not see. These were our "kangaroo" strips. We hopped and took off and landed several times before actually coming to a standstill. Taking off was the worst, lifting and touching down again before gaining enough speed to stay in the air. It seemed we were always short of runway and many a time made it by just a few feet. There was no way of knowing how these strips could handle a plane until it landed. Nor could we tell that the grass Savannah near the Zambezi River that looked so smooth was actually grass eight feet tall! As Rod came down, instead of the plane touching ground, it continued to sink into the tall grass. He couldn't see a thing except for flying grass as the propellers mowed the grass before him. Taking off in it was even worse! Sweaty palms and praying in the Spirit was part of flying.

One bush strip had trenches dug across it by the military years before. The local population filled these up and told us they had a good place for Rod to fly into. It looked good from the air, but on landing it felt like the plane would be smashed to pieces. The plane flew home with several dents and scratches in the paint. At the airport the ground staff shook their heads, wondering how Rod managed to mess his plane up so much while all other planes remained unscratched. Of course they didn't know what we had to land on most of the time.

Texas evangelist Lester Roloff tells of force-landing his

twin-engine plane on a freeway! Rod didn't have to worry about that happening to him, with neither highways, runways or roads – and certainly no traffic to try to miss!

WILD ANIMALS AND WEATHER

Wild animals like to come out of the bush into the open space of the grass strip to graze. That's how Rod hit a small deer with his wheel just before touchdown. Then on takeoff, a large herd of Kudu antelope ran across the strip. He avoided them by jerking the plane up over them. A flight with Rod is seldom smooth or uneventful.

Weather forecasts were not available and the bush strips had no windsocks. Countless times we set off for a place, then had to return or deviate into the unknown because of bad weather. Other times we had no choice but to fly through it with no IFR rating. The weather scared me more than any possible enemy attack. The worst was when one of the engines failed during bad weather. Another time one engine failed on takeoff. We had to try again; this time it worked. More often than not there was no communication with home when there were delays or if something went wrong.

Several times it rained just before we had to take off for home. The strips became muddy or water-logged. We had to lay sticks down so the plane wheels wouldn't sink into the mud. I said to Rod, "This is unbelievable. We've always had to push the truck through mud, I never dreamed we'd be pushing an airplane one day!" Perhaps one of the most incongruous incidents is when the ground where the plane was parked was so waterlogged, we had to get people to carry the plane to the top where it was drier. It was a dangerous area, and the plane could not stay there; we had to get out. With eight people under each wing lifting it as much as they could and forty people pushing uphill, the plane was finally at the top of the strip. Rod actually managed to take off in the mud. It was scary but when one is desperate one will try anything, and the more desperate we are, the more we tap into God.

RISK

Security was bad. How were we to know where and when the next attack would be? We scanned the skies, looking for enemy aircraft. We scoured the ground for any unusual activity. Sometimes we flew into trouble without knowing it. Through all the war years, our plane was only once hit with a bullet. It was hard having no backup or real contingency plans. A trip was needed and we went for it. If we crashed, there would be no medical help. If we were caught we'd be shot or imprisoned; nobody would know what had become of us. Trusting in God has proved over and over again to be sufficient, but it is difficult when one's faith is not on a high level. This happens to all of us at times.

Enemy aircraft was always a concern. Our Aztec was slow compared to any of the craft flown by Zimbabwean or Frelimo forces. Sometimes we had to leave our plane on the ground for several days while we went further inland on foot or by motorcycle. In these instances we covered the aircraft with branches to camouflage it as best we could.

We were half an hour's bike ride into the heart of the Gorongosa Forest when we heard the Russian Antonov circling overhead. I became very nervous, wondering if they would spot the plane from the air. If they did, they might drop a bomb on it and having discovered it, there would undoubtedly be a follow-up with paratroopers dropped in to shoot everybody. "Don't worry, they'll never see the plane," Rod said. I wasn't so sure. The Antonovs were used specifically for spotting unusual sightings or targets. They carried two bombs for the purpose of dropping them on anything suspicious. It wasn't long before we heard the first bomb drop. It was some distance off, not in the direction of the plane but the deep, heavy thud was disturbing. "Let's get to the plane before they do," we decided, and sped as fast as we could in and out of the trees on the bike along the winding path. On arrival at the airstrip we turned off the bike engine and could hear the Antonov coming closer. "Quick," said Rod, "take off the branches." We cleared the plane and got it to the runway; the Antonov was getting closer all the time. Rod started one engine and as it roared to life we could no longer hear the Antonov. To our dismay, the other engine failed to start. Again and again Rod tried, but the propeller turned a few times and stopped. By this time we did not know where the Antonov was, the one engine drowning out all the sound. I did what I knew to do best and began praying loudly in the Spirit. The engine started. Rod got the revs up and we lifted into the sky. Up, up, through the layer of clouds into a blue space. Above us was another layer of clouds. We flew the 45 minutes back to Blantyre sandwiched between the two layers of cloud, hidden from above and from below. It was perfect. As we approached the Chileka airport the layer of cloud below opened and we could see clearly to land. We felt so safe on that flight, cocooned by clouds, safe under the shadow of His wings.

For long trips, we had to carry extra fuel ahead of time, land in the bush and bury cans of aviation gas to hide till later, when out would come the shovel and we'd dig up the cans and fill the plane from our own little bush "gas station." I worried that someone might dig up our supply and it wouldn't be there when we landed for it. When the plane needed unexpected repair, Rod and his toolbox had to suffice. A Swiss army knife and Leatherman can work wonders! He could not carry much with him but God always provided. Like the time the wheel strut broke and Rod found a nut on an old discarded metal frame lying in the bush.

Night falls so quickly in Africa. It seemed we were always racing the sun and some of our delays on the ground were unavoidable. On one trip while flying Dhlakama and some of his men back to base we ran out of daylight. Rod had hurried and chased people all day but still there were delays. Now on landing, there was not enough light to see the strip carved out of the jungle, which was hard to land on even in daylight. Rod circled over the position and saw two bright lights at the end of what he knew must be the airstrip. Two of the soldiers had had the foresight to park the motorbikes with lights blazing at the end of the runway. On a low wing and a prayer, with all his extra senses and instincts finely tuned, Rod safely put the plane down in the dark jungle. If we **walk** by faith and not by sight, then we can surely **fly** by faith and not by sight.

A BROKEN NOSE WHEEL

Rod's trip to a place near Dombe, several hours' flight to the south ended in drama. Our newsletter reported as follows:

"We have had several close encounters in the past few months. Just recently, three abortive take-offs in a row. The sand on this particular airstrip is so soft and thick in patches that the plane just suddenly sinks when it's supposed to be gathering speed.

Right now our faithful bird is sitting on a far away patch of dirt with its nose on the ground, tail in the air, and propellers pinned into the sand. It is looking very sick and sorry. Rodney arrived home yesterday, dirty, smelly, unshaven and several pounds lighter. Praise God, he is still in one piece and smiling. He had to walk for three days in flip-flops through mined territory to a place where he could be picked up in a rescue operation. There was no place to get any food, but being mango season, God provided every day. What could be healthier than vitamin-loaded mangos?

It was some time before the children and I knew where Rod was or why he had not come home. On landing, the plane had hit a soft patch and the front wheel collapsed. The propellers slashed the ground and bent sadly out of shape. The people received the load of food but the mercy flights are on hold. Rod will have to hire a plane and return with special tools to remove the wheel and propellers. He will then have to take them all the way to Johannesburg, South Africa, for repair, fly back to Dombe and somehow get the plane flying again. This will take time, hard work and a few miracles. We know that the God Who has called us and appointed us is faithful to complete every good work He has started in us. For us it is a great honor to work in Mozambique. It is true that the price is high, but the joy in seeing lives touched and changed is far greater. Thank you for praying for us."

Three months went by before Rod was flying again. We continued the saga in another newsletter.

"The recovery operation was not easy but with the help of God and friends, nothing is impossible. The bush situation and conditions make an already complicated task rather daunting. Rodney had to hire a small plane and fly to where the Aztec was lying abandoned so he could remove the front wheel and propellers. These he brought back to Malawi and sent to South Africa for the necessary repairs. The propellers had to be replaced. He then flew commercially to Johannesburg to collect the precious plane parts himself. He again hired a small plane to go replace the wheel and propellers on the Aztec. Rod is not a qualified aircraft technician, but he is gifted and anointed by the Holy Spirit and as I always say, 'Rod can fix anything!' He flew back again and now had to find a pilot who would drop him off so he could fly the Aztec home again. Each flight is three hours there and three hours back. It has been raining consistently for a month and three days; dry weather was needed before the trip could be made. At last it was clear to fly. James, a Mozambican pilot operating out of Beira was willing to fly Rod in. A born-again Christian and a man of faith, he was a gift from God. He dropped Rod off and left him there to do all the finishing off of repairs.

On completion of the mechanics, Rod discovered another problem, fuel contamination. The wing tanks had water mixed with the fuel from standing out in the rain so long. Rod had flown cans of extra fuel with them but it was not enough to fill the tanks that now had to be totally emptied. Now what? Few planes flew in this area, but Rod could hear one not far off. He got onto his radio and started calling. He communicated with the pilot whom he did not know, and asked if he could bring him some fuel. The pilot who was flying to Beira said he didn't have enough on board, but would return with fuel after he had completed his journey. This pilot was true to his word and a ministering angel in the time of need. Rod drained the tanks as best he could but could not get every liter out, no matter how he rocked the plane. This meant he would have to fly with the risk of some contamination. He took off safely and landed periodically at various hidden bush strips, which he knew from his food-delivering route. Each time he drained off more water. Dangerous? Yes, but there was no other way."

It would have been easy to give up at this point but we're so glad we didn't. There was still so much in store for us and many victories for the Kingdom of God.

BLACK BOOK

We have a little black book signed by many of the people whom we flew into Mozambique. It is a very interesting book, especially the comments written by various individuals. The range of personalities is amazing. Some were bush people who couldn't write, they pressed their thumbprint on the page. Some were missionary friends who had come to share in our lives. Journalists came from many nations. Others were from the U.S. Senate, British Parliament and House of Lords. Almost everyone declared Rod to be the best pilot they had ever flown with. This, in spite of some hair-raising experiences encountered at times.

While some people love the adrenaline surge of bush flying in a war zone, others are terrified of flying in calm weather in the safest of situations. Rod liked to show any visitor the best of Africa when he could. Flying close to the Zambezi River he spotted a herd of hippo and swooped down so a group of journalists from Portugal could enjoy the wildlife close up. One of the men protested in terror, "What you doing, man?" "I'm showing you the hippos," replied Rod. "To h..*@#. with the hippos! I no wish to see hippos!" was the response. It was very funny. Another man once shouted, "Put me out. Let me out!" The strangest things are said and done in a panic. Dangerous too, like the man who grabbed the controls when Rod was maneuvering a tricky landing. He got such a shock at the narrowness of the strip in the forest, he decided that Rod needed some help. Rod gave him a thump to force him to let go.

The little black book also holds a message from a mother

who thought she might never see her three children again. While caught in bad weather conditions with no view of the ground except the 8,000-foot-high tip of Mount Mulanje poking through thick clouds, I was sure this was it! In the hopes that at least the little black book might be retrieved, I wrote, "Tell my children I love them."

Risks are not to be evaluated in the terms of the probability of success, but in terms of the goal. Bush flying has its hazards, but it is also a lot of fun and gives a sense of freedom and joy that is hard to equal.❖

FROM WAR TO PEACE

DHLAKAMA MEETS MUGABE

Rodney's willingness to assist in the Peace Process fast-forwarded us into situations that we would never have dreamed of. We met a wide spectrum of people and had unusual opportunities to share about Jesus. We saw this as another span of our mission work, a fascinating field to plant in.

When President Dhlakama was to meet President Mugabe of Zimbabwe face to face for the first time, it was Rodney who flew him from Gorongosa to Blantyre for the meeting. In view of our history, and being on Mugabe's "wanted" list for so long, this was ironic. More than ironic, it was hilarious. The Peace Process had advanced far enough for the age-old enemy, Mugabe, to request talks with Dhlakama. As Rod landed the plane in Blantyre, he sat talking with Dhlakama, who told Rodney of his concerns. He recognized the importance and progress of an official invitation from Mugabe, who in the past had only ranted and raved at his name. This new summit showed recognition of him as a Resistance Force leader with substantial support from the people, not simply the leader of a "bunch of bandits," as had been Mugabe's habit of referring to him.

"My friend, Joseph," Dhlakama spoke to Rod, "you know this is a very serious matter. I want you to pray for me. I need wisdom from God to know how to talk to Mugabe. He has caused much suffering in my country; his army has killed many civilians. We can forgive him, but he must not play games with us." Rodney spoke some words of counsel from his heart and prayed for his friend. "Thank you, my friend. Now I know everything will be good," answered the polite gentleman.

It was remarkably good. We were all amazed at Mugabe's favorable response. But we should not have been amazed; there were thousands of Christians praying for peace in Mozambique. Dhlakama had a winning manner. "You and I," he had said to Mugabe in Shona, "we are of the same tribal language. It is wrong that there should be war between us. We are brothers. Let us find a way to resolve our problems and bring peace to Mozambique." Something had obviously gotten through to Mugabe and we were very proud when we saw on TV that he acknowledged Dhlakama as a man of authority. "I have found him to be a very reasonable man, I believe he is a man of integrity," he said. It was fun, being on the inside and then watching the news. God has always had his people in unusual places, unseen, but effective. Rod flew Dhlakama back to his bush HQ again. As Dhlakama shared the details with him they laughed a lot and gave thanks to God. Mozambique had taken a gigantic leap towards peace through this meeting with Mugabe.

The book of Genesis acquaints us with another servant-leader known as "Joseph." He also was falsely accused, imprisoned, kept under wraps, remembered for filling men's sacks with food (incognito), navigating a nation through famine, and rising to a place of honor among rulers. And best of all (Gen. 39:21) "the Lord was with Joseph and gave him favor." Thank God for His Josephs! (Ed. note)

THE PEACE ACCORD

At last, in 1992, the Peace Accord was signed between Frelimo and Renamo. The inhumanity, suffering and despair that paved the blood-soaked road to this point, remains unknown to most of the world.

There is a historic picture of President Chissano and Afonso Dhlakama embracing one another after the signing of the peace agreement in Rome. It's an amazing picture. Staunch enemies of more than a decade, embracing in reconciliation. The picture was printed in international newspapers with a full report, parts of which are included here.

"Agreement to end the 16-year civil war was signed in Rome yesterday. One million people are reported to have died in this war.

The Italian-sponsored peace negotiations between the Mozambique government and the Renamo National Resistance Forces would have been unthinkable a short time ago.

Italy said it would step up humanitarian aid to ease the effects of a severe drought in Mozambique – three million people are threatened by death from starvation as a result of the drought.

The civil war broke out in 1975 after Mozambique received its independence. Apart from those who have died, millions more have lost their homes, forced to flee to neighboring states or into Mozambique's already over-crowded cities."

GENERAL PEACE AGREEMENT FOR MOZAMBIQUE

Rome, 4 October 1992

Joaquim Alberto Chissano, President of the Republic of Mozambique and Afonso Macacho Marceta Dhlakama, President of RENAMO, meeting at Rome, under the chairmanship of the Italian goverment, in the presence of the Minister for Foreign Affairs of the Italian Republic, Emilio Colombo, and in presence of:

H.E. Robert Gabriel Mugabe, President of the Republic of Zimbabwe;

H.E. Ketumile Masire, President of the Republic of Botswana;

H.E. George Saitoti, Vice-President of the Republic of Kenya;

H.E. Roelof F. Botha, Minister for Foreign Affairs of the

Republic of South Africa;

The Hon. John Tembo, Minister in the Office of the President of the Republic of Malawi;

Ambassador Ahmed Haggag, Assistant Secretary-General of OAU; and of the mediators: Mario Raffaelli, representative of the Italian Government and coordinator of the mediators, Jaime Conçalves, Archbishop of Beira, Andrea Riccardi and Mateo Zuppi of the Community of San Egidio;

and representatives of the observers: Dr. James O.C. Jonah, Under-Secretary-General for Political Affairs of the United Nations; H.E. Ambassador Herman J. Cohen, Assistant Secretary of State, for the Government of the United States of America;

H.E. Ambassador Philippe Cuvillier for the Government of France; H.E. Dr. José Manuel Durao Barroso, Secretary of State for Foreign Affairs, for the Government of Portugal; and H.E. Sir Patrick Fairweather for the Government of the United Kingdom; at the conclusion of the negotiating process in Rome for the establishment of a lasting peace and effective democracy in Mozambique, accept as binding the following documents which constitute the General Peace Agreement:

The President of the Republic of Mozambique and the President of RENAMO undertake to do everything within their power for the achievement of genuine national reconciliation.

The protocols have been duly initialled and signed by the respective heads of delegation and by the mediators. The present General Peace Agreement shall enter into force immediately upon its signature.

(Signed) Joaquim Alberto Chissano   (Signed) Afonso Macacho M. Dhlakama
President of the Republic of Mozambique   President of RENAMO

Both sides agreed to lay down arms. The United Nations was to activate and administer the demobilization of Renamo and Frelimo armies, a mammoth project. The agreement was that a new National Army made up of both sides would be formed. Few people had faith that Renamo would actually lay down arms.

In a private conversation Dhlakama said to Rod. "My friend. I give you my word, I make a promise to you, Renamo will not go back to war. It is time for peace. God has made the way for peace."

We believed him; he proved true to his word. Though provoked many times by Frelimo, who broke several agreements on numerous occasions, Dhlakama did not take up arms again. Amnesty was granted to all political activists. Everyone was now allowed to move freely about, regardless of political affiliation.

Amnesty was applicable to us, too; we were no longer on the "wanted" list in Mozambique or Zimbabwe. Mugabe had to pull his troops out of Mozambique.

The signing of the Peace Accord was to us a great personal victory. We had invested and risked our lives towards this goal. As we read the newspapers and followed each step we could through the media, it felt as if we were there in person. Of course the greatest thing was that the fighting would stop. Aid would come into the Renamo areas where the majority of the population lived. Rod would not be alone in distributing food. Medicines and aid workers would be available to the people. **So we thought.** We were yet to learn of the treachery and manipulation of world governments. It was not in the UN agenda for Renamo to win the elections. They continued to back Frelimo in attempt to weaken Renamo. Very little, and in most cases, no aid was delivered into Renamo zones. **People continued to starve and die while Frelimo areas received all the food and aid it could use.** People were tired of war, they were starving, and they wanted food. Within this scenario Frelimo launched its campaigning for the elections to follow in two years.

THE UNITED NATIONS

This glorious peace-keeping force that feeds the starving and clothes the naked – savior of a destitute and dying world, bringing an end to all war? We found within The McAlveny Intelligence advisor a definition of the New World Order that helped us understand how things worked. Reading it now, eight years later makes it even plainer.

"The New World Order is a world or global government under the United Nations which international elitists in the financial and power corridors believe they can install by the mid to late 1990's. The New World Order is being pushed by the world's most powerful socialists, communists, internationalists, occultists and New Agers. In January 1992, the leaders of the top 20 Western countries pledged that the UN would henceforth be used to police countries within their own borders, to put down civil wars that would no longer be tolerated. The plan is to move UN troops into any country in the world to keep the peace, put down insurrection, rebellion or opposition to the New World Order."

In the midst of all this, the Mozambique tragedy is but a small part of the game. To get rid of Renamo they would get rid of the people who supported them. Genocide through starvation. This was even simpler than bombing them. Renamo had laid down their arms; they would cease to exist when the people who supported them were dead.

Our ministry to the villages and famine relief continued. We sat with the people and wept with them when the massive food carriers flew over their villages to land in Frelimo zones. Empty promises, empty stomachs. As I sat beside a stricken girl holding her crying sister close, I penned these words on a scrap of paper.

Hush, little baby, please don't cry,
The UN plane comes in the sky
Bringing food for your little tummy
You won't have to die like our mummy.
Sissy's gonna get you a bowl of grain
To feed you, warm you, ease your pain.
Tomorrow? Next week? Never!

It was heartbreaking to see the hopes of the people fade as it finally dawned on them that the wonderful promises they had been given were not actually for them. We were angered as our own education concerning the New World Order was expanded. I started a new writing campaign, revealing incidents of food and resource manipulation being used to control the population in Renamo zones. When these reports were denied, we gave locations, photographs, factual first-hand evidence. Never underestimate the voice in the wilderness. We had friends who printed our articles and we helped make a difference, though change was slow and minimal.

The Renamo Office in Kenya was closed down. There was no need for it now, Renamo was told. They were free to operate from within Mozambique in any way they liked. This made things difficult, as all communication once more had to be made from the Main Camp now based at Maringue. The bush equipment was hopelessly inadequate. Gostode was returned to the bush too. This able young man no longer took messages over the phone nor played his part as representative. Instead, he was sent to an outpost where he waited for his turn to be demobilized. Only a core of soldiers would be kept at Maringue on standby until after elections. For many of them that day would never come. A new enemy lay in wait to steal them away before they could walk the path to freedom. The shadow of death moved swiftly and silently. Mozambique was hit by a Cholera epidemic.

KILLER CHOLERA

The famine continued for three years. During this period the Peace Accord held, though somewhat shakily at times. The food distribution was inadequate – many were still starving. Then came the terrible scourge of cholera. Inhaminga, like other places, was badly affected. The multitudes that moved through the town and those who stayed there did not have toilet facilities. People used sidewalks, empty buildings, the railway carriages, and just any place to go to the toilet. It was terrible. The town began to smell and when the first rains began to fall, the inevitable happened. Cholera spread like a flood, in refugee camps, villages, everywhere. Even places with sanitation were affected, though not as badly.

The Inhaminga hospital was full; people died daily. We did our best with medicines, and health care training. We flew in Soya protein foods for the sick who could not eat the hard maize kernels.

With the tragedy of famine, it seemed things could not get much worse, but cholera is a killer that strikes suddenly and does its work swiftly without mercy. Within hours of the onset of dysentery and vomiting, the unfortunate victim, already weakened by famine is dead. Rodney flew into one village where people lay all over the floor on mats in a bombed out building. Too weak to move, they stared into space, and died before the day was out. Villages were emptied of living souls as one after the other they buried each other, the remaining few moving on.

Maringue, the new Renamo Base Camp was not spared. The deadly disease swept through the ranks, cutting down the lives of strong young men. Rodney flew in to the Base and was shocked to find the usually active camp somber and in dread silence. No cheerful greetings, no smiles. At his desk Dhlakama sat with his head in his hands, tears on his face. "Joseph, my friend. Please, you must pray for us." Dhlakama told him in a low voice. "Today, sixty of my soldiers have died. Sixty in one day." They sat together in silence for some time and then Rod prayed. "This war," Dhlakama said. "This war could not destroy us. Frelimo and Zimbabwean troops could not destroy us. But this cholera, it can finish us. We need the help of God."

On one visit I asked to see Gostode. We had not talked for some time and I was anxious to see how he was getting on. I waited and waited, then finally a shadow blocked the light from the doorway of the hut I was sitting in. A slight figure walked unsteadily in. Hollow eyes tiredly squinted at me. A yellowed face marked with black spots from insect bite sores reflected a glimmer of hope at seeing me. "My Mother, are you well?" I could not believe this was Gostode. Gone was the round, smiling face. This was less than a shadow of the person we knew so well. I could not bear it. So close to going home, and he looked like he would surely not live. "It's OK. I am OK now," he assured me. "I have been very sick from the cholera but now I am OK." Gostode did get well and at last found his way back to Inhambane province from where he wrote telling us that he was the only son of his family, some of whom had survived the war. He found his father and various other family members for whom he took responsibility. His mother had died after stepping on an anti-personnel mine. We will always remember Gostode with special affection. He was part of our family in a time of trouble and we shared much together.

DEMOBILIZATION OF SOLDIERS

After 16 years of war, Renamo soldiers came in from the bush to hand in their weapons. Peace is so much more than the signing on a sheet of paper by warring parties. Unless the troops actually stopped fighting, there could be no peace. It was a remarkable feeling, driving along the bush roads and seeing soldiers laden with backpacks and a gun heading for the nearest demobilization camp. Hardship was not yet over for them. Barefooted, they had to cover long, weary miles with little food, sleeping in the bush just as they had been all these years. The difference was that this time the march was towards peace, not to battle. In the camps where the soldiers had to wait for weeks, sometimes months before the UN demobilized them, life was fraught with anxieties. Frequently there was not sufficient food in the camps. The men sat around with nothing to do waiting, waiting, and waiting.

They had been told a certain amount of money would be paid to them on handing in their weapons – to help them start a new life. The payments were slow in coming, some never received them. Their gun was all they possessed – their only security. It was a time for laying aside the weapons of war and looking to a future of peace and reconstruction of lives. We did our best to see that the old weapons of death and destruction were replaced with the Sword of the Spirit, the Word of God. Thousands of Bibles were stacked into the Aztec to be handed out personally. Now that amnesty had been granted, we were free to move through the borders by road again, and could load up the land cruiser and trailer with large consignments of Bibles.

The euphoria of the war coming to an end was tainted with the fears of a future without a job. Many of the soldiers did not know whether their families were alive or dead. Did they have homes to go back to? In spite of all this, optimistic hope reigned. They had been through so much, survived countless horrors; they could hold out a little longer.

Apart from continued relief flights into villages, showing the *JESUS* film in the demobilization camps became the focal thrust of our ministry for that season. Rodney made numerous trips to visit the soldiers, minister to them and give them Bibles. The response was fantastic. Having worked for so long in Renamo zones, Rod knew a great number of the soldiers personally. Coming in from far and wide, they were overjoyed to see him. Some he had not seen in several years. It was the most rewarding thing to see a soldier led to Jesus years ago, still walking with the Lord, carrying a much traveled, tattered Bible. To listen to their stories of how God had kept them through the years, listening to their hopes and dreams of finding their families, was a moving experience. Sometimes I sent in a special package to someone we had been particularly close to. The following letter of thanks was received from one of the soldiers.

"Dear My Mother, Mai. I have received your letter and box with many things. I thank you very much indeed. God bless you indeed. I was very happy to see Pastor Rodney this day of 19th May. I was full of joy. I jumped like a dog when sees its master, the tail never stop it dancing. I hope I shall see you soon also".

On one of our trips, while sitting under the shade of a scrubby bush, watching these men, I penciled the following words on a scrap of paper.

Returning Soldier

Through winter cold and summer heat
Ragged bodies with naked feet
Devour the miles of rugged track;
Gun in hand, heavy load on back.

Home is where at last they stop
At night, heavy load to drop;
Beneath the stars, bush or tree
Dream of love and liberty.

Through windmills of heart and mind
Names of those they long to find;
Smiles and faces like a flood
Are they washed away with blood?

Do you still live, childhood mother?
Where is father, little brother?
Our mud hut, does it still stand
Or wiped away by death's dark hand?

I have seen the bombs take their claim
To shatter, kill, destroy and maim.
A village, not unlike my own
Screaming in pain, in death alone.

Now guns are silent, peace is here
A chance to live and laugh is near.
Grant that I find those of my heart;
Then strength is mine, new life to start.

It was a long tightrope walk from war to peace. Some fell
and died. Others made it all the way. Some found their wives,
children and families. Some never did.❖

THESE BONES SHALL LIVE

BROKEN TOWN, BROKEN PEOPLE

Elevated fifteen feet high, standing with arms crossed over the head in the typical power pose of the Communist worker, the statue proclaimed its message of Marxist so-called freedom, ushered in by the Frelimo Regime when they came into power in 1975. The same freedom was responsible for the succession of bombings that destroyed many small towns in Mozambique. The once pretty town of Inhaminga was hit worse than most. In the park that had bloomed with beautiful tropical trees and shrubs, the statue now stood surrounded by stark devastation.

On the outskirts of the town, three kilometers (2 1/2 miles) of mass graves filled with the bones and skulls of thousands of victims serve as a stark reminder of Portuguese colonial oppression, followed by the greater cruelty of Communist persecution. Here hapless souls were lined up at the long trenches and shot, falling into the trench graves they had been forced to dig for themselves. Others were thrown in alive while bulldozers covered them with dirt. Their crime? Political insurrection against the Portuguese colonialists, and in later years those who resisted Communism suffered the same fate at the hands of Frelimo — who had learned this cruel method from their former masters. Then there was the other unpardonable offense: Christianity.

Frelimo was hard core Communist and any form of religion was forbidden. Worshippers of different creeds were machine-gunned down at their gatherings, or they were brought to the mass graves to die with others, criminals and innocent alike. These bones are there today. They speak. The blood of the martyrs cries out from the ground.

Now Inhaminga was one of the locations where the UN could land their big planes on the long grass airstrip. On hearing that thousands of people were walking to Inhaminga to line up at the food distribution point, Rodney flew in to the town we had always wanted to visit. "You've got to come and see this place," he told me.

My heart was filled with anticipation as the plane circled to land. It was as if I knew this place would play a significant part in our lives. Of course I didn't know, but I guess my spirit did. We landed on the best runway I had yet seen in Mozambique. There was a shiny new red tractor with a large trailer driven by some of our soldier friends to meet us. The tractor had been donated by an aid organization to haul bags of food from the airstrip to the town. We climbed on the back and were driven in style to town. People waved at us as we shouted "Hallelujah!" at them, and they shouted the same back to us.

It was like being in another world. What used to be a beautiful, thriving place of habitation, was now the shell of an obliterated town. Bombs had torn through buildings, demolishing roofs and walls. Rubble and decay lined the paved roads cracked and broken by the tracks of heavy Russian tanks. Gas stations stripped of their working mechanism mocked the abandoned cars and trucks littering the roads. These are burnt out, rusting heaps on disintegrated tires that will never run again. Telephone wires hang loose, trailing onto the roads. Old stoves and fridges slumped against cracked, peeling walls. Just a few weeks ago, this had been a ghost town evacuated of living humanity. Now, being one of the main points of food distribution, the empty shell was crawling with depleted life as thousands of skeletal civilians came pouring in from miles around.

As we walked through the throng, we were hailed by excited voices of recognition. "You are here!" The drought and famine had brought to a central point hundreds of Christians with whom we have worked through the years. People whose huts we had stayed in as we tramped from village to village, some of whom we had not seen for a number of years. Pastor Time and his family were there with others that had joined us on mobile missions. Their smiles appeared even wider on faces narrowed by the decrease of food intake. Laughter and slaps on the back stirred up the spirit of excitement in anticipation of the weeks ahead. Rod would leave me here to minister to the people. Marvelous how :he joy of the Lord can shine through in such devastating conditions.

With a trail of children behind us, we set off across the railway line where hundreds of carriages languish on their tracks. Overgrown with thorn and scrub, they have not moved in years. Lampposts lining the road spoke of a time when there was light in the dark streets.

A girl child with one leg came bounding up to us on crutches. It was Nina! What was she doing so far from home? She smiled happily at seeing us. This was the nine-year-old girl whose leg had been amputated at the Bush hospital after being bitten by a puff adder earlier in the year. She had journeyed for two and a half days on her crutches to accompany her family in their quest for food. Confidently she joined in the fun with the children and then actually outpaced them, her courage and clacking crutches moving her rapidly ahead of them.

The old hotel steps made an ideal preaching platform. Here travelers used to stop over on their journey to northern Mozambique. Piri Piri chicken and other delectable Portuguese meals were served in the hotel restaurant. Today we would serve the Bread of Life.

PROPHESY TO THESE BONES

Accompanied by their drum, our team sang on the steps, drawing the crowd to see who on earth had something to be happy about. Our hearts were moved with compassion as we looked across the sea of emaciated people. There were at least four thousand people stretching way down the road. For some it was too late. Their bodies would never recover from the harsh stripping of flesh from their bones. The famine mercilessly ate away at their existence. What does one say to such a people? It seemed everywhere we looked we saw **bones**. The buildings were bones, hung about with broken walls and windows. The burned out vehicles were bones, adorned with rusted paneling. Men once arrayed with strength were draped in dry, parched skin. The women were shrunken bags of bones, many with tiny bony bundles at their dried up breasts, or strapped onto their backs. The children, small skulls with enormous empty eyes.

I thought out loud, "Can these bones live? Oh Lord, Thou knowest!" Immediately we recognized the prophetic word for the hour. I called out to Luis, "Find Ezekiel 37 in your Bible, we are going to preach!"

"The hand of the Lord was upon me and set me in the middle of a valley; it was full of dry bones. He led me to and fro among them, and I saw a great many bones on the floor of the valley, bones that were very dry. He asked me, 'Can these bones live?' I answered, 'Oh, Sovereign Lord, You alone know!' Then He said to me 'Prophesy to these bones and say to them, O bones, surely I will cause breath to enter into you, and you shall live!'"

Luis read the whole chapter, the people listening intently. The quietness of the large crowd was remarkable. "Prophesy to these bones, and they shall live," we heard the Word of the Lord speak to us.

So we prophesied, and we preached, speaking hope, faith and creative life. We poured out our hearts to the people, telling them of God's great love for them. Most of them were heathens with little or no knowledge of God. Now they were hearing marvelous things, promises of life, hope of a better future. The impact of the Word was powerful. "Now prophesy to one another. Put your hand on your neighbor's shoulder and say, 'You shall not die, you shall live!' We could feel spiritual strongholds being torn down, the curse being broken as the voices of the people rose to a crescendo, speaking life to one another in the name of Jesus. It was awesome, never had we experienced anything like this. "Now prophesy to this town of Inhaminga. You see all the devastation, no vehicles moving, everything broken down and destroyed. The day is coming when you will see the walls being rebuilt, vehicles will travel again down these roads, shops will open and the market place will be full of food." The people lifted their voices in positive declaration. Then we prayed for peace. Most did not believe that peace would truly come to their shattered land. True, the cease-fire had been signed and at the moment there was no fighting, but how long before the killing starts again? They had lived so long under war and killing, they knew no other way of life. We prophesied that lasting peace would soon come to Mozambique. An encouraged people are a strong people. We saw people visibly standing up straighter. Though they had not yet eaten, it was evident that they had received strength. The food distribution was starting and it was time for them to take their places in line.

What a wonderful day it had been. I was so glad Rod had insisted on bringing me here and I knew that there was a purpose for it beyond the exciting events of the day. Standing there on the steps we made a new commitment to God. "Yes, Lord. These bones shall live. We shall help make this town live."

So began a new phase of our ministry as we started to invest our lives into the "city of bones." Commander Manuel, who had led our team the time we met up with Luis, "the Centurion, who gave his heart to Jesus," had been installed as the new administrator at Inhaminga. He had received Jesus during that trip and was baptized together with several other soldiers. Released from military duty to be effective in administration during the Peace Process, he was appointed to Inhaminga. We could not have asked for better. Here was someone who knew us and trusted us. Manuel insisted we stay at his house. After knowing him only in the bush, it was wonderful to walk into his home where his wife and two daughters now lived together with him. Separated during much of the war, they were overjoyed to be together again, and it was a happy group that sat down at a table with flowers in the center. It was certainly different from being in the army barracks or village huts. Manuel prayed over the meal, giving glory to God for bringing us together at such a place, for such a time as this.

Walking through Inhaminga was an experience of mixed emotions. To see the ruin and decline was sad, but to see people in the streets that had been empty for so long was exciting. We talked to those camping on the side of the road and watched as women lined up with their baskets for maize. Here was a problem. The maize was hard, unmilled kernels. There was no grinding mill at Inhaminga. How were these women supposed to prepare this food delivered by the UN? Traditionally, they pound maize in a huge mortar and pestle after letting it soak for two days to soften it. Then the heavy and lengthy work of pounding it begins. The people could not carry their mortar and very heavy pestles; they were too weak. Now they stood with whole maize in their baskets. We watched as the women made fires and put the seeds on to boil in the pots they had carried with them. The water was fetched from some distance, the pump wells having ceased to operate years before. The kernels boiled and boiled, more firewood was collected, more water was carried and still they were too hard to chew, especially for the little children. Families sat in huddles, children crying for the food they could see but could not eat. "How can people be so stupid as to send hard, whole maize to starving people?" We were angry. "Surely the UN can send in milled maize like we do?" Apparently not. We watched sadly as they tried to chew on the seeds. Mostly they swallowed them whole. For people in starvation, this could only be bad.

"We will have to put up a grinding mill here for the people to use," Rod, the practical helper, began to plan in his mind. "But how will you get it here? It wouldn't fit in the plane and the roads are not open because of mines. How would you run it?

You cannot buy diesel and oil here. Anyway, it would cost a fortune to buy a grinding mill!" Though I agreed with the desperation of the need, I could not see the way of doing it. "I'll find a way. I'll make a plan," were Rod's favorite words that had made so much happen already. I believed him. He would find a way, this waymaker.

We were eager to learn as much as we could about the history of the place. A few of the men and pastors we knew had grown up at Inhaminga. They knew the history of the town and told fascinating tales of days gone by. They pointed out homes, naming the people who had lived there, their job description, families. Many of these were Portuguese Colonials. "What happened to them?" we asked. Mostly the answer was "We don't know. War came and people had to run away to save their lives." They never returned.

In the town center was a beautiful twin-towered Catholic cathedral. Its stained glass windows caught the sun. There was even a bell in the tower. We climbed the steps and passed through the heavy wooden doors. Inside were wooden pews waiting patiently to once more hold worshippers. It was dusty inside from standing empty for so long. There was a headless statue of Mary and some of the stained glass windows had bullet holes; others were quite badly broken. A hole had been blasted through the roof on one side, probably by a bazooka. Bullet holes marked the walls on the outside where soldiers had sprayed with machine guns. This house of worship had been desecrated.

The clubhouse and recreational facilities were an incredible sight. Spacious buildings surrounded by gardens and a children's playground. There were swings, rusted at the hinges, seesaws, a merry-go-round with wooden horses, a Ferris wheel, a high slide and a jungle gym. These objects of delight had not moved on their hinges for at least seven years. They stood like ghosts peering out of the long grass, mourning the days of festivity. All this, waiting for the happy shouts of children, for the touch of young hands and feet to thrust them back into life. We could not resist. We shouted to the children, "Come, let's play on these things!" They looked at us blankly. They did not know what these things were. Where had they ever seen a playground before? There was only one way for them to learn – by example – so up the steps of the slide we went and slid down the other side. The children screamed with laughter, never having seen anything so hilarious as these white missionaries sliding down the weird object. It took a lot of persuasion to get them started, they were so afraid of the strange contraptions. In a few days, however, they were swinging, jumping and playing on it all. It was heartwarming to watch them. The equipment squeaked and creaked. "These bones shall live," its rhythmic baritone seemed to sing. The playground had come alive!

Exploring the grounds was amazing; we just never knew what we would find. To our surprise, there was an Olympic-sized tiled swimming pool! It was empty. A large grandstand stood on one side. There were changing rooms and plumbing facilities which of course did not work. A paddling pool with a concrete elephant slide was overgrown with a beautiful pink creeper. Through the bush and thorns, the brave flowers proudly displayed their ability to survive in the face of all odds. "Just like the people," I thought.

There was a basketball pitch and a soccer field. There were even underground dressing rooms for the soccer players to come running out of. "We'll start with soccer," Rod said. He spoke to a group of youths, promising them a real soccer ball next time we came if they cleared the field of brush. It was exactly what they needed, to be given a task with incentive in place of lolling around with nothing to do. Within two days the soccer field was being trampled into shape through play, and people were cheering on the grandstands. They had made their own ball from bits of rag, plastic, strips of tree bark, whatever they could find, rolled into a tight ball. "These bones shall live!"

We preached every day. There were a lot of Christians around, but mostly unbelievers. It was wonderful to see souls added daily to the church. Pastors of various denominations built new pole-and-thatch churches and as the people continued to flock in, they found their respective places of worship and set up camp nearby. At night we gathered the leaders together for special meetings. This was a day of new beginnings for Mozambique. People would soon begin to relocate, leaving refugee camps and places of hiding to return to their old homes. We prayed and interceded for the nation, for the church. We discussed strategies and plans that the leaders could begin to implement in preparation for the spiritual harvest that would follow freedom of speech and movement. A whole new life was opening up. We planned on finding a place where we could set up a Bible School to equip men in the Word and work of God.

We were eager to see and learn as much of the area that we could. The more we could learn, the better would be our understanding of the people and what they had been through. "Show us everything," we said to Manuel and our guides. "Everything?" Pastor Time asked, a shadow crossing his face. "Yes, we want to see everything that has touched and affected the lives of Mozambicans." That was when they told us about the mass graves. "But we cannot go there. Nobody goes there now," they said. "We want to see." we insisted. "It is important for us to know what is here at Inhaminga."

MASS GRAVES

The following afternoon the tractor took us part of the way as it was quite a long walk. We drove down what used to be a road, branches and thorns snatching at our bare arms. The driver stopped the tractor and we were told it was time to start walking as there were land mines on the road and the tractor might detonate one. We walked along a path where the grass was so tall we could barely see over the top. "Look, here is the old prison." Pastor Time pointed out a building with bars at the small windows. "This is where they put the accused, then at night they came and took them to the graves where they killed them." It was very quiet; we all spoke in low voices as we continued the journey. "We are here." It was difficult at first to discern what was around us. Long lines of earth mounds stretched ahead. "Where are the graves?" I asked. "These mounds are the graves." I stared, then realized that we were actually standing at the edge of the graves. For three kilometers, the mounds stretched like low sand dunes, row upon row. We could not see the end. Shrubs and wild brush grew in patches, but mostly it was just hard, baked earth. We were standing on the ground from which the blood of the martyrs cried out. My soul felt crushed within me. I sobbed. How could people still live in hope when they had seen so much suffering? Words from the scripture flowed through my mind. *"Through the Lord's mercies we are not consumed, because His compassions fail not." Lamentations 3:22.* Yes, it is only through the mercy of God that people can live again, hope again, and have courage for the future.

Here, people had died, some crying and pleading, some silently. As my tears fell on to the dried earth, again the Word of the Lord came to me concerning Inhaminga, *"These bones shall live."* We all joined hands and prayed together there at the mass graves. We prayed for the people who were desolate, hearts that were broken because of the war. We prayed that the time of weeping would be replaced by a time of joy, and that from the seed of the blood of the martyrs would come forth a great harvest of souls for the Kingdom of God in Mozambique.

FIRST CHRISTMAS AT INHAMINGA

It was one of those events that should be recorded in history to warm the hearts of mankind. We believe it is chronicled in the annals of heaven. In December 1992, the love and joy of Christmas came to the ruined "city of bones". "Peace on earth, good will to all men." The service was in the bullet-ridden cathedral with the bazooka hole through the roof. Joining us was our special friend, President Afonso Dhlakama. Rod made the fifteen-minute flight from Inhaminga to Maringue twice to collect Dhlakama and members of his Cabinet as well as several of his top military contingency to attend the ceremony. What a sight it was to see the gleaming tractor coming from the airstrip with the dignitaries sitting on chairs in the trailer. They wore suits and ties; even Rod was in a suit. People had come for miles, dressed in their rags – which were all they owned. They filled the church and overflowed onto the street.

Though we were in the Catholic cathedral, the service was non-denominational. The Roman Catholic priests would return some day, but in the meantime we were the only missionaries who had ventured into Inhaminga.

There were at least one thousand bush people crowded into the cathedral. They filled every inch of floor space and hung over the balcony railings as they packed in. Rodney had replaced the rope that was missing from the church bell and did we ring it! So long – too long – it had been silent. We could almost hear the bells of heaven ringing in unison to the joyful sound.

It was a momentous occasion for each person there. Chris and Fernanda had worked hard to teach a choir some songs in Portuguese. They had shown the children how to perform a nativity play and dressed them up using whatever garments and scraps of cloth they could find for costumes. The children were precious and their presentation a beautiful expression of the simplicity of the birth of Christ. To barefoot, ragged children such as these He came. A large group of our pastors and church leaders exuberantly sang carols in Portuguese and Sena. They looked so neat in their suits, shirts and ties which we had received in boxes from Christians in England. Their feet were bare, as we did not have shoes for them, but they did not look out of place in this cathedral where past splendor and the ugliness of war stood side by side. Their faces beamed with the joy of the occasion.

Rodney shared the Word of God, exhorting us all to follow the example of Jesus, who did not remain a baby but grew up to be a man of courage and vision, obedient to His Father's will. He challenged the Christian men, in particular, to take their place as leaders among the people in the new Mozambique – a place of authority, as well as servanthood; to be vitally involved in the restoration and building of the land. Most of all, to go out and preach the Gospel and make disciples.

The President of Renamo also spoke, giving glory to God for the miracle of the occasion. He shared his heart concerning his desire for the nation and stated several times that without the help of God it could not happen. He ended his talk with a forceful "Hallelujah!" and a beaming smile.

A Portuguese reporter and camera crew from one of the top media agencies was present and filmed almost the whole service. This was viewed on Mozambican as well as International TV. Excerpts from the news reports as follows:

"Today we are gathered in this church to worship God and celebrate Christmas," the President of Renamo, Afonso Dhlakama said yesterday, December 23, 1992, at Inhaminga, where Christians of various denominations came together to celebrate Christmas for the first time since Mozambican Independence, 17 years ago. With the signing of the Peace Accord last October, the population dispersed by the war is beginning to return to their hometowns. It is to this bombed shell of Inhaminga and many others like it that the people are returning and starting life all over again. The returning population is currently carrying out major clean-up efforts, but it will be some time before Inhaminga is restored.

"I have much joy in seeing these children singing and participating in this Christmas program. The Mozambican child, through Communism, was denied the knowledge of the birth of Jesus Christ. With independence in Mozambique, Christmas was no longer celebrated. The 25th of December became simply a public holiday known as Family Day. Jesus, the Messiah, came as a baby in humility. He was rejected, hung on a cross. He suffered among men, but His birth and life show us the way to God. Though we have many needs, our greatest need is to recognize that we need the help of God and of one another to build the new Mozambique in peace. The past cannot be

altered, but we can change our future. The time for reconciliation has come. I appeal for all Mozambicans to come together
and pray for God's help for our country."

A Christmas dinner following the service was served outside the church. The preparation and cooking was done by
Renamo soldiers. Dhlakama walked among the people, as he
loved to do, talking with them, playing with their children,
affirming his commitment to them and the nation. In a time of
famine the poorest of the poor were feasting. Their chattering
voices and laughter rang through the air. Christmas is such a
wonderful time of anticipation and promise. It was a miracle to
witness a celebration so exciting and joyous as here in "the city
of bones" where no wrapped gifts were exchanged. It was wonderful. Who would have ever thought this possible?

OUR BOMB-SHAKEN HOUSE

Jesus said that those who left house and home for His
sake will receive back a hundredfold on this earth. We do indeed
have many homes. At Inhaminga the house next to the soccer
field was given to us to use by the Renamo Administration. It
had survived the bombings and numerous attacks surprisingly
well. The roof was intact except for a large hole blown out by a
bazooka. A fire had broken out and burnt some of the ceiling
and blackened the walls on one side of the house. The outside
walls were pockmarked by machine guns. There was scarcely a
window that had not been shot to smithereens. The shell of a
200-kilogram bomb lay near the front door. It became a good
potplant stand.

General clean-up and some basic repairs were begun. We
were delighted to discover an underground water cistern and
cleaned it out so it would be ready to catch the first rains. Dustin
painted it with sealer so it would be fresh and not leak. He was
a great help; he filled up the numerous bullet holes in the water
storage tank on the roof that served the bathroom and kitchen.
The blocked and broken plumbing had to be cleared and
replaced. What excitement when at last the toilet had a seat and

we could flush it with a bucket of water!

The carpenter made us a double bed with a cleverly carved hunting scene on the headboard – a hunter with a bow and a small dog hunting a lion. The African dreams of success in the big hunt while he sleeps. With no electricity, we scratched around for matches and candles in the dark. We got rid of the rats during the first week – a blessed relief. The pigeons roosting in the roof added interest to home life as they flew in and out of the house through the shot-up windows. No telephones here, no television, just each other. It's a good way to live.

Our ministry to other places in Mozambique continued while we visited Inhaminga as often as we could. Life returned to normal bit by bit, day by day. We started work on the hospital, which was so overgrown with bush and trees it could barely be seen from the road, in spite of being one of the largest buildings around. At one time it had been a beautifully equipped facility. It was spacious and well planned. Now only one wing remained undamaged from the bombings. Our first task was to cut away the bush, clear out the rubble and clean the walls and floor. With little water available this was not easy. Rod started a food-for-work program involving the local population, and before too long we could use the wing. We flew in loads of medicines; Jane and her crew spent some time working there together with other periodic volunteers. We put out word to other Christian organizations to help with equipment and were delighted when Dorcas Aid from Holland sent a container with 40 beds, complete with bedding and various other supplies and medicines. In time, the Red Cross got involved, and the situation continued to improve. But for a long time it was known as "Joseph's hospital."

One day we arrived at Inhaminga to some very sad news. The tractor and trailer had taken a load of food out to Mdoro. On its way back, loaded with people, it hit a land mine. Nineteen people were killed and fourteen injured. Some of the bodies could not be recovered. Mangani, one of our team members lost his daughter and one of the Christians from Pastor

Time's church died. It was tragic. Though the fighting had stopped, the effects of war continued.

By God's grace, Rod had brought a large consignment of medical supplies a few days previously. The hospital had been depleted of supplies, but now at this crucial time drugs and anesthetics were on hand. A boy's leg was taken off with a hack saw; we would have to find an amputation saw for the hospital at Inhaminga.

God is faithful to answer our prayers, and through a lot of hard work and faith, Rodney installed a grinding mill at Inhaminga. The mill was donated by Tear Fund, a British Christian organization. We could never have done so much for the people without the generous help of Tear Fund.

To get the mill to Inhaminga was like moving a mountain. No way could it fit in the plane complete. Rod dismantled it and flew it in from Blantyre to Inhaminga in three loads. He had to bring cement to cast a floor, wait for the floor to dry before he could drill holes in so he could bolt the mill down as he assembled it again. The town began to buzz with excitement. Joseph had brought them a grinding mill! Diesel and oil had to be flown in. The people gathered to watch, and then when the engine started with a roar, pouring out soft, milled flour, they ululated and cheered with joy. It was a difficult and expensive operation, but it changed life as well as saved lives.

The mill was run by our team with Mangani in charge. Before the war he had operated a grinding mill; now he was here for such a time as this. We did not charge the people to have their maize milled. Few of them had money. They gave a small portion of their maize as payment. This was mixed together with Soya protein and milled to feed the hospital patients, the aged and infirm, and the orphans. Above the mill we hung our "Afrika Wa Yesu, Jesus is Lord" sign. Here the team sang songs of praise and shared Jesus with those who came to the mill and those who walked by. Inhaminga was beginning to live!❖

GOD HEALS THE GENERAL

The narrow footpaths that wind through the Gorongosa forest are only wide enough for one-way traffic. A collision between two motorcycles coming from opposite directions, neither rider hearing the other above the roar of their engines, caused critical injuries for General Mateus Nyogonhama. General Mateus had many times escorted us through the war zones to the villages on our preaching missions. Now, propelled several feet into the air before violently impacting the hard ground with unprotected head (no crash helmets being available), it seemed his vital life might be lost. With this incident occurring out in the bush, no medical assistance on hand, it was necessary to arrange for a mercy flight to a hospital in Malawi.

It was 12 hours before the seriously injured general landed in Malawi. He was taken to a small military hospital one hour's bumpy ride away, where we found him the following night, still untreated. He was unrecognizable, his head almost double in size, features totally lost in the massive swelling. The general's arms were tied to the bedposts to stop the wild thrashing and futile attempts to get up and out. He was out of his head and the nurses were terrified, their African superstitions and traditions overriding medical training and common sense. They ran away and the delirious man was left alone, tied down.

Rodney looked in shock at his friend. Could a man in such

condition live? Taking firm hold of the thrashing hand, he began to speak close to his ear. The response was instantaneous. The general lay still and listened. When Rod asked him to press his hand if he could understand, he squeezed it and held on as if to a lifeline as Rod started praying for him.

It was obvious that if Mateus were left here unattended he would die. Permission to take him to another hospital was refused. The concern was, who would take responsibility for getting the dead body back to Mozambique? We said there would be no dead body, but yes, we would take responsibility for whatever happened. We carried the general to our land cruiser, laid him on a mattress in the back and started off for what we believed to be the best hospital in Malawi.

The three-hour journey became the battleground for the general's life and soundness of mind. To see our friend in such a state was a terrible shock. We could not bear to see this strong, authoritative man who had frequently accompanied us on our preaching missions and ultimately accepted Jesus, so close to death. We prayed out loud as we drove, resisting the spirit of death hanging over our friend, commanding it in the name of Jesus to leave.

Before being airlifted out of Mozambique, the general, during a brief return to consciousness had told the distraught President of Renamo at his side that he was very sorry to let him down at such a crucial time, but he knew he was dying. General Mateus was a key man in the current Peace Process, the disarming of soldiers, and a vital part of the preparation of a new joint army. He apologized for leaving so many important assignments uncompleted, then lapsed into unconsciousness. Now we addressed the general very firmly as we bounced along the road. "You shall not die! You shall live to complete your work and continue to serve your country!" We spoke this over and over again.

At 1:00 a.m. we reached the hospital and finally got the patient stabilized, an IV inserted and X-Rays taken. The pictures showed four breaks in the skull with a piece of bone protruding into the brain. Then at 7:00 a.m. we were told to move him to another hospital as nothing could be done for him there. Back into the land cruiser he went. As we headed down the road a deluge of rain so heavy that we could not see two inches in front of us, held us up on the side of the road for another hour. Knowing that each moment was crucial and too much time had already elapsed, we were very concerned. After another hour we reached the Central Hospital in Blantyre where we had been told to take him, as it was the only facility with the equipment needed for brain surgery. "Sorry, we have no space; we have no room for another patient," we were told. The Central Hospital, though large, was indeed full to overflowing. Patients lay on the beds, under the beds, in the corridor, on chairs, on couches, everywhere! There was still another hospital we could try. Perhaps they could keep the patient stabilized until we could arrange a flight to South Africa, where he would certainly receive the urgent attention he needed. What a relief when the general was admitted, in spite of the overcrowded conditions. We were thankful when a doctor came quite quickly to give a very thorough examination. He told us that medication would be given to bring down the swelling before any surgery could be performed and it was inadvisable for our friend to be taken on a long flight at this time.

At last we knew that something was finally being done for the general. It was now 24 hours since the accident; exhausted, we returned home for a few hours sleep.

For five days and nights the general had a private nurse constantly at his side. We visited him several times a day, praying, reading the Word of God out loud to him, playing Christian songs on the tape recorder. All this entered his subconscious mind. He was responding to treatment and the swelling was going down. His eyes, having been totally covered over by the swelling became visible, but he could not see. The doctor had some hope for the left eye but said the right eye was totally blind. Refusing to accept this, we read James 5: 14-15 to the general. We anointed his head and eyes with oil and believed for his healing. He improved daily and the first sentence he spoke to Rodney was **"God has touched me. He has saved my life!"** His left eye opened and though blurred, there was some vision; still no vision in the right eye. By the sixth day he could sit up, then walk a bit with two people holding him up, one on either side. The medical staff were astounded and agreed a miracle had taken place.

The doctor and hospital staff did not know who this man was. They knew only that we were missionaries and this was a friend of ours from Mozambique. What they would have done if they knew they had a Renamo General in one of their beds, we do not know. The Frelimo government had a pact with the Malawi government that no Renamo soldiers should be allowed in Malawi and certainly should in no way receive help of any kind. Though Mateus was improving daily, his mind was very muddled, and he spoke often in a general's voice about military matters. He insisted he had an urgent message for the president and wanted paper to write it on. The nurses looked more than a little confused. We gave him the paper and he laboriously wrote out long messages in illegible writing. He wrote off the page onto the bed without knowing it. Sweat poured down his face at the effort of exerting his mind, but he battled on. We continued to pray for his obviously brain-damaged mind. Having seen God do so much for him already, we did not doubt that God would heal him totally. We pushed for his soonest possible discharge from hospital and on the ninth day the man who was not expected to live was released from hospital. He was still weak and in need of bed rest and great care. The doctor assured us he would not normally allow a patient in this condition out so early, but as we were certain we could take good care of him, he consented.

HIDING THE GENERAL IN OUR HOME

We brought General Mateus to our home where we nursed him for several more weeks. A Renamo bush-medic stayed in his room with him at all times. He had come in civilian clothes but the only shoes he had were military boots, which we replaced with ordinary shoes. If it were known that we were keeping the general and this Renamo soldier in our home, we would be facing trouble indeed. How we managed to keep it all secret is a miracle, especially when a group of five Renamo soldiers showed up to come and personally see for themselves that their friend and commanding officer was indeed alive. With much rejoicing, noise and laughter they visited him on several occasions while Ellie baked cakes and made them all feel at home. They all watched the *JESUS* video, and we used the time to challenge them spiritually. Adullam's Cave was in full use again.

We, as a family, enjoyed our guest. It was exciting to see him improve daily. His mind was clearer every day. We put him through the paces, throwing a lot of questions at him, and finally we were assured that his mind was absolutely sound. We were in doubt the first day he poured very hot chili sauce all over his food and ate it with gusto. How could anyone in his right mind eat such hot stuff in such quantity? He had an appetite like a horse and though he enjoyed my cooking, he asked nostalgically for some of his home favorites, such as corn and chicken roasted on an open fire outside.

What excitement when vision cleared in his left eye and also returned to the blind right eye. For some time he had double vision which made it quite difficult to maneuver through the door without walking into it when he got out of bed at dinner time to join us. He waited eagerly each day for the children to return from school. Dustin chatted with him about airplanes and motorcycles and Deborah played with her dolls on his bed. Much of his time was spent sleeping and listening to Christian preaching and praise and worship music tapes.

Halfway through his stay with us, we got him to the office when the President of Renamo called for the latest news on his progress.

"Hold on, Sir, I've got someone who wants to talk with you" Rodney told Dhlakama. The relief experienced by the president at hearing his general's voice was enormous. "Is it really you, General Mateus?" The conversation that followed proved that it indeed was, for no one else knew of the matters they discussed. Always the polite gentleman to the extreme, General Mateus apologized to the president for his absence from his post and delay in returning. He would be back very soon, he said, to make that important journey to Zimbabwe.

Within a month of the accident the general was fit enough to return to Mozambique. He would have to take things quietly for the first few weeks but could begin some of his work. By this time he was chomping at the bit to get back to the movement. Looking very smart in the new clothes we had procured for him, he thanked us over and over again for our hospitality. We simply assured him it was our pleasure and privilege to return some of the hospitality we had for so long enjoyed from him. Rodney flew him home while he keenly watched out the window for familiar landmarks, which he pointed out with much enthusiasm. He had flown many times with Rod and the two have shared many adventures together. As the plane approached Maringue, Rodney circled low over the camp. They all knew this was the day of the general's return and already some people were waiting on the airstrip while others came running through the bushes to witness the event. Many had not believed the report that General Mateus was alive. Having seen him at the time of the accident, they did not believe he could live. Then there were rumors that he was alive, but quite mad. There was a hushed silence as Rod opened the door for the general to climb out of the plane and then loud cheers of greeting. The people were positively beside themselves with joy to see their military leader. They came to greet and salute him, their fears and doubts wiped away. The man they had so much confidence in was alive and well, to continue to fill his part in leading the nation through the tricky Peace Process.

Within the arena of our mission work in rural

Mozambique, we enjoyed the unique privilege of meeting and making friends with a wide range of people hidden from most of the world. From the little child who has never before seen a white face, the woman who has never owned a dress, the man who fights for the survival of his family with bare hands out of barren fields in vain hope of food, to the high-ranking army officer who fights for them all in hopes of a better country, a better life, a greater dream. To see some of these greater dreams become reality is tremendously exciting. One year after the accident General Mateus was given a top position as Chief of Staff of the New Mozambican Army.

With the Peace Process well under way, the cream of both Frelimo and Renamo forces was put into joint training under British soldiers in Zimbabwe for the purpose of forming a new, non-political Mozambican Army. The Chief of Staff was chosen on merit, and General Mateus passed through the course with the highest honors. This was significant in that regardless of who won the elections, this Renamo general would hold a high position in the new army! God had a purpose in sparing the general's life.❖

MEANWHILE, BACK
AT THE RANCH

Incredibly, while all these events were taking place in Mozambique, the Malawi Mission continued to grow. When we were not in Mozambique, much of our time was spent on outreach, seminars and periodic six-week Bible training courses in Malawi.

Then the day of trouble came. Pastor Chakanza's sudden death affected the church badly. The cause of death was never known; an autopsy is seldom carried out in Malawi. Superstition and the power-seeking greed of man caused much confusion; wild rumors of witchcraft being the cause of death were circled about. There was no man to adequately fill Pastor Chakanza's place, and we had a succession of disasters as corrupt men tried to take control and rule the church. For a couple of years they succeeded. This was not one of our mission success stories. It was a fight for survival and much rot was revealed. We really could not afford the energy and trauma of fighting this spiritual war in Malawi, as well as what we were facing in Mozambique. So many times we were tempted to wash our hands of the situation and continue only in Mozambique, but we couldn't. Too many voices from the congregation begged us to stay on and help restore order and purity. It seemed an impossible task, and if it were not for the faithfulness of many of the brethren who had risked their lives alongside ours in Mozambique for so long, we would have given up. We could not abandon them now. They were as sheep without a shepherd, and plenty of wolves were about. Rod's perseverance and patience at last won through. During this period his own ministry developed into something deeper; he became more than an instructor and innovator, he became a father. As the Apostle Paul writes in *1 Corinthians 4: 15, "For though you might have ten thousand instructors in Christ, yet you do not have many fathers; for in Christ Jesus I have begotten you through the gospel."*

The church building project, started just before Pastor Chakanza died, was completed. Rod worked incredibly hard on it while many mocked. It is a great building, and today the church at Nsanje is totally run by Malawians with Pastor Rodgers Alufazema as the leading pastor. Together with Pastor Kennedy Ndaluza and four other men, the church is autonomous and runs without the help of white missionaries. Africa reaching Africa; men who have been through the fire and have come forth purified to the Glory of God, fulfilling the great commission in every sense. This is true missions success, when the missionary is no longer needed. We remain in close fellowship with the church at Nsanje, visiting when we can, and receiving visits from them at the Inhaminga Base.

FAMILY TRIALS

Our days were difficult, overcrowded with many responsibilities. In the midst of it we were trying to keep a family together – something we failed to do as well as we would have liked. Tammy finished school and left home to find a job in Zimbabwe. It was a terrible wrench and we missed her sorely. Dustin finished school and his wish was to take a year out just to be with his Dad before deciding on any career. We were very happy with this, but then just four days after his 17th birthday, he had a terrible motorcycle accident. It was not his fault; a careless driver turned in front of him and smashed into him. Dustin was thrown over the top of the car. Fortunately, the lady in the car behind him, who witnessed the accident, picked him up and took him to hospital. Dustin was able to give our telephone number and we were with him very quickly. His left leg was too badly damaged for the doctor to handle and they advised that we should take him to the government hospital, where a foreign specialist was visiting. Dustin had lost a tremendous amount of blood and was very weak. The Queen Elizabeth Hospital in Blantyre was short of medicine, over-crowded, and woefully inadequate. For four hours Dustin lay waiting for a doctor in a humid, airless ward packed with patients whose families lived under the beds to help care for them. The specialist never came. Rod arranged for a private emergency flight to South Africa, but as we were about to take Dustin to the airport, the doctor came and advised us not to move him as his condition was too serious to stand the five hour flight. He would clean the leg immediately; Dustin needed blood and should be stabilized overnight before being flown out the next day. It was a nightmare. One of the doctors warned us about something we already were concerned about: Aids. We asked that Dustin should receive blood from us, and not from the hospital blood bank. Malawi is near the top of the list for Aids in Africa. Some of the staff became very angry, accusing us of being racist. It was most unpleasant and we had to fight for over an hour while our son became weaker and weaker. Finally they conceded and our son received our blood.

THANK GOD FOR FRIENDS

Our friends, Tim and Sally Salmon, were there for us in the time of need. They arranged an ambulance and hospital for Dustin on arrival in South Africa. The flight was a time of near-ness to one another and to God. Dustin kept wanting to know, "What are we flying over now?" We flew over Mozambique for much of the way and Rod would say, "We're over the Zambezi River now, remember when....?" or "We're near the Main Camp now, remember when.....?" Dustin was incredibly brave and uncomplaining in spite of being in so much pain. He was not allowed to drink anything because they expected him to have surgery on arrival, so he was very thirsty. I helped him rinse his mouth frequently and kept his cracking lips as moist as I could. We shall never forget that flight.

He had the best care at Klerksdorp and Pastor Tim's church members were wonderful. The young people visited Dustin daily through six long, painful weeks on his back. His leg was in traction and had an eighteen-inch-long steel pin in place of the badly shattered bone. He also had a fractured wrist. On arrival he was wheeled into surgery to have his spleen removed. With us praying outside the surgical ward, and our friend, Dr. Mig, who had been to Mozambique with us on mission, praying in the O.R., a final examination revealed Dustin no longer needed the operation. They warned that it would be 48 hours before we would know if Dustin's life was out of danger. How grateful we were to be told later that he would be OK.

I spent two weeks at his bedside and we spoke about so many things, big and small. We could not stay with him the whole time and after two weeks had to return to Malawi where Deborah was still in school, and hungry people waited in Mozambique for food. How grateful we were and are to Tim and Sally Salmon and those who loved and cared for Dustin during that difficult time.

At last we drove the long way from Malawi, through Mozambique and through Zimbabwe to South Africa to bring Dustin home again. It was our first time to be in Zimbabwe since we had to flee eight years before. With amnesty having been granted through the Peace Process, we were free to return. It felt good to drive through our own land, but we had one goal in mind: to get to our son in South Africa.

We were shocked to see how thin Dustin was. He was very weak still and needed to use crutches for a long time. We took a few days vacation and went to the fun park where Dustin tried every ride he could get on. Christmas was just a few days away and we had so much fun. It was a great time but not without incident. While we felt free and at ease from the tensions and years of danger we faced in Mozambique, the enemy had another scheme of attack. South Africa was not without its problems and today has one of the highest crime rates in the world. We were appalled to see a taxi van with a sticker on the back "Kill a White a day." While happily chatting as we drove along the road we realized it was time for Dustin to have his medication. The water bottle was out of reach, so we stopped on the side of the road to get it for him. Suddenly, there was a loud crack and the car filled with gun smoke. A passing car had driven very close and shot at Rod's open window. Hey! This was supposed to be our time of rest and relaxation! Thankfully none of us were hurt. The next day as we drove through Pretoria, a police car behind us was shot at. We were not sorry to leave South Africa for our journey to Zimbabwe to spend Christmas with all of Ellie's family for the first time in eight years. Dustin's condition did not keep him from his usual mischief. He had bought a box of firecrackers and delighted in setting them off at unexpected times and throwing squibs under the adults' chairs, scaring everyone. It was a brilliant Christmas. We had sorely missed the family and enjoyed a very precious time together.

After Christmas we drove to Beira where the guys left the girls. Deborah and I camped on the beach while Rod and Dustin made a trip to Inhaminga by road for the first time. I was sure Dustin was not up to it, but he insisted he was and thoroughly enjoyed the adventure. We returned to Malawi to face a major crisis of another nature. We call it our cooking pot experience.❖

MISSIONARIES IN THE COOKING POT

IN THE COMPANY OF DAVID LIVINGSTONE

Most of us have seen or can imagine a cartoon sketch of a missionary sitting in a big cooking pot over an open fire with a group of natives standing around with spears, licking their lips. Any person in ministry knows what it's like to come under the pressure of persecution, or in other words, to be in the cooking pot. We have been through many difficulties in our ministry, but a new experience in the cooking pot was awaiting us. All the work we had done in Mozambique was about to be misrepresented as a work of evil. The media unleashed lies so extreme they were laughable. We did laugh in the cooking pot; some of it was very funny. We also cried in the cooking pot; the heat was turned up very high. But praise God, we **survived** the cooking pot!

One of the promises Jesus made to His disciples was this – persecution. *"If they persecuted Me, they will also persecute you."* *John 15:20.* We should not be shocked when His Word comes to pass in our lives. He said we are to rejoice when our good is spoken of as evil. Persecution will come. We cannot run from it. We must stand firm and face it. When we face our fears, they will turn and run from us!

"Beloved, think it not strange concerning the fiery trial which is to try you, as though some strange thing happened to you. But rejoice,

inasmuch as ye are partakers of Christ's sufferings, that, when His glory shall be revealed, you may be glad also with exceeding joy." 1 Peter 4:12,13. (KJV)

The Apostle Paul, too, knew the meaning of persecution. He says he *"suffered in abundance, above measure, frequently in prison. Flogged more severely, exposed to death often, beaten with rods, stoned, shipwrecked, on long journeys often, in perils of the sea, robbers, his own countrymen, the heathen, in the city, in the wilderness, and in danger of false brothers." 2 Corinthians 11:23-27*

These sufferings are spiritual as well as physical. Character assassination through lies and misrepresentation can be more painful than physical abuse. All through the ages Christians have been falsely accused and persecuted. This will not stop, but as we get nearer to the coming of our Lord it will get worse. We need to prepare ourselves and take courage from those who have gone before us on the road of persecution. An example of great encouragement to us has been the life of that famous missionary-explorer, Dr. David Livingstone.

Africa's greatest pioneer missionary, Livingstone suffered tremendous persecution and cruel attempts of character assassination. It is interesting to see that much of his persecution came from the government, the Boers who were zealously upholding the Dutch Reformed faith, and fellow missionaries.

The following is taken from a book written about Livingstone, printed in 1927.

"Livingstone made two journeys to the Magaliesberg on the borders of newly occupied Boer territory with the object of extending missionary operations in that direction and installing a native teacher there. The Dutch settlers in the area refused to permit any attempt at evangelism among the natives, and some went so far as to intimate they would kill any native teacher operating anywhere near them. In the face of this threat, the idea had to be abandoned for a time.

"Ere long, the hostility thus evinced became more menacing. The

Boers suspected, or at least accused Livingstone of selling arms to the Bakwains and denounced him to the Cape government for this offense, demanding his withdrawal and the disarming of Secheles tribe. They also forbade the continuance of building operations for a permanent mission station at Chonuane. The facts of the case were that Sechele possessed no more than five muskets, which he had purchased from traders and the only lethal weapon that Livingstone had was an iron pot for cooking. Writing long subsequent to the event, Livingstone makes merry over the terror excited in the Boer mind by this iron pot which they persisted in believing to be a cannon. The British officials at Cape Town were wary of offending the Boers and unsympathetic with the aims of the missionary; they seem indeed to have regarded Livingstone as a troublesome person likely to create difficulties for them.

We find Livingstone using his natural gifts and talents in matters not solely confined to missions. Livingstone's achievements in geographical knowledge resulting from his expeditions, gained the missionary official recognition that opened up a new chapter in his career. He met continually with opposition. Some of his missionary brethren believed that he was actuated by selfish motives and was deserting his proper service for a venture outside the limits of his vocation. His answer to the criticism was: 'So powerfully convinced am I that it is the will of our Lord I should, I will go, no matter who opposes!' He wrote to his brother- in-law, 'I will open a way to the interior or perish!'"

IT'S HOT IN THE POT!

We can personally identify with so much that happened to Livingstone, having tasted some of the same. This was triggered when the Malawi political situation became increasingly volatile as the election date drew near. The hated "Malawi Young Pioneers," an arm of President Banda's government, was disbanded and attacked by the Malawi army, supportive of the party in opposition to the government. The Young Pioneers fled for their lives and some were reported to be hiding in Mozambique. It was claimed that a new army was being trained in Mozambique to overthrow the opposition, who expected to win the elections. Like wildfire, rumors spread and before we knew it, Rod was said to be the one who was training this supposed army and accused of flying weapons in to them. This was ridiculous; we had never ferried weapons in our lives, nor had we any contact with the Young Pioneers.

The first we heard of our supposed crimes was when we were waved down by a friend as we drove down the road into Blantyre City Center. "Have you seen today's paper?" "No, why?" "You'd better buy one and go home and read it. You're the news headlines!"

Now imagine you were us, operating a vital work in Mozambique from Malawi, trying to keep a low profile so your work will not be stopped and your safety jeopardized. You buy The Malawi Democrat with the front page blazing,

"The Flying Reverend, Linkman or Agent?" The second report is worse, "Renamo's Fake Missionary." Starting to get the feel of it? It gets a lot worse. We were actually being used as a political pawn and scapegoat while the parties fought out their ugly battles. Advice from friends in ministry was, "Don't say a word; keep silent." It is hard to remain silent when being falsely accused, but for nine months this is what we did while newspaper reports became more and more incongruous. Rod was grounded, no more flying. We went about our daily business pretending nothing was wrong, (or trying to). We did have a lot of laughs over some of the things printed by amateur newsmen. We also had some tense and trying experiences.

THE FLYING REVEREND, LINKMAN OR AGENT?
The Malawi Democrat

"Under the guise of a reverend, a certain white man, now called Reverend Hayne came to Malawi in 1993 and took flying lessons at Chileka airport. He had already mastered the flying before the normal period required.

"In normal circumstances a pilot files in his flight plan with a briefing officer at the airport before he flies off but my good reverend never does. The Mozambican government always wondered about this small plane flying into its territory and sent an agent

spy to the airport as a pilot trainee.

"Reverend Haynes has the authorities in his hands and may leave earlier than the airport is officially opened, and even makes suicidal night landings after dark after the airport is closed."

RENAMO'S FAKE MISSIONARY
The Guardian

"Recently it was confirmed by the Minister of State that at one time or another Renamo leaders were given territorial access on their way to Kenya for peace talks. As we went to press Hein had disappeared into South Africa.

"Hein posed as a priest. He was always in short trousers and resided in Nyambadwe, Blantyre.

"According to Voice of America, Dhlakama has accused Malawi's opposition leaders of fabricating the story."

THE BLUE PLANE
The Inquirer

The owner of the Blue Plane has been identified at last. And for all we know — layman and legal experts alike, he should be in a cold prison or police cell surrounded by five police officers and men with their needles and pliers all asking him questions at the same time.

The man, using his blue plane is strongly suspected to have ferried weapons to the Young Pioneers movement. This blue plane villain should not be allowed to get away with murder.

This one was written by a columnist who signed himself Mr. 'T'.

There was a lot more than these edited portions. It was awful; there could be no greater insult than being called a "fake missionary." Sadly, people are inclined to believe what they read and we began to see negative reactions. Some who had been friendly in the past no longer greeted us. This was largely among the White population; the Black people were friendly as ever and sympathetic. Wik and Sue were wonderful; they were there for us and came to pray with us. They too suffered unkindness from some people because of being our friends.

AIRPORT ARREST

We waited for encouragement and moral support from fellow missionaries, which never came. One pastor of a leading ministry came in the night to see if we were OK and apologized that they could not risk being seen with us in daylight. Rather like Nicodemus.

The atmosphere during Malawi's political upheaval was sinister and threatening. For us, because of the newspaper reports, even more so. Rodney was called in for questioning by the police on several occasions. Our friend Marcos was powerless to help us. His own position was in jeopardy, and he was later imprisoned and then released after a long time as there was no evidence against him, the charges being fabricated. Elections had ushered in a new government whose leaders knew nothing about us. In short, as we read in *Exodus 1:8*, *"There arose a new Pharaoh over Egypt who knew not Joseph."*

Each time Rodney was called to the police we did not know what the repercussions would be. The army had received an anonymous call saying that Rod had been seen loading suspicious looking boxes into the plane. He had in fact not been near the plane. Who made the call? We never knew. The army stationed soldiers with machine guns around the plane all night and the following morning informed Rod that he was to go to the airport. On arrival they grabbed hold of him, pushed him about and started hitting him on the back of the legs with their guns while they yelled accusations at him and demanded to know where his wife was. Through it all Rod remained calm and did not react except to tell them it was none of their business where his wife was. "You are under arrest!" they yelled at him as they shoved him into an army land rover and drove off. All this took place at the public terminal, a rather humiliating experience. He was taken to the plane so they could search it and pull out the supposed weapons in his presence. They threw him to the ground and made him sit with his head between his knees, but he got up, insisting on entering the plane with them so he could try to observe if they were trying to plant something inside to falsely incriminate him. The soldiers searched and searched, disappointment marking their faces, as they could, of course, find nothing. The whole time the guns were trained in Rod's direction. Finally they let him go, not much worse for wear except for some bruises.

When we have lost our reputation, we have nothing more to lose. Should we lose our life, we shall find it in Christ. The Christian sold out to God, therefore, has nothing to lose and everything to gain.

It was the famous missionary Jim Elliot, murdered by Auca Indians who said, **"He is no fool who gives what he cannot keep to gain that which he cannot lose."**

BACK TO OLD HUNTING GROUNDS

The best way to survive the cooking pot is to keep focused on the vision and call of God. Never doubt in the dark what God has shown you in the light. Though our circumstances may change, our commission remains the same. This is not the time to slow down or let up.

For eight years until amnesty, we could not drive openly on any roads or through any towns in Mozambique. We could only fly, walk, or ride the motorcycles on bush paths. Now Rod was grounded: we could not fly, but there was nothing to stop us using our wheels into Mozambique. The Gospel and our work would continue. When one door shuts, God will open another. Now was our chance to return to visit one of the first churches we had ever ministered at in the city of Tete.

The Toyota land cruiser groaned under the weight of Bibles, clothes, food and gifts for the Christians we were about to surprise. Dustin and I were on mission, together again, while Rod answered the call to another area of Mozambique.

Memories flooded my mind as we approached the Mozambique border post at Zobue. Our last visits had been fraught with dangers and uncertainties. We entered the building to have our documents stamped. The atmosphere was very different from what I remembered. Whereas previously the place had crawled with armed soldiers and officials barking orders in rough manner, all was now at ease. The officials were polite and even smiled! A rare sight in Communist days past. They did not even ask what we had in our vehicle and in a short space of time, the barrier was lifted for us to pass through. We were stunned.

Initially the road was good, and then we started hitting potholes. I was glad Dustin was on board; he could change the tires if needed. Within two hours we reached the bridge that spans the Zambezi River and takes one into Tete. This was very exciting. Soon we would see the amazed faces of our friends. Nobody was expecting us and they would be in shock. Would I be able to find the church in the shanty houses on the outskirts of town? My sense of direction is not the best, but yes, there it was. Mud houses rose out of hard-baked earth, not a tree in sight. This part of Tete had certainly not changed. We maneuvered the truck in and out of people, pigs, ducks, goats and market stalls, and there was Pastor Wilson's house on the hill. He stood looking down at us with a blank face. We waved at him and he waved cautiously back; then in a flash of recognition he started jumping and clapping and shouting "Hallelujah!" His wife and eight children came tumbling out of the surroundings and stood open-mouthed. "I was seeing but not believing. Then I looked and looked and I believed." Pastor Wilson's joy knew no bounds and it matched ours exactly.

In the evening the church was packed with excited Christians. Years of suffering and streams of blood and tears lay between us and our last meeting in this place. Yet the church had grown amazingly. My heart pounded and my eyes burned. "Oh God. Thank you for this precious, precious moment."

The folk were excited and responsive, devouring every word, their beaming faces lit up by the single light bulb hanging from the roof and the light within their souls. Our last meeting here was not forgotten. With some visitors from the USA, we had slept on the church floor after the church meeting. Loud thundering just before daybreak shook us awake. We thought our prayers for rain had been answered but this illusion was quickly shattered. We looked outside to see flashes of fire from mortar rockets as they exploded. There was no danger of that now and we lifted our hands to praise and thank God for the miracle of peace. There were many in the church who had been present at our very first meeting there eleven years before. They raised their hands towards us. A strong spiritual cord binds us with an everlasting bond. They had been tried in the fire and had come forth as pure gold.

It was ironic that we now had more freedom in Mozambique than in Malawi. We made various trips to places where we used to minister. Unable to fly to Inhaminga, we started going by road. We continued with ministry in the demobilization camps. There was much to do. Land mines were the biggest danger and several cars got blown up and passengers killed. God kept us safe, though we had several close encounters. We came around a corner and saw two men who had been walking on the road due to having no transport, pointing with a stick. They had spotted the top part of a land mine sticking out from under the dust. We left them there to warn the few motorists on the road, while we drove to the nearest police station to report the mine-sighting. On another occasion Rod stopped on the side of the road to repair a puncture. On his return, he saw a massive hole caused by a boosted mine on the spot where he had stopped. Somehow he had just missed it.

ENOUGH IS ENOUGH! MR. "T"

For nine months the crazy reports periodically appeared in the papers. They got worse and worse, then more serious, as one of the journalists whom we had flown in previously sold out on us. Breaching his promise not to disclose logistical information on us, he not only gave accurate information, but a load of false reports as well. He gave our real names, the airport we flew from in Malawi and the routing we took. These were printed by the British paper he worked for, and then picked up by the Malawi papers, which had led to Rod's arrest by the army. We were betrayed by a man we had assisted to the best of our ability. On his pleading request, we had allowed him to walk with us through the bush on a preaching mission so he could film and interview the local population in their normal setting in a war zone. When food was short, we shared our meager supplies with him. Our limited water supply on hot walks in dry regions was shared with him also. He was interested in everything we did and said, showing appreciation for the way he gained entrance into the lives of the people and won their trust through our reputation. At the end of the trip he hugged us warmly and said, "I cannot thank you enough. This trip has been very tough but you have made it so much easier and been such a help. I have learned a lot from you." We were pleased, as we had truly done our best for him and had shared much about God and our vision for winning Mozambique to Christ, hoping to reach his heart. Here was a Judas in person! We were shocked to read the things he reported about us. Among other things, he claimed that we were not missionaries at all, but using the cover for subversive activities.

Finally, we'd had enough and it was time to speak. Various friends and contacts of good repute helped us with the problem in Britain. "The Guardian" received a succession of phone calls and faxes from reputable people whom we had taken on fact-finding missions into Mozambique. They spoke up on our behalf and challenged the accuracy of the reports and credibility of the newspaper. These distorted and untrue reports were not only discrediting us, but actually placing us in danger. By the end of it the said journalist was reprimanded and an apology and retraction printed in "The Guardian." Typically, the apology was in small print in an obscure corner on page five while the accusations had received bold print and large headlines. Why would this journalist who had been so friendly and whom we had so generously assisted sell out on us? Power-hungry and greedy, he lacked sufficient self respect and honor, stopping at nothing to make a story more sellable. He did not care about risking our safety either.

This man can periodically be heard on the BBC reporting on hot spot events in Africa. Though we have forgiven him and do not disclose his name, we cannot be blamed for doubting the accuracy of what we hear.

In Malawi, I telephoned the Enquirer; they were the ones who wanted Rod in prison; I asked to talk to Mr. 'T'. "Are you a reputable paper? Do you print the truth or lies?" I asked. "Oh, we always print the truth. We are a very respectable paper," he said. "Well, in that case, I have some very interesting information for you. I have all the missing details about The Flying Reverend who wears short trousers and flies a blue plane." "You have? That is marvelous. I want this information badly." "Get your fax machine ready," I said, "I am sending you the hottest and the latest. I'll watch the papers to see if you have the courage to print it." Mr. 'T' was very excited; he had the top story of the nation as far as he was concerned. I proceeded to send him a detailed report of our mission work and involvement in peace talks. We had nothing to hide anymore; we just wanted the truth out. I concluded the report with these words, "The Heins are honored to have played the part of peacemakers in Mozambique as well as having the opportunity to preach the Gospel throughout the length and breadth of Mozambique. For these efforts, it has been suggested that the owner of the blue plane should be imprisoned and tortured. To those who have mercilessly attacked us, we say 'Peace; no hard feelings. We forgive you.'" Rodney & Ellie Hein, Blantyre, Malawi.

I also sent copies to some other papers. The "Daily Times" printed the full report. Mr. 'T' printed a few lines, a weak effort on his part. Some people started to talk to us again. However, the pressure from the army and police did not lift. They got in touch with the authorities at the Mozambique border post where Frelimo arrested Rodney after having cleared customs into Mozambique. Here, the Frelimo police attempted to take his car away. Rod refused to hand over the keys. He simply dug in his heels and said "No." "You are under arrest! We are taking you to the police station at Moatize. If you will not give us your car, move over and we will drive you there." "No," said Rod. "I will not give you my car to drive; I drive my own car." The policemen were perplexed; they didn't know what to do with this man. In Africa you do not refuse men with guns. They didn't know how to respond to this refusal. Eventually, the Commander told the two policemen to get in the back with their guns and allow Rod to drive them all to the police station one hour's drive away. There they kept him for most of the day, while nobody could make a decision as to what to do with him. Rod used his time to hand out Christian literature to everyone he saw. Exasperated, and with no evidence against him, they finally let him go.

On the whole, the journalists we took in to the Mozambique war zones were great. We enjoyed getting to know them and it is a pleasure to see some of them continue to do well in their field. Jeremy Thompson, currently on British Sky News is one of these.

"I WANT MY GIRLS OUT OF HERE"

When Deborah came to the end of her school year, Rodney had only one thought and that was to get us out of the country. He sent us to Zimbabwe for a week from where we would fly out to the USA while he stayed on to sort out the logistics of our final departure. Deborah and I started our ministry tour. She was incredibly excited to be going to the States. I was horribly churned up at going ahead without Rod, but at the same time knew it was the right thing to do and that it would also help him. Our first stop was Dallas, Texas where we spent some time at Christ For The Nations. Deborah affirmed the decision she had made at the age of seven years when she confidently had told us, "One day I will be a student at Christ For The Nations."

Our work in Malawi was over. The plane was grounded;

we could no longer use it and had no idea how long it would be before we'd be allowed to fly again. The church was stable, under good leadership; they could carry on without us. Rod stayed on a few more weeks to tie up loose ends and to pack up our belongings. Tension intensified daily; he was glad that the children and I were all safely out of Malawi.

It was great to be with friends in America, and a special time for the two of us to be together. Though only eleven years old, Deborah was tremendously supportive. We prayed together and she sat through my ministry and cheered me on. We had loads of fun and did some crazy things together; she declared her mom was her best friend ever.

It was difficult not knowing what was going on with Rod and of course I worried terribly. He was away from home a lot and out of contact range, and we only received an occasional message. His biggest complaint was that he missed having wings and jokingly said he would have to start sniffing avgas to help with the withdrawal symptoms of not being able to fly. Deborah and I often had to share a bed as one does when traveling, and at night we'd lie chatting to each other and talking to God. One night as we were in conversational prayer with the Lord, Deborah piped up, "And Lord, please keep Daddy safe and help him so he doesn't have to sniff avgas." We started laughing and laughing and couldn't stop for ages.

At last it was time for Rod to join us. We were beside ourselves with excitement, but I was experiencing some gnawing fears. Would he safely get on the plane or would he be stopped at the border post and arrested again? Would they lock him up in that cold prison after all? Rod was to land in Colorado while I was preaching in Missouri. We were booked to fly out in the morning and meet him there. It took some discipline to keep focused on ministry that night, and after the meeting I rushed to the phone to receive Rod's call. Finally it came. We both cried and could barely talk. Just to be connected through the air was enough. God's faithfulness reaches to the skies. The following day we would meet in Colorado.

Just two days before Rod was to fly out of Malawi, he was issued with a document canceling our work permit in that country. God's timing was perfect. We had exactly the right time in which to do everything he had sent us to do in Malawi, and exactly the right amount of time to settle up our affairs and move out again. We knew exactly what we would do. Conclude the ministry tour in the States together then go home to Zimbabwe where Tammy and Dustin were both working now, and from where we would continue our Mission Mozambique.❖

Part Three

BEAUTY
FOR ASHES

To comfort those who mourn,
to give them beauty for ashes,
the oil of joy for mourning,
The garment of praise for the spirit of heaviness;
that they may be called trees of righteousness,
The planting of the Lord, that He may be glorified.

And they shall rebuild the old ruins,
they shall raise up the former desolations,
And they shall repair the ruined cities.

Isaiah 61:3,4

RETURN OF THE EXILES

NEW BEGINNINGS

December 1994 was a month of extreme contrasts. From Rocky Mountain snow and the Christmas winter wonderland of Colorado, we flew into the hot, sticky embrace of our African homeland. Over Zimbabwe, the barren ground where lush vegetation should have been growing was a stark reminder that the drought had continued to devour during our absence. In contrast, Harare was dotted with the blazing red, orange, purple and yellow bougainvilleas blooming defiantly in the face of the drought. As we touched down at Harare airport, an emotional lump rose in our throats and we wiped away several tears. Filled with gratitude to be safely home, we stepped off the plane into a new phase of our lives and ministry. Tammy and Dustin were at the airport to meet us together with my mum, sisters and family members. How wonderful to be enfolded in that welcome of love. We spent a few days with the family, catching up with each other's lives before setting off for Inhaminga.

Three months previously, in the uncertainties of the cooking pot, we had promised the folk at Inhaminga we would be back for Christmas. There had been no way to communicate with them since we left Malawi, and it was important that we keep this promise. Reports of continued drought and failure of crops hastened us on to where we knew the people were in need of encouragement.

The Inhaminga trail was the usual slow drive through wild bush country where baboons languidly watch solitary vehicles trundle by. It was intolerably hot; we were melting by the time we finally rolled past the market stalls. Children came running alongside us with shrieks of "hallelujahs" and "Josefo, Josefo!" They were beside themselves with excitement. We quickly learned that tales of dread had been spread and people thought we would never be back. The African bush telegraph had picked up the wrong message and it had stretched and stretched as bits were added on to the tales of woe about our arrest and imprisonment. Now here we were, just in time for Christmas as we had promised.

The elections had been held and the same ruling Frelimo party came in again. Massive rigging of votes in spite of UN peacekeeping forces at polling stations had kept the Communists in power. Except they no longer called themselves Communists. Renamo had lost, but not by a large margin and they had several members in Parliament now. We had assured the folk that we would continue our ministry regardless of the results of the elections. "Our commission does not change, even if our circumstances do. Our cause is Christ, and our cause will never change."

ANOTHER INHAMINGA CHRISTMAS

Shifting from Colorado to Inhaminga mode was quite a culture shock. Had it ever been so hot before? Perspiration streamed incessantly down our faces and bodies. The house felt like an oven and the mosquitoes whined and dined with gusto. Every window pane having been shot out during the war, there was no way to shut out the mosquitoes. It was Christmas Eve. No lights in town, no decorations, no Christmas tree to brighten up the festivities. We had so enjoyed the lights and beauty of decorated cities in the USA, but for these people there was no respite from the pressures of the daily grind and pain of a dry, thirsty and hungry land. The crops they had planted in hope lay shriveled in the fields. Still, on this Christmas Eve there shone a light in the hearts of those that believed. The joy and hope that only Jesus can give refused to be extinguished. The war had come to an end, the season of Peace was drenched in the reality of peace. Rod and Deborah arranged the few gifts we had brought on the table. Most of the space in our vehicle had been taken up for food to ensure that the Christians would eat well this Christmas. I thanked God for Deborah's cheerful attitude and enthusiasm for a Christmas so different from that of her friends.

We slept on and off, tossing and turning in the oven of the night. Finally we gave up on sleep and rose at dawn to the sounds of pigeons cooing in the rafter at the bedroom window and babies crying. At 08:00 a.m. drums and singing called us to the church. News of our arrival had spread like wild fire during the night. "You are our gift this Christmas," they told us. It felt good to be a Christmas gift. When the offering was taken up the drum was placed in the center of the church and the people placed their coins on it. They sang a song, "What you have, give with all your heart. If it be money, a shirt or a pair of trousers, what you have, give with all your heart." Some had no money to give, they did not even have clothes on their bodies, just strips of rag. Pointing at the drum, we shared the Christmas song of "The Little Drummer Boy." They were very touched by the words, also by the fact that the shepherds too had nothing to give Jesus other than their worship and adoration. "That is what God wants from us, more than gifts and offerings," we told them. "He wants our love, our worship." It was a precious Christmas service, beautiful in its simplicity and sincerity.

Christmas dinner under the shade of the trees was a fight with the flies. Rice, potatoes, beans and corned beef followed by bread and jam was wildly luxurious for these folk who never saw such fare. Unfortunately, the flies were equally enthusiastic about the feast. Never have we seen such flies. It happens in time of famine; even the flies are hungry, I guess. We spent more time trying to chase flies off our food with leafy twigs than eating. No matter how hard we tried, the flies managed to settle on our laden forks before we could get the food into our mouths. The local Inhaminga folk laughed at our shooing antics. They were accustomed to the flies and were not about to allow such a small problem to spoil their Christmas dinner. They did not waste time swatting, but busied themselves with the important task of making the most of their blessings. The children sitting on reed mats ate happily. After licking the last of the jam off their lips, hands and arms, they stood up to go and play. Like overfed puppies they wobbled onto their feet and toddled off.

Finally, the day's festivities came to an end and we fell into a sweaty sleep in overpowering heat. We had not had a decent wash since our arrival; there just was not enough water. Then in the night a loud burst of thunder shook the heavens and almost immediately the rain began to fall. Rain, wonderful rain! It was the best gift we could have wished for. As soon as it was light enough to see, the whole town scampered about to put out buckets and containers to catch as much water as possible. Now we could wash the pile of dirty clothes and have a thorough bucket bath. We could wash our hair that felt as if it was about to crawl off our heads. The morning was full of joy and laughter. No babies cried. The sound, smell and touch of rain had broken the tensions that had stretched ragged nerves for months.

Ever the farmer at heart, Rodney wasted no time in getting on the tractor and plowing a field to plant corn. Deborah learned to drive the tractor too; it was great fun. She busied herself finding plants that had survived in old wasted gardens, making a new garden. The week leading into the New Year passed speedily with people coming each day to bring us the Season's greetings. Shortage of food forced people to spend much of their day digging for wild roots. The softened ground yielded these more easily and soon new shoots would grow on edible shrubs. This would help, but was not enough to keep people till the next harvest. We worked hard and Rod also managed to get the roof on the first dormitory we planned to use to house Bible School students. It was exciting to see the beginnings of a vision take place. We knew this was a long-term, difficult project, but how good to make a start!

The New Year was not without its problems. Renamo leader Afonso Dhlakama had proved true to his word and did not return to war after losing the elections as many had thought he would. However, the aftermath of war and continued famine did not help matters. A bunch of bananas was good payment for an AK-47 rifle. All soldiers had been commanded to hand over their weapons, but there were those that didn't. They traded them for what they could get. This placed lethal weapons in the hands of common thieves, highwaymen and marauders as well as ex-soldiers from both armies.

These armed men did not take long to show their muscle. They shot at passing vehicles, robbed and killed passengers and drivers. The Inhaminga road was especially bad for this and we were thankful to never encounter anything but baboons, normal travelers and a few lions, on the many trips we made as time moved on.

A New Home

1995 was a year of transition. Having left Malawi, we needed to find a new home. We had two choices. The first was to live in Mozambique, placing Deborah in boarding school and leaving Tammy and Dustin working in Zimbabwe. Second was to live in Zimbabwe where Deborah could attend day school and we would be near Tammy and Dustin. Both choices would mean a lot of traveling back and forth. We didn't have to think hard about it, and settled for the small town of Mutare in Zimbabwe, the town closest to the Mozambique border. Here we found a lovely home set on a hill, a good school for Deborah, and we were not far from the family.

Peace at last! We had lived and worked for years in a war situation, and now it was over. No newspapers reported on us, we were just ordinary folk moved to town. Sometimes it's only when something is over, that one realizes how tough it really was. To live without the continual stress of danger and persecution was very refreshing. Family members were nearby, some old friends still lived in the vicinity and we made new friends. We seldom spoke to others about our eight years in Malawi and the work we had done in Mozambique from there, sharing with only a handful of people a little of what we had been through. Most people had no idea of our lives other than the fact that we were missionaries. It took some time for us to get used to our new lifestyle. We wanted to leave the past behind and move into a new thrust in our work and lives. We prayed that the newspapers would not pick up on any stories about the Flying Reverend moving to Mutare!

We live just three hours by road from Chipinge, the small town from which we had made our great escape. Eight years previously we had said goodbye to family and friends. My mother had thought we'd be away on a two-week trip, never dreaming how long it would be before our return. Many times it had seemed that we never would return.

Deborah started high school at Hillcrest College where she will shortly complete her school career. She has been very happy there and has done well. Tammy and Dustin periodically came home for weekends when they got time off from work. It felt so good to have all three of them around the dinner table again.

Those of our friends who had kept in touch with us during the years of trials and extreme action, were concerned that we might find life too dull now that we were "normal people" again. We were not flying into war zones, not getting shot at. The truth is, we were so thrilled with our plans and vision for a Mozambique at peace, that we wasted no time in putting heart and soul and hands to the task. There was no time to rest on our laurels or gather dust. There was much work to be done. Serving God is the most exciting thing in the world!❖

COMMAND POST

STRATEGY

Before God closed the door of a completed work, He showed us glimpses of the new. This way there was no coming to a dead end, but simply a flowing through and out of one into the other. We did not lose momentum, did not struggle to find our feet in a new place or to adjust to changed lifestyle. How faithful He is.

On one of Rod's flights to Inhaminga, he had spotted a ruined complex of buildings close to the landing strip. The bush was thick, obscuring the buildings totally from anyone on the ground. From the air Rod could make out the walls with no roofing standing in the midst of tall trees and brush. He determined to investigate.

Leaving the plane on the airstrip, he footed 500 meters to the buildings. Pushing through the overgrowth, he fought his way to the steps of a large structure. On either side of the entrance walls was painted a faded Red Cross. Walking through a broad corridor and through the building, it was obvious this had once been a small hospital. There were several buildings dotted about. Why all this outside of town? Inhaminga was three kilometers down the road, with its own hospital. As Rod continued to walk and push through the debris, the Holy Spirit planted ideas and thoughts into his mind. **"This is perfect for a Bible School. Look at these old wards – they can be turned into lecture rooms and staff quarters. Outside there is the kitchen, and those buildings can be turned into dormitories."** Rod began to plan with the Holy Spirit and right there, amongst the debris of broken walls and roofing lying in the middle of the rooms, with trees growing through cracks in the floors, together they made a pact to rise up and build.

This was the right man for the Holy Spirit to get hold of. Creative, hard-working and always ready for a challenge, Rod could see with the eyes of faith beyond the bush and broken walls. He saw the walls rebuilt, a roof put on, paint, plumbing and lighting. (I think the "footprints on the sands of time" are most likely made by work-shoes.) Most of all, Rod could see the place full of people worshipping God, praying, sitting at desks studying. He saw them going out from those very walls, filled with joy and zeal, endued with power from on high to preach the Gospel throughout the nation. Hallelujah!

Making his way back to the airstrip, Rod had a sense of destiny about the place. Already we had committed to help make Inhaminga live. This would be part of it. Not only would the place live, it would also send out life.

We learned that the area had been the original Portuguese settlement of Inhaminga. The office of administration, the hospital and a few other posts were established at Commando, which we learned was the name of the place. It had been the Command Post of the early settlers. Now it was to become a spiritual Command Post where leaders would be trained in the work of God, where strategies would be planned, and from where teams would go out to spread the Gospel. If you go to Inhaminga today, simply ask for Commando. You will be directed to the Commando road, at the end of which you will find the Afrika wa Yesu ministry base and Bible Training Center. When looking at the map of Mozambique, Inhaminga is a strategic dot right in the middle. Hard to get to, far away in the wilds, yet the place God told us to bring to life.

OPERATION NEHEMIAH

A wonderful example of courage and fortitude is found in Nehemiah. Here was a man who succeeded against all odds in rebuilding the destroyed walls of Jerusalem. He had every form of opposition come against him. His life was threatened numerous times, and still he never gave up. Physically, the task was impossible, but with God all things are possible. Our story turned out to be much the same. Nehemiah succeeded in his God-appointed task. *"And so built we the wall: for the people had a mind to work." Nehemiah 4:6.* By the grace of God and the help of the many faithful folk who supported us and worked with us, we too have succeeded. The impossible has been and is being accomplished.

The First person to whom Rod showed the ruins at Command was John Miles of REAP. This is a ministry that works out of Riverside Fellowship, UK. Nick & Lois Cuthbert, who pastor Riverside, are special friends of ours. John had asked to see Inhaminga so Rod flew him in, also showing him the buildings with the bush partially cleared away. The cleaning-up exercise we had started revealed human bones, empty bullet shells and cartridges, all evidence of the war and many lives that had been lost on the site.

Looking at the main structure, John said. "This building needs a roof. We can send you a team to put on a roof." He returned to England to put together a team for Inhaminga. A group of young people would come out to help us. In the mean-time Rod had to get all the building materials to Inhaminga. This proved to be the hardest part of the exercise.

Every bit of material we needed had to be bought in Zimbabwe, taken across the border and driven down the long, hard, Inhaminga road. To this date the Inhaminga road remains the nemesis of our ministry operations. It is an indescribable stretch of 150 kilometers that takes six hours on a good dry day, or can take three days to a week during the wet season. Instead of improving it, as had been promised by the government, it has become worse year by year. We had been confident that as Inhaminga was on the main highway to the north, the road would surely be rebuilt. No such thing. Had we known that the road would eat away at our lives, our vehicles, our money at such a rate, would we have established the Bible School at Inhaminga? Probably not, which is why God hid all that from us. In spite of all the hardship and difficulties, we remain convinced that we are in the right place. In preparation for the REAP Team, we drove to Inhaminga with Dustin and Deborah some days ahead of the team's arrival. Rod would return to collect the team. We arrived at our bomb-shaken house late at night, worn out after long hours of traveling. It was winter now, and we could think only of warm beds with clean linen. It was not to be. During our absence, a colony of mice had moved in. Our linen box was the choice place of habitation and they had efficiently tunneled through sheets, blankets and bedcovers, leaving very few articles whole. The smell forbade the use of the linen and we had to make do with a few untainted pieces. Nevertheless, it was good to be home again in Mozambique.

We prepared for the team as best we could, washing and cleaning so they would not have to suffer worse culture shock than necessary. They arrived thoroughly shaken up by the rough ride and astounding sights of derailed railway carriages and burned-out vehicles on the side of the road, as well as the broken shells of buildings that made up Inhaminga. They looked a little more than dazed as they climbed out the back of the truck. This bunch soon proved to be a team of tough, game young people, serving and giving of themselves far above what we had dared to hope and expect. They worked incredibly hard and gave not only their physical labors but also their hearts to the people. They ministered, shared testimonies, and played with the children, bringing the voice of joy and gladness to the "city of bones."

It was wonderful to see how our first visiting team to Inhaminga responded to the people and to the challenge. We were greatly encouraged by the way they picked up on the vision for life in place of death. They had sacrificed their summer vacation to come, saving money and raising funds to cover their costs as well as pay for the roof. For them it was an experience nobody could have prepared them for. God did a great work in their lives too, as we see in some of the testimonies they wrote.

Patrick: *"One of the most striking images on my mind is the Communist statue which is in the town park. It lies face down in the dirt, having been removed from its pedestal by the local people. It stood for oppression and fear, and the fact that it lies fallen to the ground speaks to me of hope and freedom come to this country. My experience of the local church has been inspiring, and more than fifty people were baptized. Dustin filled up the bullet holes in the old water tank with putty so it could hold the water. With all this real life experience I am aware how for many years I have seen television reports of war and famine stricken countries, yet because it was on television, part of me treated it lightly because it wasn't real to me. I have learned that as a Christian I need to be aware of and act on the truth of what is around me."*

Jenny: *"'Break into shouts of joy, you ruins of Jerusalem! The Lord will restore His city and comfort His people.' Isaiah 52:9. What a privilege to be part of the restoration. As the shape of the roof on the Bible training Center has emerged I have felt very hopeful for Mozambique. The most exciting thing about the project is that at the same time as doing the physical job of building the roof, we have been able to minister at the mill, in the church and at the Bible School."*

Jonathan: *"I know we came here to build a roof but I'm so thankful for being able to teach at the Bible School and preach at the mill. The outreach to Ndoro was incredible – what a privilege to be allowed to baptize young Christians, and what a setting to baptize them in. Was that really water we were standing in under the thick green algae and what creatures were swimming about in the murky depths?"*

Dustin: *"I have enjoyed working with my Dad and being a general "gofer" for him. Driving the tractor to fetch water was good. I have enjoyed working with the REAP team on the roof; they* *are fun to be with. There are lots of old bombs around. I found some 500 lb. bomb cases, the kinds that are dropped by air; also some bazooka tails and carrying tubes. We have to be careful of land mines. I am glad I have been able to help the people here."*

Deborah: *"The people here are very poor but friendly. The Team works really hard putting rafters up for the roof. I made a hat rack out of planks and nails for them to hang their hats on. I played with the kids at the building site and taught them to play hopscotch. Today I went right to the top of the cathedral tower where the bell is. The stained glass windows are pretty but a lot of the glass has been shot out. Everyday Dustin and Patrick have to fetch water as there is a drought and there is no water for miles. We baptized a lot of people in a tank we filled with water. I was sorry for them as it was cold and they have no other clothes to change into. They had to walk a long way home afterwards. Lots and lots of people got baptized and they were very excited and happy. They were singing and dancing and didn't seem to mind that they were shivering with cold, they were so happy."*

As the team built up the walls, erecting the giant roof trusses and hammering away, so we built spiritually. Eager to waste no time, we brought in 35 bush pastors for one month of Bible Training. We sat on rocks for chairs, under the trees for a roof, used laps for desks and studied the Word of God. Putting the spiritual vision into practice while the others continued to build, made significant impact on our faith. It also made a bold statement of confidence and assurance of success to those around us. We could see the day when the buildings would be complete, the lecture rooms filled with chairs and desks. The team visually saw the reason for their labors. Some of them participated in the teaching sessions. What a thrill to lay down the tools of physical service for a time, and to pick up the tools of the Word of God and build in the lives and hearts of these men.

The drought continued for three years with a few sporadic downpours, which were not sufficient for crops or water supplies. As Inhaminga began to breathe and live, the decreasing supply of water threatened to take the life of a town struggling in the infancy of new beginnings. Thirst was a killer more merciless than the bombs; one could not run and hide from thirst. The one and only operating well in town where people lined up to get a turn at the pump, yielded a slow trickle. The well of life had become a pit of despair. Hope of a future merged into the shimmering mirage of African heat and evaporated into oblivion.

Death stretched its long claws across the dry dirt and claimed parched humanity. At the well where 300 people stood in line for water, a woman collapsed near the back and breathed her last. She had been in line for three days and had no more strength. She died in line, waiting for her turn to drink.

Outside the town is a swamp where people had dug shallow wells. These had no protective walls or casing. As they dug further, several of the wells collapsed, burying people alive. At night, some women went to the wells with their buckets, hoping that during the cool of the night perhaps some water had come to the surface. Having no light, some fell into the treacherous holes and died there. Was there to be no end to the pain and sorrow of the Mozambican people?

Deborah, aged 12 at the time, wrote her prayer in a poem.

Rain

Today I cry out to the Lord, I cry for rain.
We need both physical and spiritual rain.
Who will cry out with me?
Who will cry unto the Lord?
I will cry out to the Lord
I will cry out till the rain comes.
Until the rain of the Lord fills the land.
THANK YOU, LORD!

The line at the pump grew longer and longer while the October heat pressed down on bodies slouching against whatever they could find to lean on. Then the dreaded happened. The trickle ceased to flow. Ashen faces stared in shock. The only other pump in town was broken, and spare parts had to be brought in from Zimbabwe.

Rodney looked to the sky, darkened with the smoke of bush fires. The acrid smell hung heavily in the air, making the heat so much hotter and the dryness drier. Detecting a different kind of darkness behind the smog, Rod called to the people. "Get every container you can and place it where you can catch water. It's going to rain!" The hopeless villagers groaned in disbelief. Then the sky began to rumble; electricity hung suspended in the lifeless air. Tension rose; anything could happen. Either the rain could begin to fall, or the dark clouds could dissipate and the deadly, dry stillness intensify. "Go! Get your pots and buckets," Rodney yelled. They began to peel off in the direction of their homes as a few wet drops woke their senses. BOOM! The clouds exploded in flashes of brilliant lightning and deafening thunder and the floodgates opened up with pouring, pounding RAIN! Rod stood for a long time, welcoming the heavenly flood – which was drenching, washing, refreshing him, inside and out. As he stood there soaking in the sweet mercy-rain thanking and praising God, his cup was running over, his strength and resolve renewed.

That night everyone went to sleep with thirst assuaged. Inhaminga had experienced a miracle. When there was no way, when all else had failed, God sent the rain. This was only temporary help for a few days but it came at the most desperate moment. The water level rose a bit and Rod returned to Zimbabwe to buy spare parts for the broken pump which once repaired, yielded water from the other well.

We continued with our endeavors to establish a water system at Command. This proved to be a long and difficult task and it was three years before we were able to sink a well deep enough to supply adequate water. Even so, we have to use it frugally. In the meantime the tractor and trailer continued to carry water. Building and living under these conditions was extremely difficult. The REAP Team was wonderful and did not complain as showers became less and less and clothes were not washed as frequently as before.

Hardships become insignificant when we see the fruit of our labors, physical as well as spiritual. We rejoiced at each load of debris carted away and each step of building progress. To experience the glory of God in our midst as we worshipped Him and to see the joy of the pastors as they devoured the Word of God, made it all worthwhile.

It was important for us not to lose contact with the people whom we had visited during the war, and as we built physically, we continued to build relationships.

PANGO

We had visited Pango several years previously on motorcycles. The people were of the poorest we had yet seen; almost all were clad in sacks and the beaten bark of the Baobab tree. Their poverty and nakedness pulled at our hearts. We had made a promise that proved very difficult to keep. "We will bring clothes for you."

There were no roads open to Pango during the war, and no airstrip close by. The clothes would have to be dropped off at some far-off point and walked in to the people on the heads of couriers. As the intensity of the war increased in that area, this had proved impossible also. Rodney could not forget the promise we had made to the people of Pango. So determined was he to keep that promise that he kept that load of clothes hidden away for the appointed time. Frequently, as we saw the need so many people had for clothing, we were tempted to take those clothes and give them out. Rod would say, "No, these are promised to the people of Pango."

The REAP Team was eager for a mission outreach into the wilds and we had the big white truck at Inhaminga. The time to visit Pango had come! Sacks of clothing were loaded onto the back, making good seats for the team members. Each carried with him a bedroll, change of clothes and a bottle of water. We had never been to Pango via this route. We knew the road was now open but had no idea what it was like. Our destination was sure but the journey there totally unknown. We estimated the two-and-a-half-day journey on foot would take us six hours by truck.

Thorn trees grew along the way, their spiky branches hanging over the road, which had not been used in years. We had not had the truck very long and as yet it had no canopy. The team sat on the bags of clothes and their bedrolls, as comfortable as was possible over the bumps and potholes. Deborah had brought her monkey, Jaques along. Jaques was no trouble, except for urinating on someone's bedroll when pit stops were not frequent enough for him. This caused much dismay, but kept everyone alert. They had to be alert, as the thorny branches snatched at their clothes and bare arms. The pace was very slow and we got stuck many times, but we had a good push-me-pull-me team. From all appearances we were heading to the ends of the earth and over the edge. There was not a single road sign, we saw no vehicles on the way and the six hours turned out to be nine. The team experienced the vastness and isolation of Africa at its rawest. No tour agency could have organized such an expedition for them.

We had sent messengers on foot several days ahead to prepare the people for our arrival. As we finally approached, children were waiting miles down the road for us, singing hallelujahs, shouting and clapping in their excited welcome. The hardships of the journey were immediately forgotten and Jaques was instantly forgiven. What a privilege to be here!

Darkness was creeping on us and weary bodies disembarked to greet the happy people and set up for the *JESUS* film. We were delighted to see so many familiar faces. Many stories bind us together eternally. Sufferings in famine and war, victories in the joy of knowing Jesus, these are things that form strong ties which cannot be broken.

Many of these children and teenagers had never seen a vehicle. The big white truck loaded with clothes was a giant loaded with blessing. We had shown the *JESUS* film several times before, and folk had walked for miles to come and watch the wonderful story of Jesus. It was a very precious evening and the drums and singing continued into the early morning hours, long after we had laid our weary bodies down on the hard, rocky dirt.

Giving the clothes out was a joy. These bush people were totally unspoiled, protected from the greed and pushing of city life and modern influences. They sat quietly in long rows, men in one line, women and children in the other to make distribution easier and fair. We wished we had more to give but the people were grateful for what they got. Rod explained that we had wanted to come long before but it had been impossible. All understood the difficulties of the situation and the spokesman said, "You promised you would come, and you have come. It has taken a long time, but you have come, and we thank you." Rod was satisfied. He had kept his promise.

Excerpts from some of our newsletters help to convey the difficulty of putting Operation Nehemiah into practice.

May 1996

We left home early Thursday morning to be at Inhaminga the same night. The road was so bad it took us a whole day extra to get there, and we arrived late, missing the Easter Friday evening service.

The many potholes have become small dams big enough to fit a car and deep enough for the water to reach the windscreen of the land cruiser. Some of the holes are just a couple of meters apart; it's like riding a roller coaster. Up and down, in and out, it was unbelievable. We counted 635 holes. One round trip makes for 1,270 of these dams to be forded through. Rodney had to make two extra round trips to carry cement and building materials for the Bible School restoration. So much time is wasted on the roads. En route we found several trucks thoroughly stuck in the mud. We helped winch them out, feeling very sorry for people who had been stuck on the road for up to a week, sleeping in the rain with very little food to eat.

December, 1996

We are happy to share with you that the 4x4 DAF truck is fully paid for. The money for this incredible vehicle was raised by Wayne Myers. We have named the giant "Big Foot."

We drove to Inhaminga in Big Foot just before Christmas. Our excitement was soon replaced by aches and pains from being thrown about. The suspension of the truck is very hard, the springs are the toughest, (just what we need!) The cab sits above the wheels so every bump is felt. We averaged a speed of 20 kilometers an hour on that horrific road, and were tossed about like corks on a stormy sea. Deborah and I passed from hysterical giggles to agonized silence, near to tears at times then back to laughter. It really was awful and by the end of the day we had several bruises from the bumping.

While we were at Inhaminga it rained some more, the road was churned into a bigger mess. If it were not for Big Foot we would not have made it back to Zimbabwe for Christmas. Nothing can stand in that brute's way. It plowed through the mud and pulled out many stuck vehicles along the way. We are very, very grateful for Big Foot.

March, 1997

Floods have overpowered and immobilized vast stretches of land in Mozambique. Hundreds of people have been evacuated by helicopters as they were left stranded on small islands. In some regions people fled into the forests where they could hold onto trees and branches to keep from being swept away.

Needless to say, the roads that are appalling at the best of times are now worse, and in some cases, nonexistent. Rodney, while traveling in the land cruiser got stuck in a porridge bowl of mud so deep he couldn't open the door to get out. He eventually got out on the opposite side which was lifted a bit higher. Supplies were needed at the Bible School and miraculously, Big Foot pushed through. Then on the return journey, even Big Foot was overcome by the mire. Eventually a bulldozer came to the rescue and pulled him out.

Rod arrived home four days late, the Pungwe river having flood-

ed the approaches to the bridge on both sides. He drove three kilometers on a road filled with water, then could go no further. Unable to turn around, he drove in reverse all the way back, precariously close to the eaten-away edges of the road. A bus full of passengers was swept away. Cars slipped over the edge of the road. How glad we were when at last he was safely home. And so built we the walls and carried supplies to Inhaminga.

Operation Nehemiah continues to this day as we restore more buildings and take teams out to build in the lives and hearts of the people of Mozambique. From our Command Post at Inhaminga, we are fulfilling every dream and vision that God showed us at the time when all was "bones". He had said "Prophesy to these bones and I will make them live." Our vision continues to grow as we reach out, making disciples, teaching them to be missionaries and leaders on their own continent.❖

Three

INHAMINGA BIBLE SCHOOL

MOBILE BUSH SCHOOLS

Throughout our bush walking ministry, we saw the tremendous lack of basic biblical teaching. In the scattered mud-hut churches, the saints meet regularly to pray and worship. On Sundays church starts early in the morning and ends at dusk. All night-prayer meetings are part of life. Their zeal and commitment are phenomenal, but they lack the knowledge of the Word of God. Instead of preaching from the Word, pastors share African folklore stories with a moral, as they know so few Bible stories. "Please teach us the Bible," they beg. Men in leadership of the flock mostly do not even own a Bible. Many of them could not read one if they did, but they are desperately hungry for the Word.

As we walked, men and women from the villages being keen to catch every teaching they could, walked with us as we continued on. Our "Mobile Bible School" was born. We talked as we walked, teaching around the campfire at night. Every day held more biblical examples than we could cover. Walking as Jesus and His disciples did, meeting with people, praying for them and counseling with them, was like living within the pages of the New Testament. When someone got healed, delivered from demons, whatever happened, there was an example already written in the Word. While these people have great faith in certain areas, fear rules them in others. Not only fear of war, but fear of witchcraft and the spiritual forces of darkness. Generally only those who are full of the power of the Holy Spirit can overcome these ancestral strongholds that have controlled and ruled their lives for centuries. *"One day soon, we shall have a Bible School where men can be taught the Word of God, be filled with His power and equipped to lead their people out of darkness into the light."* We spoke these words to ourselves, to the Mozambicans, to the creation around us. We believed it, it was our goal, our vision. One day as we were walking it occurred to us that this vision was already in first stage operation. It was a school on foot, a mobile Bible school.

Since 1987 we have held countless training seminars of four to six weeks where bush pastors come in from afar to attend the training sessions. These were held mostly in Malawi and the refugee camps. Now we had a place to use in Mozambique.

Starting from scratch at Command in 1994, the facilities were very rough. No desks and chairs, with only a reed mat on the ground to sleep on. Meals consisted of maize meal porridge and beans. There were not enough cups and plates for everyone, so the students had to share, taking turns to eat. We started with thirty students, but they kept coming. Soon there were forty eager men with six women earnestly pleading to be allowed to attend the lessons. "We cannot read or write," they said. "But we will sit very quietly and listen carefully and we will write the words of God on our hearts." We could not deny Living Bread to the spiritually hungry, so they joined the classes. Though the classes were for the pastors from the surrounding areas, the Holy Spirit brought in students from other provinces too. This was prophetic for the time when we would receive students from seven provinces for every school session.

In a time when the nation was trying to pick itself up out of the dust and ashes of war, the people too were struggling to find direction. Displaced peoples returned to their homes, some finding their families, some not. Others found their partners lost for many years, were now married to someone else, each presuming the other dead. Children had been born from other fathers. How did one begin to unravel the matted web of tangled lives? Many returned home maimed, with limbs missing, no money or means to start a new life. Within this situation, the church had to look up and live. People depended on direction from pastors who had little direction themselves. Attending the school helped these men find healing and purpose and new vision. There was little time to spend on dealing with personal trauma or counseling individuals. Together we met with God and He sent His Word and healed them. We worshipped together, wept together and laughed together while the Holy Spirit did the work.

In those early days we established through our prayers and faith a course that would take us on a path of growth and development that would amaze us all. It was largely done through the help of faithful friends.

WAYNE MYERS AND GOD'S BEST

To this back-of-the-woods outpost, God brought, and continues to bring, friends and ministers from across the oceans to encourage, inspire and help us. Speakers accustomed to addressing large crowds where they are recognized as some of God's best, continue to come to Inhaminga to preach and teach to small groups who have no knowledge of their significance at home.

The task ahead of us required a mammoth insurgence of faith. We had exercised immense faith through the past years. It was largely a faith to survive the dangers of war and to keep people alive in time of famine. It was a time packed with miraculous incidents of deliverance from death and danger and pushing through into the impossible. But it was not enough. We needed loads more faith for the work He has commissioned us to. To push us further on the faith experience, God sent His best man on the subject to spend time with us in Mozambique.

Wayne Myers, missionary to Mexico for over 50 years, was coming to Mozambique to teach on "Living to Give." He did this very effectively, but looking back, we think God brought Wayne more for our own personal benefit than for that of the Mozambicans!

Here was a man accustomed to preaching to thousands at a time, giving his very best to 50 bush pastors. He taught on the principles of greatness; serving and giving. It was revolutionary to the listeners. They had thought that in their poverty they had nothing to give. When the Word revealed how we rob God as we withhold our tithes and offerings, conviction fell heavily. Said one man, "Though we are still sitting here in our seats, in our spirits we are running away because we are ashamed of what we have been doing." Another cried out, "We are very convicted. It is like the bombs falling in the time of war. Yes, we are being bombed with the Word of God."

It was unbearably hot in the lecture room. All were wilting in their seats but Wayne preached with a vengeance, his bald head gleaming. It was more than the perspiration; the oil of the Spirit was poured out on him as he spoke with power and anointing.

His demonstration of *"Give and it shall be given unto you,"* brought the house down. Taking a teaspoon he measured a portion out of a bag of grain. "If this is how much you give, this is how much God will give back to you." Then he took a big shovel, filled it to overflowing and hurled it across the room. Men ducked and dived. "If that's the measure you'll give to God, that's how much He'll measure back to you." The principle made a powerful impact. If we will freely give, God will freely give back to us.

Wayne and Martha walked around the premises, not so much looking at all the improvements we had made, but observing what needed to be done. "You need a large generator so you can have lights at night," said Wayne. Sure we needed a generator, but we did not have the funds for one. You don't say things like that to Wayne, though. He kept telling us that if we had faith to believe, God would provide our every need according to His riches in glory. "The students need desks and chairs," he continued. We agreed. Wayne related story after story of incidents of God's miraculous provision in his life and in the lives of others. Our faith grew with each illustration. Wayne made mental notes and before he left for the USA, gave us the money for a new generator plus various other needs.

The school sessions were of such benefit we determined to increase the four weeks of training to three months three times a year. This meant we'd need full-time live-in teachers on staff. Where would we find teachers willing to live in this isolated wilderness of Inhaminga, and how would we be able to fund them? Our first intake of students arrived before we had the teachers. Pastor Rodgers and I started classes. Within three weeks we had some assistance from missionaries who were involved in another project. This was helpful but still not satisfactory. We needed people who would be totally committed to the school. We continued to pray for three full-time teachers. God had it all worked out. When He sent us three Brazilian teachers to work on a three year program, fully funded, we were over the moon. Now we had resident teachers who could take personal time with the students as well as teach daily classes.

With each student intake, the quality of lessons and materials continue to improve. It has been one-step-at-a-time progress, and the three-month sessions have now grown into two five-month schools a year, 45 to 60 men at a time who can read and write. Seminars are held for the illiterate. The premises continue to grow also, as more buildings are restored and facilities are added. The school, once a heap of ruins, is now an attractive oasis in the wilderness. Though simple and basic, it is neatly laid out, well-kept, and a source of amazement to all who wander far enough into the bush to see it. The buildings are painted brown to blend in with the natural surroundings.

There is a sense of peace as well as purpose; we just love it. "Who would ever have thought we'd see anything like this at Inhaminga!" is an exclamation commonly heard. Though there remains much to be done, we are very proud of the school that God has planted and is raising in the wilderness.

This is a growing period for us, just as much as it is for the church of Mozambique. Various visitors come and go, each adding blessing and growth to our lives as well as the school.

Our most precious visitor to the school is Mbuya. This is the Shona name for "Grandmother," and the name by which the African people call Ellie's mum, Batsie Snyders.

Mbuya is much loved in Zimbabwe where some years ago she sold her house and gave the money towards the building of a Children's Home, on the farm belonging to Don and Lorraine Odendaal, Ellie's sister and brother-in-law. This group is doing a great work there and Batsie is very active in the ministry. Among other things, she spends time visiting the old people (she is 75 years old), preaching and teaching in the rural areas and schools. She visited us many times in Malawi when we were cut off from our family, playing a vital role in our lives and ministry. She continues to do so. We were delighted to have her return to visit Inhaminga, and eager for her to see the renewed Bible School facilities. Rod flew her in to a very excited crowd of people. "The Mbuya who visited us during the dangers of war is coming back again!" She had been to Inhaminga when it was at its worst, in times of hardship and danger. She had even braved and survived the Inhaminga road. Now she was back and couldn't believe her eyes at the transformation around her. She ministered to the students and women's group and in the churches. They all loved her to bits.

It is such a privilege for us to have our mum visit the work and be part of it. She is our prayer warrior and we cannot thank God enough for giving us such a wonderful woman of God for a mother, grandmother and great-grandmother!

SCHOOL OF THE SPIRIT

While most of the students are from Pentecostal churches very few have experienced the Baptism of the Holy Spirit.
Each intake of students receives instruction from the Word of
God and most are filled to overflowing long before they prepare to go home again. It is amazing to see how they respond
to the teaching on the Holy Spirit. What they see in the Word
they believe, and thus they receive the baptism very simply and
easily. It is a joy to share these Holy Spirit times with visitors.
A team from Resurrection Fellowship was with us on an occasion when the Holy Spirit fell powerfully on the students.

The 43 students from 7 provinces of Mozambique were
thrilled to have visitors from across the big ocean. Sharing testimonies from different language and tribal backgrounds
enlarges their thinking. Because travel is difficult, many people
never move outside of their home province. At the school they
learn about what God is doing elsewhere in Mozambique, and
when foreigners come, they learn about what He is doing in
other parts of the world. They were hungry to receive the ful-
ness of the Spirit. We preached the Word of God with power
and the results were immediate.

*Isaiah 6. "I saw the Lord seated on a throne, high and lifted up,
and His glory filled the temple. The angels cried 'Holy, Holy, Holy is
the Lord, The whole earth is filled with His glory.' And the posts of the
door were shaken, the house was filled with smoke. Then said I 'Woe is
me, for I am undone, a man of unclean lips!' Then one of the angels flew
to me and touched my lips with a coal from the altar – and said to me,
'Behold, this has touched your lips; your iniquity is taken away and your
sin is purged.' Also, I heard the voice of the Lord saying: 'Whom shall I
send, and who will go for us?' Then said I, 'Here Am I, Lord, send me!'"*

We prayed for God to do all this in our lives. For the students to see His glory, to cry out, **Holy, Holy, Holy** till the
door posts of their hearts were shaken and filled with the glory
of God. For them to see their uncleanness and for God to
touch their lips with His fire till they were filled with His Spirit

and ready to answer to His call. It happened!

These students have never heard of the Toronto Blessing or the Brownsville Revival. The unusual manifestations of the Holy Spirit were brand new to them. As the power came down, many of them started to shake and weep. Some fell down under His power, some spoke in new languages. Two were supernaturally transported from one side of the room to the other, two bounced like the fastest rubber balls for a long time. Oh, the glory of His Presence! It was awesome, like the sound of a distant thunder, the sound of a pouring rain. Thirsty, thirsty, thirsty for the Spirit. Hungry, hungry, hungry for more of God.

The testimonies afterwards were beautiful in their simplicity.

"I don't know what happened to me. I began to shake all over. I became weak in my legs, then I began to speak in another language. I don't know this language. I have never heard this language before, yet I was speaking and speaking!"

"I felt something come all over me, and I felt that I could not stand. It was like a heavy bag of rice being put on my shoulders. It was so heavy I could not stand though I tried very hard to keep from falling over, but I could not. I fell to the ground and lay there for a long time while a bright light was shining around me." (A genuine case of being slain in the Spirit or what?)

"I don't know how it happened, but I was standing on that side of the room. Then I woke up and found I was lying on this side of the room. I do not know how I came to be here!" Another said, *"I was also on the other side of the room, then two angels came and lifted me up. They carried me, one at each elbow, and they placed me on this side of the room!"*

"I was weeping and weeping, yet I felt great joy. I don't know what has happened here today, we have never seen anything like this before. Surely the power of God is here with us."

What is this? This is THAT! which was spoken by the prophet Joel, *"And it shall come to pass afterward that I will pour out my Spirit on all flesh." (Joel 2:28,29)*

The Holy Spirit continues to pour Himself out on us all at the Bible School. We want no less than ALL God has for us, and as we grow in Him, He is able to fill us more and more.

The Bible School continues as the heartbeat of our ministry. Though we travel far and wide, everything we do ultimately returns to the school. It is here where disciples are being made, men who will in turn disciple others.

The student body is made up of diverse personalities. Some are already in the position of pastoring a church. Others are deacons and evangelists. Still others are new converts, with little experience in the Christian walk. Though it is not easy teaching such a mixed group, there are many advantages. Students learn from each other and grow together. Varying tribal customs and languages as well as various levels of maturity provide good opportunities for hands-on training in learning to flow and work together with people different from oneself. It is challenging to teach such a mixed group; there is never a dull moment, especially with lives as dramatically changed as that of Marco.

MARCO, THE WILD MAN BECOMES A PREACHER

He was a wild-looking man, uncombed bushy hair standing several inches high. His tempestuous eyes mirrored the chaos of his soul. They said he was mad for he lived the existence of a hermit, seldom speaking a word to any man. His lone hut was visited by no person. People pointed and laughed at him whenever he passed by. He kept company with himself and his garden.

Marco's garden was his pride and life. He planted pawpaw, bananas and vegetables. He also grew marijuana, hence the crazed eyes. Waking with the birds he rose early at dawn to tend his garden at Dimba. Dimba is the main water source for the Inhaminga region, situated three kilometers out of town. He carried water in buckets from the spring for the thirsty plants and watched over them like a hen watches over her chicks. He was rewarded with results like nobody else saw from their own gardens. His portion of land was the envy of all the other men, and there were those who were ready to kill for it.

There was one man who did not think Marco was loco. Rodney made a point of stopping to talk to Marco whenever he saw him walking along the road. A rapport quickly built up between them as he would stop the truck to chat with the man everyone else avoided. "How is your garden growing?" was a good place to start. The avid gardener was forever needing new seeds and wanting to try something different. One cannot buy seeds at Inhaminga and Rod periodically brought some from Zimbabwe.

One day, Rodney found Marco on his way out of town. Asked where he was heading, Marco replied that he was walking to Marromeu, over 100 kilometers away. "But why don't you get a ride on one of the trucks going that way?" asked Rodney. "I have no money but I must go, so I will walk." Rodney dug in his pocket to find enough for Marco to ride there and back. The man was overwhelmed. Never before had he received anything for nothing and without even asking.

The relationship bond continued to strengthen, then two Portuguese-speaking missionaries visited Marco in his field and challenged him to receive Christ. Both missionaries had been marijuana smokers before their conversion and could from experience testify of the deliverance that came through Jesus Christ. Marco believed and repented. He immediately started pulling out the marijuana in his field by the roots. He was not delivered from the desire for it, however, and still managed periodically to find it from somewhere.

In the meantime the local Christians were alerted to show love and encouragement to the man who had accepted Christ. He seldom attended church though, because each time he left his field, jealous neighbors who did not have such good results in harvest would come and steal his produce. The neighbors became increasingly malicious, and one night a group of them attacked Marco with pangas (long knives). They slashed at his back, neck and head. Marco managed to break loose and started running up the mountain to Command. We were getting ready for dinner when we heard the pounding of running feet and wild yells. The pursuers had stopped short of entering the premises. Blood covered the ripped shirt and by the light Rodney examined the wounds. They were not too bad but the woolly head needed stitching. Rod repaired the gash. We gave Marco a bed for the night; it was not safe for him to return to his hut. During that night the marauders chopped down his paw-paw trees, slashed the bananas and stole the produce.

Persecution of the new convert intensified, fuelled by the village chief, who was also deeply involved in witchcraft. Then someone burned Marco's hut down. We hired someone to build a new one. In spite of all the adversity, Marco continued to grow in his faith with much encouragement from the team members. Water baptism brought a tremendous breakthrough for him. When preparing to satisfy his addiction, Marco began to feel intensely ill at the smell of the marijuana. He could not touch it. He was delivered of the addiction when he took the step of obedience to Christ through water baptism!

With this deliverance, his testimony took on a powerful dimension. As Marco witnessed to people, conviction fell upon them and they repented. Soon there was a sizeable group praying regularly with him at Dimba. This number included the very chief that advocated persecution against Marco. So affected was he by the change in this "madman" he repented of his own sin and has left his witchcraft practices. Now several of Marco's former persecutors have also received Christ. When a widow in the area lost the thatch off her hut due to a fire, Marco put on a new roof for her, as she had no husband to help her. His testimony is not only in word, but also in deed.

Marco continues to plant vegetables, working hard in God's field as well as his own. The one-time hermit is now a messenger of Christ. The people in his group wanted him to become their new pastor. "But I feel I am not yet ready to take the position of pastor," Marco confided in Rod. "I need to study the Word of God. Please, may I attend the Afrika wa Yesu Bible School?"

We took Marco in as a student. He did not find studying easy, but he worked hard at the course. The Bible School exists for people like Marco, as well as for pastors and leaders who already have had quite a lot of training. It is for all men who hunger to grow in the knowledge and love of the Word of God, and who desire to equip themselves to serve the flock of Jesus Christ.

If you go down to Dimba today you will find Marco there, a living testimony of God's power to change the heart of man through the love of Jesus Christ. He has evangelized and planted more churches in a short space of time than any of the experienced pastors in the region.

"Faith cries out from our hearts today, declaring the power and joy that comes from daring to believe God. Where do you stand in faith today? Are you gaining good ground on the road of your destiny in God... Or have you grown weary and slowed down? Faith challenges you today to reach beyond any boundary that you've set yourself or crossed before. It's time to cross the line and dare to believe for the impossible in God's provision for your life and ministry.

We as a team have received a revolutionary insurgence of faith. Not merely name it and claim it, but pure faith as in Hebrews 11:1 "Now faith is the assurance (the confirmation, the title deed) of the things we hope for, being the proof of things we do not see and the conviction of their reality (faith perceiving as real fact what is not revealed to the senses.)"

-Newsletter, June 1996

STATEMENT OF PURPOSE

Afrika wa Yesu (Africa for Jesus) Bible School exists to equip believers to affect their areas of influence through the love of Christ. To inspire them to receive and impart vision, direction and knowledge of the Word. To assist them to find God's place in their lives as well as in their nation. To become true and faithful disciples of Jesus who will make disciples also.

This training center offers balanced teaching from the Word of God – with emphasis on praise and worship, prayer and intercession, life in the Spirit and practical ministry preparation.

Above all, the school strives to be a school of prayer and worship. The focus is practical rather than theological.

The school draws students from seven provinces in Mozambique, thus teaching them to work together with different tribes, using this also as a tool to carry the spirit of worship and truth into the regions beyond.

The Commission continues till Jesus comes again.❖

BRAZIL COMES TO
MOZAMBIQUE

A CHINESE MEAL IN BIRMINGHAM

God has His own way of putting His children together for His projects. I can imagine Him having a certain plan in mind, and looking around at His children to see whom He will pick to do certain tasks. It does not matter to God where we are from or what language we speak. We are all His children and He knows us each by name. He knows our gifting, character and potential, and with these in mind, He puts together a group which may seem mismatched in the natural, but is actually perfectly matched for the job. Now the groundwork for a far greater purpose than we had envisioned was being laid.

Our friends Nick & Lois Cuthbert had invited us to visit and minister at their church, Riverside Fellowship in Birmingham. Nick mentioned that he was meeting with a Christian businessman, Bob Edmiston, whom he believed we should meet also. Bob Edmiston is the President of the UK-based ministry Christian Vision. This ministry operates internationally, largely through Christian Broadcasting programs. Bob also happens to be a multimillionaire. Nick communicated with Bob who the same day heard about us from a different source. This confirmed to Bob that he should meet us.

We seldom get to eat Chinese food, which we love, so when we met with Bob and Tracie at a top Chinese restaurant in Birmingham, we had big plans to enjoy Chinese at its best. Nick and Lois had the same plans; theirs were fulfilled, ours were not. Bob and Tracie are a great team with a love for the nations of the world. They plied us with questions about Mozambique and we were so keen to answer each question fully, neither of us got to eat more than a few small mouthfuls. However, it turned out to be one of the most beneficial meals of our lives, the food (or lack of it) being of no importance.

"What strategy would you use to reach Mozambique for Christ?" We shared the plan that had been in our hearts through the war years, waiting to be birthed during the time of peace. If we could put a team of seven or eight people in each of the five most Northern provinces, we could impact the nation significantly with the gospel. These teams would evangelize and plant churches out of new converts. Few missionaries were moving in the North. The South was being touched, though in a limited way through Zimbabwe and South Africa. We like to work where the need is the greatest. The Inhaminga Bible School was top of our agenda. Drawing prospective leaders from the new converts who would be won through the provincial church planting program and training them at Inhaminga would be an ideal way to raise up Holy Spirit empowered leadership. It was a good plan, but a plan we could never institute on our own. We needed mature Portuguese-speaking Christians who were prepared to brave the unknown and sacrifice much, perhaps more than they could even imagine, in order to fulfill the call to Mozambique.

Bob talked a bit about his vision to reach a billion people with the gospel through Christian radio. Already he had a radio station and ministry base set up in Zambia where Christian Vision has a farm, Primary School and a Bible School. He was very interested in Mozambique and encouraged us in our work, blessing us with a significant financial gift for the work before we parted company. We had no idea what God was setting in motion through that meeting which he had planned. It turned out to be the Chinese meal of a lifetime.

Some weeks after meeting us in Birmingham, Bob made a scheduled visit to Brazil. While talking to Pastor Samuel Camara of the Brazilian Assemblies of God, and hearing his vision to send missionaries from Brazil to Portuguese-speaking countries around the world, an idea came into Bob's head. This idea became the seed of an amazing project, which the Holy Spirit would birth and bring to fruition. The idea was, "Rod needs missionaries for Mozambique, Samuel wants to send missionaries. Perhaps I can put this together!"

Bob telephoned Rod in Africa and in his direct manner got straight to the point. "If I send you one hundred missionaries for Mozambique, can you handle it?" "Yes, let's go for it," Rod did not hesitate. The wheels began to turn.

Pastor Samuel Camara was at the time based in Manaus on the Amazon River. Through a selection process he gathered together the missionaries who would come out on a three-year-project. In the end it was not one hundred, but over fifty who came, plus eleven children. We would not be reaching only five provinces, but the seven most Northern provinces of Manica, Sofala, Zambezia, Tete, Niassa, Nampula and Cabo del Gado. National Mozambicans joining the project made up the figure of one hundred.

The strategy was formed through numerous faxes and visits back and forth. Each province would have a married couple living in the provincial capital city. Five or six single missionaries known as local pastors, (a few of them came out as married couples) would be located to various parts of the respective province. These would relate and work under the leadership of the married couple in the capital, known as the Regional Pastors. Each Provincial pastor would report to the overall leader, Pastor Aldenor Do Vale who was to live in Beira with his wife Ercelia and their three sons, Thiago, Lucas and Andre.

Our part would be to assist in the initiation and logistics of the project. We would put the missionaries through practical training as they arrived in groups. We would also visit the missionaries on location, show the *JESUS* film to bring in the harvest and act as a general backup. Rod would also be responsible for the maintenance of eight white land rovers assigned to the provinces.

HANDS-ON TRAINING

The Visao Crista (Christian Vision) missionaries arrived in 1996 for their three-year-project, full of excitement and anticipation. On the first night of meetings in Mutare before they were to go into Mozambique, Rodney showed some of our slide pictures and gave a brief talk. He shared about the spiritually dry years when few missionaries would venture into Mozambique and how we had cried out to the Lord of the harvest to raise up laborers.

"You are the answer to many years of prayer and intercession for God to send workers into Mozambique. God has heard the cries of suffering Christians throughout Mozambique. You are the response to the cry of the blood of the martyrs that has drenched Mozambican soil."

So overwhelmed were the young Brazilians by the presence of God, they prostrated themselves on the ground in weeping and worship. When hearts are as soft and pliable as this, there is no end to what God can do.

Ours was the task to initiate these missionaries into Mozambique. Where does one start and how does one adequately prepare and train a group of people for three years in Mozambique? All the theory had been taken care of in Brazil. It remained for us to give a few lectures, but most of all, hands-on training. An outline can be planned, but most hands-on training happens naturally as we stay on the alert, recognizing the moment of opportunity as it comes up.

It was good to have Tracie as well as Steve Chase who is the Director of African Division for Christian Vision with us on some of the hands-on training programs. Thirty-eight of us headed for the Mozambique border, and then on to Inhaminga.

Our first hands-on lesson was right at the border post.

The Brazilians were wound up with excitement. They could not wait to put their feet on Mozambican soil. We stopped the truck at the border post and Rod went in to start the crossing formalities. A tired-looking man in his thirties joined the long waiting line. We started talking to him and he revealed the reason for his dejection. "I can't wait to get out of this country," he said. "Mozambique is a corrupt, rotten nation. The government robs you day and night. It is impossible to achieve anything without paying heavy bribes all the way. I've tried for eighteen months, now I've lost all my money. I'm getting out and I'll never set foot in this place again. I know some missionaries who are packing up, too. How long did you say these Brazilians would be in Mozambique? Three years? I feel sorry for them; they probably won't last."

These were just a few statements that echoed the disappointments of others who were finding Mozambique too difficult. While this disillusioned man was feeling pity for the Brazilians, they were having the time of their lives. They started singing in the parking lot, and immediately a group of people gathered around. They ministered Jesus to them, and within fifteen minutes five souls were added to the Kingdom of God. Here in this so-called hopeless nation is a magnificent harvest ripe for the picking. **God's best gifts to us are not things, but opportunities.** Here, opportunity lies around every corner; what a great nation to be in!

We arrived at Inhaminga late in the afternoon after a wearying journey. Sunday dawned and aching bodies dragged themselves off reed sleeping mats to enjoy a meal of coffee and rolls before setting off on a mission they had already been briefed on. Rod took them to a central point where they were met by National church leaders from various churches. They were divided into groups and sent out on foot to preach the gospel, heal the sick, cast out demons and all else that happens on mission outreach when teams eat, sleep and live in the mud-hut villages. The added value of this experience would be when they all returned and shared what they had seen, heard and done. Discussions on questions asked and first hand experiences shared are often the best way to teach. This way topics get covered that would otherwise never be mentioned in a normal topical lecture.

The groups returned rejoicing with testimonies of victory.

"The moment our feet touched the soil of Mozambique, God gave us souls. This was prophesied in Brazil before we left, that the Holy Spirit would be upon us in power the moment we entered the land."

"Something happened in the skies. I could see the glory of God. The sun is shining on us. Many angels, there is glory all around."

With so much progress made on the Bible School premises, it is hard for someone who did not see it before to imagine what the empty ruined shell was like. In place of cracked and broken walls and rubble are strong walls freshly painted. Window frames and panes, plumbing and electric wiring have transformed the place. This is not true for most of Mozambique, however. It was vital for the Brazilians to comprehend what Mozambique has come out of if they were to truly know the people and fully understand their own role in bringing life and restoration.

One does not have to look far for a practical example of destruction in this country. A few hundred yards from the main school complex stands the shell of a once lovely house. We took the group over and walked in silent prayer through the rooms. For many Mozambicans, little has changed since the cessation of the war. The poverty and hopelessness remain, just as this shell remains among the restored buildings. The Holy Spirit spoke to individual hearts. Tears wet their faces. We joined in a central room where weeds and thorns grew through the cracked foundations. Then someone pointed out a small white flower growing in the center of the room. What a message of hope we found in that brave, pure white blossom struggling through the debris with its head held up. "This is a new day. This is the time for restoration, for hope, for seeds to grow and multiply. The past is over and gone, we reach out for new things in Christ Jesus and His work in Mozambique." The prophetic prayer triggered off a time of thanksgiving. *A baptism of gratitude washed over us. It was as if we felt the gratitude of many generations who had given their lives for the Gospel.* And we felt the gratitude of the thousands who would receive new life through this Brazilian project in years to come.

The few days of training passed very rapidly. Our worship times in the main lecture room at the Bible School were precious. God continued to confirm and strengthen things He had spoken to us. We realized that He had a unique purpose in bringing all these Brazilians to Mozambique. I shared a prophetic word that had been growing in me. *"God has saved the best wine for last. Many missionaries have come and done a good work, but God has brought Brazil to Mozambique at this appointed time. They are the best wine saved for last."*

Three years later at the conclusion of this particular project we still believe this. Brazil will continue to feature significantly in the harvest of souls in Mozambique. Perhaps the final harvest before Jesus returns will be gathered by the Mozambicans themselves who are in training and already gathering the souls as missionaries to their own nation.

STAKE YOUR CLAIM

The Brazilians did not have it easy. There is only one vehicle per province, for the use of the Regional Coordinator. The rest must catch a lift, ride a bicycle or walk. Each missionary was dropped off at their specific location and left very much on their own to stake a claim for their spiritual gold mine. This means finding a place to live, planting a church from new converts, then putting up a building in which to meet together. We traveled around and visited them periodically, always touched by what we saw.

We drove for ten hours through magnificent mountain scenery to visit Andre in Angonia district. As we were asking for directions to Andre's house, a bicycle hurtled down the road in a cloud of dust. A figure leapt off and hugged Rod's neck, expressing welcomes in Portuguese. Andre was so happy to see us his eyes were swimming in tears. It gets lonely out there. We had arrived a couple of hours later than he had anticipated and he was getting worried that we might not pitch up. "People have walked for miles to come and see the *JESUS* film tonight," he told us. We went straight to the soccer field to set up the equipment so the people could see we had truly arrived. Soon the loudspeakers were reverberating the good news across the town. "Tonight, free of charge, come and see the life story of Jesus Christ, Who loves you and died for you." A multitude of people attended. Here the people were largely animistic in religion. They came openly to hear about yet another god, and many met with the One True God.

In the morning we spent some time chatting with Andre, encouraging him in the work and listening to the details of his ministry in the region. He was starved for Western fellowship and talked and talked while we fired questions at him. He told us how he had lived in a mud hut for the first few months after his arrival. Then some folk he had befriended made a way for him to rent a small brick house with secure windows and doors as the thieves had visited his hut regularly to steal the few possessions he owned.

Andre is a worshipper and loves to play the guitar and sing to God. Not knowing a soul when he arrived, he started the only way he knew how, through worship. Out in the open, under a eucalyptus tree in full view of passers-by, Andre got down on his knees. He played his guitar, sang and prayed out loud. Day in and day out he worshipped God. Each day some folk would stand around and watch. Who can know the extent of God's work in the lives of those who watched this young Brazilian unashamedly worship his God?

Finally, a woman came to ask him questions. "Like Lydia in the Bible," he told us. She understood the message of salvation and persuaded three more women and a man to meet with Andre also. A church was born.

Ronaldo arrived at Nacala on a Saturday morning with two bags of his clothes, blanket and study materials, plus a few personal belongings. Nacala is a beautiful seaport but a tough location spiritually as the coastlands of Mozambique are predominantly Islamic. Ronaldo knew nobody and had no place to stay. He was a stranger in a strange land with the commission to plant a church. By late afternoon he was feeling a bit worn and hungry. He got chatting to some people who gave him some food. He found a room to stay in and held his first meeting that night with some folk he had gathered by speaking to them on the streets and inviting them in. He harvested four souls.

Breakthrough came when Ronaldo was asked to visit a Muslim in hospital who was not expected to live. He prayed for the man and immediately there was a change. He returned a few times and soon the man was released from hospital. The patient in the bed next to him was also healed. Healing is a powerful testimony of the love of God. People were amazed and the church grew in numbers.

Ronaldo was excited to have us visit and we showed the *JESUS* film twice. The Muslims came in droves under the cover of night to watch the movie. Not wanting to be recognized by their religious leaders, they wait until it is dark. Funny enough, their leaders often do the same. We left a happy missionary saying, "Now my work will be much easier here. The people have been deeply moved by the film."

Sumaia and Fransisca are two young girls from the Amazon who heard God speak to them in their hearts as He spoke to Abraham. *"Get thee out from thy country, and from thy kindred, and from thy father's house unto a land that I will show thee."* *Genesis 12:1. (KJV)*

So they left their homes, families and friends for a three year commitment to Mozambique. They were dropped off at Nhamatanda with the usual Brazilian commission. "Find a place to live, get to know the people, plant a church and raise up future leaders." Wandering around and making inquiries in their Brazilian Portuguese, they found a room to rent where they stayed till they got the feel of things. They decided to move on to Metuchira just 13 kilometers away, where there is a greater concentration of people. On the 13th of March 1997, they started visiting people and witnessing from house to house. Within a few weeks they had a congregation of 35 adults, all new converts, and a horde of children meeting under a tree for Sunday church. In April they selected a piece of land on which to build and within a year completed a 16x6-meter brick church. This is no small achievement for two girls in a strange land. Theirs was the first church building to be completed on the project. Not bad for a couple of girls! Today the church is full, and they have also built another one at Nhamatanda where they originally stopped the first time.

We continue to visit these churches and others throughout Mozambique. The tracks of our land cruiser are imprinted deep into the heart of Mozambique. On one specific trip to the North, we bounced and rolled from village to village for three weeks, carrying the precious cargo of the Gospel to thousands waiting to see the *JESUS* film. One group joyfully spoke out, "For two years we have been waiting for you to come. Now you are here and we are very happy." During this trip, over 50,000 people saw this powerful movie. Thousands responded to the invitation to receive Christ as Savior. In some places the congregations doubled in size after our visit. The mosques were left with some empty kneeling-places.

Of course the roads were terrible. It was a tough and tiresome journey, taking six hours to cover 90 miles in some places. At times our progress was so slow the bicycles and even pedestrians passed us. We also had the normal fun of getting stuck in the mud and having to winch ourselves out.

So what's a trip like this really like? The landscape is magnificent. Mountains and rock formations to delight the eye. It is a time for reflection as the miles are slowly eaten up. That rare and precious commodity, "time" is present in all its fullness. For some, this is the most difficult thing. In an age where we are all crying out for more time, many don't know what to do with it when they have it. It has been said, *"To do nothing is often more difficult than to do the greatest exploits, and to submit requires more faith than to achieve."* For us as a family, it is a great gift when we can just be together, day in and day out without the usual separations. For three weeks Deborah hung on her Daddy's neck from the back seat almost all the way while he was driving.

We ate when we could, showered when there was water and slept on the side of the road many times. We had our tents and sleeping bags, which worked well except when the ants got in and tried to carry us out. No hot showers. A bucket in the middle of the floor is a luxury. Dip in the cup, wet the body all over, soap and scrub and rinse off. The toilet facilities (or lack of them) are the worst thing to get used to. Sparse thatch staked around a hole in the ground. No roof; hopefully nobody will peer over the top. The problem is that a couple of hundred people at the meetings are using the same hole, a lot of them inaccurately. Hold your nose, watch your step and woe to him who has to go at night. This is all part of preaching the gospel in rural Mozambique. It's not all glory stories and romantic canoe rides, but the reward is pure gold and eternal.

THREE-YEAR-PROJECT CONCLUDES

God is not limited by man, but He does use man to release His blessings. He has big pockets that never empty, and He loves to use the heart of man through which to pour His resources.

For this Mozambique project, God chose one of the biggest hearts available. Bob Edmiston has been and is the heart of provision for this project. Bob is not just a rich man. He is a man that works very hard for his money and seriously considers the stewardship of it. God blesses and multiplies it back to him as he pours it out into the harvest fields. Bob's wife Tracie, has a heart that matches his own and enough enthusiasm to shake the foundations of a nation.

As we wind down the project for missionaries to begin to return home in groups, questions leap to the mind. What is the true success of this project? Are the National pastors able to carry the work? Where do we go from here?

Twelve of us joined up in Beira to commence a ten-day journey flying from province to province to see the work in action and the churches that have been built. Christian Vision hired a Cessna Grand Caravan for the trip. Rod finally got to fly in his **dream plane!**

It was a great team made up of the leaders of the project from the UK, Brazil, and us two from Zimbabwe. The flow of love, unity and vision in the team made up of all these nationalities was a beautiful experience.

At each provincial airport we were met by singing Africans and the Brazilian missionaries who have planted the churches. We were then bundled into whatever transport was available and driven from location to location. What a thrill to see the church buildings. They are built simply and practically, fresh paint and strong structures making them stand out impressively like beacons in the midst of the drab and bedraggled surroundings of Mozambican towns and villages.

Through this project 154 church buildings have been erected. These consist of 34 brick and cement churches with metal roofs; 50 brick and cement buildings with thatch roofs, and 70 pole-and-mud churches with thatch.

Some of the churches have been in use for a while, others completed just in time to be inaugurated during our visit. How proud the missionaries and the congregations are! In some cases the finishing touches of the paintbrush were being applied at the time of our arrival. All had worked so hard to try and get the building finished in time.

This project has turned out to be an amazing method of impacting a nation. For years the land has lain desolate with little visible evidence of a strong Christian representation. Roman Catholic cathedrals and Islamic mosques built a long time ago dominate the landscape and have dominated lives for too long.

Though many missionaries have come in since the cessation of the war, mostly they are small groups doing what they can with little resources on hand. Some have given up and gone home, finding Mozambique too difficult a place in which to work. One of the Pastors thanked Bob Edmiston with tears on his face. *"I have no words to say what we feel, no words that are enough to thank you. We have had people come here before, and then they say, 'No. It is impossible to plant a church in this place. It cannot work, it is too difficult,' but these Brazilian missionaries have done it."*

Evangelical and Pentecostal Christians have struggled to find places of worship. Too poor to put money into buildings that can house more than a very small group, it has been difficult to make a forceful statement in the community. Now these new church buildings, most of them placed in strategic, highly visible places, proclaim a message in themselves. **"We are here to make an impact for Christ! We stand strong and sure, and we shall not be moved!"**

Certainly as far as we know, Mozambique has never before experienced such an onslaught on the kingdom of darkness by a single organization. The combination of funding from Christian Vision and workers from Brazil has brought about the fruit of true success, in that the face of a nation has been affected and changed through the work of the Gospel.

While we rejoice to see these church buildings, our real joy is in the people that gather inside. The church is people, not bricks and mortar. Men and women, young and old, teenagers and small children, singing and dancing to the rhythm of Africa's heartbeat for Jesus.

Few things can touch the heart as the testimonies of lives changed by the power of God. At Alto Molocue, we heard a man testify of his total deliverance from evil. He had been an alcoholic. His wife was unable to bear children and had three times miscarried a child. Theirs was a miserable life dominated by alcohol and witchcraft. Then he made a decision to follow Jesus. The chains of darkness and bondage fell off as he was delivered from alcohol and other strongholds in his life. God saved, cleansed and set them free. Before long his wife was again pregnant and this time she carried the child to full term. They proudly held up a boy for everyone to see. The whole church clapped and cheered, sharing in their joy and victory! This is also a powerful testimony to the unbelievers. When they see the power of the God these people serve, many times they say, **"This God of yours, we want Him to be our God, too."**

At Lichinga we saw the dents in the roof where persecuting Muslims had thrown rocks at the Christians when they came to worship in the new church. It was so bad they had to shut the windows and doors for protection while praying. When a Muslim is converted to Christianity, he is usually excommunicated from his family and suffers much persecution. The congregation had chosen to build the church right in the Islamic center of town. This bold proclamation angered the people and the forces of darkness, but the church is not here to appease the devil. We are here to reclaim the territory he has stolen. Today, the Muslims are no longer stoning the Christians. The completed church and the stand they have made is a strong testimony of God's power. They have won the respect of the community! Several Muslim families have converted to Christianity.

On our journey we had the joy of seeing the Bible students in action back in their home churches. When the students return to their home towns after being at the Bible School, they are filled with zeal and energy, ready to share with others the things they have learned. As time goes by, it is not always easy for us to know how they are really doing, as some come from very far. Traveling around like this enables us to gain a better idea of how successful their training really was. There are those who have not done very well. Because the churches are being planted from new converts, there is not always time for students to be tried and tested before being sent to the school. On the other hand, some of the newer converts make up the better part of ministry potential, as they are not full of dead traditions as is often the case of those who've been in churches for a long time.

Either way, we do our best and God does the rest. Mostly, the students do well and it is a great joy for us to see them on their home field and to see the fruit of the labors of those that have taught and nurtured them at the school.

IMPACTING A NATION

National Mozambican church leaders have taken over the reins of the churches. All but twenty missionaries will return to Brazil. Those who remain will continue to be involved with the churches for two more years. During this time any problems and difficulties that arise, areas where the new leaders may be struggling in, can be taken care of. This ensures the success of the National takeover. As the congregations grow in number and the churches multiply through new churches being planted, students will continue to flow through the Afrika wa Yesu Bible School at Inhaminga.

It is always hard to say goodbye. The services we've attended in each church have been joyful in giving thanks for the work that has been done, and sad in saying farewell to the missionaries who are returning to Brazil. Laughter and tears are the natural combination of the saints of God. It has been touching to see the genuine love that the local people have for the Brazilian missionaries. These are they who came from a far country to tell them about the saving power of JESUS. These are they who have lived with them, shared their hearts, partaking of their joys and sorrows. Together they have fought the spiritual wars and attempts to destroy the work of God. Together they have won the victory and established strong churches.

Now the time for farewell has come and it hurts to say goodbye. Just as the disciples sorrowed to hear Jesus say He was going away, these people are feeling the loss and insecurity of being left on their own. Yet Jesus said, *"I will not leave you comfortless, but the Holy Spirit will come not many days from now."* In the same way, these churches are not being left on their own, they have trained leaders to carry on the work. Most of all, they are the responsibility of the Holy Spirit.

The missionaries too are feeling a great loss and for some of them it will be difficult integrating back into their Brazilian society and work. As one of them said, "It was easier for me to come out to Africa to a land I did not know, than it is to leave Africa and return to my own land."

THE COST

Can one measure the volume and depth of a soul poured out to its last drop? The homesickness of not seeing family and loved ones for three years? The loneliness and isolation, malaria and hardships of a strange land?

The cup of desolation, desperation and uncertainty brimmed over many a time for these brave missionaries who left all that was familiar to them for three years to obey the Macedonian call: **"Come over into Mozambique and help us!"**

How does one measure the depth of pain of the grave where three-year-old Leticia lies buried in Pemba after malaria took her young life? We stood together around that small grave where the ultimate sacrifice a missionary couple can give, lay buried. Surely a great harvest is promised from this little seed planted here. We prayed for Lourival and Nazoeme who must soon board the plane home without Leticia sitting beside them. God in His amazing grace has blessed them with another little girl. While no child can replace the loss of another, we rejoice that they do not go home with empty arms. Smiling, bouncing Carolina will ease their pain.

The graveyard at Pemba is situated on a hill surrounded by the turquoise bay of the Indian Ocean – a place of sorrow situated in such a place of beauty. It's the most amazing location of a graveyard one can imagine. As one looks out onto the sparkling ocean, it is impossible not to marvel at the greatness of God and His creation. It gives hope and the assurance of wondrous things to come, for we know that heaven is far more beautiful than anything on this earth.

Our routing took us from Beira to Alto Molocue,

Nampula, Pemba, Lichinga, Songo, Tete, Chimoio, then our last stop through Inhaminga to visit the Bible School before going back to Beira for the Grande Finale Celebration. The Bible School is the joy of our hearts so for us it was a case of saving the best for last.

The tractor and trailer met us at the grass airstrip to transport the visitors to the Bible School. It was very special to see the lecture hall packed full of students, the school grounds men and workers, and the visiting team. We had just come from the various provincial homes of the students, and here they were gathered all together to be sent back, equipped in the Word and full of the Holy Spirit. To have Bob and Tracie there who together have contributed so much to the Bible School was a great honor.

Some years ago we had on our "goals" list, the need for a vibrant church at Inhaminga housed in a good structure. Restoring the Bible School kept us so busy, we never had the time to put up a big church building. Now Danilo, who is one of the missionaries who concluded his three years with us as a teacher has built and planted a church not far from the school. After the group visited the Bible School we all climbed back into the trailer to visit the church for the inauguration service. We rejoice to see this day. It is a tremendous spiritual victory for Inhaminga, the so-called place of bones, which has now come to life!

The teachers who gave three years of their lives to the school will ever live in our memory and hearts. Their commitment and sacrifice has contributed enormously to the success of the school, and the overall project in training up men in the Word of God. Our special thanks go to Danilo, Lindalva and Nailza for their faithfulness.

All things considered, the project has been a great success. All that remains now is to see the churches running themselves and raising up from within their own congregations enough finances to support their own pastor, do outreach and in turn plant another church. In other words, the church must be able to operate and multiply without any dependence on outside support. It has been concluded that the greatest need remaining is for continued leadership training. Though we have many plans for missions growth in Mozambique, the Bible School at Inhaminga remains our chief focus. What a wonderful way to end 1999 and prepare for 2000!

The year 2000 ushered in the gift of three new teachers, this time from Christ For The Nations, Brazil. Our special thanks to Pastor Gary Haynes and the staff who selected to send us Arnaldo, Gilda and Patricia. Lindalva opted to return for another two years. These four teachers are a dynamic force and we delight in seeing the level of the teaching and the school in general grow from glory to glory.❖

AMERICA,
LAND OF BLESSING

FRIENDS

Friendship is a priceless gift. It is the special ingredient
that brings to perfection any relationship, whether it be in marriage, family, work or business.

We as a family have been blessed with friends that have
stood with us for years. They love us, pray for us, support us,
inspire us and give encouragement and advice when we need it.
These friends are the strength and courage without whom we
would never have been able to do the work to which God has
called us. They come from various nations, of a wide diversity
of character and gifting, and of amazing generosity. We
acknowledge and appreciate each person who has touched our
lives and touched others through us.

It was Don and Cindy Normand who took us in and
began to connect us to contacts of their own. This spread into
a network of supporters which continues today. Don and
Cindy, born and raised in Africa, were used dynamically for
God in Africa for many years before they moved to the USA.
Today, Don is accepted as a great teacher throughout the
States. This couple adopted us and helped us get our network
of ministry going in America. We are eternally indebted to
them for their faith in us, for looking past the very unpolished
exterior and believing God could do something with us.

Cindy worked hard typing and mailing our newsletters, while Don worked on people, convincing anyone he could get hold of that they should have us minister in their church. Don is very persuasive and there are not many people who get away with a "No!" He called Christ for the Nations in Dallas and told them as only Don can, "You have **got** to meet these people." We found ourselves on our way to Dallas with our three children, and that was the beginning of an amazing relationship that has grown over the years. Thank you, Don and Cindy. We love and appreciate you very much!

Through the love and acceptance of Freda Lindsay and those at CFNI, we met many others who have vitally impacted our lives. We gained remarkable acceptance at CFNI and have had the honor through the years of speaking at several "Prime Time" sessions as well as teaching in some of the classes. These are the folk who gave us the funds to buy the white land cruiser in 1987, which we still drive today. This vehicle was the breakthrough we needed in Africa. No longer did we break down in our old truck in "Ambush Alley", but forded through war zones, rivers, mud valleys and mountains with the Gospel. CFNI also printed our first book, **"Mozambique, The Cross and the Crown."** They promoted our book through their own advertising network and have used it for missions training in their school. Now we are linked even more closely through being part of CFNABS (Christ For The Nations Association of Bible Schools).

PEACE BEFORE THE STORM

On average, we visited the States once in three years. Each visit was always in the midst of some crisis, due to the war and famine. Boarding the plane from Africa was always hard. We were torn away from loved ones we might never see again. Sometimes we returned to find that pastors and friends had died in our absence.

Now, in 1997, we would visit in a time of peace. It was a new and glorious experience. We had no pressures beyond those of normal ministry on the field. Tammy and Dustin were both grown up and settled in good jobs. Deborah was still at school; we had made every provision for her care during our absence. We had nothing to worry about, nothing to fear; or so we thought. We intended to have a great trip, spending time together as husband and wife and visiting dear friends as we traveled around in ministry. We had never felt so free and at ease. It was wonderful.

Our ministry started in Texas, from where we took a first-time visit to Mexico. Wayne and Martha Myers met us at the airport in Mexico City. It was a brand new experience; never had we imagined anything like Mexico City. We fell in love with the Mexican people! Spending time with Wayne and Martha in their home, seeing the city and visiting churches with them was a very special experience. We returned to the United States and drove across to Florida from Texas. It was here that without warning, the most devastating storm of our lives erupted in full force. Our hearts are forever scarred by the effects of this tragic event that took the life of our only son.❖

DUSTIN

On 11th October 1997, our son passed through heaven's gates. It is not possible to put into words the emotions and pain of such a loss. One cannot measure the depth of pain that lies in the grave. It is also impossible to find the words to tell of the love and power of God at such a time as this. One cannot measure the depth nor height of His love, grace and comfort.

November Newsletter, 1997

Dear Friends,

This is a very difficult letter to write, but we have chosen to share with you some of the things we have experienced in the tragic death of our beloved son, Dustin. We know that many of you have carried us in love and prayer, and through events we share, you will see how wonderfully God has answered your prayers.

Since the beginning of time, starting with Adam and Eve, and through all the ages, mothers and fathers have wept and grieved over the death of their sons. Mary wept over Jesus, the heart of the Father was in anguish over the death of His only begotten Son on the Cross.

Some of you have never personally encountered death at such a close range, many of you have. Death will come to us all, and to all of our loved ones. How will we respond in the face of the worst devastation? For Ellie, it was as if Dustin had been torn out of her womb. For Rod, the desolation that only a father can know when his only son is taken from him.

Several friends have spoken to us of their fear of being unable to cope should such a tragedy hit their lives. To those of you who are concerned about the same, we say, fear not. God has never been more real to us, Jesus never a closer friend, and the Holy Spirit never more comforting. He even does our thinking for us when sorrow clouds our understanding and we don't even know where we are. In the spaces of empty despair that come when we have no more strength, God is there. When we can no longer hold on, He holds on to us. He simply requires that we trust Him. Friends, there is no one else to trust. God is the beginning and the end. After Him, there is nothing. Trust Him. His Love never fails.

"Whom have I in heaven but Thee? And there is none upon the earth that I desire beside Thee. My flesh and my heart faileth: but God is the strength of my heart, and my portion for ever." Psalm 73:25,26. (KJV)

The Flowers Bloom Brighter in Heaven

Jacaranda season is a special time of year. The enormous trees are robed in purple magnificence. It is sheer delight to drive or walk through the avenues under such a brilliant canopy. The early blossoms start appearing in late September. "The trees are getting ready for Daddy's birthday!" is a joyful exclamation made each year by our children since they were very small. Sure enough, by September 29th there are enough blooms on the early trees to proclaim a celebration. Then later in November with the first rains, most of the blossoms fall off, spreading out a thick royal carpet.

It was in October, at the peak of Jacaranda season, when the trees are at their very best, that our son Dustin was born to us. A son, a son! What joy! It was also at this time, just two weeks before his 21st birthday, that he left us. He entered another world, where the flowers and trees are far more beautiful, their brilliance beyond the confines of our earthly imagination.

That God Might Be Glorified

Like a wounded or dying animal seeks to hide in the bush, the temptation was to close ourselves in and hide away in our pain. We had thought to return home and bury our son quietly, with only closest family members in attendance. This was not what God wanted.

When Tammy phoned with the news of Dustin's death we were in Titusville, Florida, almost half way through our USA trip. We had spoken at a Missions Conference the night before. Pastor Larry Linkous and his team were wonderful in their support and in helping us change our tickets to get back home so we could be with Tammy and Deborah. Africa is a long way off and the journey ahead would not be easy. With this in mind, folk began to pray for our flight home. The Holy Spirit had already started planning.

At Orlando airport we walked beyond the boarding gate to find a quiet corner where we would be least noticed. We were so broken we wanted to melt into obscurity. While huddling in a corner, Rod looked up to see a man walking past. It was Bob Edmiston, the founder of Christian Vision. Bob was as amazed to see us as we were to see him. He had just visited China and then Florida where he was setting up another Christian Radio station. Waiting to board the same flight to London, he was, like us, looking for a quiet place to be alone. Neither of us was at the boarding gate where we were supposed to be. Coincidence? No!

Bob was shattered to hear about Dustin, who had been on a trip Rod and Bob had made together in Mozambique. Kneeling on the carpet at our feet, he took our hands and prayed for us. We wept together in that public place.

This man was as a ministering angel on divine appointment. Not only did he hold us up in our immediate hour of need, but prepared the rest of the way for us. A man of success and influence, both physically and spiritually, Bob spoke to the British Airways crew and requested that we should be upgraded to Club Class. This type of luxury is seen by most of us only on the commercials. During the night flight as we moved in and out of pain and sleep, stretched out on those marvelous seats that tilt all the way back and even have foot rests, we kept saying,

"God, do you really love us this much? Are you really so personally interested and concerned about us that that you organized the best possible comfort for us? It was as if He was cradling us all the way in His loving arms. We had a 14-hour layover at Gatwick Airport. Imagine us spending all that time in the waiting lounge in our grief, but we didn't have to. On arrival we were escorted by British Airways crew through customs and given a room for the day in the very nice airport hotel, compliments of the airline in sympathy with our loss. Free meal cards at excellent restaurants were included, though we could not eat and gave up the cards. The room gave us a place to pray and mourn in private. We had our son's funeral to arrange as soon as we arrived home. "Father God, what do you want us to do; what type of service do you want us to prepare for?"

As we knelt together on the carpet, God spoke to our hearts. "I will be glorified through this service and through the sacrifice of your son." As thoughts came to our mind, we jotted them down; where, what, how and who. We saw every idea fulfilled, and marveled at how the Holy Spirit directed each detail.

We also prayed that when our feet touched African soil we would stop being "basket cases" and receive strength to be the support that Tammy and Deborah needed. God came through for us. There they were waiting for us at the airport, Tammy holding Raurie in her arms with Deborah beside her. We were able to smile through tear-filled eyes and hug our precious daughters, rejoicing in the fact that we are so very blessed to have them. To hold Raurie in our arms, stroke the little blond head and cuddle the little boy who strongly resembles Dustin was the balm of Gilead to our souls.

We are very proud of Tammy in the way she handled the responsibility of the many matters that arose out of her brother's death. She and Dustin were incredibly close and this was a shattering blow to her. Yet she held herself together and did everything that would have fallen on our shoulders had we been there. Thank you, Tammy. Well done.

Deborah has been very brave too, a testimony to her faith and trust in Jesus with whom she has a very close relationship. You're doing great, Deborah.

MINISTERING ANGELS

While we were still in that hotel room trying to pack our bags, our friend Tim Salmon phoned from South Africa. "Rodney, when you arrive in Zimbabwe, I will be at the airport waiting for you with a plane. I am coming to serve you. Whatever you need, whatever I can do for you, I'll be there," he said. "Tim, I want you to be there, I want you to take the service." During our troubled years in Malawi and Mozambique Tim and Sally have been stalwart friends. Tim flew into the war zones many a time with Rod, partaking in the dangers, joys and sufferings of our ministry. Here he was again, ready to help in the greatest crisis of our lives. Together with Tim was pilot Ron Wayner and Richard, a young man from Tim's church. They flew us home to Mutare, saving us the long drive. On our arrival home, we found Ellie's mum, sister and brother-in-law arriving at the same time. They took over the household responsibilities and for that week nine of us lived together, cried together and even laughed together.

Christian brothers and sisters cooked meals, visited and prayed with us. We have a fuller understanding of the Body of Christ, and the importance of each member. How true that when part of the Body hurts, the whole Body suffers. We saw people enter into mourning with us, deeply grieved and hurt because of the pain we suffered. It is a beautiful thing. What a hope-filled, challenging and very moving service. We have never attended any funeral even remotely like it. Nor had any-one else who was there. Our heart cry was that somehow, something good would come out of Dustin's death. Tim was ready to use the opportunity for God, and ten people responded to the altar call. Life out of death! God had given Rod a Word, "I will turn your sorrow into joy." He did. Other people's joy at finding Christ as Saviour and great joy for us, too. Maxwell, one of our

African workers, put it very well. "Ah, ah. Satan, he is totally defeated in this thing that has happened!"

Every person who participated in the service did so with hearts exposed, fully yielded to God. Only such a heart can celebrate and weep alternately. The whole congregation, many of whom are committed to Christ, and others who attend church only for "hatch, match and dispatch," were visibly affected by the anointing, ministry and comfort of the Holy Spirit.

It was a wonderful service! Who would have thought one could ever say that about the funeral of one's only son? It's a mystery, this knowing and loving Jesus. The hymns and songs were rich and meaningful; strength and tears intermingled. A precious experience, to be gathered under His mighty wings, safe, warm and secure from the storm that raged about us.

The graveside service was very simple. Some of our African friends sang, and Tim related a couple of escapades Dustin had gotten into during his young life. He was always in trouble for some boyish prank. He also told of how Dustin had been baptized in the Holy Spirit at the age of six. Never will we forget that shining little face, red with emotion, turned up with praise flowing out in the language of the Spirit. Now the Glory of God illuminates him through and through.

When Ron flew the plane over the gathering in salute to Dustin, we saluted the memory of our son. The sound of the reverberating engines thudded in our souls. Dustin had loved this plane and had flown in it in Mozambique. "Dusty, if you were here, you'd think this is real cool."

That night as we lay in bed talking about some of the stories various people had told about Dustin when we had talked together after the service, it happened. Quiet joy welled up in our hearts in thankfulness for the son God gave us – thankfulness for his life. The stories were all very funny, just Dustin. We lay chuckling in bed. Together with the souls saved and happy memories, God turned our sorrow into joy on the night of Dustin's funeral. It was also the day of our

26th wedding anniversary. Yes, we grieved and mourned, we wept every day, several times a day, for a long time. Pain comes unexpectedly, and our hearts ache with such longing for Dusty. But God allows us the healing of tears, and the smiles come through again.

THE INJURED PASSENGER

The cause of the air crash has not been verified. It is possible that a wind shear could have brought the small craft down.

Initially, we were told that the passenger Dustin was flying on the "Bushbird's Flying Safari" over the Victoria Falls and Game Park was not seriously injured. To our dismay, we learned on the day of the funeral that Mark Bulpit, a young man from Britain, was in critical condition with lung injuries and a badly fractured femur.

We took this deeply to heart; he must not die! Perhaps he did not know Jesus as Saviour. We arranged for someone to go and see him in the hospital. The pastor told us that he had shared Jesus with Mark, who was unable to verbally respond but had given a positive indication to the Gospel message. Praise God!

Then Mark was flown to Johannesburg, as he needed better care than he was getting in Zimbabwe. Tammy managed to locate his family and fiancé at a hotel near the hospital. Excited, she called us back, "Mom, Dad, can you believe this? They are Christians, too!" She had spoken to Mark's future mother-in-law, who told her that Mark had become a Christian four months previously and was totally committed to Jesus, as were she and Mark's fiancé. Immediately, we felt that bond that can only come in Christ and began to communicate with one another. They were very sad about Dustin while in great concern over Mark whose life hung in the balance for weeks. He went through a bad time with the pain and trauma of the accident and kept asking about Dustin. When we heard that Mark was a Christian we were greatly comforted. The coroner judged that Dustin had lived for about an hour after the accident. His legs were badly smashed, and he died of internal injuries. To imagine what he must have gone through was too much to bear. That a Christian was with him when he died was a great comfort.

It was some months before Mark could write to us. His letter is a God-send to us.

"I had only met Dustin briefly. When we flew together he asked numerous times how I was, was I anxious, etc. I felt a real concern for my well being and warmed to him greatly. I do not want to increase your sadness, but I feel that perhaps I can help you by filling in some details about your son's death.

"I am absolutely convinced (as I hope you already know) that I do not blame Dustin for the accident. Dustin was a caring and sensible man, he did not fly unsafely, and I knew he was concerned for my well being. The plane just suddenly fell, at an angle, nose first. We were both unconscious when the plane hit the ground. My left foot was trapped under Dustin. Dustin was trapped by the plane in a sitting position. Neither of us could move to free ourselves because of our broken legs and other injuries. Dustin tried desperately on numerous occasions to help me free my foot from under him. He was a strong man emotionally, the type of man we always would like to think ourselves being, in such a situation. Dustin was that man. Despite the severity of our situation he never panicked. He tried the radio, but found it was broken and turned off the plane's ignition to stop a possible explosion, as the fuel tanks were leaking.

"He had concern for me and complete unselfishness. Most of the time until he died we were both quiet, drifting around the peacefulness of semi-consciousness. I remember praying out loud to God; it is possible that Dustin heard and was comforted by it. He died quietly and peacefully, there was no screaming or fright. I looked at him, and though he was still in the same position, something inside told me he had died and gave me peace about it. No feeling of panic, worry or fear rose up. There was peace and acceptance of his death."

Six hours passed before the search and rescue team found Mark and Dustin. While Mark writes a glowing report about Dustin, it seems to us that Mark showed exactly the same courage and fortitude. He and Sandy are married now, and we continue to communicate by e-mail.

"Are not two little sparrows sold for a penny? And yet not one of them will fall to the ground without your Father's consent and notice. But even the very hairs of your head are all numbered. Fear not, then; you are of more value than many sparrows."
Matthew 10: 29-31. (Amplified)

AND I WILL SEND THE COMFORTER

Where or what would we be without the prayers of the saints? In our darkest hours, days, weeks, we have felt ourselves lifted up out of the earthly realm of sorrow and pain into a place of peace and safety. Prayer has preserved our sanity. We have stood amazed as we've watched God intervene in the smallest and biggest details of our lives as He has sent people to us, paved the way and done a thousand things to bring us comfort and reassurance that He is indeed in control.

The Holy Spirit has revealed Himself to us in a new way through the comfort of God's people. He is closer to us than our skin. Not only do we feel the strength and comfort of the Holy Spirit Himself as He puts His arms around us, but we feel His comfort through words of encouragement, a touch, a look, a hug. We have a new awareness of the power and love of the Spirit, which indwells every believer.

"Oh, I have slipped the surly bonds of earth
and danced the skies on laughter-silvered wings;
Sunward I've climbed, and joined the tumbling mirth
of sun-split clouds — and done a hundred things
you have not dreamed of — wheeled and soared and swung
high in the sunlit silence. Hov'ring there,
I've chased the shouting wind along, and flung

my eager craft through footless halls of air.
Up, up the long delirious, burning blue
I've topped the windswept heights with easy grace
where never lark, or even eagle flew.
And, while with silent, lifting mind I've trod
the high untrespassed sanctity of space,
put out my hand, and touched the face of God."

(By John Gillespie Magee, Jr., a 19-year old American serving with the Royal Canadian Air Force in England. He composed this sonnet "High Flight" several months before he was killed when his Spitfire collided with another aircraft inside a cloud.)

We recently planted a palm tree and placed a simple headstone on Dustin's grave, inscribing Psalm 63:7 *"Rejoicing Under The Shadow Of Thy Wings."*❖

Seven

WALKING WOUNDED

THE LION

In Africa, the most feared predator is the lion. Like other cats, lions have deceptively soft padded paws with strong claws that can be drawn back into sheaths. One powerful swipe can kill a man, claws shredding him to ribbons. Just one blow can break the back of a zebra or crack open the skull of a large antelope. A full-grown male can drag off a whole horse in its jaws. Even young elephants, hippopotami and rhinoceros are not safe from the attack of a lion. The tawny coat blends very well with the background of sun-scorched Africa. A full-grown male, standing just over three feet high and weighing about five hundred pounds, can move its ten-foot tip-to-tail length with silent stealth through the long grass. You'll smell him before you see him, and he's upon you before you know it. The only escape from a lion is up. He is not a good tree climber. Lions have frequently been seen near Inhaminga, and a couple of people have been killed and eaten by these fearsome beasts.

The deep-throated, thunderous roar of a lion is one of the most terrifying sounds in nature. It can be heard for a distance of twenty kilometers. The roar of the lion causes the earth to tremble. Sleeping out in the bush you will feel the ground vibrate under you. Adrenaline surges to the brain and you get that awful taste in your mouth, while your sweat glands expand to send out the bitter scent of fear. One night on a ministry trip, as we walked a trail through high grass, a lion cut across our path. We froze – too afraid to move. He took a look at us, then nonchalantly sauntered off into the bushes ... (reminiscent of the attitude of Daniel's den-mates ... thank God.)

Lions are stealthy hunters and not afraid to tackle big animals. However, given the option, the lion will choose to go for the wounded. Those who have been crippled or weakened through some misfortune are easy prey for the greatest predator on earth, who fears only one thing – man.

The Apostle Peter warned, *"Be sober, be vigilant, because your adversary the devil, walks about like a roaring lion, seeking whom he may devour." I Peter 5:8.*

The death of our son left us wounded. Though we received strength from God daily, we were weakened by the gnawing pain and grief. Like wounded animals we wished for a place to hide. It was during this time of pain that the devil came as a roaring lion, launching successive attacks in a mammoth attempt to break our backs and that of the ministry forever. We could not run anywhere; there was only one way to go – UP. God is faithful and as we reached up to Him, He reached down to us.

The Frelimo government officials at Inhaminga were not happy with the influence we had among the people. They did not like us having a Bible school. Suspicious of our motives, they often followed us and continually dug for information in the hopes of bringing something against us. Everything we did was above board; they could find nothing of which to accuse us.

Then the devil entered into the heart of Pastor Time. (Name changed for his sake.) Here was a man with whom we had walked during the war. We had risked our lives to keep him and his family alive during the time of famine. Landing the Aztec at great risk onto an old cornfield near his house, Rod had taken loads of food to him and his family, as well as his church members. Pastor Time was one of Rod's right-hand men at

Command Bible School. He had a position of responsibility and we worked together for several years.

Pastor Time fell into adultery. Of course he denied it, but there was much evidence against him. Rod counseled with him and offered him the best help we could give. We had to stand him down from ministry and would work through restoration with him. For one year we would continue to pay him the salary he had been getting as a leader in the ministry. During this year he was to put his life in order and find some means of employment, as we would not pay him after one year. This was not enough for him. Just like Judas, he decided he would do far better to sell us out to the authorities.

Time (we can no longer call him Pastor), went to the police with a list of lies as long as his arm. Among other things, he told them that we were training a secret army of soldiers at the Bible School to overthrow the government. He added that we had weapons caches hidden away at Command. He also told them some true things which they already knew but of which we were absolved, such as our flights across the border during the war, our visits to the Renamo camps and walking missions escorted by the soldiers. All in all, he made a very big story, enough to hang us with.

The police came to Command to arrest Rod. They kept him at the police camp for questioning for three days, allowing him to return to Command at night. The accusations, though untrue, were serious. Already a number of Mozambicans had been imprisoned at Inhaminga and died of supposedly natural causes while in custody. Time was there with his accusations, and Rod was treated with utmost contempt. The police threatened to close down the Bible School and send the students home. All our work in Mozambique was to be stopped. We knew the threat was real. Once the government picked up on these lies they could use them against us to suit themselves. Not only was Rod in danger, the whole work was in jeopardy.

During these days, the students prayed earnestly. The

local people of Inhaminga came out of their huts and homes and formed groups around the police camp. They stood there for three days, sending in delegations to demand that the police release Rod as they knew him to be an honorable man who had committed no crime. This was a brave thing to do. While one betrayed us, the hundreds stood with us, and through the faithfulness and perseverance of these men the police finally let Rod go.

WE ALMOST LOST COMMAND

The Lion continued to roar! The Bible School at Command was his target. How he hates that place where the glory of God continues to fall and lives are changed and equipped through the power of His Word.

The property had been given to us during the Peace Process. For twenty years it had lain desolate and there was no hope that it would be restored. An agreement was passed by the United Nations that all transactions made with Renamo during the Peace Process in the areas which they ruled, would be honored after elections. We had signed documents stating that the property was ours, free of charge, to be restored as a ministry base and Bible School.

Now, the Frelimo Government department started pressing for payment of Command. They wanted $38,000 for what had once been rubble and what we had restored at our own expense. We laughed; they were surely not serious? Was it worth paying this sum even if we had it? Wasn't it perhaps time to close the door on Inhaminga and move on to an easier location? Ellie was tempted, but Rod remained steadfast. It was not pleasant. Letters and documents, police and government officials hounded us. We tried to negotiate a more realistic price, we traveled back and forth to various offices. They kept telling us we had to move off the property and we kept telling them we were working on getting the money.

The Bible tells us that the enemy comes to steal, kill and destroy. He came again and again to Inhaminga. Our faithful co-worker, Alex, a member of our board of directors, fell off the back of the tractor and was run over by the big wheel. Alex had the warmest, biggest smile. He was Rod's top man at the Bible school, acting as chief translator, as well as carrying many responsibilities. Alex had worked diligently to get Rod free from the police camp, showing the boldness and courage needed. Just as our son had been torn from our womb, Alex was torn from the womb of the ministry. It was a tough year.

Some of our Afrika wa Yesu crew had gone out with the tractor and trailer to the bush areas to buy maize to feed the Bible School students. Alex fell off under the wheel while traveling over a rough part of the road. Quintao leapt off and begged Alex to forgive him. Alex was able to speak these words, *"Don't worry, it was not your fault. Just pray for me."* They prayed for Alex as he lay dying of severe internal injuries. Alex left a young widow, Dominga, and two-year-old David. It was a trying time. While the ministry grieved the loss of a valuable and dear co-worker, the police moved in and arrested Quintao, the driver of the tractor, confiscating the vehicle. Rod went to the prison to pray with the trembling Quintao. Filled with fear, not without cause, he struggled to stand in faith, and won through. There had been several witnesses, Alex had not died through any fault of Quintao, and after some days the police released him from prison.

"We are waiting for you to come to Mozambique, Mai (mother) Ellie. Everybody is happy and expecting you for many meetings!" The very morning of the day that Alex died, he and I spoke excitedly to each other over the HF radio. Rod was to fly me in the next day and leave for two weeks of ministry, the agenda having been arranged by Alex. I could not believe how full he had packed the programme. Was it physically possible to walk all day to a village, hold several meetings then walk back to Inhaminga for more meetings the next day? Yes, if one got up with the sun, then had afternoon and evening meetings. "These people are waiting for you, Mai; we must do it." Alex had great confidence that all things are possible for the sake of the Gospel.

Now, shattered lives and shattered plans lay in a crumpled heap. Rod flew in to Inhaminga by himself as he would need to spend several days there, and we could not both be away at the same time. There would be much to sort out at Inhaminga.

DEATH IN THE AFRICAN CULTURE

Though we are accustomed to African culture, we were unprepared for all that followed.

Alex was a Malawian married to a Mozambican. Laws and culture vary from country to country. Malawian law demands that all the man's goods plus his wife and family go to his family. The wife is usually married off to one of the brothers, regardless of how many wives he already has or whether or not this pleases her. Alex's family are not Christians. Mozambican law defends the wife to some extent. She can keep her husband's belongings and cannot lawfully be forced to go and live with his family.

Foreseeing a problem, Rod, with Dominga's consent, locked all their things up in our container. The Malawi family arrived, demanded all her worldly goods, few as they were, and said she was to accompany them to Malawi. When Dominga resisted, they started practicing witchcraft against her and all of us on the Bible School property. The students stood firm in prayer and encouragement of Dominga and the situation. They prayed in turns, day and night.

Rod returned home and Ellie went to Inhaminga with Armando, a young man God brought in to help us at a crucial time. It worked out in the end that he stayed on with us and has become a member of the Afrika wa Yesu Team.

An intense spiritual battle broke out. Dominga's mother-in-law threatened to kill her, scaring the wits out of the poor girl, who was given no chance to catch her breath and mourn her beloved husband. Little David became sick and Dominga's young cousin, who had been living with her and Alex, was bitten by a snake. The demonic oppression was such as we have seldom felt – physical manifestations, as well as spiritual. A colony of bats moved in to hang under the eaves of our thatched entrance. Snakes and frogs were everywhere! We killed three snakes in one day; one was hanging above our heads on the beams of the roof. It was so hot everything that could creep or crawl came out in search of air.

Alex's family plagued us day after day, demanding money and refusing to get off the property. After much dialogue during which we were sorely tried, Armando won through for us. This young man has the patience of a saint and the boldness of a lion. He knows all the cultural tricks as well as the Word of God. Finally poor Dominga and David were able to go to Beira to live with her parents. Rodney would deliver all her things to their doorstep. The whole thing was a nightmare. In the midst of all this, we were preaching, visiting villages and teaching at the Bible School. No matter what the spiritual opposition, when we exercise the power, life and love of God, we can never lose.

NDUNGU YANGA (MY SPEAR)

Usually a trip to Inhaminga is a step into the flow of the Holy Spirit. The peace and joy, particularly while Bible School is in session, is tangible; we just love it. This time it was very different. Losing Alex and the resulting problems, as well as the unusual activity of witchcraft took its toll. It was especially difficult for us as we were separated from one another as a family when we really needed each other. Because the dates of my trip had to be changed, I was in Mozambique on the first anniversary of Dustin's death. Also for Tammy's birthday, and then our 27th wedding anniversary which was also the day of Dustin's funeral. All in one week. These little things that mean a lot can really take it out of one. Still, God is faithful, and we saw many victories.

Marco (the wild bushman-turned-searching-shepherd), organized a new ministry program for me. Having a heart for the sinner, Marco's program was different from the one Alex had organized. Alex would major on teaching the church. Marco majors on walking across the mountain in search of the one lost sheep. "I want you to come with me to Ndungu Yanga," said Marco "It's the place where I greatly long to see souls saved. This is the place where I used to travel to all the time for 'mbanje' (marijuana). The people knew me as a bad man. They need to see how I am changed."

It was extremely hot and we sweated over the rocky hills, arriving at our destination just before dusk, the dust and smoke from bush fires turning the setting sun into a ball of fire. Several of Marco's congregation had walked with us, including the ten-year-old drummer with his drum. Under the tree we sat while the small group of Christians sang, and the drum announced the impending meeting. We sang and sang; nobody came. Ndungu Yanga is steeped in witchcraft, the husband and wife under whose tree we were sitting being the only Christians for miles. "Keep worshipping God," we told the group. "Our praises will pierce the darkness and make a way for the light and truth of Christ to come into this place. We have the spear of the Lord. It is greater and more powerful than the spear of Ndungu Yanga."

At last one man came through the scrubby thorn bushes. He was a neighbor and had responded to the words of the song, "Bwerani, bwerani - Come, come, it's time to hear the Word of God." We testified, prayed, sang some more and preached a Gospel message. The visitor responded, stood to his feet and asked Jesus to come into his life. One sheep had been found. Marco was ecstatic and we know the angels rejoice in heaven when one soul comes to repentance!

We laid sleeping mats under the stars behind the hut to shield us from the worst of the dust blown around by the gusty wind. The place crawled with ants! In our blankets, in our hair, across our faces. I wished for home and my bed!

On our way to Ndungu Yanga, Marco had directed us to a cluster of huts. "There is a man staying there who has been sick for many months. Can we take time to go and pray for him?" Lying on a reed mat was the emaciated form of a man. His skinny legs lay limp and he held one arm out at an odd angle. The relatives of the man gathered around and introduced him as Mr.

Portugal. They told us he had been lying there for four months and could hardly move about. His eyes were glazed and his mouth caked with dried saliva. I did not feel inspired to pray for Mr. Portugal. He looked too near death's door. I could sense the spirit of death hanging over him. "We'll just sit here on the ground and chat to him and the family for a while," I told the team.

The ants crawled over Mr. Portugal. He had not the strength to brush them off and it did not seem to occur to any of his family that they could assist him with this problem. Perhaps when ants crawl on you day and night for months one loses the incentive to do anything about it. "Come, let's clean the mat of ants." I suggested.

As we chatted, telling of our purpose in visiting Ndungu Yanga, Mr. Portugal began to show a bit of interest. We asked him some questions about himself, learning that he used to be a Christian, and a leader of a church group. Then he became ill. Nobody in the church stood with him in his trials; they did not visit him at his hut; so in time he asked for help from the witch doctor. He showed us scars on his body from huge abscesses. He then showed us the abscess under his arm, the painful reason of having to keep it at an angle. He said his bones suffered great pain and because of this he could not walk. All this he told us with gasping breath and hopelessness written all over his face.

Armando was a great help, and together we read scriptures to him and exhorted him to return to the Lord and believe for his deliverance. His main concern was what would happen to him after we had gone. Who would visit him and who would help him in prayer? Marco gave his word to visit him till he was well and able to come to church himself. Mr. Portugal agreed and we led him through repentance. We prayed for his healing and helped him pray out loud, too. Finally we left him, promising to visit him on our return journey.

The next morning we could hardly believe our eyes. Mr. Portugal was washed, his eyes were clear and he could speak normally. He was not gasping for breath and could even walk with the support of his relatives! We were elated. The spirit of death was gone!

Once at the Inhaminga base we put together a parcel for Mr. Portugal. New clothes, soap, milk powder, protein mix and a Bible. He is growing stronger day by day, body, soul and spirit. His greatest cause of illness was a sick heart. Disillusionment, hopelessness and despair convinced him to accept death. Now, the love of Christ shown through God's people had restored him to God and given him a future and a hope.

We once read the following words somewhere, and they stuck with us forever, **"A love for souls will heal all your diseases."** Being active in ministry in the midst of our pain helped bring healing to us. Forced to take our eyes from our own needs and situation, we were from the start, caught up with ministering to the immediate needs of others. While a period of grieving is very necessary for healing, there is no reason why in the midst of our grieving we cannot be of help to others. We have found medicine and peace for our souls in doing just this. However, as all who have lost loved ones know, the pain returns, fierce and deep, at the most unexpected moment. But God has not left us comfortless and reaches out to us in countless ways.

Magnificently arrayed in the indescribable shade that flows somewhere between purple, mauve and lilac, the Jacaranda trees have burst forth again to declare a glorious message of hope and promise. How beautiful heaven must be! (We think often now of heaven.)

"Sweet rain is on its way.... to wash the dry, dusty, choked-up months out of your scorched mind and heart."

As I sit writing this, I can see the giant Jacaranda tree in our garden from our window. Not only are the enormous branches heavy with this indescribable color, but on the ground lies a thick carpet of blossoms. You see, in the night the rain came, laying a royal carpet just for us in our garden. We're going out right now to walk on it!❖

Eight

WE SHALL FLY AGAIN

FAITH TAKES TO THE SKIES

After we sold our Piper Aztec due to its needing engine replacement, we badly missed having wings. It was three years before Rod would fly again, and this time in a World War II Piaggio P149 military trainer. Rod had bought it for a song as it had not flown in 18 years. He and Horace Masauli, a friend and engineer based in Malawi had spent three years working on it while we were still in Malawi. Spare parts had to be ordered from all over the world. Often it seemed they had come to a dead end, but always they found a way. Congratulations to Horace for reviving a bird that had been given up for dead. At last the Piaggio was certified, ready for flight. We had already moved to Zimbabwe, so Rod had to get up to Malawi for the special thrill of test-flying the Piaggio as there were no pilots around who were rated on that model. Nor was Rod, but the job had to be done. It was the unforgettable combination of trepidation that comes with hanging over the edge of a precipice by a thread, and the joyous achievement of scaling the highest mountain after a long and hard climb. The view from such a place cannot be described. As Rod took the Piaggio into the air and began to fly through the brilliant sky, something new was born. On the ground as many airport staff as could leave their positions gathered to watch the Flying Reverend do the craziest thing. Everyone knew that bird could not fly and would come crashing down. Everyone except Horace and Rod, though both admit to great sighs of relief and prayerful thanks as the wheels touched ground.

Rod flew the plane out of Malawi into Zimbabwe just three days before Wayne and Martha Myers arrived for a trip into Mozambique with us. They would share the joy of our first mission into Mozambique in the Piaggio. We were so proud to have the Piaggio flying, that we didn't much care about the drawbacks it had as a Missions plane. After all, the **wings** were what mattered; they could carry us over and above the dreadful Inhaminga road! The Piaggio has two seats in the front and a little bench seat at the back. Martha and I shared the same safety belt on the back seat and we fitted well enough, but luggage space was limited and there was no space for Missions supplies.

To climb into the aircraft is an acrobatic feat. There is no door. The roof rolls back and one climbs in from the top after hoisting oneself up on the wing. Well done, Martha! Not many ladies in their seventies could do it so gracefully. The noise and vibration of the engine prevented us from hearing each other even when yelling. One hour after takeoff we circled over Beira to land for customs clearing. I watched Rod closely as he began to push and shove a handle that was obviously not responding. "Oh no! The wheels won't come down!" I was not wrong. By this time Rod was on finals for landing and had no wheels. He grabbed hold of the manual lever and, praise God, the wheels came down.

We caused quite a commotion at the Beira International Airport. People laughed and pointed, shaking their heads. We could not imagine why, until some came running over to take a closer look at the "antique". In contrast to the sleek new planes in the parking bays, the Piaggio looked like something out of an old movie. "What is this? Ah, you should put this in the museum." Finally we landed at Inhaminga. The journey that would have taken us a full day at the very least was accomplished in just two hours flying time.

We completed our mission at Inhaminga, enjoying a tremendous time under Wayne's anointed teaching. Several days later we landed safely back in Zimbabwe. Wayne was not as impressed with the plane as we were and climbed out with the words, "You people need a new aircraft!" "Whatever for?" we wondered. "The Piaggio had done a good job, had it not?"

A couple of weeks later Rod flew to Mozambique again. On his return journey the plane started losing power soon after takeoff. He decided to turn back and land at Beira airport from which he had taken off. The plane stayed there for several months before the needed repairs could be done. On taking it for inspection to South Africa, it was discovered that there was corrosion on the right wing spar. The wing would have to be replaced. Where to find another wing for this rare old bird, and at what cost? After long struggles, Rod had to let the broken-winged Piaggio go. Our excitement at being airborne again was short-lived.

OUR FIGHT TO FLY

Now that we were no longer in danger of being shot at, surely mission work should become easier? For us, not. With no plane, we found ourselves spending days on a journey that took a couple of hours by air. It was ironic that in a time of peace our work was slowing down. Surely it should be speeding up!

Dare we reach higher and believe God for another plane? Nervous about the enormous amount of money needed for a plane, we asked God. "Lord, if you want us to have another plane, please show us clearly." The following week we received a fax from Wayne and Martha Myers stating, "If God were to allow us to invest $20,000 into your ministry how would you use it?" We both immediately said to each other, "Towards a plane!"

We dialogued with God about the matter and came up with – "O.K. Lord, if Wayne and Martha agree to this money starting off a plane fund, we'll know it's from You. If not, we'll scrap the idea of getting a new plane." We asked the Myers to consider the idea and confirm if they felt this was a right move. They replied, "We are delighted for you to use the money we are sending as seed towards your much-needed plane."

We needed a reliable six-seater, single-engine plane. It was hard to find the faith for this, but possibly it takes **more** faith to build two planes from scrap and fly through the dangers of war. Surely it should be easier to simply believe God for a good plane? Rodney remembered the words of the great German evangelist, Reinhardt Bonnke. Bonnke had experienced repeated troubles with the trucks he used for carrying the big tent through Africa. He spoke to God about it and finally God said to him, "Stop looking for Me on the scrap heap." In order to try to be frugal with God's money, Bonnke had been buying old trucks that continually broke down. God wanted him to buy good trucks that would serve well, it did not matter that they cost more! "I feel God is telling us the same thing," Rod said. "We must stop looking for God on the scrap heap and buy a good plane." Working from Zimbabwe into seven different provinces in Mozambique and also into Malawi is difficult because of the distances. We needed to increase our efficiency in soul harvest. Too much time was being wasted bouncing over potholes and being stuck in the mud, being cut off by overflowing rivers and broken bridges. Not to mention the wear and tear on our vehicles and bodies. God would make a way. We believed!

APRIL, 1998 – WE HAVE WINGS! WE CAN FLY!

Thank you, Dear Friends, for………. the magnificent gift of a 1980 Cessna 206 Aircraft. New Engine, fresh paint job, white with blue & gray trim. Very smart looking!

The real beauty of this aircraft is in the many hearts that have been invested in it. It was not bought with a sweeping offering from a wealthy source ………but rather, this aircraft was purchased with the love, faith, and generosity of hundreds of saints. Some gave $10.00, some $50.00, many gave $100. Others gave $1,000, $3,000 and so on. Several gave $5,000 and a few $10,000, and one couple gave beyond $20,000.

If each person who gave something were to engrave his or her name on the aircraft, there would be little space left! Certainly, every name has an eternal share in all the Holy Spirit is doing through the use of these wings.

Each contribution has been specially wrapped with the prayers of people who have personally involved themselves with our vision and the need. Without this personal investment of hearts and lives, we would never have reached our target. Sure, God can give all by Himself, and sometimes He does. Mostly, we have found that He gives through His people. He loves to see us need each other and to see us meet each other's needs. That's how a real family works!

Most of the funds came in through pledges. People felt the desire and prompting of the Holy Spirit to give, but did not have the money on hand. They made a decision to believe God to supply the amount they wanted to give. Faith pledges were made, and God proved Himself faithful to folk as they saw the money start coming in.

"To the best of our ability, we pledge to use this plane for the glory of God. Not to grow weary, but to give, to serve, and to be ready for any mission to which we feel the leading of the Holy Spirit. We pledge to give our best."

"When someone carries our burden, how light we travel." We are never alone. Jesus is with us through friends as well as in person. When Dustin died, we were so shattered we didn't even care about the plane anymore. We abandoned the project and left it lying in the ashes of our sorrow. It was picked up again by some of the most faithful friends in the world, Wayne and Martha, who had been nurturing the project ever since they helped initiate it. They carried it for us when we were too weak, and through continued efforts in sharing with numerous friends of theirs, it all came together. Folk who didn't even know us contributed on the testimony of Wayne and Martha. We are grateful to so many people, but none lifted the plane as high in faith and prayer as did Wayne and Martha Myers! ❖

JESUS SAFARI

MAZAMBA

The Christians at Mazamba cheered as the truckload of visitors trundled into their village. Two messengers had arrived at the Bible School on foot some days previously. *"Please come and visit us and pray with us. We have not had Holy Communion for more than ten years. Please come and lead us in Holy Communion."*

Now we had arrived, and they were very happy to see us. An uninhabited brick house, devoid of any furniture was offered to us as accommodation. We were warned, however, that the house was haunted and at night footsteps could be heard, as well as knocking on the doors. "This is because many, many people died here during the war and their spirits are wandering about with no peace." We opted to sleep outside, not because we were afraid, but because it was hot. We had another REAP team with us and they loved to lie and watch the stars that are so much bigger and brighter than in England.

Early in the morning we set out to see the chief, who was a woman, to take her gifts of clothes and blankets, as her hut had burned down with all her possessions. We spoke to her about Jesus but she shook her head sadly. She explained that it was impossible for her to become a Christian as her first responsibility was to her tribe. Her position as chief required the fulfilling of certain obligations that did not mix with

Christianity. For example, it was necessary for her to offer sacrifices and pray to the ancestral spirits, particularly in time of drought and famine. Her people depended on her intercession. Though we told her how she could lead her people in a far more excellent way, the way of eternal life, she would not change her mind. She had attended some of our meetings before and had seen the *JESUS* film, but she did not wish to change. She did allow us to pray for her, however, and we did so, laying hands on her and asking God to remove the darkness from her mind and let His light shine in. She thanked us for the prayers and was obviously moved that we should care about her.

Several church groups joined together for the meetings. They were all eager to partake of the Lord's table. We first taught some lessons on the power of the Blood of Christ and the importance of communion. One of the leaders stood up and said, "Our church does not allow us to partake of communion without an ordained minister being present. No leader has visited us for ten years. Mazamba is a forgotten place, but now we have been remembered through your visit." We assured them that Jesus had told the disciples to *"do this often in remembrance of me,"* and that this was a very important ordinance for the church. "As long as you have given your life to Christ and are walking with Him and with one another in love and truth, you are free to partake of the bread and cup. You do not have to wait to be baptized; you do not have to wait for visitors to come; you can do this yourselves." They cheered and clapped their appreciation. How we struggle with the rules and laws made by man. Many missionaries have laid a heavy yoke of bondage on the people and it is part of our mission to set people free, not only from the powers of darkness, but from man-made laws also.

The people also expressed their desire to be baptized by immersion, but all surface water had dried up. "When the rain comes again, your own leaders are free to baptize you. Follow the Word of God, repent and be baptized." It was a joy-filled and liberated group that saw us off the next day. How wonderful to see people hungry for God receive the truth and determine to put it into action. Our long drive back to Inhaminga passed quickly as we sang and rejoiced at being allowed the privilege of preaching and teaching in rural Mozambique.

FLYING IS A BREEZE

It was a special joy for us to fly Steve and Betty Bishop, friends of Wayne and Martha, in our newly acquired Cessna 206. This was to be our first Jesus Safari on Wings since taking ownership of the plane. This couple had responded tremendously with raising the funds for it. We loaded the Cessna 206 with the heavy film equipment, and our immediate priorities, which were two small tents and bedrolls. Camping out in the winter cold, one needs to be prepared. Rod, being extra cautious about weight on small bush runways, left the teakettle behind, a move he lived to regret. The kettle is Ellie's highest priority.

Landing on the airstrip next to the Bible School was like a bird homing to the nest. Our guests were thrilled to see the Bible School and all the work that has transformed the shell into a living habitation; but shocked to see the poverty and destruction of the town. They had never seen anything so desolate and hopeless. "No, no!" we cried. "This is wonderful, this is progress, this is life, things are happening!" Only those who saw Inhaminga dressed in famine and bones can see and recognize the life that is there now.

We climbed down the escarpment to Dimba to preach at Marco's little church. This young man who was on drugs and considered insane just two years before, is totally transformed by the Spirit of God. Marco is planting churches faster than any other pastor in the Inhaminga region. He was overjoyed to have us minister to his congregation at Dimba. We jumped the small muddy stream, walking through the fields until we finally reached the pole-and-thatch church building where about thirty people were gathered. Throughout the meeting, a young man filled with home brew moonshine kept interrupting the service. He was not aggressive, just very friendly. "No, don't throw him out," we said. "Just sit him down and take no notice of his interruptions." Some of the folk laughed and jeered. Looking at the young man, seeing his desperate need and the hunger for acceptance in his face, we made a point of telling him he was welcome and we were glad he had come. This stopped the jeers. The young man quieted down, listening intently to our words. "Yes, yes, it is true what they say!" Finally, no longer able to contain himself, he shouted out his identity and the fact that he recognized who we were. "I know you. I heard you preaching in Malawi in the Refugee Camp eight years ago." Now here he was, back in Mozambique, at Inhaminga of all places, and very happy to see us too. No wonder he had been so anxious to shake hands frequently through the service.

When we gave the altar call, four men came forward to receive Jesus as Savior. The drunk cried out, "I want to be delivered of alcohol!" We prayed for them all – it was great. Afterwards, we invited people to give their testimonies. One after another the men stood up and told of how God had delivered them from a life of sin and hopelessness. Almost all of them said, "One day Marco came to me and spoke to me about Jesus......... He showed me the love of God."

The walk back up the mountain was more difficult than down, but we had seen lives touched by the Holy Spirit, and that made the going a great deal easier. That night we showed the *JESUS* film to an excited crowd of 3,000 people on the soccer field. The film was in the local dialect, Sena, thus the cause for extra excitement. In the morning Rod drove the tractor while the rest of us bounced around in the trailer. We stopped to chat to some folk when a man in uniform came walking up to us. He was a government official, and to our surprise he told us with a proud smile that his had been the voice of Pontius Pilate in the Sena translation of the *JESUS* film. "Please, can you help me get a copy of that video cassette?" he said. We assured him we would. Amazing whom one meets up with at Inhaminga!

MUNGARI

The one-hour flight from Inhaminga to Mungari would have taken us 18 hours by road. We were glad to go as the crow flies. This route took us over our old wartime locations. Rod flew low over the Gorongosa Forest, searching out the narrow strip cleared in the forest where he had landed over 200 times during the heat of the war. There it was, a jagged brown scar ripped through the lush forest. The Cessna dipped low, just a few feet off the ground, trees above wing level. "We're not landing are we?!" "No, not this time." The landing space was smaller and narrower than ever, the forest already having encroached around it. It was a bit like being on a fast train rushing through a tunnel of trees, except our wheels were not on the ground. Wow! It felt good, though our hearts were pumping pretty fast. Rod was on a positive high from the rush of adrenaline and the memories of some of the best ministry opportunities of our lives. We all laughed and shouted and hal-lelujahed. God is good and we've had and still are having such a wonderful life in His service.

As we approached Mungari, a spread-out bush village, we wondered what the airstrip would be like, never having landed there before. We saw a clearing that we took to be the strip – it must be, there's no other clearing? Yes, but look at those bushes and trees; there doesn't seem to be much space! "It's fine," said Rod, his trained bush-pilot eye able to judge so much better than ours. We landed and bounced off again a cou-ple of times before coming to a thankful stop. Out from behind bushes and huts people came running and shouting. This was the event of years. The children crowded round excitedly, watching and exclaiming at every move.

Humberto, the Brazilian missionary stationed at Mungari, welcomed us together with his two national workers who have already been through the Inhaminga Bible School. "Well, this is where we make our home." Rod pulled out the equipment. "You put your tent beside that wing; we'll put ours beside this one. That way we can keep guard over the plane during the night."

Putting up tents proved to be quite a task with people pressing in on every side to see what the white people were doing. Most of them had never seen a tent before. "Nyumba a Zungu!" (white man's house). Very impressive, with zip, mosquito netting and all. Oh, for a cup of tea. But there was none! Much later we got someone to boil water on their fire for us and it was such a treat to sit on that airstrip drinking tea and watching the sun spread its magnificence across the bush sky. It did not matter too much that there was no bathroom, only the bushes, and there was no water for bathing.

The *JESUS* film was a tremendous success as always. It was cold out. People shivered through the two-hour viewing, most of them standing on their feet the whole time, not wanting to sit down in case they missed something.

The poverty of the village was far greater than at Inhaminga. How do these people manage to survive? Truly they have nothing, and we have so much. Humberto showed us the church they are building. The walls were already at roof level and they were waiting to have enough funds to roof it. "It is a very tough area," Humberto told us. "These people are born into witchcraft. It is their culture and religion; they know no other way." All around us were signs of witchcraft. At the footpath crossroads stood the clay bowls of food sacrificed to the spirits to ensure a safe journey. It was unthinkable to go on a journey without the blessing of the spirits. Throughout the village stood moonshine stills. Enslaved by drunken stupor and evil spirits, the people to whom God has sent Humberto are in great darkness. Our hearts went out to Humberto and we marveled at his commitment to live for three years in the midst of this gross darkness, upholding the light of Christ. Humberto is the only non-Mozambican at Mungari. Surrounded by thousands of some of the poorest people in the world, loneliness and discouragement were a continuous battle. Humberto stood firm and finished his course.

It's great to fly to the village, but once you're there, you may have to walk. Sometimes the airstrip is several miles from the village and there is no transport available. There may be no place to sleep, bathe, or buy anything to eat. The picture of missions made easy by air is quickly dispelled, but it's a lot of fun, too. This way we reach the people off the beaten track and cover a vast territory we would not otherwise be able to reach.

From Mungari we flew for one and a half hours to Buzi. The small town is divided by the Buzi River. The problem is that the airstrip is on one side and Brazilian missionaries Carlos and Ernandes live on the other side. There is no bridge or way to get a vehicle across. To carry our heavy equipment to the river was a task too formidable. "What should we do, Lord?" Within minutes a pickup truck came onto the scene driven by a South African man who worked at Buzi. Curiosity at the sight of the plane had drawn him to come and see who we were. Very friendly and helpful, he loaded our stuff and took us to his house – for tea! An angel in disguise. Afterwards, he kindly drove us to the riverbank where we loaded our baggage onto a small boat. Carlos had a car waiting for us on the other side, and away we went.

Carlos and Ernandes live in a small but solid little house. No running water, but they have electric lights. Power cuts are frequent, but while we were there we had light.

We pulled up to the sound of drums and singing. No, it was not the Christians welcoming us. Stationed a few meters from the house was a crowd of people totally absorbed in ancestral worship.

Ten days of devil worship at the gate! Carlos ran his fingers through his hair in exasperation. "This has been going on for nine days now. Day and night, they worship their ancestors, calling up demon spirits and supposedly consulting with their ancestors. As one part of the crowd grows weary in singing another takes over. Thus they cease not to worship, day or night."

This unholy conference was initiated by a professional group of spirit callers. They move around from area to area, giving a ten-day setting and opportunity for people to talk to their ancestors about various problems, seek direction and protection. They are then paid for their services. It just so happened that they were next door to Carlos and Ernandes while they were having visitors come to show the *JESUS* film. These were just ordinary people, lost in sin, blinded by Satan, and drowned in deception. They were doing what they had been taught. Rod walked over to them, much to the dismay of the local Christians who were with us. "Doesn't Pastor Rodney know what these people are?" Rod sat down and talked with some of them. They inquired of him what his purpose was in coming to Buzi. "To tell about Jesus. We will be showing a very wonderful film tonight. It's all about Jesus, His birth, His life on earth, the miracles He did. It is also about His death and resurrection. It is a very exciting film; please come and see it!" Some of them said they would.

That evening as we left to show the film, the drums were quiet, the space was vacated. Most of them had gone to the field to see the *JESUS* film. Much later after the film they started up again and banged all night. We believe they were now fewer in number. Who knows how many of those people saw the *JESUS* film and how many lives were touched by it? We got to thinking....... If these people can be so dedicated as to worship their gods for ten days, day and night, how do we as Christians compare in dedication and commitment?

Two sleepless nights in Buzi had us more than ready for the next stop, which was Beira. Here we camped at a holiday resort with a restaurant and hot showers on the beach. It was bliss and a good way to round off our flying trip. 5,000 people showed up to see the *JESUS* film where we set it up in the slum area. Betty who loves the ocean like Ellie does, had the joy of pitching tent as close to the waves as is wise. It was a first time for her to camp on the beach. In fact, it was her first time to sleep in a tent at all..... Praise God for adventurous souls who are willing to leave the comfort of house and homeland to join with us on the mission field. Friends like these are a great encouragement, and when they leave we are strengthened and built up in the Holy Spirit, refreshed and ready to "go into all the world and preach the Gospel."

FROM ROCKY MOUNTAINS TO ROCKING ROADS

It has been our great joy to host a team from Resurrection Fellowship, Loveland, Colorado. The team was led by Missions Pastor Mark Lucks. Together on the team was Mark's wife Kyle Anne, Chuck & Elaine, Jeff and Nicky, Tom, Steve, Joy and Carrie.

Big Foot, our 4x4 ex-military DAF truck donated by Wayne and Martha Myers, stomped through the potholes and over the ridges for days on end, rattling its precious cargo around in the back till their teeth clattered. Deafening was the noise of the metal canopy clanging like giant cymbals. Above all that noise, laughter, singing and stories could be heard most of the time. Then there were times of silence as fatigued bodies swayed along from side to side, trying to get a bit of rest, only to be rudely awakened when Big Foot tripped over an exceptionally big pothole.

Metushira was our first stop for the *JESUS* film. We camped outside the church Sumaia and Francisca had built. Then in the morning we started the eleven-hour-long journey to Inhaminga. It was dark by the time we got there, the journey taking even longer than anticipated. How glad we were to get out and place our feet on steady ground. The meal prepared for us by the Inhaminga Afrika wa Yesu team was spectacular. Heaps of chicken and rice with a magnificent salad from our Bible School vegetable garden. Since the premises were jam-packed with 43 students plus staff, the team needed to put up tents for their time there.

Teaching the students was much enjoyed and the students begged us, "Please, can these people stay longer? We are being blessed greatly through their ministry!"

The village visits were undoubtedly one of the highlights

of the trip. The teams walked out of Inhaminga in three groups with bedrolls and minimum provisions, to visit and sleep in various villages. Each group was accompanied by an Afrika wa Yesu guide. For the Americans to visit the local people in the homes, talk, eat and become partakers of their lives was an unforgettable experience. They shared Jesus in mud huts, homes and mud churches, prayed for people, leading souls to Jesus. It was a precious time for both visitors and hosts alike.

Muanza is a village en route to Inhaminga. Frequently, the people there have asked us to stop and show the *JESUS* film, but it seemed we were always pressing on to another assignment. This time we would stop over with the team.

During the long civil war, Muanza was one of the many locations under control of the Renamo Rebels fighting against Communism. Since the end of the war, the Frelimo government has moved back into all the previously held rebel territory and established their administrative offices. When driving through most towns, one will see a Frelimo flag flying over their office, and a Renamo flag flying over theirs. Renamo is no longer in control of these areas but is free as a political party to have its own flag. As we have many friends among the Renamo movement due to years of preaching in their zones during the war, it is most natural for us to stop and speak with them. At Muanza, they were excited to see us and offered us a place to camp under a mango grove next to their offices. It was the perfect spot, under the leafy trees, plus our camp would be safely guarded while we were out ministering. They welcomed us with the words, "Today our house is blessed of God because you, the people of God, have come to us."

We unloaded all the gear, set up seven tents, unpacked our food and supplies, then gathered to catch our breath and plan some evangelism strategy. Then arrived two Frelimo policemen who told us we could not camp next to the Renamo Party offices. "Why not?" "Because there is no water here." "No matter, we have our own water." "Oh, but there is no toilet here for you to use." "Oh, but there is, round the back here. We've already used it." "Well you cannot stay here next to the Opposition Party." "Why not? There is peace now, Mozambique is a democratic country, people are free now. Aren't they?" "Yes, but the Frelimo Administrator says you are not to stay here. We want to take you to another place where we will give you water and take care of you." "We appreciate your concern for our welfare. It is most kind of you to care about us. However, we have already set up camp, it was hard work, we do not want to take it down again. Also, it will soon be dark and we are here for Jesus and we have much work to do." And so it went on and on.

Finally Rodney and Mark went off with the policemen to see the Frelimo hierarchy themselves. To cut a long story short, the truth of what Mozambique is really like for the local people under the facade of so-called "change" was revealed.

"Mozambique is **not** a democratic country. We the Frelimo Party rule the country, nobody else can say anything. Everyone will do as we say, Frelimo says." The Frelimo administrator of Muanza spoke for his supposedly democratic government. No amount of tact, diplomacy or complaint could move him. Finally, for the sake of the work we have been commissioned to do, Rodney agreed to move our camp far away from the Renamo Party, but said that we would move right out of town after the *JESUS* film and not sleep in the place appointed by Frelimo.

The heaviness from this battle was evident. As a team we were definitely affected, and as we moved through the people talking to them about Jesus, their fears and uncertainties were evident. Only one thing to do! Steve got out his saxophone and began to play. The team gathered around and began to worship God. As the atmosphere began to clear in the heavens, the people began to flock around. The Word was preached, God was glorified and soon the liberty that we were accustomed to began to return. Glory be to Jesus!

However, that night, for the first time ever, the field where we had set up the film equipment was empty of people.

Usually we have hundreds of children and some adults swarming around in anticipation long before the film starts. This night, nobody. The Team began to worship and intercede.

"Here comes the army of God!" Suddenly, seemingly out of nowhere, came a throng of people. Singing, clapping, worshipping, they danced their way down the soccer field. It was the Christians of the region, coming out of their huts to join together in unison to make a stand against spiritual wickedness in high places. Oh, it was thrilling! The team moving forward to join them was caught up in the wild stomping dance of spiritual warfare. We trampled the demons into the dust where they belong. Victory was ours as the anointing of the Lord rolled over us all in a great cloud of Glory. Hallelujah!

The large crowd listened intently to the words spoken on the film. Only on rare occasions have we witnessed such absorption. Out of the silence they broke for periodic exclamations of awe and cheers of appreciation as they saw the disciples bringing in the massive catch in their nets, Jesus multiplying the loaves and fishes and calming the storm. Such weeping and intense mourning we have seldom seen. The people poured out their hearts as they lived through the sorrow and death of their Saviour. Loud sobbing and wailing expressed their grief. En masse they lifted up their hands to receive Jesus or recommit their lives to Him as the altar call was given.

Stationing team members down the side of the field, several meters apart, we invited those who needed prayer to move into groups in front of the different team members. What a time of praying we had! Lives were forever changed as we prayed for and laid hands on the multitude who came forward to receive a touch from Jesus. How aware we were that we are His hands upon this earth. It was a very humbling experience. It was all very different; could it be because of the spiritual battle we had won? No wonder Satan tried his best to get us out of town. We were so glad we stayed to show the film rather than leave in an offended huff at the reception we had received from the Frelimo authorities. The devil really does try every trick.

IN THE JUNGLE, THE MIGHTY JUNGLE, THE LION SLEEPS TONIGHT!

Finally, it was all over, and we hit the trail in the dark to find a clearing large enough for us all to camp in. The forest is thick in this area, but after over an hour's travel Rod pulled off into a clearing where some trees had been chopped down. Right there, in the middle of the jungle, we set up camp and boiled the kettle for coffee. Everyone was hyped up from the excitement of the day and the move of God we had experienced. Chatter, shrieks and giggles rang through the jungle as the joy of the Lord bubbled out of God's people. When everyone was at last safely zipped up in their tents, Rod and Ellie were tempted to start the song, "In the jungle, the mighty jungle, the lion sleeps tonight." We decided not to; the possibility of a lion visit was too real. Rod didn't tell anyone till the next day that this was the place where he had seen three lionesses on the road some time ago. We were sleeping in the midst of lion territory!

Ministry and travel in Big Foot continued for several more days. Each place was different and everywhere God changed lives. Here were people who were prepared to rough it in Africa for souls. Most visitors come to our continent to see the lions and other wildlife. While it is exciting to experience the magnificence of these animals God has created, how much more thrilling to experience the people He has created!

After the tough but glorious mission, we took the REZ team on a spectacular visit to some of Zimbabwe's greatest tourist attractions. At Hwange Game Park they experienced the vastness of Africa – the sights and sounds of wild animals roaming in the sunset.

The Magnificent Victoria Falls, "the smoke that thunders," is a must for every visitor to Zimbabwe. The famous missionary David Livingstone said of the Falls, "Here angels pause in their flight in awe of the splendor." This sight our son had gazed upon many a time also during his time at Victoria Falls.

White Water Rafting on the Great Zambezi River is every rafter's dream come true. Huge volumes of water pound the rough valley floor boiling up and exploding into the most exciting rapids in the world. Deborah loved it.

Bungee-jumping 111 meters down the world's highest commercial jump could cause your heart to measure "10" on the Richter scale as you break the accepted bounds of reality. Personal videos are taken and sold to the jumper. We have a great one of Dustin, who did this jump shortly before he left for heaven. Fun, fellowship, praise and prayer, a wonderful way to conclude a Mozambique / Zimbabwe Safari Mission.

This team had been a very special gift to us. They brought a flood of love and healing to our lives. Personally, I did not have the courage and strength to join the trip and visit Victoria Falls where we had spent time with Dustin just weeks before his death, so I stayed behind in Mutare. But through the ministry and love of the team, parts of us that were lying dormant have been awakened. Parts that had died through the pain we have been through have been resurrected. Oh, what a mighty God of love we serve! His work and healing in all of us is progressive, constant, and continual.

For three months before coming out, the REZ team met together each week. Under the guidance of Pastor Mark they prayed – for each other, for us, for the people to whom they would be ministering. They worshipped and interceded. They were trained in group ministry and evangelism, as well as one to one. They got excited, filled with joy and anticipation and faith. They were prepared and toughened up for the biggest hardships imaginable. Most of all, they were filled with love. This is just a brief mention of the preparation, which was part of their key to success. Relationship, unity and a servant's heart in acting out what they had learned did the rest.

How can we ever thank you, Pastor Mark and the Resurrection Fellowship Team? You have done us GOOD!❖

Ten

MOURNING TURNS
TO DANCING

MIRACLE PAYMENT FOR COMMAND

In December of 1998 we flew to the USA to complete the trip we had been called home from when Dustin had died. Leaving Zimbabwe in the December heat, we landed in a snow blizzard. A white Christmas comes to Loveland, Colorado once in 7 or 8 years. This was just for us! The Christmas lights and decor inside and outside stores and homes delighted us. On Christmas Eve we attended the service at Resurrection Fellowship. We had never seen anything like it. We tried to count the candles on the platform and stopped at 150. Pastor John Stocker sat on the platform steps with all the little children around him and read the Christmas Story. The music was heavenly and holy communion was served. The three Heins cried throughout that sacred evening, so touched by the Spirit of God. It was good for our souls, washing us clean in preparation for the two months of ministry ahead. We spent the first two weeks over Christmas and the New Year in the home of our special friends, Mark and Kyle Ann Lucks and family. Their kindness to us is unforgettable.

Ten days before we left for the USA, we had received a letter of demand for payment of Command. It was final; the price was not coming down. Feeling sick at heart, we continued preparations for the trip. The purpose of this visit was to renew relationships and give praise reports to friends and supporters, not to appeal for funds. "I don't want to go to America anymore," I whined. "I'm just not going from church to church begging for money! You can go if you want to, I'm staying. Maybe God doesn't want us to have that school anymore. The road is so awful anyway. Maybe we should just give up and go some place nice and easy. Somewhere like on the beach!"

"Don't even think about the payment again," Rod replied. "It's not your problem, it's God's. Put it out of your head. He will provide." I was glad to put it out of my mind; there was so much to do before we left I didn't have time to worry about it anyway. Rod told the officials that we would pay them on our return!

Soon after our arrival in Colorado, Pastor Mark Lucks asked if we had any special needs. Rod told him we needed funds for Command but that we're not worried about it as we knew God would make a way. We were given an opportunity to address the congregation. Pastor John Stocker told us to tell the people of the need. During worship, Pastor John was lying on his face before God and heard God speak to his heart, "I want you to send this couple away with the full amount they need." He talked quietly with two other staff members, who confirmed his prompting.

Not knowing what God had spoken to Pastor John, we took our place on the platform. We shared about what God was doing in Mozambique, thanked them all for their tremendous support but could not bring ourselves to say, "We need loads of money!" So we never mentioned any need. Pastor John stood up when we finished and shared what God had shown him. That morning, the total amount was given! To write on paper what we felt is impossible. The power and greatness of God, His wonderful provision, the love of the saints, all these together confirming God's hand on our work in Mozambique was overwhelming. At our very first meeting, God did it all. We could proceed on our ministry tour without the burden of a heavy financial need!

After New Year, we started our 7,000 mile journey through twelve states in a lovely Ford van loaned to us by Resurrection Fellowship. Rod did not miss the Inhaminga road one bit. The snow was not a problem; it's clean mud! Amazing love, the finest friends, hearts and homes opened up to us everywhere we went. The American people must have the biggest hearts in the world. Kindness received us, comfort cared for us, and generosity carried us on our way from state to state for two glorious months. Our testimony and unprofessional preaching were graciously received, and with the help of the Holy Spirit we were able to impart vision and encouragement to many. It was wonderful to see and visit with old friends and make new ones also. Having Deborah with us added to the joy. Everywhere we went folk organized fun events; we had the time of our lives! Spiritually, we were greatly built up by the quality fellowship we enjoyed with friends, as well as the praise and worship and Word in many different churches. It truly was a time of restoration and healing. We are deeply indebted to the Christians of the USA for their generosity in love, friendship and giving. **"God Bless America!"**

PRESIDENT CHISSANO VISITS BIBLE SCHOOL

This is one of the most spiritually significant events that has happened in our ministry. President Chissano is the leader of Frelimo, the former Communist party. The effect of the Berlin Wall coming down ricocheted across the world, and even faraway Mozambique, a country that had been at war for 25 years was finally released from Communism – sort of. The regime continues in power and there are some things that have been slow to change. During the guerrilla war the Communists were after our necks and we had to run for our lives on several occasions. When the Mozambique Peace Accord was signed, amnesty was granted and we were free from threat... or so we thought. Since then, Rod has twice been arrested by Frelimo, the last time just one year ago. We have had many false accusations brought against us, have suffered persecution at the Bible School and have been followed by Frelimo police while on preaching trips, just like in the old Russia KGB days!

A year ago, when our co-worker, Alex, tragically died after falling off the back of our tractor and trailer, the Frelimo police confiscated our tractor. They have illegally kept it for almost a year, allowing us to use it only sometimes, mainly when the community needs some service performed.

Inhaminga area is a strong opposition area. The people have not forgotten the terrors and sorrows of Communist rule. They do not support the government. President Chissano had never ventured here and suddenly, the town was informed that Chissano was coming for a presidential visit, preceding the upcoming elections. We received official notification that he would be visiting the Bible School! We even received an official invitation to be present.

It was the responsibility of the Frelimo Party to make all arrangements for the visit. An enormous amount of people would come in with the president. Food, water, firewood for cooking, a host of things would be needed. One by one, the requests came in. Our old enemies were asking us to help them.

Please, would we use our tractor (the one they had unfairly kept in confiscation) to carry firewood and other supplies? "What a cheek!" said Ellie. Rod said, "Sure you can use it, I'll send my driver to pick it up from the police station." *"Bless those who persecute you." Romans 12:14*

Please, would we donate some food to help feed the visiting delegation? We gave 20 kg of rice and a duck and some cooking oil. *"Therefore, if your enemy is hungry, feed him." Romans 12:20*

Please, would we let them use our public address system – the president must be clearly heard. "Sure, I'll set it up for you." Rod assured them.

The morning of Chissano's arrival, a delegation of Frelimo officials arrived at the Bible School to ask for more favors. The Chief of Police was with them, holding in his hands a document of release for the tractor. Hallelujah! Please, would we lend them some mattresses, blankets, cooking pots, plates, cups, you name it; they don't have enough for all the officials accompanying the president. "With pleasure," said Rod. "Thank you for the tractor document; we will deliver everything to you by tractor and trailer."

As the entourage came up the drive, they were not greeted with the usual political songs as happens everywhere else, but instead, our workers sang songs of praise to our God. They disembarked and were welcomed by Rod, Bible School staff and workers. Chissano was all smiles and friendliness, shaking hands all round. The Press had accompanied him; this was a big deal. After being shown around it was time for speeches.

Rod and the team told of the purpose and vision of the school, sharing about what God had been doing.

Christian Vision, UK, had put together a lovely Bible Study book titled "Pura Verdade," (Simple Truth). It is customary to give visitors, especially those of high status, a gift when they visit your home. Nailza presented President Chissano with a Bible with underlined scripture, and a copy of "Pura Verdade." Each member accompanying him received the "Pura Verdade" also. Over 30 copies were given out. The next morning a request was sent for more Bible Study books!

The president commended Rod on his hard work and perseverance in rebuilding the premises, especially in view of the fact that the road is so bad. He promised that a new road would be built soon!

"I have heard that you are a very good farmer," President Chissano said to Rod. "You should go to Gurue and plant tea and coffee. We have big developments there. You are wasted here at Inhaminga."

"No, thank you," replied Rod. "The reward here at the Bible School is far bigger than anywhere else. This is an eternal harvest."

On three occasions years ago, Rod was given a prophetic word. *"See a man diligent in his work? He shall stand before kings."*

(Proverbs 22:29)

During our involvement in the Mozambique Peace Process, we saw this fulfilled several times as Rod met with magistrates in high places. Now, he was standing before the President of Mozambique. He had the opportunity to testify of Jesus. Amazing how God works. Nothing He does should ever surprise us!

"When a man's ways please the Lord, He makes even his enemies to be at peace with him." *(Proverbs 16:7)*

We have won battles over the kingdoms of darkness that tried many times to run us out of town, through discouragement, false accusations and dangerous threats. Those who were against us, making life as hard as possible for us, are now friendly and helpful. If the president says it's OK, who's going to argue? God has made our enemies to be at peace with us!

GRADUATION

The week prior to the president's visit, Rod had to brave the Inhaminga road driving Big Foot to take supplies for the next Bible School intake, and to get students back home after graduation. It was a nightmarish journey but a glorious graduation. It hadn't rained for six weeks; then as Rod started down the road, the clouds gathered and deposited their load. Rod was stuck for six hours at a time, several times. It took three days and two nights to travel 190 kilometers.

An overhanging branch smashed the window and the rain poured in. All the supplies got wet, as potholes the size of small swimming pools were so deep with water, the trailer was submerged; also the back of the truck, many times. Rod's sleeping bag and clothes were wet too. African winters are cold at night.

Rod came across some other trucks stuck in the road so he couldn't pass. The men had been without food for some time. "I've got food if you've got fire," Rod said to them. They whooped. Africans always make a fire wherever they stop. Out came the food, and everyone got fed. With the help of a tractor and some other trucks, Big Foot was pulled out of the mud. When Rod wasn't stuck, someone else was, and so they helped one another until finally they got to Inhaminga.

The graduation was very moving. The students were so thrilled to receive their awards; some could hardly speak. The two top students each received a bicycle as a prize. A bicycle is a great asset to a pastor who usually travels on foot. The students sang and worshipped with all their heart and returned home full of the Word of God, confidence and vision. Rod said, "As soon as I get to the Bible School, I'm so grateful for all God is doing here, the pain of the journey is nothing." It's rather like what Jesus said concerning the birth of a child; at the time there is much pain, but the pain is forgotten the minute the child is born.

Amos Saide, a 23-year-old student from Cabo Delgado gave the following testimony at the graduation.

"I was mightily snatched from the claw of the devil to live in abundant life in Christ Jesus.

"In the year of 1997 in a period of nearly three months I was completely demon possessed and mentally disturbed and there was a time when I would walk in the streets totally undressed. In the vastness of the neighborhood bush where I lived for a long time by the will of Satan, without water many times, and no food in my stomach I resisted for a whole month without fainting but instead I became stronger each day, for nothing could detain me.

"Whatsoever my eyes could see, whatsoever I could contemplate was similar to a great multitude in a very high voice shrieking: 'Amos... you are certainly dead for there is no one who can liberate you... What is left then? SUICIDE YOURSELF now because your death is inevitable!'

"Numbers of suicide attempts I have, whether using gallows through rashness of jumping from trees with rope... and many ways. Various medium spirits were consulted and great resources were spent in vain.... throwing myself in a profound abyss of disgrace and hopelessness.

"Praised be the Holy Name of Jesus who had mercy for me and

sent his servants Visao Crista (Christian Vision) invited by my uncle to come and pray for me. It happened while they were praying I felt that something like great power and force was pulled out of me, it was the multitude of demons. Right from that hour I was totally free and accepted the Lord Jesus as my Savior. Soon after I had accepted the Lord, my family rejected me because they are the Muslims. For I don't consider Islam of great importance because now Jesus is all that I need.

"I am now a student at the Bible School at Inhaminga being better trained to serve the Lord Jesus in Whom I rejoice. Great things the Lord has done for me, for this reason I am happy. Hallelujah! Beloved pray for me."

MOZAMBIQUE FLOOD

While the year 2000 dawned with dramatic, thundering fireworks throughout the nations, places like Inhaminga saw only the magnificent stars studding the black velvet sky. The world held its breath to see what effects Y2K would have on power systems that run the machines and oil the wheels of this computerized age, while folk at Inhaminga and throughout rural Mozambique slept soundly. They were unconcerned at the possible failure of power, not being connected to electricity supplies anyway, nor to telephones to which computers are linked. Christians praised God and prayed all night as is their custom at the turn of a new year. Others were filled with fear as they had heard that the world was soon to come to an end. For many of those in the floodplains of the Buzi, Limpopo and Olifant Rivers, this was true. Their world was about to become a watery grave.

Video footage and newscasts of the floods that swept away parts of Mozambique gripped the international heart like no other disaster before. God was touching the heart of the nations for the broken land emerging from long years of mourning the effects of war, famine and death. Caught up in our own crisis caused by the same Cyclone Eline in Zimbabwe, we watched in horror at the far worse scenes in Mozambique that appeared on the television. With tear-blurred eyes, and a groaning pain in our inner being, we read the reports that came through, some of which are included below.

February, March 2000

.....Efforts to save thousands of people stranded in trees and on roofs are taking place in central and southern Mozambique, where muddy floodwaters stretch for miles in every direction.

.....Thousands of people are feared dead, most near the submerged town of Chokwe and dozens of villages in the Gaza region.

.....Residents had less than 10 minutes warning before the Limpopo River came cascading through the town.

.....Seven South African helicopters have flown more than 8,000 people to safety, the British Broadcasting Corporation said. The official death count at the time was 200, but it is possible that thousands more bodies are under water, or trapped in homes or the brush, news reports said.

.....About 100,000 people are still at risk. Most of the stranded have had no food or clean water for three days, news reports said. More flooding is expected because of heavy rains in neighboring Zimbabwe.

.....As many as 1 million people have been forced from their homes. Mozambican families have taken in refugees and several camps have been established. The population of one camp grew from 2,000 to 15,000 in less than 48 hours and still is increasing, the BBC said.

.....Fresh supplies of medicine, food, and clean water are vital, relief workers say. The danger of starvation is growing, and decomposing bodies are contaminating the water, threatening outbreaks of cholera, dysentery, and malaria. "We need to ensure we get enough medical assistance and enough water supplies in the next few days or we're going to see a lot of deaths," UNICEF said.

.....World Relief workers also rescued a 7-year-old boy from the roof of his hut as water was covering his feet, the men said. Holding a 2-week-old baby, the boy told the men that his mother had drowned inside the hut.

.....Mozambique, one of the world's poorest countries, had been recovering from a devastating 16-year war that ended in 1992. In recent years, foreign investors had opened factories, tourists had flocked to its beaches, and highways and bridges were being rebuilt. It had been held up as an example of the kind of recovery that can come out of a terrible humanitarian disaster.

....."The waters have wrought as much damage as a war," said an economic analyst in South Africa. The flood has washed away bridges, destroyed crops, and drowned thousands of livestock.

.....Land mine-clearance restarts. The United Nations Development Programme is working out an emergency mine-clearance programme. It is feared that the floods have moved land mines into areas that previously had no land mines, or even to areas that had already been cleared of these devices.

..... "There has been an almost total wipeout of animals in flooded Mozambique and veterinary supplies are vital to rescue surviving livestock," warned a spokesman for the World Society for the Protection of Animals.

OUR FIRST FLOOD RELIEF FLIGHT WAS TO OUR OWN FAMILY

Though Cyclone Eline also hit the Beira area where we do some work, and Mutare, our Zimbabwe home base, the worst affected areas are south. Inhaminga was not affected at all.

Parts of Zimbabwe were badly affected. A mighty wind swept through Mutare, uprooting trees and causing quite a bit of damage. The wind was incredible, and just kept on and on blowing. Four trees in our garden were uprooted, and there was only one way to describe the town, "It looks like a hurricane has hit the place!" Power and telephone lines were down for five days and more.

The surrounding farmlands were devastated, bridges down, roads swept away. Chipinge, (where Ellie's relatives live) was totally cut off for over a week. They had no power, no telephones, no communication, and nobody could get there to assess the damage. It was a week before Rod could fly there, the bad weather making it impossible to fly.

We had no idea how bad the Chipinge area was; we had no communication with our family and didn't know what to expect. When we saw signs of possible sunshine, we went to town to buy blankets and food for the people that must be in need, as much as would fit in our plane. We loaded some extra supplies of fresh fruit and vegetables and bread for Ellie's mum. We knew her house was sturdy and therefore would be OK, but did not know what her food situation was. There was no way of notifying anyone of our coming. The weather could prevent Rod from getting there, but we had to try; we could not allow the first opportunity of a break in the skies to pass by. It was very much a "Faith Flight", and it worked out wonderfully.

Rod took a man from the Electricity Commission with him. They had no way of knowing where the damaged pylons were as the roads were cut off. As the plane lifted off, a light rain began to fall again. It would be a miracle if they could get to Chipinge, an hour's flight away.

Along the route the devastation of broken bridges and swept-away mud huts lay beneath the wings. Low level flying enabled them to pinpoint power pylons lying in the mud. Identifying the problem areas would help speed up the restoration of power.

As Rod came in low over her house, Ellie's mum came running out, waving her arms excitedly. The rain had lifted again and the sun shone weakly. Who could know the relief and excitement she felt as she watched her beloved Rod circle the house. She knew he would be heading back to Chipinge, the only place he could land, and leaped into her little VW Golf car and drove over the roads, which she had to be towed out of a few days previously. It was drier now and wild horses would not keep this intrepid 75-year-old veteran from meeting Rod at the airstrip. Rod was horrified at how quickly she made the supposedly 20-minute journey!

It was a happy reunion. Rod said to me afterwards, "When I saw Ma running out of the house waving so excitedly, I could have happily turned back even if I had not been able to land. Just to see she was safe was so wonderful!"

Ellie's mum does a lot of ministry among the village population, visiting old people in the tribal areas and preaching the Gospel. She almost cried when she saw all the stuff, knowing that there were many needing the supplies. A few days later she told us of a particular family. The husband had drowned, the hut flooded away and every item they possessed had been lost. His wife and children were the first to receive provision from this batch of supplies.

It was not logistically viable for us to take supplies in our Cessna 206 to the South of Mozambique where the greatest needs were, so we helped nearer home ground. Here, the disaster was not as great in magnitude, but losing loved ones, home and possessions was equally traumatic for those affected. We were thankful for the fast action of international relief agencies, as well as 700 Club, Christ For The Nations, James Robison's Life Outreach and other large ministries.

FLOOD? WHAT IS FLOOD?

Millions of Mozambicans who have no access to TV only heard about the floods on the radio or from people passing through their villages. They could not imagine the destruction or terror being faced by those in the south. At Inhaminga there is no surface water. Most people living there have never seen a large mass of water in their lives. Rod took video clippings of the flood to show the students so they would understand better how to pray and intercede for their fellow countrymen. He also showed the clippings to the villagers before starting the *JESUS* video at the soccer field. Every living soul for miles around turned up to come and see what a flood looks like. Mouths gaping and eyes stretched wide, they gasped and cried in shocked horror at what they saw.

Rudyard Kipling's "Best Beloved" stories captivated my heart as a child. I was fascinated to learn how the elephant got his trunk and how the leopard got his spots. The *"great green, greasy Limpopo"* as Kipling described the Limpopo dividing Zimbabwe and South Africa, was a river I vowed I would see when I grew up. Imagine my disappointment to see shallow trickles creeping over river sand the first time I crossed the border at Beit Bridge. But now, with the thick, heavy surges inundating man, animal, vegetation and property, I thought, "Kipling must have visited the Limpopo during heavy rains". It is unlikely, however, that he saw anything like this raging madness.

The waters cut through homes, separating mother and child, carrying away family members and possessions as a wave of water two meters high surged down the Limpopo and swallowed the town of Chokwe. Many small villages were totally obliterated and the larger town of Xai Xai drowned.

Where the waters rose more slowly but persistently, some families built tree-houses, stacking blankets, firewood, a cooking pot and food. It wrenched the heart to see a family with little children huddling over a small fire struggling to burn off wet wood balancing on a few poles in the tree. We were filled with admiration for those who had made this desperate effort to keep their families safe in the midst of near impossible conditions. Others camped on roofs of buildings. Surely the waters would not come this high? In some cases they did, sweeping people off the thin thread of life they were hanging onto.

Branches swayed or broke under the weight of too many

people in one tree. The paths and roads had disappeared, there was only one way to go, and that was up. Days and nights without food or sleep while hanging onto branches waiting for help to come was too much for some. Exhausted and hopeless, their strength failed and they slipped off their precarious perches and tumbled into the hungry waters together with the corpses of cattle, goats, dogs and cats.

Helicopters battled bad weather and used every shred of sunshine and light that broke through to help locate and rescue people. Terrified by the noise of the chopper, and in danger of being shaken out of the trees by the wind caused by the rotor blades, people held on more tightly than ever. Making the transition from the tree to the chopper was precarious. The skill of the pilots was tested to the limits as the brave crews continued relentlessly in their efforts to save lives. Though help from the International Community seemed slow in arriving, once they started operations it was phenomenal, and certainly, without the commitment and sacrifice of those teams, thousands more lives would have been lost.

The Mozambican people who had lived for so many years in refugee camps, and thought themselves free of that misery, now found themselves crowded together again with insufficient water, shelter and food. This time it was worse, but they bravely held together, showing resilience and strength that amazed aid workers. Cholera and malaria claimed lives that had been rescued from the waters. There was no way aid workers could reach everyone. Starving people ate rotten corpses of animals that floated on the river. Cooking was difficult as firewood was wet, and there were few cooking pots to be found. In the midst of this, compassion for one another and sharing the little they had, showed the heart of a people who had been there before and knew their survival depended on each other. Over one million people were displaced during these floods which affected 500 kilometers of landmass.

Christians joined together to worship God and pray. They

clapped their hands in rhythmic thanks and praise to God for saving their lives as they sang, "God is our deliverer." In the midst of the sorrow, joy broke through for those who were reunited with family and friends thought to be lost forever to the floods.

The rain continued and the rivers flooded again and again. As soon as it seemed there was hope for the sun to show its face, angry clouds would darken the sky and down came yet another deluge.

Weeks later, a few people began to return to what was once their homes. Mud huts were no longer in existence; houses of brick and cement still stood but were often three feet deep in mud. Pieces of furniture, personal possessions and in some cases, bodies were dug out of the mud as folk endeavored to clean out their homes. It was not a happy return, but they were anxious to try and rebuild their lives.

At the height of the flood crisis, Chihaquelane Camp was sheltering 80,000 people. By mid-June, about 90 per cent of the population of Chokwe district, in the southern Mozambican province of Gaza, who fled from their homes in February had now returned. Even with ongoing assistance from the international community, it will take years to rebuild the nation.

HUSH, LITTLE BABY IN THE TREETOP

Sofia, the woman who achieved media fame by giving birth tied down in a tree while awaiting rescue during the floods on the Limpopo, and her baby Rosita, symbolize the suffering of women and children in the worst flood in the country in living memory.

The 1-hour-old baby girl was rescued by helicopter after a medic was lowered into the tree and cut the umbilical cord. Sofia said the baby was lucky because when she went into labor on top of the tree, she was accompanied by her mother-in-law, and it was she who helped deliver Rosita. "The delivery was not very difficult. The baby came out quickly. She did not create any difficulties for me. She came out when nobody expected."

Undoubtedly, this traumatic scene, flashed upon the screens of the world, served to awaken hearts to serve and give more than ever, to save the lives and alleviate the suffering of the Mozambican people. Aid workers spoke continually of the resilience and bravery they saw displayed. Out of the crushing of war had come strong vessels who would not give up, but clung tenaciously to floating logs, rooftops, trees, hope and life. With this kind of resilience and determination, we can believe to see the day when this beloved nation, once despised and scorned by her neighbors for her rags and desolation, stands tall and strong in Africa.❖

VISION 2000

"A woman, when she is in labor, has sorrow because her hour is come; but as soon as she has given birth to the child, she no longer remembers the anguish, for the joy of the life she has brought forth." John 16:21

Imagine the young Mozambican mother, Sofia, looking down at the raging waters below her, holding her newborn baby in her arms. Sorrow, death and destruction raging around her, new life, joy and hope, held tightly to her heart.

This is how it is in much of the work of the ministry. It's not easy, but every inch of territory gained in the name of Jesus is worth the pain and price we sometimes have to pay. It is with confidence in God, and great expectations of a tremendous harvest that we continue with His work into a new millennium.

"Being confident of this very thing, that He Who has begun a good work in you, will complete it until the day of Jesus Christ." (Philippians 1:6)

Join with us, the Team and students at the **Afrika wa Yesu Bible School** in these words from Chris Christensen's song ......"Can I Go With You?"

CAN I GO WITH YOU?

Can I go with You?
Do what You do?
All I want to know
Is can I go with You?

To the hungry heart waiting for Your Word
To the thirsty soul who has never heard
Of the Father's love and a sinner's load
Of His sacrifice and the blood that flowed.

To the enemy camp, to the dungeons deep
To the gates of hell, where the lion roars
Against Your church they shall not prevail
With Your weapons of life we shall never fail.

Give me wings to fly far from the curse
To the outer edge of the universe
Where the stars all call and the angels sing
And the saints fall down before the King.

Can I go with You?

EPILOGUE

The Heins continue in their mission to Mozambique through the operation of the Inhaminga Bible School, and ministering the Word of God throughout the nation.

Tammy lives in Malawi with her husband David. The Heins delight in their first grandson, Raurie Dustin Michael, who was born in August 1996.

Dustin grew up to be a pilot. He passed through heaven's gates on October 11, 1997. God heals; scars remain, but we have a future together with Dustin in eternity.

Deborah is completing her last year of school in Zimbabwe and is preparing to enter Christ For The Nations Institute, Dallas, Texas in the year 2001.

DEFINITIONS

Rodney & Ellie Hein – Missionaries to Mozambique, citizens of Zimbabwe (Rhodesia).

Frelimo – The ruling Marxist Government Party of Mozambique. Officially no longer called Communist after the fall of Communism in the Soviet Union and Europe. President – Joaquim Chissano.

Renamo – A Popular People's Resistance Movement formed to resist repression of Communist rule. President – Afonso Dhlakama.

Joseph – Rodney Hein's alias; the name used in essentially secretive communication.

Bush – reference to areas of rural, undeveloped villages in Africa.

Bush telegraph – word-of-mouth, village-to-village.

SNASP – equivalent to Russian KGB.

Inhaminga Command Post – Former ruined buildings of a Portuguese Command Post, restored and turned into a Bible School and Ministry Center by the Hein family.

ICRC – International Convention of the Red Cross.

Adullam's cave – Heins' home/office, often a hideout and rendezvous point during civil war. Taken from I Samuel 22:2.

BBC – British Broadcasting Corporation.

JESUS **film** – 2-hour film, major tool in bush evangelism, impacting thousands.

Rome Peace Accord – Climax of negotiations to end 16-year civil war, signed in Rome on Oct. 4, 1992.

Kilometer – 5/8 of a mile.

Meter – approximately three feet plus three inches.

SELECTED OTHER BOOKS
published by Christ For The Nations, Inc.:

- Mozambique, the Cross and The Crown - Ellie Hein
- Before We Kill and Eat You - H. B. Garlock
- John G. Lake, Apostle to Africa - Gordon Lindsay
- Bible Days are Here Again - Gordon Lindsay
- My Diary Secrets - Freda Lindsay
- "Freda" - Freda Lindsay
- The Gordon Lindsay Autobiography - Gordon Lindsay
- Prayer and Fasting - Gordon Lindsay
- A Book of Miracles - Freda Lindsay
- The Second Wind - Freda Lindsay
- Christ For The Nations Golden Jubilee - (50-year history, many photos)
- While Children Slept - Trena McDougal

Write for more information concerning:
- Additional books available
- Bible study series by Gordon Lindsay
- Creation Science series by Dennis Lindsay
- Catalog of Worship Music Products (1-800-GOD-SONG)
- Information on our Dallas Bible Institute, or specialized programs, including Pastoral Ministries; Missions, and Worship and the Arts

To receive a 1-year FREE subscription to our monthly magazine contact:
Christ For The Nations, Inc.
P. O. Box 769000
Dallas, Texas 75376-9000

Ph. 1-800-933-2364 or (214) 376-1711
e-mail: info@cfni.org
Web-site: http://www.cfni.org